Lecture Notes in Computer Science 1382

Edited by G. Goos, J. Hartmanis and J. van Leeuwen

T0223271

Springer
Berlin
Heidelberg
New York
Barcelona
Budapest
Hong Kong
London
Milan
Paris
Santa Clara
Singapore
Tokyo

Egidio Astesiano (Ed.)

Fundamental Approaches to Software Engineering

First International Conference, FASE'98
Held as Part of the Joint European Conferences
on Theory and Practice of Software, ETAPS'98
Lisbon, Portugal, March 28 – April 4, 1998
Proceedings

 Springer

Series Editors

Gerhard Goos, Karlsruhe University, Germany
Juris Hartmanis, Cornell University, NY, USA
Jan van Leeuwen, Utrecht University, The Netherlands

Volume Editor

Egidio Astesiano
University of Genova, Departmenmt of Computer Science
Via Dodecaneso 35, I-16146 Genova, Italy
E-mail: astes@didi.unige.it

Cataloging-in-Publication data applied for

Die Deutsche Bibliothek - CIP-Einheitsaufnahme

Fundamental approaches to software engineering : first
international conference ; proceedings / FASE '98, held as part of the
Joint European Conferences on Theory and Practice of Software,
ETAPS '98, Lisbon, Portugal, March 28 - April 4, 1998. Egidio
Astesiano (ed.). - Berlin ; Heidelberg ; New York ; Barcelona ;
Budapest ; Hong Kong ; London Milan ; Paris ; Santa Clara ;
Singapore ; Tokyo : Springer, 1998
    (Lecture notes in computer science ; Vol. 1382)
    ISBN 3-540-64303-6

CR Subject Classification (1991): D.2, D.3, F.3.4

ISSN 0302-9743
ISBN 3-540-64303-6 Springer-Verlag Berlin Heidelberg New York

© Springer-Verlag Berlin Heidelberg 1998
Printed in Germany

Typesetting: Camera-ready by author
SPIN 10632029   06/3142 – 5 4 3 2 1 0   Printed on acid-free paper

Foreword

The European conference situation in the general area of software science has long been considered unsatisfactory. A fairly large number of small and medium-sized conferences and workshops take place on an irregular basis, competing for high-quality contributions and for enough attendees to make them financially viable. Discussions aiming at a consolidation have been underway since at least 1992, with concrete planning beginning in summer 1994 and culminating in a public meeting at TAPSOFT'95 in Aarhus.

On the basis of a broad consensus, it was decided to establish a single annual federated spring conference in the slot that was then occupied by TAPSOFT and CAAP/ESOP/CC, comprising a number of existing and new conferences and covering a spectrum from theory to practice. ETAPS'98, the first instance of the European Joint Conferences on Theory and Practice of Software, is taking place this year in Lisbon. It comprises five conferences (FoSSaCS, FASE, ESOP, CC, TACAS), four workshops (ACoS, VISUAL, WADT, CMCS), seven invited lectures, and nine tutorials.

The events that comprise ETAPS address various aspects of the system development process, including specification, design, implementation, analysis and improvement. The languages, methodologies and tools which support these activities are all well within its scope. Different blends of theory and practice are represented, with an inclination towards theory with a practical motivation on one hand and soundly-based practice on the other. Many of the issues involved in software design apply to systems in general, including hardware systems, and the emphasis on software is not intended to be exclusive.

ETAPS is a natural development from its predecessors. It is a loose confederation in which each event retains its own identity, with a separate programme committee and independent proceedings. Its format is open-ended, allowing it to grow and evolve as time goes by. Contributed talks and system demonstrations are in synchronized parallel sessions, with invited lectures in plenary sessions. Two of the invited lectures are reserved for "unifying" talks on topics of interest to the whole range of ETAPS attendees. The aim of cramming all this activity into a single one-week meeting is to create a strong magnet for academic and industrial researchers working on topics within its scope, giving them the opportunity to learn about research in related areas, and thereby to foster new and existing links between work in areas that have hitherto been addressed in separate meetings.

ETAPS'98 has been superbly organized by José Luis Fiadeiro and his team at the Department of Informatics of the University of Lisbon. The ETAPS steering committee has put considerable energy into planning for ETAPS'98 and its successors. Its current membership is:

André Arnold (Bordeaux), Egidio Astesiano (Genova), Jan Bergstra (Amsterdam), Ed Brinksma (Enschede), Rance Cleaveland (Raleigh), Pierpaolo Degano (Pisa), Hartmut Ehrig (Berlin), José Fiadeiro (Lisbon), Jean-Pierre Finance (Nancy), Marie-Claude Gaudel (Paris), Tibor

Gyimothy (Szeged), Chris Hankin (London), Stefan Jähnichen (Berlin), Uwe Kastens (Paderborn), Paul Klint (Amsterdam), Kai Koskimies (Tampere), Tom Maibaum (London), Hanne Riis Nielson (Aarhus), Fernando Orejas (Barcelona), Don Sannella (Edinburgh, chair), Bernhard Steffen (Dortmund), Doaitse Swierstra (Utrecht), Wolfgang Thomas (Kiel)

Other people were influential in the early stages of planning, including Peter Mosses (Aarhus) and Reinhard Wilhelm (Saarbrücken). ETAPS'98 has received generous sponsorship from:

Portugal Telecom
TAP Air Portugal
the Luso-American Development Foundation
the British Council
the EU programme "Training and Mobility of Researchers"
the University of Lisbon
the European Association for Theoretical Computer Science
the European Association for Programming Languages and Systems
the Gulbenkian Foundation

I would like to express my sincere gratitude to all of these people and organizations, and to José in particular, as well as to Springer-Verlag for agreeing to publish the ETAPS proceedings.

Edinburgh, January 1998   Donald Sannella
                                           ETAPS Steering Committee chairman

Preface

Within the ETAPS'98 event, the Conference on Fundamental Approaches to Software Engineering (FASE), aims at providing a forum where rigorous methods for the software production process, bridging the gap between theory and practice, are presented, compared and discussed.

While keeping the acronym, FASE'98 replaces the conference on Formal Aspects/Approaches to Software Engineering, which took place within most editions of TAPSOFT. The new name of FASE has been chosen to mark a significant shift of emphasis towards approaches to SE, which are "fundamental" more than "formal", i.e. address basic issues by means of rigorous, but not necessarily formal, methods; in particular, the integration of formal and informal methods are encouraged, as well as reports on industrial experiences and experimental studies on the application of formal methods.

The FASE'98 Programme Committee members are

Egidio Astesiano (Italy, chair)
Michel Bidoit (France)
Dan Craigen (Canada)
Hartmut Ehrig (Germany)
Carlo Ghezzi (Italy)
Heinrich Hussmann (Germany)
Cliff Jones (UK)
Tom Maibaum (UK)
Fernando Orejas (Spain)
Gérard Renardel de Lavalette (The Netherlands)
Doug Smith (USA)
Jeannette Wing (USA)
Martin Wirsing (Germany)
Zhou Chao Chen (Macau)

Out of 59 submissions, in order to comply with the intended spirit and the novelty of ETAPS as an event of federated conferences, after some discussion within the PC, three rerouted to ESOP and two to FoSSACS. Then, after a rigorous refereeing process, followed by an intensive, ten-days-long, electronic selection meeting, 18 were selected for presentation and are included in this volume,which also includes two invited papers and three presentations of demos.

The first invited paper is by Kent Beck, one of the two invited speakers on behalf of the overall ETAPS'98 (the other being Amir Pnueli). His contribution is a much shortened version of a manifesto he had in mind on what he calls Extreme Programming, a discipline of software development emphasizing "productivity, flexibility, informality, teamwork and limited use of technology outside programming". Following the author's rather dialectical wishes, I welcome its inclusion in these proceedings, because, first of all, a much broader and more dialectical view of the software production process is very well in the spirit of the new FASE, as it is also witnessed by the paper of Cliff Jones, the specific FASE invited speaker. Moreover, the debate this inclusion (and the talk, I am sure) will undoubtedly generate will have the benefit of helping the new, but obviously still much overlooked, nature of FASE emerge. Indeed, as anticipated, the other invited paper by Cliff Jones, with the significant title "Some Mistakes I Have Made and What I Have Learned from Them", intends "to argue that some formal methods research is going in a direction which has little chance of making an impact on computing practice" and strongly emphasizes the somewhat obvious (but not to all) fact "that for formal methods to be used they must be usable by engineers". In the spirit of this talk, and concerning the current contributions, let me add my feeling that, while we have already made a move toward more viable directions, there is still a long way to go and I pass the witness to the future chairpersons of FASE with the wish they pursue with more success the change in attitude and results.

I acknowledge the extremely efficient cooperation of the PC during the refereeing and selection process and of the other referees, as listed. I also want to express my conviction, after many experiences, that well-run electronic meetings (here it was by Web plus email), are very effective in allowing a much more rigorous and well motivated selection than by old-fashioned meetings.

Also I cannot forget to mention the efficiency, fairness and adherence to the principles of ETAPS of Don Sannella, the Coordinator of the Steering Committee. Moreover, being guilty for having proposed him and convinced him to accept such a frightening burden, it is a relaxing pleasure to witness day after day the skill and diplomacy of the organizer José Luis Fiadeiro in driving the whole event so smoothly, notwithstanding the intrinsic difficulties of the practical matters and those added by the strong personalities involved.

In all matters concerning the handling of the Web and the interface with the authors and the publisher I have been invaluably supported by my colleague and friend Gianna Reggio, helped by our secretary Elisabetta Ferrando; I will keep forever the nice memory of Gianna's unlimited cooperation in a difficult period of my life.

Genova, January 1998   Egidio Astesiano
                                                        FASE PC chairman

External Referees

We apologise if, inadvertently, we have omitted a referee from the above list. To the best of our knowledge the list is accurate.

Table of Contents

Invited Papers

Contributed Papers

Demos

Extreme Programming: A Humanistic Discipline of Software Development

Kent Beck

CSLife and First Class Software
P.O. Box 226
Boulder Creek, CA
email: 70761.1216@compuserve.com

Once a farmer and his friend were sitting at a battered kitchen table. The farmer said, "It's time for the mule's lesson." Out they went into the yard. The farmer picked up a thick tree branch lying on the ground. He walked up to the mule and hit it over the head so hard the branch shattered. The mule staggered. His friend's jaw dropped. The friend said, "You can't teach a mule a lesson like that." "That wasn't the lesson," replied the farmer, "that was just to get his attention."

Introduction

Extreme Programming is a discipline of software development. It is intended to guide development of medium sized projects by small teams, getting ordinary programmers to achieve extraordinary goals. It emphasizes productivity, flexibility, informality, teamwork, and limited use of technology outside of programming. This paper presents the values underlying Extreme Programming, its assumptions, and some ways to begin incorporating its ideas into your work.

My plan was not to write this paper for these proceedings. My plan was to write a 25 page manifesto from which you could infuriate, amuse, enlighten, and motivate yourself. Instead, I'm typing this with three day old Joëlle Karen on my chest, trying to decide what all to leave out. If there's one lesson in Extreme Programming, it is that life and software development must balance. So, instead of a carefully reasoned argument leading you gently step by step to the conclusions of Extreme Programming, I'm going to take the time I have to hit you over the head with XPs most bizarre and surprising assumptions. I'll trust you to keep an open mind, and incorporate those practices that make sense to you.

Values

Any discipline has to start with a set of values. What does the discipline hold dear? How will it measure its success? Extreme Programming emphasizes four values:

Communication The bottlenecks in software development all stem from the difficulty in communication between people. XP aims to enhance communication developer-to-developer, developer-to-client, and developer-to-manager.

Simplicity Every bit of complexity on a project adds a little to the required effort, but it adds a lot to risk. XP reduces risk by constantly asking "What is the simplest thing that could possibly work?" Requirements should be simple, programs should be simple, and the discipline itself should be simple. Communication enhances simplicity by making it easier to find unnecessary complexity. Simplicity enhances communication because it is much easier to communicate simple structures.

Testing If a program feature has no automated test, it doesn't work. If it does have an automated test, it might work. XP relies on two levels of testing: developers write their own unit tests in minute-by-minute synchronization with their code, and separate functional testers write tests from the client's perspective. Testing enhances communication by recording the interfaces of the program. Communication enhances testing by improving the odds that a test will discover a defect. Testing enhances simplicity because with tests you can refactor code much more readily. Simplicity enhances testing because there is that much less to test in a simple program

Aggression With the first three values in place, the team can go like hell. Nothing beats experience for dispelling fear. XP developers throw code away when it isn't going well. XP developers spend as much time refactoring as they do coding, even late in development. Communication enhances aggression because two people together are much more likely to try something difficult but valuable than one person alone. Aggression enhances communication because developers are not afraid to learn about new parts of the system. Simplicity enhances aggression because you can much more easily manipulate a simple program. Aggression enhances simplicity because it is often late in development when you discover how the system really should have been structured to be simple, and if you are aggressive you will make it so. Testing enhances aggression because you are much more likely to try something if you can test it afterwards.

Lying beneath all of these values is the recognition that software development is a human process. People want programs. People write programs. People use programs. Computers have a profound effect on all of these people's lives. Acknowledging and honoring humanity in this process is the only way to realize the potential of computers. Treating them like balky bits of machinery will not provide the best results for anyone.

If you believe that humanity is part of software development, then you have to pay attention to how everyone feels. People will be afraid, everybody, whether because my job might disappear, because I haven't learned about Java yet, because I've forgotten how to program, or because I don't like giving so much power to nerds. You have to address those fears with listening, with victories, with celebration, with punishment where necessary. The good news is that if you pay attention to emotions, you will find them a sensitive barometer of progress, risk, and deviation.

Assumptions

This section hints at how XP is a different way of developing software. I have tried to state the assumptions without much justification (in deference to the shortness of time and this fussing baby). Each assumption also hints at XPs reaction to the assumption. It's been frustrating writing this section, as I want to explain each assumption enough to convince you, and explain the practices that follow from it enough to let you try them. I keep reminding myself of the mule story – I'm just trying to get your attention.

Most developers have no idea of the cost or benefits of their decisions. Therefore, begin each project by making a chart listing five years' income and expenses for the company with the project and without it. Refer to this business justification when "How much is enough?" arises.

Many, perhaps a majority of, projects fail to deliver any value beyond experience. Therefore, do whatever you can to reduce the chance of project failure. Simplify requirements, ignore reuse, eliminate useless documentation, ignore unfamiliar technology.

Planning has limited accuracy. Therefore, only give it limited investment at first. Before you commit to a schedule, implement enough of the tricky bits to be comfortable. Be prepared to revisit planning as you learn throughout the project.

Requirements will change. Therefore, be prepared to change with them. Collect brief stories from the client describing everything the system has to do, and which set of stories would constitute a useful first release. Implement the most valuable features first. Invest no more than necessary in the features you do implement. Create a dialog with the client so you know as soon as possible that they are changing the requirements.

Clients need to see progress. Therefore, break the schedule up into bundles of stories no more than four weeks long. Implement functional tests for each story and try to make sure they pass before the end of their iteration.

Many systems never have a big picture, or the big picture is so vague as to be useless. Therefore, agree on a common metaphor before beginning. Make the first iteration of the system fully functional in some way (print a real check, make a real phone call).

The users don't need everything they ask for. The users don't know what is hard and what is easy. The developers don't know what is important. Therefore, make real users a full-time part of the development team. Let them decide what order to implement features. Let them decide what will be in a release based on estimates from the developers and a fixed amount of available development.

Most features implemented in anticipation of future requirements are never used. Therefore, implement today what you need today. Trust your ability to refactor should your design prove naive.

Most program documentation is never read. Therefore, don't write the parts that won't be read. Instead, make every effort to communicate through code (common metaphor, coding conventions, small procedures, separation of concerns). Write information that doesn't fit well in the code in the form of technical memos.

Technology gets in the way of communication. Therefore, avoid it whenever possible. In particular, CASE tools and project management tools interfere with communication, so don't use them. Write information on index cards, stacked, stapled, color coded, and rubber-banded as necessary.

Face-to-face communication is far more effective than any other kind. Therefore, locate your entire team in the same office and ask everyone to keep roughly the same hours. Program in pairs, two developers at one machine, when writing production code.

Developers need freedom to make changes where they make the most sense. Therefore, integrate and test several times a day. Throw away unintegrated code after a couple of days and start over. Ignore code ownership. Program in pairs. Don't integrate without unit tests.

Changing analysis and design decisions is easy. Therefore, don't make lots of big decisions early in development when you don't have any experience. Make them later when you actually have a chance of being right. Accept refactoring as part of the price of doing business this way, but do refactor a little each day.

Tuning the performance of a simple, well-factored system is easy. Therefore, ignore performance as long as possible. Half way through development, create an automated performance test and graph the results of the test weekly.

First Steps

If you are saying, "I want to throw away everything I am doing now and adopt Extreme Programming on my current project," you have missed the point of XP. (Unless you know you are going to fail and you're desperate. Then a leap might be called for.) Instead, I'd like you to think about little things that you can change that might make a big difference. Here are some suggestions.

If you are a programmer:

Pair Programming The next time you have a couple hours of programming to do, ask a colleague to sit beside you while you do it. Offer to reciprocate for their next programming task. You will be much more successful doing this if you move your computer out of the corner and onto a flat table or even better the protruding end of a table, where you can pass the keyboard and mouse back and forth without moving your chairs.

Unit Testing The next time you have a programming task, write a test before you begin that will only succeed when you are done. If you are using Smalltalk or Java, try a programmatic testing framework like the one at http://ic.net/~jeffries. Run your tests after every compile.

Literate Programming The next time you write a tricky bit of code, before you go on to the next task, write it up as a story. Interleave text, pictures, and source code in the document. Rewrite the code if necessary to make it easier to explain. When I wrote my first literate program, I realized just how much more I could say with my code than I was.

If you are a manager:

Stories Write down (or better yet, have a real user write down) the next 20 or 50 things your system has to do. Write each feature on an index card – a name and a couple of sentences are enough. In a meeting with developers and users, have the users sort the cards into three piles: must have, should have, and like to have. Schedule the must have's next.

Iterations Next Monday, have all the developers tell you what 2 or 5 things they are going to do that week and how long (in ideal engineering days) each will take. Next Friday, review what was actually accomplished and how long it took.

Conclusion

You should have been able to conclude by now that XP is not a polished edifice. Indeed, it would be against its own spirit if it ever were. Instead, it is and should always be an evolving fabric of mutually supporting practices. These practices will continue to evolve, perhaps radically, over the next few years.

XP discards much of the received wisdom of the past. Some baby has certainly been thrown out with the bath water. I expect to see some familiar practices return to XP, although in reduced form. For example, diagrammatic notations are entirely ignored by XP currently. There is certainly a role to play for graphics as a design tool.

If you are skeptical about Extreme Programming as presented here, great. It has only been used in its pure form on one project. That makes me suspicious, as I have seen far too many one-project-methodologies. However, if it does no more than make you take a fresh look at what you see as essential to software engineering, I will have partly achieved my purpose. However, none of the ideas in XP is new. The novelty is in putting them all together, and asking that they be taken seriously as a whole discipline of development.

Extreme Programming is named after the currently popular trend of extreme sports. There is a macho, chest-thumping, "I can get closer to dying than you" aspect to extreme sports that I find repugnant. However, underlying all the extreme sports (and all traditional sports at their highest level), is a marriage of courage and skill that I find an apt metaphor to strive for in software development.

The twin waves of business and technology change are heading for the beach. You can get out your shovels and your buckets and dig like mad, and make bigger buckets and bigger shovels when that doesn't work, or you can get on your surf board and ride.

Acknowledgments

Short iterations/lots of tests came from Jon Hopkins. Many of the scheduling ideas came from Ward Cunningham's Episodes pattern language. Ward was also the person who first began preaching pair programming. Baptism under fire was provided by the brave folks in C3: Ron Jeffries, Bob Coe, Chet Hendrickson, Rich Garzaniti, Margaret Fronczak, Denny Gore, Ralph Beattie, Don Wells, Marie DeArment, Brian Hacker, and Matt Saigeon. Stories are Ivar Jacobson's use cases in warm, fuzzy clothes. Courage to talk about this as more than just a better way to hack came from Alistair Cockburn. Martin Fowler kept reassuring me that I did analysis and design, I just did it weird.

Some Mistakes I Have
and What I Have Learned from Them

Cliff B Jones

Harlequin plc
Queens Court, Wilmslow Road, Alderley Edge, Cheshire, SK9 7QD
e-mail: cbj@harlequin.com
Department of Computer Science, Manchester University, M13 9PL
e-mail: cbj@cs.man.ac.uk

Abstract. The purpose of this paper is to make a number of points about the selection of topics, research style, and dissemination of ideas. The writing style chosen is to present past personal decisions which might be regarded as technical or strategic mistakes and to indicate what positive messages can be derived from the experiences.

Introduction

An invited contribution is an opportunity to do something different: for a start, I write in the first person singular. In a sense, I intend to preach: to argue that some formal methods research is going in a direction which has little chance of making an impact on computing practise; to try to persuade senior researchers to direct students –or anyone who is susceptible to influence– to look more seriously at new applications and less at polishing ways of treating problems which have come to be seen as classical.

Just preaching is not likely to sway people so I have chosen to don a "hair shirt" and describe some decisions that I have made which could be regarded as mistakes. At the end of each of my four "confessions", I try to draw lessons from the story. Of course, there is a degree of self-justification in these lessons. Furthermore, I should concede that I could probably not have presented some of these lessons without a gap of (in some cases, many) years. What follows certainly does not present the only examples I could have drawn from about thirty years of trying to develop and disseminate what have become known as "formal methods". But I believe that each of these four enable me to make a positive point.

1 Handling partial functions in proofs

I first met the problem of how to reason about partial functions in the IBM Vienna Laboratory in the late 1960s; I remember an intense discussion with Peter Lucas during the period that he was writing [Luc69]. The early Vienna (operational semantics) VDL work had used McCarthy's conditional expression interpretation of logical operators and I had found that these presented a number of difficulties which went beyond solving the problem that initially presented itself. The reason for my first stay in Vienna was to experiment with using the VDL (cf. [LW69]) language definitions in proofs about implementation correctness of compiling algorithms and I suspect that I encountered difficulties earlier than many precisely because I was one of the first people to make such use of the definitions.

I have had several tries at this problem since and have –I guess– to view all but the last as mistakes (and to continue to question the last!). Most important is that the criteria for success have been motivated by efficacy in the construction of proofs.

Problem

The difficulty of reasoning about partial functions is apparent to anyone who has faced other than the most trivial of specification tasks. Terms arise in logical expressions which for certain values of their free variables fail to denote an (obvious) value. One source of this problem is operators on basic data types such as sequences: taking the head of an empty sequence does not denote an obvious value so an expression like $\mathsf{hd}\, t$ might or might not denote a value. In

$$\forall t \in \mathbb{N}^* \cdot t = [\,] \vee t = append(\mathsf{hd}\, t, \mathsf{tl}\, t)$$

it is obviously intended that a value be denoted but perhaps less obvious as to how to explain in a compositional way why it is.

The more troublesome terms come from partial functions. In large specifications, one needs many auxiliary functions and they are often defined by recursion. What makes their handling more delicate than monadic operators is that the domain over which they are defined can depend on relationships between their arguments. Examples of moderate difficulty could be cited from work on databases etc. A simple example which I have used in several papers is intentionally just complex enough to illustrate the problem.

$diff : \mathbb{Z} \times \mathbb{Z} \to \mathbb{Z}$

$diff(i,j) \quad \triangleq \quad$ if $i = j$ then 0 else $diff(i, j + 1) + 1$ fi is a perverse definition of subtraction over the integers; its intended domain appears to be summarised by

$$\forall i, j: \mathbb{Z} \cdot i \geq j \;\Rightarrow\; diff(i, j) = i - j \tag{1}$$

But here again a denotational understanding founders on the need to provide a value for terms like $diff(2, 3)$.

The conditional interpretation of the logical operators outlined in [McC63] extends their meaning to cover undefined operands so that the implication in Eq. 1 evaluates to true with false as its left operand and undefined as its right. As indicated above, the conditional expression approach works but is less than ideal in proofs: the familiar commutativity property of conjunction and disjunction are lost and –in the case in hand– the contrapositive does not hold.

$$\forall i, j: \mathbb{Z} \cdot diff(i, j) \neq i - j \;\Rightarrow\; i < j \tag{2}$$

Moreover, although less likely to arise, there is no reason why the following should not be true

$$\forall i, j: \mathbb{Z} \cdot diff(i, j) = i - j \lor diff(j, i) = j - i \tag{3}$$

but this cannot hold in the conditional interpretation.

The real rub with the conditional view is that every operator is forced to be understood via its conditional expression meaning whether or not this is necessary. This observation has prompted a number of computer scientists (e.g. [Jon72,Dij76,Gri81]) to experiment with mixed sets of classical and conditional operators. The difficulty then is that the number of rules for manipulating the double set of operators is far greater and less intuitive than one would wish. None of the above cited contributions provide a full set of rules and surprises like right distribution of "conditional and" over the "conditional or" are unintuitive.

I made a further attempt to stay with classical logic in [Jon80] by using quantifiers to bound variables so as to make any term only meet values of its free variables for which it is defined. This experiment was also unsuccessful in proofs although it is broadly what is much more systematically worked out in *Order-Sorted Algebras* – see [GM92].

One of my earliest exposures to classical predicate calculus came from reading [Kle52] and I am sure that I had retained a memory of Łukasiewicz's "three-valued" logical operators. These are presented in Kleene's "blue book" only by truth tables but a student of Peter Aczel had provided an axiomatisation in [Kol76] and I misused the absence of his real supervisor to get Jen Cheng interested in the challenge of giving a natural deduction proof style for such operators (this led to [BCJ84,Che86,CJ91]). This logic has become known as the *Logic of Partial Function* (or LPF) and its use in [Jon86] and subsequent publications on VDM have convinced me that this provides a usable proof system. (As Kees Middelburg pointed out, Cheng had only provided a justification for an untyped version of the logic whereas VDM proofs typically used a typed version – this hole was closed in [JM94].) LPF is not classical logic, but the only

significant casualty is the "law of the excluded middle" – which with expressions
such as

$$hd\,[\,] = 5 \vee hd\,[\,] \neq 5 \qquad\qquad (4)$$

is a loss I can tolerate.

There are of course other approaches to the thorny problem of reasoning
about partial functions – see [JM94,CJ91,Jon95] for further references.

Lessons

The lessons which I believe it is important to draw from my series of attempts
to find a satisfactory way to reason about partial functions include the fact the
a real difficulty should be faced rather than ignored (I can accept any approach
to this problem much more readily than pretending it does not exist). But the
main lesson is that the mathematics that we require to handle computer science
problems may not be classical; it might or might not exist in textbooks. Kline
wrote

> More than anything else Mathematics is a method

Which I take to indicate that a mathematical approach exists and that there is
not some sacrosanct body of results within which we must expect to find the
tools to handle all (computing) problems.

2 Operation decomposition rules

An earlier (but yet to be published – see [Jon92] for a preprint) paper, traces one
view of a history of work on program verification. One interesting observation
that one could add to those made in the history is that all the way from Turing, through Floyd to Hoare and Dijkstra, there has been a reliance on proving
programs satisfy specifications in terms of predicates of a single state. Since the
purposes of a program are likely to be some sort of input/output relation this restriction being applied to post-conditions is surprising. In effect this odd decision
causes people to invent a number of auxiliary tricks such as extra "variables"
which cannot be changed by the program but have to be employed to remember
the initial state.

In contrast, the earliest work (post my first stay in Vienna) on what was
to become VDM [Jon73] used post-conditions which directly related initial and
final states. This section relates the discovery of usable operation decomposition
rules for such post-conditions.

Problem

In [Jon92], Hoare's seminal contribution of [Hoa69] is taken as a fulcrum around
which earlier and subsequent efforts can be conveniently surveyed. The rule

(axiom) there which facilitates reasoning about partial correctness of repetitive while constructs is both well known and a model of clarity.

$$\boxed{Hoare} \quad \frac{\{P \wedge b\} \, S \, \{P\}}{\{P\} \text{ while } b \text{ do } S \text{ end } \{P \wedge \neg b\}}$$

It is the reward of the single state view of post-conditions that such concise rules are available. (One can see this perhaps even more clearly with Dijkstra's weakest pre-condition work – see [DS90] and the considerable literature that this has spawned; but the Hoare rules provide a better comparison with the VDM work.)

In [Jon80] there are a number of rules which make it possible to establish results about iterative constructs. Interestingly, the first rules presented are for initialised while constructs. There is some virtue in this decision since the rules were intended to be used in program development and it is a fact that most useful iterative constructs have to be preceded by initialisation: the combined rules in some sense included the statement composition with the initialisation in a way which prompted reasonable design decisions. But even comparing the rules in [Hoa69] and [Jon80] for simple iteration the latter look heavy: they are presented as two separate domain conditions, two conditions about the relational meaning of the components and desired post-condition in addition to separate clauses about termination.

Peter Aczel wrote in [Acz82]

But a more flexible and powerful approach has been advocated by Cliff Jones ... His approach is to allow the post-condition of a specification to depend on the starting state of a computation ...

but went on to add that

His [CBJ] rules appear elaborate and unmemorable compared with the original rules for partial correctness of Hoare.

which is a considerably more polite commentary than they deserved. Aczel's unpublished note went on to show how a form of rule to cover post-conditions of two states could be formulated neatly (and be memorable). In the following, P is a predicate (truth-valued function) of a single state and R is a (transitive, well-founded) relation over state pairs. The rule

$$\boxed{AczelJones} \quad \frac{\{P \wedge b\} \, S \, \{P \wedge R\}}{\{P\} \text{ while } b \text{ do } S \text{ end } \{R^r \wedge \neg b\}} \quad R \text{ twf}$$

captures termination which was treated separately in the Hoare rule. (As a further confession here, [Jon80] presents the stupid compromise of using a termination function whose domain was a single state as in Hoare's rule).

Lesson

The lesson that I wish to draw from this story is that it is sometimes necessary to use a somewhat inelegant formulation until a better solution can be found. The path to the improvement might need to look at "simplifications" (such as Hoare's choice to rely on post-conditions of a single state) but one must also be prepared to look at the untidy solution to see what needs simplifying.

Hardy wrote in [Har67]

> there is no permanent place in the world for ugly mathematics

but there might be times when an ugly formulation is the best we have and its use is more honest than ducking the problem. Perhaps if we all had Hardy's skill and taste, we should always have clean formulations; I suspect not; I am sure that mere mortals can make a contribution be presenting something on which others can develop improvements.

Just before concluding this section, it is worth pointing out that the elegant formulation in the *AczelJones* rule above does actually lose something which was present in [Jon80]. In the original rules –quite apart from the question of including composed initialisation– there was a distinction between forward and backwards composition of the overall loop relation for the repetitive construct with the relation for the loop body. In [Jon80] they were called "up versus down" loops. Essentially the difference is whether the intermediate results of the loop are best understood in terms of a relation from the initial state or a relation with the end state. Use of the Hoare-like axioms tends to force non-overwriting of initial state information and can mostly be viewed as relations with the initial state; programs which compute the same result by destroying their inputs (e.g. computing n factorial whilst subtracting 1 from the variable containing n at each iteration) are often better understood via relations to the final state. The [Jon80] rules reflected this directly; there is an open piece of work to show how to do this with the new rule.

3 A challenge from parallel object-based languages

The events related in this section are much more recent than those discussed above and are to some extent are still unfolding. I developed a compositional way of developing some parallel (shared variable) programs during my work in Oxford: rely and guarantee-conditions were proposed in [Jon81,Jon83] as a way of recording and reasoning about interference; the work then lay somewhat dormant (a significant exception is the transfer to Temporal Logic in [BKP84]) until picked up and significantly developed in [Stø90,Xu92,Col94]. I returned to the challenge of finding usable methods for the design of interfering programs during a Research Council Fellowship from 1988-93. Although the developments of Ketil Stølen and Pierre Collette had made interference reasoning more useful, it was still clear that the proof work involved would be unlikely to find favour with working engineers who were already difficult to wean away from testing to reasoning about sequential programs. Ideas like rely and guarantee-conditions had shown that it was possible to specify interference in a way which facilitated constructing proofs about compositional developments but there were simply too many things to be proved. (Furthermore, it took considerable experience to juggle items between the various predicates – this is a point reviewed in [CJ98].) Late on in my Fellowship I realised that parallel object-oriented (or perhaps object-based since inheritance is a quagmire) languages offered a marvelous way to constrain interference and thus to put in the hands of the program designer a way to indicate precisely where interference was –and was not– an issue; POOL [AR89,Ame89] was the major inspiration.

The research led to the development of a design language which became known as $\pi o \beta \lambda$ in which there are three levels at which interference can be controlled

- all instance variables are strictly local to the object in which they are contained
- objects which can only be reached via local references form islands within which no interference can be experienced
- objects which can be reached by general references are subject (via their methods) to interference from elsewhere

There was then a linguistic framework in which decisions about interference could be expressed and complex reasoning with rely and guarantee-conditions could be restricted to those areas where the designer made a conscious decision that intimate interference between two processes was necessary. An unexpected bonus of the move to object-based languages was that there was a clear way of introducing some forms of concurrency by transforming sequential programs into ones which were observationally equivalent at the input/output level but could run faster if there were sufficiently many processors available (and a few scheduling problems were resolved).

Problem

A simple example of two allegedly equivalent $\pi o \beta \lambda$ programs can be given in the context of a linked list implementation of a sorting vector: Figures 1 and 2 show two $\pi o \beta \lambda$ programs which ought be equivalent.

A sequence of integers is represented by a linked-list of *Sort* objects. The first object behaves as a server containing the whole queue but, in fact, each object holds a single element of the sequence (in v) and a unique reference to the next object in the list (in l). The method *insert* places its argument such that the resulting sequence is in ascending order; *test* searches the sequence for its argument. The implementation of both of these methods is sequential: at most one object is active at any one time. In Figure 2 concurrency has been introduced by applying two equivalences. The *insert* method given in Figure 1 is sequential: its client is held in a "rendezvous" until the effect of the insert has passed down the list structure to the appropriate point and the return statements have been executed in every object on the way back up the list. If the return statement of *insert* is commuted to the beginning of the method as in Figure 2, the client is able to continue its computation concurrently with the activity of the insertion. Furthermore, as the insertion progresses down the list, objects "up stream" of the operation are free to accept further method calls. One can thus imagine a whole series of *insert* operations trickling concurrently down the list structure.

```
Sort class
vars v: N ← 0; l: unique ref(Sort) ← nil
insert(x: N) method
   begin
      if is-nil(l) then (v ← x; l ← new Sort)
      elif v ≤ x then l.insert(x)
      else (l.insert(v); v ← x)
      fi;
      return
   end
test(x: N) method : B
   if is-nil(l) ∨ x ≤ v then return false
   elif x = v then return true
   else return l.test(x)
   fi
```

Fig. 1. Example Program *Sort* – sequential

One task facing the $\pi o \beta \lambda$ research was then to have a justified set of equivalence –or transformation– rules (I rejected the suggestion that I just put down the transformation rules as the (only) language definition both because I did not initially see the prospect of getting a complete set of rules and because this would have simply shifted the burden onto anyone interested in implementing such a language).

Well, this sounded like a familiar challenge — one for which I had been equipped by over two decades of work on language definition topics. One writes a model-oriented (operational or denotational) description of the language and proves the putative equivalences are consistent with the model-oriented semantics. I dismissed the idea of writing a denotational definition in terms of power domains (my views on the real advantages of denotational semantics are somewhat heretical) and opted to write an SOS definition. Although I realised when reviewing the work of some PhD students who picked up this line of research that there is little real guidance in the literature as to how to formulate a clear operational semantics definition, the task is not difficult for someone who has written several definitions. But then the problems start: one could say that there is no natural algebra for SOS definitions. Initial attempts at proving the putative equivalences sound with respect to the SOS definition were cumbersome and unrevealing.

```
Sort class
   vars v: N ← 0; l: unique ref(Sort) ← nil
   insert(x: N) method
      begin
         return;
         if is-nil(l) then (v ← x; l ← new Sort)
         elif v ≤ x then l.insert(x)
         else (l.insert(v); v ← x)
         fi
      end
   test(x: N) method : B
      if is-nil(l) ∨ x ≤ v then return false
      elif x = v then return true
      else delegate l.test(x)
      fi
```

Fig. 2. The concurrent implementation of *Sort*

As well as stumbling on POOL at what appears to have been the right time, I also read the early papers (cf. [Mil92,MPW92]) on the π-calculus at about this point. Independently of David Walker, I decided to give the semantics of my parallel object based language by mapping it to the π-calculus (David was actually there first and, when Ito-sensei kindly sent me a copy of [IM91], I saw [Wal91] as a confirmation of what I was attempting). A mapping was not difficult to write although here there was less experience on which to base the style and I think it is fair to say that David and I have influenced each other in subsequent choices. There are clear notions of equivalences for process algebras so I was naively optimistic that it was just a case of choosing the most appropriate to the context of $\pi o \beta \lambda$ and it would be straightforward to justify the putative equivalences. Well, there are certainly no shortage of notions of bi-similarity! In fact I conjecture –based on my search– that there are far more notions than there are examples of proofs. It quickly became clear that the process expressions which resulted from my mapping of the $\pi o \beta \lambda$ programs of Figures 1 and 2 to the π-calculus resulted in process expressions which are not bi-similar in any obvious sense. The full story of the search for proofs has yet to be written. I was flattered that scientists like David Walker, Davide Sangiorgi and Benjamin Pierce found the problem interesting (cf. [Wal93,Wal94]). Suffice it to say that the task of proving particular cases of the equivalences (but one related to what I termed in [HJ96] as delegation is more delicate than the one illustrated here) was tractable but prompted new variants of bi-similarity; the task of justifying the general equivalences via the mapping to the π-calculus has proved far more taxing; [HJ96] does contain arguments via SOS for the general case. (It would also be interesting to trace how the SOS proof attempts and those via the mapping have yielded insights which have influenced each other.)

Lesson

I will risk offending some colleagues by maintaining that the notions of process algebraic equivalences have proceeded as an end in themselves rather than being clearly motivated by applications. The lesson that I would wish to draw from the $\pi o \beta \lambda$ story is that a clear need for notions of equivalence might be a better guiding light for research than a pure mathematical taxonomy of variants.

In [Jon96] and in my invited talk at ICFEM in Hiroshima, I argued strongly for looking at new application areas far more exotic than the parallel object-oriented languages discussed in the previous section; examples such as Virtual Reality modelling languages, CORBA, Java etc. seem to me much more potentially stimulating than honing formal description techniques on well worn abstractions of older computing paradigms. I hope the the $\pi o \beta \lambda$ story illustrates the potential payoff.

4 Deploying formal methods

This section relates a strategic rather than a technical mistake. It prepares the way for a comment in the summary. To make clear my starting point here, I assume that the purpose of developing formal methods is to influence practical engineering of computer systems (whether hardware or software). It is a measure of my unease with some research in the area of computer science that I feel it necessary to state this fact.

At one stage of my career, I spent a lot of time trying to transfer technology into practical computing environments. Most notably this was associated with VDM in IBM but there were many other contacts and it is perhaps less well known that I was also involved as a consultant in the Z work for CICS. During the late 1970s and early 80s, I consistently advised that the only way to get formal methods into real use was to insist that everyone in a team became familiar with their use. This advice was the result of several earlier rather negative experiences. Firstly I had repeatedly seen groups of "architects" design systems and record their work in natural language which was passed to a group of formalists who attempted to build a model from their understanding of the English. Anyone who has experienced this process for a significant system will know the upshot: streams of questions and contradictions are generated in the formalisation; the direct reward for passing these back to the architects was a further stream of English (with sometimes a grudging acknowledgement that these formalists were asking very interesting questions). As way of arriving at a coherent model of a system, this left much to be desired. It seemed to me that the only way forward was for everyone to work on the same (formal) model. Furthermore, in teaching VDM, I always insisted on teaching proof concepts because I felt that –even if not used– they deepened people's understanding of the formalism. I had also seen –in IBM Hursley as it so happens– the waste that occurred when one or two people in a large group went off to learn some formal method and came back into a group where even the notation was a complete barrier to interchange. In contrast, I had had some positive experiences where we were able to brainwash whole project groups at the same time.

Whether these experiences really justified my austere advice is not really the most important point here. It was some time before I saw that not only are there are some engineers who question the need for formal notation but there are some people who find it impossible to extract useful abstractions from the level of detail with which they normally work.

In more recent pronouncements on the application of formal methods I have modified my position considerably. I now recommend that something like Operations Research groups are formed where different members bring different skills. Thus there might be domain experts, implementors and formalists all involved in an architecture group.

Towards the end of the time when I was teaching at Manchester, I also taught a (Master's level) course on defining models of systems which put minimal emphasis on the notation itself and none on formal proof.

The lesson I draw from the above is that computer scientists have to think about how there ideas might be deployed; this might include addressing tool support before expecting users to adopt a new method; it almost certainly involves tackling a significant range of examples; my advice would also be to work together with real engineers (not just students) before thinking that one has the "silver bullet" for which industry has been waiting.

Summary

The above four personal stories are certainly not the only ones that I could have used to illustrate my themes: I could have chosen examples such as the decision in VDM language definitions to use an "exit combinator" rather than continuations, or the risk of deliberately using a data reification rule which was known to be incomplete. I could perhaps have chosen a catalogue of mistakes that I believe have been made by other scientists. But the examples chosen do serve to illustrate a number of points that I feel are in danger of being ignored by some researchers today.

Before reiterating the points of this sermon, I should make one thing absolutely clear. Nothing in what I have to say argues against the search for fundamental concepts which really do change the way we think about key concepts. With Algol-like languages we were lucky enough to find a ready concept for their denotations; for parallel languages, the search has been much harder and has not really yielded a universally agreed result. It is clear that finding the right concept here could make considerably more difference than detailed differences between one notation or another. Nor do I underestimate the importance of notation. Hoare's major supplement to Floyd's work was notational but it bought about a complete change of emphasis from operational reasoning to compositional design. But it must be remembered that significant steps in science are likely to come from long experimentation.

To take my points in the reverse of the order above: if we claim that we are doing research for the practising engineer we must make sure that the ideas proposed have at least some chance of being deployed in a way in which those building systems will actually be able to use them. Every esoteric mathematical concept must really be worthwhile (or carefully hidden in the way that my good friend Michael Jackson did so successfully in his design methods).

If we only look for mathematical elegance without clear applicability, we should be honest enough to list ourselves as (pure) mathematicians and not rely on a spurious contact with some simplified computing problems to justify our research.

We must look at today's applications and learn from them. Much has happened in computing since the "stack" and the problem of the "Dining Philosophers" were first taken as important paradigms on which to test formal approaches. Whatever the disadvantages of modern software (and I know many of them), significant systems are now constructed on top of a flexible and general interfaces to packages which handle much of the detail of –for example– the precise presentation on the screen. Attention has turned from closed systems which compute a particular input/output function to reactive systems.

We must not expect to find solutions to all of the problems presented by building computer systems in standard mathematics. Nor –unless we are unbelievably fortunate– will we always find beautiful mathematical solutions first time; but publishing an attempt which does solve a problem could spur others to show the way to a cleaner formulation. In any case, this is a more honest approach than ignoring all aspects of a problem which do not fit our current formalism. We should perhaps avoid massaging known problems: don't spend too much time on esoteric mathematics unless you're convinced it can all be hidden from engineers — remember that for formal methods to be used they must be usable by engineers.

References

[Acz82] P. Aczel. A note on program verification. manuscript, January 1982.

[Ame89] Pierre America. Issues in the design of a parallel object-oriented language. *Formal Aspects of Computing*, 1(4), 1989.

[AR89]   Pierre America and Jan Rutten. *A Parallel Object-Oriented Language: Design and Semantic Foundations*. PhD thesis, Free University of Amsterdam, 1989.

[BCJ84] H. Barringer, J.H. Cheng, and C. B. Jones. A logic covering undefinedness in program proofs. *Acta Informatica*, 21:251–269, 1984.

[BKP84] H. Barringer, R. Kuiper, and A. Pnueli. Now you can compose temporal logic specification. In *Proceedings of 16th ACM STOC*, Washington, May 1984.

[Che86] J.H. Cheng. *A Logic for Partial Functions*. PhD thesis, University of Manchester, 1986.

[CJ91]   J. H. Cheng and C. B. Jones. On the usability of logics which handle partial functions. In C. Morgan and J. C. P. Woodcock, editors, *3rd Refinement Workshop*, pages 51–69. Springer-Verlag, 1991.

[CJ98]   P. Collette and C. B. Jones. Enhancing the tractability of rely/guarantee specifications in the development of interfering operations. In G. D. Plotkin, editor, *to be published*. MIT Press, 1998.

[Col94]   Pierre Collette. *Design of Compositional Proof Systems Based on Assumption-Commitment Specifications - Application to UNITY*. PhD thesis, Louvain-la-Neuve, June 1994.

[Dij76]   E. W. Dijkstra. *A Discipline of Programming*. Prentice-Hall, 1976.

[DS90]   Edsger W Dijkstra and Carel S Scholten. *Predicate Calculus and Program Semantics*. Springer-Verlag, 1990. ISBN 0-387-96957-8, 3-540-96957-8.

[GM92]   J. Goguen and J. Meseguer. Order-sorted algebra I: Equational deduction for multiple inheritance, overloading, exceptions and partial operations. *Theoretical Computer Science*, 105:217–273, 1992.

[Gri81]   D. Gries. *The Science of Programming*. Springer-Verlag, 1981.

[Har67]   G. H. Hardy. *A Mathematician's Apology*. Cambridge University Press, 1967.

[HJ96]   Steve J. Hodges and Cliff B. Jones. Non-interference properties of a concurrent object-based language: Proofs based on an operational semantics. In Burkhard Freitag, Cliff B. Jones, Christian Lengauer, and Hans-Jörg Schek, editors, *Oject Orientation with Parallelism and Persistence*, pages 1–22. Kluwer Academic Publishers, 1996.

[Hoa69]   C. A. R. Hoare. An axiomatic basis for computer programming. *Communications of the ACM*, 12(10):576–580, 583, October 1969.

[IM91]   T. Ito and A. R. Meyer, editors. *TACS'91 - Proceedings of the International Conference on Theoretical Aspects of Computer Science, Sendai, Japan*, volume 526 of *Lecture Notes in Computer Science*. Springer-Verlag, 1991.

[JM94]   C.B. Jones and C.A. Middelburg. A typed logic of partial functions reconstructed classically. *Acta Informatica*, 31(5):399–430, 1994.

[Jon72]   C. B. Jones. Formal development of correct algorithms: an example based on Earley's recogniser. In *SIGPLAN Notices, Volume 7 Number 1*, pages 150–169. ACM, January 1972.

[Jon73]   C. B. Jones. Formal development of programs. Technical Report 12.117, IBM Laboratory Hursley, June 1973.

[Jon80]   C. B. Jones. *Software Development: A Rigorous Approach*. Prentice Hall International, 1980. ISBN 0-13-821884-6.

[Jon81]   C. B. Jones. *Development Methods for Computer Programs including a Notion of Interference*. PhD thesis, Oxford University, June 1981. Printed as: Programming Research Group, Technical Monograph 25.

[Jon83]   C. B. Jones. Specification and design of (parallel) programs. In *Proceedings of IFIP'83*, pages 321–332. North-Holland, 1983.

[Jon86]   C. B. Jones. *Systematic Software Development Using VDM*. Prentice Hall International, 1986.

[Jon92]   C. B. Jones. The search for tractable ways of reasoning about programs. Technical Report UMCS-92-4-4, Manchester University, 1992.

[Jon95]   C.B. Jones. Partial functions and logics: A warning. *Information Processing Letters*, 54(2):65–67, 1995.

[Jon96]   C. B. Jones. Some practical problems and their influence on semantics. In
           ESOP'96, volume 1058 of *Lecture Notes in Computer Science*, pages 1–17.
           Springer-Verlag, 1996.

[Kle52]   S. C. Kleene. *Introduction to Metamathematics*. Van Nostrad, 1952.

[Kol76]   G. Koletsos. Sequent calculus and partial logic. Master's thesis, Manchester
           University, 1976.

[Luc69]   P. Lucas. Note on strong meanings of logical operators. Technical Report
           LN 25.3.051, IBM Laboratory Vienna, 1969.

[LW69]   P. Lucas and K. Walk. *On The Formal Description of PL/I*, volume 6 of
           Annual Review in Automatic Programming Part 3. Pergamon Press, 1969.

[McC63]   J. McCarthy. Predicate calculus with 'undefined' as a truth-value. Technical
           Report AI Memo 1, Stanford Artificial Intelligence Project, March 22nd 1963.

[Mil92]   R. Milner. The polyadic π-calculus: A tutorial. In M. Broy, editor, *Logic
           and Algebra of Specification*. Springer-Verlag, 1992.

[MPW92]   R. Milner, J. Parrow, and D. Walker. A calculus of mobile processes. *In-
           formation and Computation*, 100:1–77, 1992.

[Stø90]   K. Stølen. *Development of Parallel Programs on Shared Data-Structures*.
           PhD thesis, Manchester University, 1990. available as UMCS-91-1-1.

[Wal91]   D. Walker. π-calculus semantics for object-oriented programming languages.
           In *[IM91]*, pages 532–547, 1991.

[Wal93]   D. Walker. Process calculus and parallel object-oriented programming lan-
           guages. In *In T. Casavant (ed), Parallel Computers: Theory and Practice*.
           Computer Society Press, to appear, 1993.

[Wal94]   D. Walker. Algebraic proofs of properties of objects, 1994. Proceedings of
           ESOP'94.

[Xu92]   Qiwen Xu. *A Theory of State-based Parallel Programming*. PhD thesis,
           Oxford University, 1992.

Specifying and Analyzing Dynamic Software Architectures*

Robert Allen, Rémi Douence, and David Garlan

School of Computer Science, Carnegie Mellon University, Pittsburgh, PA 15213, USA

IRISA, Campus de Beaulieu, 35042 Rennes Cedex, France

rallen@cs.cmu.edu douence@irisa.fr garlan@cs.cmu.edu

Abstract. A critical issue for complex component-based systems design is the modeling and analysis of architecture. One of the complicating factors in developing architectural models is accounting for systems whose architecture changes dynamically (during run time). This is because dynamic changes to architectural structure may interact in subtle ways with on-going computations of the system.

In this paper we argue that it is possible and valuable to provide a modeling approach that accounts for the interactions between architectural reconfiguration and non-reconfiguration system functionality, while maintaining a separation of concerns between these two aspects of a system. The key to the approach is to use a uniform notation and semantic base for both reconfiguration and steady-state behavior, while at the same time providing syntactic separation between the two. As we will show, this permits us to view the architecture in terms of a set of possible architectural snapshots, each with its own steady-state behavior. Transitions between these snapshots are accounted for by special reconfiguration-triggering events.

1 Introduction

Recently, there has been considerable progress on the development of architecture description languages (ADLs [12]) to support software architecture design and analysis. These languages capture the key design properties of a system by exposing the architectural structure as a composition of components interacting via connectors. Examples include Wright [1], UniCon [14], Rapide [10], Darwin [11] and ACME [5].

There are many aspects of a software system that can be addressed in an architectural description, including functional behavior, allocation of resources, performance, fault-tolerance, flexibility in the face of altered requirements, and so on. Each ADL tends to focus on one or more of these aspects.

---

* Research sponsored by the INRIA, the Defense Advanced Research Projects Agency, and Rome Laboratory, Air Force Materiel Command, USAF, under agreement number F30602-97-2-0031, and by the National Science Foundation under Grant No. CCR-9357792. The U.S. Government is authorized to reproduce and distribute reprints for Governmental purposes notwithstanding any copyright annotation thereon.

The views and conclusions contained herein are those of the authors and should not be interpreted as necessarily representing the official policies or endorsements, either expressed or implied, of INRIA, the Defense Advanced Research Projects Agency Rome Laboratory, or the U.S. Government.

In this paper we address the problem of capturing *dynamic* architectures. By "dynamic" we mean systems for which composition of interacting components changes during the course of a single computation. We distinguish this aspect of dynamic behavior from the *steady-state behavior*, by which we mean the computation performed by a system without reconfiguration.

We argue that it is both possible and valuable to separate the dynamic re-configuration behavior of an architecture from its non-reconfiguration functionality. While there exist ADLs, such as Darwin, that capture reconfiguration behavior, and facilities such as object-oriented languages that permit the combined description of both dynamic aspects and steady-state behavior, we believe that, at the architectural level, it is important to provide a notation that supports *both* aspects of design *while maintaining a separation of concerns*. In this paper we illustrate a new technique by which these two aspects can be described in a single formalism, while keeping them as separate "views". This facilitates the understanding of each aspect in isolation while still supporting analysis of the combined interaction between the two.

By providing a notation that provides a precise interpretation of each of these aspects, we permit the description to be analyzed for consistency and completeness, as well as for whether the system has application-specific properties desired by the architect. For example, we would like to guarantee that reconfigurations occur only at points in the computation permitted by the participating components and connectors. Also, whenever a new connection is established, we would like to show that the participating components exist at the moment of attachment. By considering interactions between the two forms of description, we can consider whether changing the participants at run time will result in inconsistencies among participants' states.

In the remainder of this paper we present our technique using the Wright ADL as our notational basis. We first review related works (Section 2). We introduce Wright (Section 3) and illustrate the problem of specifying dynamic architectures (Section 4). Then we show how a language originally designed for steady-state architectures, such as Wright, can be extended to handle dynamic aspects of architecture (Section 5). Next, we present the semantic model on which the approach is based (Section 6). Then we illustrate the kinds of analysis that such a formalism supports (Section 7). Finally, we discuss possible extensions of our work (Section 8).

2 Related Works

Our work is most closely related to two general classes of research. The first is architecture description languages. While there are a large number of such languages, only a few are capable of modeling dynamic architectures. The most prominent among these are Rapide and Darwin. In the case of Rapide, the notation takes an object-oriented view: new architectural components can be created much as one would create new objects in a object-oriented programming language [10]. A consequence of this design is that it is in general undecidable what topologies will be created during a Rapide execution. For this and other reasons, Rapide focuses on simulation and analysis of sets of execution traces. In contrast, Wright focuses on static checking.

In the case of Darwin, the language is solely concerned with the *structural* aspects of an architecture [11]. Thus, the issue of how reconfigurations interact with on-going computations does not arise. However, their use of the Pi-Calculus to give semantics to reconfiguration is elegant and suggestive of the power of a more flexible "dynamic" process algebras.

The second area of related work is general formalisms for reasoning about architectural designs. Among these two are most closely related. The first is term rewriting systems. For example, Inverardi and Wolf have shown how to model architectures using the CHAM [7]. As a general term rewriting system, CHAM is can describe arbitrary reconfigurations of architectures. While this approach has considerable power, the cost is that the description of systems and reconfigurations must be encoded in system rewriting rules, which may be far removed from the intuitive descriptions used by system designers. In contrast, Wright has tried to provide a notation that makes explicit the intentions of a designer for handling reconfigurability.

Another general-purpose formalism applied to dynamic architectures is the use of graph grammars to describe the allowable topologies of architectures [9]. Graph grammars provide a nice notation for capturing patterns of transformation. However, thus far they have not been used to relate the reconfiguration aspects of an architecture with its behavior. Thus, as before, it is not possible to reason about when it is legal to carry out architectural reconfiguration.

3 Motivating Example

Consider the simple client-server system shown in Figure 1. It consists of one client and one server interacting via a link connector. Such a system is easy to describe in an ADL such as Wright [1,2]. There are two essential aspects of a Wright description of a system architecture: architectural structure, and architectural behavior. We illustrate both aspects using the example, which is described in Wright in Figure 2.

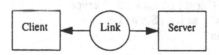

Figure 1 Static Topology : Simple Client-Server System

3.1 Architectural Structure

Wright represents architectural structure as graph of components and connectors. Components represent architecturally-relevant units of computation and data storage, while connectors represent the interactions between components. In Wright components and connectors are typed. Thus to define a system, one first declares a set of component and connector types, termed as a *Style*. Then one declares a set of instances of these types and the way in which they are assembled.

Figure 2 opens with a definition of the *Client-Server* style by declaring a *Client* and *Server* component types, as well as a *Link* connector type. Components have interfaces, which in Wright are called *ports*. Any component may have multiple ports, each port defining a logically separable point of interaction with its environment. Here, both our client and server component types have only one port *p*. Connectors also have interfaces, which are termed *roles*. The roles of a connector identify the logical participants in the interaction represented by the connector, and (as we will see shortly) specify the expected behavior of each participant in the interaction. In Figure 2, the *Link* connector has a role c for the client and one s for the server. Finally, the constraints define a set of predicates that every configurations conforming to that style must satisfy.

Style Client-Server
  Component Client
    Port p = $\overline{\text{request}}$ → reply → p ⊓ §
    Computation = internalCompute → $\overline{\text{p.request}}$ → p.reply → **Computation** ⊓ §

  Component Server
    Port p = request → $\overline{\text{reply}}$ → p [] §
    Computation = p.request → internalCompute → $\overline{\text{p.reply}}$ → **Computation** [] §

  Connector Link
    Role c = $\overline{\text{request}}$ → reply → c ⊓ §
    Role s = request → $\overline{\text{reply}}$ → s [] §
    Glue = c.request → s.request → **Glue**
      [] s.reply → c.reply → **Glue**
      [] §

  Constraints
    ∃! s ∈ Component, ∀ c ∈ Component : Server(s) ∧ Client(c) ⇒ connected(c,s)
EndStyle

Configuration Simple
  Style Client-Server
  Instances C : Client ; L : Link ; S : Server
  Attachments C.p **as** L.c ; S.p **as** L.s
EndConfiguration

Figure 2 Static Wright Specification : Simple Client-Server System

---

A small configuration is also shown in Figure 2. It uses the Client-Server style (making the components and connector types available) to declare a single client-server connector. These part are then assembled. Specifically, the port p of the client C fills the role c of the connector L, while the port p of the server S fills the role s of the connector.

3.2 Architectural Behavior

Wright focuses on architectural behavior characterized in terms of the significant events that take place in the computations of a components, and the interactions between components as described by the connectors. It allows the user to formally specify behavior such as: "the client makes a request, which is received by the server, and the server provides a response, that is communicated to the client; this sequence of actions can be repeated many times". The notation for specifying event-based behavior is adapted from CSP [6]. Each CSP process defines an alphabet of events and the permitted patterns of events that the process may exhibit. These processes synchronize on common events (i.e., interact) when composed in parallel. Wright uses such process descriptions in computation, port, role and glue specifications.

A *computation* defines a component's behavior: the way in which it accepts certain events on certain *ports* and produces new events on those or other ports. As illustrated in Figure 2, a *Client* iteratively makes a request ($\overline{p.request}$) and waits a reply (*p.reply*) on port *p*, or terminates successfully (§*). The use of internal choice (⊓) in the specification indicates that it is the client that decides whether it makes a request or terminates. In contrast, the use of external choice (□) in the *Server* specification indicates that the server is expected to respond to any number of requests, and may not terminate prematurely. Moreover, because we are interested in how different components control interactions, Wright distinguishes initiated events from observed events by an overbar. For example, the client initiates requests (e.g., $\overline{p.request}$) while the server observes them (e.g., *p.request*).

A *port* process defines the local protocol with which the component interacts with its environment through that port. This protocol is effectively the projection of the component's computation onto the particular interface point. For example, the client single port *p* faithfully reproduces the client computation pattern, but hides the internal computation modeled by the event *internalCompute*.

A *role* specifies the protocol that must be satisfied by any port that is attached to that role. In general, a port need not have the same behavior as the role that it fills, but may choose to use only a subset of the connector capabilities. In our simple case, the link role *c* and the client port *p* for example are identical.

Finally, a glue specification describes how the roles of a connector interact with each other. In the example, a client request (*c.request*) must be transmitted to the server ($\overline{s.request}$), and the server reply (*s.reply*) must be transmitted back to the client ($\overline{c.reply}$). We have described in [1,2] how these formal descriptions can be used to check the consistency and completeness of architectural descriptions. We come back to this topic in section 7.

In this description, the server does not terminate until the client is ready. But, what of a more realistic situation, where the server is running on an unreliable processor over a network, and may crash unexpectedly? In this case, the architect must consider two aspects of a robust architectural design. First is the simple view of the normal system behavior, in which the client makes a request of the server, and receives a response. Second is the architect's solution to the problem of server crashes (i.e., the way in which a server is restarted or replaced so that there is always a service available for the client). In the next section we look at one approach to unifying these two aspects of design.

4 Simulating Dynamism

Let us now consider one possible solution (see Figure 3) in which there are two servers: a "primary" server, which is more desirable to use, but which may go down unexpectedly, and a "secondary" server, which, while reliable, provides a lesser form of the service. One way to use these is to alter the architecture such that both servers are present, and when the

---

* § is similar to the CSP process TICK, except that § represents a *willingness* to terminate rather than a *decision* to terminate. So, § can occur at choice points (e.g., P □ § and P ⊓ §), which is illegal in standard CSP. An alternative definition of the sequencing operator ";" makes this kind of expression consistent. See [1] for details.

primary server goes down, the client uses the secondary server until such time as the primary server returns to service. (This kind of fault-tolerant architecture is actually used by the Simplex System [13].) The topology of the system is shown in Figure 3.

A Wright description of a possible client is shown in Figure 4. In this solution the primary server communicates its status to the client with *down* and *up* events when it is about to go down or come up (resp). (In practise, such events might be supplied by a time-out service.) These events appear in the *Client* definition. The port *Primary* expresses the client assumptions that the primary server can go down anytime, except in the middle of a request (i.e., not between *request* and *reply*), and once it goes down it provides no service until it comes up. The secondary server is a safe one that is always ready to serve. It is not concerned with *down* and *up* events (which do not occur on the port *Secondary*). The client computation now has two states (*UsePrimary* and *UseSecondary*) encoding which is the active server. The down and up events switch from one state to the other.

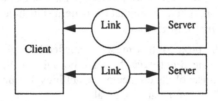

Figure 3 Static Topology : Fault-Tolerant Client-Server System

Component Client
    Port Primary = § ⊓ ($\overline{\text{request}}$ → reply → Primary) [] down → (§ ⊓ up → Primary))
    Port Secondary = § ⊓ $\overline{\text{request}}$ → reply → Secondary
    Computation = UsePrimary
        where UsePrimary = internalCompute → (TryPrimary ⊓ §)
            TryPrimary = $\overline{\text{primary.request}}$ → primary.reply → UsePrimary
                 [] primary.down → TrySecondary
            UseSecondary = internalCompute → (TrySecondary ⊓ §)
            TrySecondary = $\overline{\text{secondary.request}}$ → secondary.reply → UseSecondary
                 [] primary.up → TryPrimary

Figure 4 Static Wright Specification : Client Component (Fault-Tolerant Client-Server)

While this accomplishes what we set out to do, the description of the new architecture has several disadvantages:

• The simple client-server functional pattern and topology have been lost. In particular, its specification is now muddied by the need to consider the effects of reconfiguration at almost each step, and the client-server style constraint (see Figure 2: exactly one server is connected to every clients) is no longer true.

- It has been necessary to significantly alter the original simple client in order to accommodate a change that arguably should occur on the server's side. We have had to duplicate Client's Port, so this component now must keep state to know which port to use (i.e., which is the active server). Ideally, the client should be able to continue to operate as before, but have the *system* handle rerouting of requests to the new server.

- Distribution of the configuration state and re-configuration actions in the components makes the modifications of this system difficult. For example, adding a third backup, or permitting only the primary to go down once before abandoning it, requires extensive changes to all parts of the system, thus reducing the reusability of the constituent elements.

Instead of rigid encoding of the dynamism in the steady state behavior of the components, what we would like is to provide constructs to describe the dynamics of the system explicitly. In this case, rather than using a *fixed* topology of two servers and hiding the changes inside a client component' "choice" about which server to use, we could describe the server's failures as triggers that change the topology during computation. In effect, instead of the single configuration shown in Figure 3, we would have *two* configurations, shown in Figure 5. These configurations, each simple in itself, alternate as the primary server goes down and comes back up.

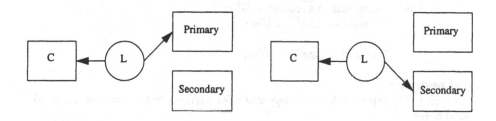

Figure 5 Dynamic Topology : Alternating Configurations of a Fault-Tolerant Client-Server

In order to achieve this effect, we must introduce notations for characterizing changes in the architecture during a computation. Such a characterization includes: (a) what events in the computation trigger a re-configuration, and (b) how the system should be reconfigured in response to a trigger.

5 Our Approach

Our solution consists of two parts. First, special "control" events are introduced into a component's alphabet, and allowed to occur in port descriptions. In this way, the interface of a component is extended to describe when reconfigurations are permitted in each protocol in which it participates. Second, these control events are used in a separate view of the architecture, the configuration program, which describes how these events trigger reconfigurations.

To illustrate, consider the fault-tolerant client-server style described in Figure 6. The architectural types (*Client*, *FlakyServer*, *SlowServer*) are declared in the usual way, but they also include events like *down* and *up*, now explicitly marked as "control" rather than "communication" events. The *FlakyServer* indicates the states in which it may go down (with *control.down*) and come up (with *control.up*). Specifically, it may go down at any-time, except in the middle of a transaction (i.e., not between *request* and $\overline{reply}$) and it may come up anytime after a *down*. These events indicate the states in which the server accepts a reconfiguration. In the same way, a *SlowServer* component can be turned *on* then *off* any-time, except in the middle of a transaction. And a *FTLink* can be reconfigured (*changeOk*) between request and reply transmissions.

Style Fault-Tolerant-Client-Server
    Component FlakyServer
        Port p = § [] (request → $\overline{reply}$ → p ⊓ control.down → (§ [] control.up → p))
        Computation = § [] (p.request → internalCompute → $\overline{p.reply}$ → **Computation**
                      ⊓ control.down → (§ [] control.up → **Computation**))

    Component SlowServer
        Port p = § [] control.on → μLoop.(request → $\overline{reply}$ → Loop [] control.off → p [] §)
        Computation = § [] control.on → μLoop. (control.off → **Computation** [] §
        [] p.request → internalCompute → $\overline{p.reply}$ → Loop

    Connector FTLink
        Role c = $\overline{request}$ → reply → c ⊓ §
        Role s = (request → $\overline{reply}$ → s ⊓ control.changeOk → s)[] §
        Glue = c.request → $\overline{s.request}$ → **Glue**
          [] s.reply → $\overline{c.reply}$ → **Glue**
          [] §
          [] control.changeOk → **Glue**

    Constraints
        ∃! s ∈ Component, ∀ c ∈ Component : Server(s) ∧ Client(c) ⇒ connected(c,s)
End Style

Figure 6 Dynamic Wright Specification : Fault-Tolerant Client-Server Style

---

This new style can be used to build different systems. For example, Figure 7 pictures our version of the fault-tolerant client-server system. The *Configuror* is responsible for achieving the changes to the architectural topology (triggered by *up* and *down*) using in-stances of architecture types (e.g., *Client*, *FlakyServer*, *SlowServer*), and *new*, *del*, *attach*, and *detach* actions, as illustrated in Figure 8.

In this reconfiguration program, unlike the previous solution, the *Client* component type is identical to the original one in Figure 2. The initial sequence of actions (*new* and *at-tach*) builds the original system. Then *WaitForDown* describes two situations: the system can run and successfully terminate (§) or a fault can occur. If the primary server goes down, the secondary server is in state *on* and the link connector is reconfigurable, the pri-mary server is detached from the link and is replaced by the secondary server. The new configuration then resumes its execution until it terminates or the primary server comes up. In this latter case, *WaitForUp* specifies that when the secondary server is *off* and the link connector is reconfigurable (*changeOk*), the secondary server is detached from the link and is replaced by the primary server.

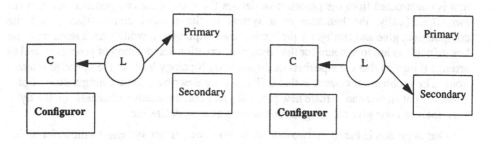

Figure 7 Dynamic Topology : Alternating Configurations of Fault-Tolerant Client-Server

      Configuror DynamicClient-Server
        Style Fault-Tolerant-Client-Server
            new.C:Client
            → new.Primary : FlakyServer
            → new.Secondary : SlowServer
            → new.L : FTLink
            → attach.C.p.to.L.c
            → attach.Primary.p.to.L.s → WaitForDown
   where
   WaitForDown = (Primary.control.down → Secondary.control.on →
                    L.control.changeOk → **Style** Fault-Tolerant-Client-Server
                          detach.Primary.p.from.L.s
                          → attach.Secondary.p.to.L.s
                          → WaitForUp)
                 [] §
   WaitForUp   = (Primary.control.up → Secondary.control.off →
                    L.control.changeOk → **Style** Fault-Tolerant-Client-Server
                          detach.Secondary.p.from.L.s
                          → attach.Primary.p.to.L.s
                          → WaitForDown)
                 [] §

Figure 8 Dynamic Wright Specification : Configuror (Fault-Tolerant-Client-Server System)

    Thus, this configuror describes three configurations (an initial one, and two alternating configurations). In the configuror, a style annotation specifies the set of component and connector types a configuration can use and the constraints it must satisfy. Here we use the same style. In general, each configuration can use a different style. In this example, it is easy to see that the *Fault-Tolerant-Client-Server* style constraint is verified in each of the three possible configurations: in each configuration, the client is connected to one server.

6 Semantics

Thus far we have relied on the reader's intuition and good faith that the notation outlined above makes sense. In this section we present the formal basis for this.

The basic idea is to translate the notation into pure CSP [6]. The behavior of the system is constructed from the process that defines the constituent components and connectors. Specifically, the behavior of a system is the parallel composition of all the computation, glue and configuror processes. In attempting to provide such a semantics, the key difficulties are to account for the "dynamic" creation and deletion of processes, and to arrange things so that the alphabets of the evolving topology leads to the intended interactions. The problem, of course, is that CSP can only describe a static configuration of processes. (That is, one can't create new processes and communication channels "on the fly"). How then can one give meaning to such actions as *new*, *delete*, etc.?

Our approach is based on two key ideas. First we restrict systems to those for which there are a finite (albeit potentially large) set of possible configurations (see section 8 for further discussion of this issue). Second, in the translation to CSP we "tag" events with the configuration in which that event occurs. (Because of our restriction to finite set of configurations, there is a finite number of possible tags.) The effect of a reconfiguration action is to select the properly tagged version of CSP expressions so that the interactions occur as defined by the new configuration. Thus an (untagged) e, in one configuration might end up (after tagging) synchronizing with one process in one configuration, but with another in a different configuration.

More formally, each event $p.e$ of the component Cp^* is relabelled as $Cp.p.e.Cn.r$ when the port p of Cp is attached to the role r of the connector Cn. For example, in our fault-tolerant client server system when the $\overline{FTLink}$ connector interacts with the *Primary* server, the "reply" case of L (s.reply $\rightarrow$ c.reply $\rightarrow$ **Glue**) is translated to:

$$L.s.reply.Primary.p \rightarrow \overline{L.c.reply.C.p} \rightarrow \textbf{Glue}$$

This indicates that a reply received by L on role s (from the *Primary* server port p) must be transmitted (by L on the role c) to the client C on port p.

Our transformation also introduces the "plumbing" that allows selection of the proper version: each version of a transformed component begins with a $Cp.go.p_1.Cn_1.r_1...r_n.Cn_n.r_n$ event selecting the version of Cp, where its port p_1 is attached to the role r_1 of $Cn_1,...$ and its port p_n attached to the role r_n of Cn_n. For example, the connector L is translated to:

$$L \quad = \quad L.go.c.C.p.s.Primary.p \rightarrow \textbf{Glue}_1$$
$$[] \quad L.go.c.C.p.s.Secondary.p \rightarrow \textbf{Glue}_2$$
$$\textbf{Glue}_1 = L.c.request.C.p \rightarrow (\overline{L.s.request.Primary.p} \rightarrow \textbf{Glue}_1 \, [] \, ...$$
$$\textbf{Glue}_2 = L.c.request.C.p \rightarrow (\overline{L.s.request.Secondary.p} \rightarrow \textbf{Glue}_2 \, [] \, ...$$

Finally, the configuror definition is transformed into a CSP process too, where the *new*, *del*, *attach* and *detach* actions are transformed into the previous $Cp.go...$ events that select the proper configuration of the components at each reconfiguration step. For example, the following configuror portion:

$$new.L \rightarrow Attach.C.p.to.L.c \rightarrow Attach.Primary.p.to.L.s \rightarrow ...$$

is transformed to $\quad$ $L.go.c.C.p.s.Primary.p \rightarrow ...$

---

* In the rest of this paper, Cp designates a Wright component, p a port, Cn a connector, r a role, and C a component or a connector.

The component transformation $\mathcal{T}Comp$ is formally defined in Figure 9. The transformation $\mathcal{T}Comp_1$ introduces a main label (to restart the component in its initial state) and enumerates the different versions of the code with the help of the CSP notation $\forall\, i : \{1, 2, 3\}$ $[]\, P_i = P_1\, []\, P_2\, []\, P_3$. In each version the events are renamed according to the current attachments (an unattached port is treated as attached to the role *void* of the dummy connector *Void*). The next to last substitution renames the internal events, and the last one restarts the process in its initial state after each control event, so that a different version can be selected. If a control event occurrence is followed by an arbitrary expression (rather than the label **Computation**), an auxiliary definition should be introduced and compiled similarly.

$\forall$ Cp: Component and Ports(Cp) = $\{p_1, \ldots p_n\}$

    $\mathcal{T}Comp\,[\![\, Cp\,]\!] = \mathcal{T}Comp_1[\![\, Computation(Cp)\,]\!]$

$\mathcal{T}Comp_1[\![\, P\,]\!] = \mu Cp.main.$

  § []

  ($\forall$ Cn$_1$: Connectors $\cup$ {Void},...,$\forall$ Cn$_n$: Connectors $\cup$ {Void}

  $\forall$ r$_1$: Roles(Cn$_1$),...,$\forall$ r$_n$: Roles(Cn$_n$)

  []

  (Cp.go.p$_1$.Cn$_1$.r$_1$...p$_n$.Cn$_n$.r$_n \to P$ [Cp.p$_1$.e.Cn$_1$.r$_1$ / p$_1$.e]

          ...

                  [Cp.p$_n$.e.Cn$_n$.r$_n$ / p$_n$.e]

                  [Cp.e / e]

               [Cp.control.evt $\to$ Cp.main / control.evt $\to$ **Computation**]))

Figure 9 Component Cp Semantics

The connector definitions are "compiled" in the same way. The Glue transformation (not shown here) is symmetric: rather than enumerating all possible roles that may attach to the given port, we vary the ports, while holding the role fixed. The renaming pattern is similar to that of Figure 9 (i.e., *Cp.p.e.Cn.r*), so that it matches the "compiled" component events.

The grammar in Figure 10 defines legal configurors. An initial sequence of action events building the original system is followed by re-configuration rules. Basically, a re-configuration rule is defined by a triggering sequence of control events followed by a sequence of action events. Several rules can compete in parallel (Rule$_1$ [] ... [] Rule$_n$); one of them is selected as the components produce the proper control events. Every rule is followed by a piece of configuror (i.e., the next rules to apply). The success process § terminates the reconfigurations and recursion permits infinite reconfiguration sequences.

Main = Action$^+$ $\to$ Configuror   where A$^+$ = A $\to$ A$^+$ | A

Configuror = (Rule$_1$ [] ... [] Rule$_n$) | μX.Configuror(X)

Rule = § | C.control.evt$^+$ $\to$ Action$^+$ $\to$ Configuror

Action = new.C | del.C | attach.Cp.p.to.Cn.r | detach.Cp.p.from.Cn.r

Figure 10 Configuror BNF Grammar

The Configuror transformation $\mathcal{T}Conf$ is defined in Figure 11 with the help of a *cfg* argument recording the current configuration. In order to make the transformation simpler, we assume a first pass has reordered all actions so that each reconfiguration rule follows the sequence: detachments, deletions, attachments and creations. The first rule in Figure

11 reproduces the control events, the second and fourth ones maintain the *cfg* argument. The rule for *new* produces *go* events according to *cfg*. The rule for *del* produces nothing, since according to our transformation in Figure 9 after a control event the component or connector is in its initial state waiting for a go. The seventh case detects the end of a rule and resumes (go events) the components and connectors which triggered the current rule and haven't been deleted, then it calls $\mathit{TConf_2}$. The four $\mathit{TConf_2}$ rules reproduce the config-uror structure.

$\mathit{TConf}[\![\ C.control.e \to P\ ]\!]$ $cfg = C.control.e \to \mathit{TConf}[\![\ P\ ]\!]\ cfg$

$\mathit{TConf}[\![\ detach.Cp.p.from.Cn.r \to P\ ]\!]cfg = \mathit{TConf}[\![\ P\ ]\!]\ (detach\ Cp.p\ Cn.r\ cfg)$

$\mathit{TConf}[\![\ del.C \to P\ ]\!]$ $cfg = \mathit{TConf}[\![\ P\ ]\!]\ (del\ C\ cfg)$

$\mathit{TConf}[\![\ attach.Cp.p.to.Cn.r \to P\ ]\!]$ $cfg = \mathit{TConf}[\![\ P\ ]\!]\ (attach\ Cp.p\ Cn.r\ cfg)$

$\mathit{TConf}[\![\ new.Cp \to P\ ]\!]$ $cfg = Cp.go.p_1.Cn_1.r_1...p_n.Cn_n.r_n \to \mathit{TConf}[\![\ P\ ]\!]\ (new\ Cp\ cfg)$

$\mathit{TConf}[\![\ new.Cn \to P\ ]\!]$ $cfg = Cn.go.r_1.Cp_1.p_1...r_n.Cp_n.p_n \to \mathit{TConf}[\![\ P\ ]\!]\ (new\ Cn\ cfg)$

$\mathit{TConf}[\![\ P\ ]\!]$ $cfg = Cp_1.go.p_{11}.Cn_{11}.r_{11}...p_{1n}.Cn_{1n}.r_{1n} \to$

                 $...$

                 $Cn_m.go.r_{m1}.Cp_{m1}.p_{m1}...r_{mp}.Cp_{mp}.p_{mp} \to$

                 $(\mathit{TConf_2}\ [\![\ P\ ]\!]\ cfg)$

$\mathit{TConf_2}\ [\![\ Rule_1\ [] \ ...\ []\ Rule_n\ ]\!]$ $cfg = (\mathit{TConf}[\![\ Rule_1\ ]\!]\ cfg)\ [] \ ...\ []\ (\mathit{TConf}[\![\ Rule_n\ ]\!]\ cfg)$

$\mathit{TConf_2}\ [\![\ \mu X.P(X)\ ]\!]$ $cfg = \mu X.(\mathit{TConf}[\![\ P(X)\ ]\!]\ cfg)$

$\mathit{TConf_2}\ [\![\ X\ ]\!]$ $cfg = X$

$\mathit{TConf_2}\ [\![\ \S\ ]\!]$ $cfg = \S$

Figure 11 Configuror Semantics

---

7 Analysis

Having specified a system and given its semantics, we would now like to analyze it. The formal semantics based on CSP allows us to adapt or extend the consistency and complete-ness analysis provided by (static) Wright. First, we formally present these checks in our dynamic context. Then we apply them to our fault-tolerant client-server example. Finally we show how to check the equivalence of a dynamic system with a static one.

7.1 Formal Tests Definition

As a configuror describes a sequence of steady state systems, the original Wright checks can be easily adapted to the dynamic extension. In this section, we review and adapt two of the most relevant Wright checks in our example. (A complete presentation of the original tests can be found in [1,2].) We then propose a new test dealing with the configuror and the dynamic aspects of the system.

7.1.1 Connector Consistency

In Wright the connector roles specify the expected behaviors of connected components and the glue specifies the coordination of these behaviors. Thus, inconsistencies between the participants in an interaction and the coordination of the glue are detected by the fol-lowing check (using the CSP process labelling operator *label:process*):

Check 1 $(C.Glue\ ||\ r_1{:}(C.r_1)\ ||\ ...\ ||\ r_n{:}(C.r_n))$ *is deadlock free.*

Another kind of inconsistency is also detectable as deadlock: if a role specification is internally inconsistent. In a complicated role specification, there may be errors that lead to a situation in which no event is possible for that participant, even if the glue were willing to take any event. This is detected by another test:

Check 2 *Each role* $r_1,...r_n$ *of the connector C is deadlock free.*

Both checks can be directly reused in our dynamic extension. They are easily performed with the help of the FDR model checker [4]. In case of failure, the tool provides the execution traces leading to the deadlock. This information may help the user to debug his specifications.

7.1.2 Attachment Consistency

In Wright, a port is a specification of a component, as it is seen from the point of view of a single interaction. A role, on the other hand, acts has a placeholder representing the range of potential participants in the interaction described by a connector. An important check is whether the port of a component is "consistent" with respect to a role to which it is attached (see especially [2]). Specifically, the port-role consistency check must ensure that when in a situation described by the role protocol, the port must always continue the protocol in a way that the role could have. This property can be expressed with a CSP refinement check. When the role r of the connector Cn is attached to the port p of the component Cp, we must check:

Check 3 $R \subseteq (P \mid\mid \det(Cn.r))$ *with* $P = Cp.p \mid\mid \text{Stop}_{\alpha r \backslash \alpha p}$ *and* $R = Cn.r \mid\mid \text{Stop}_{\alpha p \backslash \alpha r}$

As the role specifies the range of behavior that the component may have, and it circumscribes the behaviors over which the connector's rules are expected to apply, the check uses its deterministic version $\det(Cn.r)$ to constraint the port behavior. The CSP refinement operator $P \subseteq Q$ requires P and Q have the same alphabet. Stop processes, in the previous check, are used to extend the port and role alphabets.

This check must be redefined in our dynamic context. First, because of reconfigurations, it may not be a port which is attached to a single role in a dynamic system, but a sequence of ports as described by the configuror. For each role, a corresponding "virtual" port must be constructed using the configuror and port definitions. If a control event e has several occurrences in a port (e.g., $p = ... control.e \rightarrow E_1 ... control.e \rightarrow E_2 ...$), we cannot select either E_1 or E_2 when e occurs. We must assume the component can be in any of these states and use the virtual port expression $control.e \rightarrow (E_1 \sqcap E_2)$. Second, the ports and roles use different control events, which are associated by the configuror rules. So, the configuror must appear on both sides of the refinement checks. Third, a re-configuration rule expresses the rendez-vous of several components (the re-configuration actions are performed once *all* parts are ready). To express this synchronization, the control events of the port and role, and the control events sequences of the configuror rules are bracketed by a shared event *Synchro* (see example in section 7.2). With these transformed expressions (noted as E''), the port-role compatibility check becomes:

Check 4 $(Cn.r'' \mid\mid Configuror'') \subseteq (Virtual.p'' \mid\mid \det(Cn.r'') \mid\mid Configuror'')$

Wright provides other tests, which are easily adapted to our extension. We do not detail them here. These tests include: component consistency checks (is a port a projection of the computation?), attachment completeness checks (does an unattached port expect to interact with its environment?), style checks (is a style constraint satisfied by a configuration?) and initiator checks (are the initiated-observed annotations consistent?). However, our dynamic context provides also new opportunities for checking.

7.1.3 Configuror Consistency

Consistent configurors must guarantee that when the event *new.C* occurs, *C* does not already belong to the current configuration. As the configuror is defined in CSP, the test of this property can be formally expressed as a CSP refinement check:

Check 5 (prop = (new.C $\rightarrow$ (del.C $\rightarrow$ prop[] §)) [] §) $\subseteq$ configuror

Similar properties dealing with attachments can be expressed and checked in the same way. Also, more configuror checks can be defined. These tests include: configuror-connector consistency (do a glue and the configuror agree on next control events?), and configuror-component consistency (do a computation and the configuror agree on next control events?).

7.2 Applications

In this section, we apply the previously-defined checks to our fault-tolerant client-server system specifications (Figures 6 and 8).

7.2.1 Connector Consistency

The *FTLink* connector consistency checks are expressed as:

Claim 1 (FTLink.Glue | | c:(FTLink.c) | | s:(FTLink.s)) *is deadlock free.*

Claim 2 *Roles* FTLink.c *and* FTLink.s *are deadlock free.*

Checking these properties with FDR, we discover that the connector of Figure 6 is, in fact, not deadlock-free (Claim 1 fails). Indeed, if a reconfiguration (*changeOk*) occurs after the client has sent a request (*c.request*), but before it has been transmitted to the server ($\overline{s.request}$), the connector will deadlock. On the other hand, we do not have to worry about reconfiguration when the Link is transmitting a reply back to the client. In this case we can postpone the reconfiguration until the end of the transaction.

This failure has an intuitive explanation. In a concrete implementation, if the active server goes down in the middle of a request transmission (between *c.request* and $\overline{s.request}$), the reconfiguration must be taken into account or the connector will try to send the request to the wrong server. But, if the active server goes down in the middle of a reply transmission (between *s.reply* and $\overline{c.reply}$), the *FTLink* connector can still send the reply to the client, before reconfiguring its attachments with the servers.

This specification and its analysis can help the programmer modify the original Link definition (Figure 2) to achieve a fault-tolerant one. In practice, the code dealing with reconfiguration (e.g., switching the communication channel) should not be simply inserted in the original Link definition as a new fourth case, but it must also be interleaved with the transmission of a request. A correct version of Link's Glue is detailed in Figure 12.

Finally, this example reveals a point about fault-tolerance: this kind of system requires a buffer to handle transient states. In our case, a request is stored in the connector until a stable configuration with a working server is reached (see **RequestToSend**).

Glue = c.request → ($\overline{\text{s.request}}$ → **Glue** [] control.changeOk → **RequestToSend**)
    [] s.reply → $\overline{\text{c.reply}}$ → **Glue**
    [] §
    [] control.changeOk → **Glue**
where RequestToSend = $\overline{\text{s.request}}$ → **Glue** [] control.changeOk → **RequestToSend**

Figure 12 Dynamic Wright Specification : Deadlock Free FTLink Connector

---

7.2.2 Attachment Consistency

In our dynamic fault-tolerant client-server system, the *FTLink* connector is alternatively attached to a *FlakyServer* and a *SlowServer*. So, the "virtual" server port attached to *L.s* is:

Virtual.p_1 = § [] (request → $\overline{\text{reply}}$ → Virtual.p_1 ⊓ Primary.control.down → Virtual.p_2)
Virtual.p_2 = request → $\overline{\text{reply}}$ → Virtual.p_2 [] Secondary.control.off → Virtual.p_1 [] §

Then, the shared event *Synchro* is introduced in the port, role and configuror definitions. Because of space constraints we have abstracted the sequences of actions in the configuror as a single *actions* event. The resulting process definitions are:

Virtual.p_1" = § [] (request → $\overline{\text{reply}}$ → Virtual.p_1"
                ⊓ Synchro → Primary.control.down → Synchro → Virtual.p_2")
Virtual.p_2" = request → $\overline{\text{reply}}$ → Virtual.p_2"
                [] Synchro → Secondary.control.off → Synchro → Virtual.p_1" [] §
Link.s" = (request → $\overline{\text{reply}}$ → Link.s"
                ⊓ Synchro → Link.control.ChangeOk → Synchro → Link.s") [] §
Configuror = actions → WaitForDown
where
WaitForDown = § [] (Synchro → Primary.control.down → Secondary.control.on →
                          L.control.changeOk → Synchro → actions → WaitForUp)
WaitForUp = § [] (Synchro → Primary.control.up → Secondary.control.off →
                          L.control.changeOk → Synchro → actions → WaitForDown)

Finally, the attachment consistency of the connector *L* role *s* is checked as:

Claim 3 (Link.s" || Configuror") ⊆ (Virtual.p_1" || Configuror" || det(Link.s"))

We do not detail here the configuror consistency checks of our simple system.

7.3 Equivalence

The previous analysis ensures that the system satisfies certain consistency properties. Another application of our semantics is to prove that a dynamic system (or sub-system) is equivalent to some steady-state one. This is a useful result because for certain purposes we can treat the dynamic system as a static one. For instance, as in the previous example, we might like to show that the reconfigurable client-server system is equivalent to a simple client-server system in which the server never goes down.

In order to compare a dynamic system with a static one, the *control* and *go* events must be hidden, the remaining communication events should be stripped of their configuration encoding part (i.e., renaming *Cp.p.e.Cn.r* into *Cp.p.e*) and some components may have to be renamed (e.g., *Primary* and *Secondary* are unified with *S*). The following check ensures that our fault-tolerant system has the functionality of a simple client-server system:

Rename(Strip(DynamicClient-Server \ {_.control._, _.go...})) = Simple

With the tool FDR [4], we discover that these two systems are nearly equivalent: they have the same traces and failures, but *Simple* never diverges, while the left-hand side system may diverge (performing no "useful" communication, but only an infinite sequence of re-configurations). This discrepancy indicates that without some additional guarantees of fairness, the two systems are not, in fact, identical. However, although it is not possible to add fairness to our CSP description, in practice it would not be difficult to ensure this property for an implementation.

Finally we can examine the reusability of code. Our definitions of the client component are the same in the first Client-Server steady-state system (Section 3) and in the fault-tolerant Client-Server dynamic system (Section 5). We did not have to introduce control events in the client definition. So, in an implementation the same client code could be used in both steady-state and dynamic systems.

8 Future Work and Discussion

We believe that a number of technical extensions of the research are worth exploring. First, fault-tolerance introduces notions (e.g., time-out, preemption) along with idiomatic encoding (e.g., replacing the absence of event by a time-out event, or set an interruptible interpretative cycle). We think style libraries with specialized analyses and transformations might support these idioms.

Wright provides abstract specifications of software architectures. Our central configuror may not be realistic in a concrete implementation. In this case, a partial evaluation of the specifications could distribute the configuror actions in the components and connectors to be closer to real code.

Our semantics is a formal basis to further develop analysis and transformations. Intractable analysis could be replaced by proofs based on the semantic expressions and CSP. For example, a case study in [1] does not rely on model checking to study the deadlock freedom of a buffered connector style. Also, we restricted our study to dynamic systems with a finite number of configurations. The subordination CSP operator (//) can be used to dynamically duplicate processes by recursion. For example, [6] gives a definition of a factorial process where each level of recursion declares a new local process to deal with the recursive call. This technique might allow us to express semantics of dynamic architectures with regular pattern topology involving an unbounded number of configurations.

The present work focuses on protocols and deadlock freedom. Other properties should be studied in Wright. For example, [3] proposes a security analysis based on information flow in CSP expression. We think, this work could be adapted to Wright by introducing extra information specifying information flows hidden by the specifications. Finally, all interesting properties can't be expressed in CSP, but our framework and the tagging technique of our semantics could be reused with another formalism (e.g., CSP which lacks fairness must be replaced by temporal logic [8]).

In this paper, we have described an approach to architectural specification that permits the representation and analysis of dynamic architectures. The approach is based on four ideas:

- *Localization of reconfiguration behavior*, so that it is possible to understand and analyze statically what kinds of dynamic (topological) architectural changes can occur in a running system.

- *Uniform representation of reconfiguration behavior and steady state behavior*, so that interactions between the two can be analyzed.

- *Clearly delimited interactions between the two kinds of behavior through the use of control events*, so that one can explicitly identify the points in the steady state behavior at which reconfigurations are permitted.

- *Semantic foundations based on CSP*, so that we can exploit traditional tools and analytic techniques based on process algebras.

To make this approach work we have limited ourselves to dynamic architectures that have a finite number of possible reconfigurations. Thus we have made a tradeoff between generality and power: by considering a restricted set of dynamic architectures we are able to provide strong support for static reasoning and automated analysis.

Because of space constraints, we illustrated the approach with a very simple example, showing how specification and analysis could help us detect and then fix a bug in the description. However we are confident that our extension scales up to realistic systems, as static Wright does [1]. Indeed, our checks remain local, and identical checks can be shared in systems with a high degree of symmetry (e.g. multiple instances of the same component). Further study would be necessary.

References

[1] R. J. Allen. *A Formal Approach to Software Architecture*. Ph.D. Thesis, Carnegie Mellon University, School of Computer Science, May 1997.

[2] R. J. Allen and D. Garlan. A Formal Basis for Architectural Connection. In *ACM Transactions on Software Engineering and Methodology*, July 1997.

[3] J.-P. Banâtre, C. Bryce and D. Le Métayer. Compile-time detection of information flow in sequential programs. In *Proc. of ESORICS'95*, LNCS 875, 1995.

[4] *Failures Divergence Refinement: User Manual and Tutorial*. Formal Systems (Europe) Ltd., Oxford, England,1.2β edition October 1992.

[5] D. Garlan, R. T. Monroe and D. Wile. ACME: An Architecture Description Interchange Language. *Submitted for publication*, January 1997.

[6] Hoare, C.A.R. *Communicating Sequential Processes*. Prentice Hall, 1985.

[7] P. Inverardi and A. Wolf. Formal Specification and Analysis of Software Architectures Using the Chemical Abstract Machine Model. *IEEE Trans. SW Eng.*, 21(4), 95.

[8] L. Lamport. The Temporal Logic of Actions. In *ACM TOPLAS*, 16(3), 1994.

[9] D. Le Métayer. Software Architecture Styles as Graph Grammars. In *Proc. of FSE'96*, ACM SIG-SOFT.

[10] D. Luckham, L. Augustin, J. Kenney, J. Vera, D. Bryan and W. Mann. Specification and Analysis of System Architecture Using Rapide. In *IEEE Trans. on Soft. Eng.*, 21(4), 1995.

[11] J. Magee and J. Kramer. Dynamic Structure in Software Architectures. In *Proc. of FSE'96*, 1996.

[12] N. Medvidovic.A Classification and Comparison Framework for Software ADLs. *Univ. of Irvine, Dept. of Information and Computer Science*, 1997.

[13] L. Sha, R. Ragunathan and M. Gagliardi. Evolving Dependable Real-Time Systems. *Carnegie Mellon University SEI Report* CMU-SEI-95-TR-005, 1995.

[14] M. Shaw, R. DeLine, D. Klein, T. Ross, D. Young and G. Zelesnik. Abstractions for Software Architecture and Tools to Support Them. In *IEEE Trans. on Soft. Eng.*, 21(4), 1995.

Observational Proofs with Critical Contexts

Narjes Berregeb   Adel Bouhoula   Michaël Rusinowitch

LORIA – INRIA Lorraine
615, rue du Jardin Botanique - B.P. 101
54602 Villers-lès-Nancy Cedex, France.
E-mail:{berregeb,bouhoula,rusi}@loria.fr

Abstract. Observability concepts contribute to a better understanding of software correctness. In order to prove observational properties, the concept of *Context Induction* has been developed by Hennicker [10]. We propose in this paper to embed Context Induction in the implicit induction framework of [8]. The proof system we obtain applies to conditional specifications. It allows for many rewriting techniques and for the refutation of false observational conjectures. Under reasonable assumptions our method is refutationally complete, i.e. it can refute any conjecture which is not observationally valid. Moreover this proof system is operational: it has been implemented within the Spike prover and interesting computer experiments are reported.

1 Introduction

Observational concepts are fundamental in formal methods since for proving the correctness of a program with respect to a specification it is essential to be able to abstract away from internal implementation details. Data objects can be viewed as equal if they cannot be distinguished by experiments with observable result. The idea that the semantics of a specification must describe the *behaviour* of an abstract data type as viewed by an external user, is due to [9]. Though a lot of work has been devoted to the semantical aspects of observability (see [2] for a classification), few proof techniques have been studied [17,5,14,13], and even less have been implemented. In this paper we propose an automatic method for proving observational properties of conditional specifications. The method relies on computing families of well chosen contexts, called *critical contexts*, that "cover" in some sense all observable ones. These families are applied as induction schemes. Our inference system basically consists in extending terms by critical contexts and simplifying the results with a powerful rewriting machinery in order to generate new subgoals. An advantage of this approach is that it allows also for disproving false observational conjectures. The method is even refutationally complete for an interesting class of specifications. From a preliminary implementation on top of the Spike prover [8] computer experiments are reported. The given examples have been treated in a fully automatic way by the program.

2 Related works

Hennicker [10] has proposed an induction principle, called *context induction*, which is a proof principle for behavioural abstractions. A property is observationally valid if it is valid for all observable *experiments*. Such experiments are represented by *observable contexts*, which are context of observable sort over the signature of a specification where a distinguished subset of its sorts is specified as observable. Hence, a property is valid for all observable experiments if it is valid for all corresponding observable contexts. A context c is viewed as a particular term containing exactly one variable; therefore, the subterm ordering defines a noetherian relation on the set of observable contexts. Consequently, the principle of structural induction induces a proof principle for properties of contexts of observable sort, which is called *context induction*. This approach provides with a uniform proof method for the verification of behavioural properties. It has been implemented in the system ISAR [1]. However, in concrete examples, this verification is a non trivial task, and requires human guidance: the system often needs a generalization of the current induction assertion before each nested context induction, so that to achieve the proof.

Malcolm and Goguen [14] have proposed a proof technique which simplifies Hennicker proofs. The idea is to split the signature into *generators* and *defined functions*. Proving that two terms are behaviourally equivalent, comes to prove that they give the same result in all observable contexts built from defined functions, provided that the generators verify a congruence relation w.r.t. behavioural equivalence. This proof technique is an efficient optimization of Hennicker proofs.

Bidoit and Henniker [4] have investigated how a first order logic theorem prover can be used to prove properties in an observational framework. The method consists in computing automatically some special contexts called *crucial contexts*, and in enriching the specification so that to automatically prove observational properties. But this method was only developed for the proof of equations and for specifications where only one sort is not observable. Besides, it fails on several examples (cf. *Stack* example), where it is not possible to compute crucial contexts.

Bidoit and Hennicker [5] have also investigated characterization of behavioural theories that allows for proving behavioural theorems with standard proof techniques for first order logic. In particular they propose general conditions under which an infinite axiomatization of the observational equality can be transformed into a finitary one. However, in general there is no automatic procedure for generating such a finite axiomatization of the observational equality.

Puel [16] has adapted Huet-Hullot procedure for proof by consistency w.r.t. the final model. Lysne [13] extends Bachmair's method for proof by consistency to the final algebra framework. The proof technique is based on a special completion procedure whose idea is to consider, not only critical pairs emerging from positioning rewrite rules on equations, but also those emerging from positioning equations on to rewrite rules. This approach is restricted to equations and requires the ground convergence property of the axioms in order to be sound (in our case, ground convergence is needed only for refutational completeness).

3 Basic notions

We assume that the reader is familiar with the basic concepts of algebraic specifications [18], term rewriting and equational reasoning. A many sorted signature
Σ is a pair (S, F) where S is a set of *sorts* and F is a set of function symbols. For
short, a many sorted signature Σ will simply be denoted by F. We assume that
we have a partition of F in two subsets, the first one, C, contains the *constructor
symbols* and the second, D, is the set of *defined symbols*. Let X be a family of
sorted variables and let $T(F, X)$ be the set of sorted terms. $var(t)$ stands for the
set of all variables appearing in t. A term is *linear* if all its variables occur only
once in it. If $var(t)$ is empty then t is a *ground* term. The set of all ground terms
is $T(F)$. Let A be an arbitrary non-empty set, and let $F_A = \{f_A \mid f \in F\}$ such
that if f is of arity n then f_A is a function from A^n to A. The pair (A, F) is
called a Σ-*algebra*, and A the *carrier* of the algebra. For sake of simplicity, we
will write A to denote the Σ-algebra when F and F_A are non-ambiguous.

A *substitution* assigns terms of appropriate sorts to variables. The domain
of η is defined by: $dom(\eta) = \{x \mid x\eta \neq x\}$. If t is a term, then $t\theta$ denotes the
application of θ to t. If η applies every variable to a ground term, then η is a
ground substitution. We denote by $\equiv$ the syntactic equivalence between objects.
Let N^* be the set of sequences of positive integers. For any term t, $Pos(t) \subseteq N^*$
denotes its set of positions and the expression t/u denotes the *subterm of t at
a position u*. We write $t[s]_u$ (resp. $t[s]$) to indicate that s is a subterm of t
at position u (resp. at some position).The top position is written ε. Let $t(u)$
denote the symbol of t at position u. A position u in a term t is said to be *a
strict position* if $t(u) = f \in F$. A position u in a term t such that $t(u) = x$
and $x \in X$, is a *linear variable position* if x occurs only once in t, otherwise,
u is a *non linear variable position*. The depth of a term t is defined as follows:
$|t| = 0$ if t is a constant or a variable, otherwise, $|f(t_1, \ldots, t_n)| = 1 + max_i|t_i|$.
We denote by $\succ$ a transitive irreflexive relation on the set of terms, that is
noetherian, monotonic ($s \succ t$ implies $w[s]_u \succ w[t]_u$), stable per instantiation
($s \succ t$ implies $s\sigma \succ t\sigma$) and satisfies the subterm property ($f(\cdots, t, \cdots) \succ t$).
The multiset extension of $\succ$ will be denoted by $\gg$. An *equation* is a formula
of the form $l = r$. A *conditional* equation is a formula of the following form:
$\bigwedge_{i=1}^{n} a_i = b_i \Rightarrow l = r$. It will be written $\bigwedge_{i=1}^{n} a_i = b_i \Rightarrow l \to r$ and called a
conditional rule if $\{l\sigma\} \gg \{r\sigma, a_1\sigma, b_1\sigma, \cdots, a_n\sigma, b_n\sigma\}$ for each substitution σ.
The *precondition* of rule $\bigwedge_{i=1}^{n} a_i = b_i \Rightarrow l \to r$ is $\bigwedge_{i=1}^{n} a_i = b_i$. The term l is the
left-hand side of the rule. A rewrite rule $c \Rightarrow l \to r$ is *left-linear* if l is linear.
A set of conditional rules is called a *rewrite system*. A constructor is *free* if it
is not the root of a left-hand side of a rule. Let t be a term in $T(C, X)$, t is
called a *constructor* term. A rewrite system R is *left-linear* if every rule in R
is left-linear. We define $depth(R)$ as the maximal depth of the strict positions
in its left-hand sides. Let R be a set of conditional rules. Let t be a term and
u a position in t. We write: $t[l\sigma]_u \to_R t[r\sigma]_u$ if there is a substitution σ and a
conditional equation $\bigwedge_{i=1}^{n} a_i = b_i \Rightarrow l = r$ in R such that:

(i) $l\sigma \succ r\sigma$.

(ii) for all $i \in [1 \cdots n]$ there exists c_i such that $a_i\sigma \to_R^* c_i$ and $b_i\sigma \to_R^* c_i$.

(iii) $\{t[l\sigma]_u\} \gg \{a_1\sigma, \ b_1\sigma, \ \cdots, a_n\sigma, \ b_n\sigma\}$.

Rewriting is extended to literals and clauses as expected.

```
specification: STACK
sorts: nat, stack
observable sorts: nat
constructors:
0:        →nat;
s:        nat →nat;
Nil:      →stack;
push: nat × stack →stack;
defined functions:
top: stack → nat;
pop: stack → stack;
axioms:
top(Nil) = 0
top(push(i, s)) = i
pop(Nil) = Nil
pop(push(i, s)) = s
```

Fig. 1. Stack specification

A term t is *irreducible* (or in *normal form*) if there is no term s such that $t \to_R s$. A term t is *ground reducible* iff all its ground instances are reducible. A symbol $f \in F$ is *completely defined* if all ground terms with root f are reducible to terms in $T(C)$. We say that R is *sufficiently complete* if all symbols in D are completely defined. A *clause* C is an expression of the form : $\bigwedge_{i=1}^n a_i = b_i \Rightarrow \bigvee_{j=1}^m a'_j = b'_j$. The clause C is *positive* if $n = 0$. The clause C is a *logical consequence* of E if C is valid in any model of E, denoted by $E \models C$. We say that C is *inductively valid* in E and denote it by $E \models_{Ind} C$ if for any ground substitution σ, (for all i, $E \models a_i\sigma = b_i\sigma$) implies (there exists j, $E \models a'_j\sigma = b'_j\sigma$). We say that two terms s and t are joinable, denoted by $s \downarrow_R t$, if $s \to_R^* v$ and $t \to_R^* v$ for some term v. The rewrite system R is *ground convergent* if the terms u and v are joinable whenever $u, v \in T(F)$ and $R \models u = v$.

4 Observational semantics

The notion of *observation technique* have been introduced as a means for describing what is observed in a given algebra. An observational specification is then obtained by adding an observation technique to a standard algebraic specification. The observation technique we use in our method is based on sorts [1]. The semantics we choose is based on a relaxing of the satisfaction relation. The

---

[1] but it can be easily extended to observations based on operators

notion of *context* is fundamental in all approaches based on such observational semantics. An observational property is obtained by taking into account only observable information. Thus, to show that it is valid, one has to show its validity in all *observable contexts*.

Let $T(F, X)$ be a term algebra and let (S, F) be its signature. A *context* over F is a non-ground term $c \in T(F, X)$ with a distinguished occurrence of a variable called the *context variable* of c. To indicate the context variable z_s occuring in c, we often write $c[z_s]$ instead of c, where s is the sort of z_s. A context reduced to a variable z_s of sort s is called an *empty context* of sort s. The application of a context $c[z_s]$ to a term $t \in T(F, X)$ of sort s, denoted by $c[t]$, is defined by the substitution of z_s by t in $c[z_s]$. The context c is said to be *applicable* to t. By exception, $var(c)$ will denote the set of all variables occurring in c but the context variable of c. A context c is *ground* if $var(c) = \emptyset$. We denote by $|c|$ the depth of c. A *subcontext* (resp. *strict subcontext*) of c, is a subterm (resp. strict subterm) of c with the same contextual variable. A *clausal context* c for a clause C is a list of contexts $< c_1, \ldots, c_n, c_1', \ldots, c_m' >$ such that for all $i \in [1..n]$: c_i is applicable to $a_i = b_i$, and for all $j \in [1..m]$: c_j' is applicable to $a_j' = b_j'$. The application of c to C, denoted by $c[C]$, gives the clause $\bigwedge_{i=1}^{n} c_i[a_i] = c_i[b_i] \Rightarrow \bigvee_{j=1}^{m} c_j'[a_i'] = c_i'[b_i']$. Let $c[z_s]$ and $c'[z_{s'}']$ be two contexts such that c is of sort s', let t be a term of sort s and σ be a substitution such that $z_s \notin dom(\sigma)$. We use the following notations: $c'[(c[t])]=(c'[c])[t]=c'[c[t]]$ and $(c[t])\sigma = (c\sigma)[t\sigma] =c[t]\sigma$.

A specification SP is a triple (S, F, E) where (S, F) is a signature and E is a set of conditional equations. An *observational specification* SP_{obs} is a couple (SP, S_{obs}) such that $SP = (S, F, E)$ is a specification and $S_{obs} \subseteq S$ is the set of *observable sorts*. The Stack specification in Figure 1, is an observational specification, where $S_{obs} = \{nat\}$.

An observable term is a term whose sort belongs to S_{obs}. The set of observable contexts is denoted by C_{obs} . An equation $a = b$ is observable if a and b are observable. The precondition of a rule is observable if all its equations are observable. Consider the specification in Figure 1. There are infinitely many observable contexts: $top(z_{stack}), top(pop(z_{stack})), \ldots$, $top(pop(\ldots(pop(z_{stack}))\ldots)), \ldots top(push(z_{stack})), top(push(i, pop(z_{stack}))), \ldots$

The notion of observational validity is based on the idea that two objects in a given algebra are observationally equal if they cannot be distinguished by computations with observable results. These computations are formalized by contexts.

Let a and b be two terms. We say that a and b are observationally equal, and we denote it by $E \models_{Obs} a = b$ iff for all $c \in C_{obs}, E \models_{Ind} c[a] = c[b]$. Consider the stack specification in Figure 1. It is easy to see that $push(top(s), pop(s)) = s$ is not satisfied (in the classical sense). However, intuitively, it is observationally satisfied if we just *observe* the elements of the sequences $push(top(s), pop(s))$ and s. This can be formally shown by considering all observable contexts.

The next theorem gives a useful characterization of observational theorems (see e.g. [15]):

Theorem 1. *Suppose that all the preconditions of E are observable. Then $E \models_{Obs} \bigwedge_{i=1}^{n} a_i = b_i \Rightarrow \bigvee_{j=1}^{m} a'_j = b'_j$ iff for all ground substitutions σ, if (for all $i, E \models_{Obs} a_i\sigma = b_i\sigma$) then (there exists j such that $E \models_{Obs} a'_j\sigma = b'_j\sigma$).*

5 Induction schemes

Our purpose in this section is to introduce the ingredients allowing us to prove and disprove behavioural properties. This task amounts in general to check an infinite number of ground formulas for validity, since an infinite number of instances and an infinite number of contexts have to be considered for building these ground instances. This is where induction comes into play. Test substitutions will provide us with induction schemes for substitutions and critical contexts will provide us with induction schemes for contexts. In general, it is not possible to consider all the observable contexts. However, cover contexts are sufficient to prove behavioural theorems by reasoning on the ground irreducible observable contexts rather than on the whole set of observable contexts. In the following, we denote by R a conditional rewriting system with observable preconditions.

Definition 2 (cover set). A *cover set*, denoted by CS, for R, is a finite set of irreducible terms such that for all ground irreducible term s, there exist a term t in CS and a ground substitution σ such that $t\sigma \equiv s$.

We now introduce the notion of *cover context* that is used to schematize all contexts. Note that a *cover context* need not be observable, (unlike *crucial contexts* of [4]). The intuitive idea is to use *cover context* to extend the conjectures by the top in order to create redexes. Then the obtained formulas can be simplified by axioms and induction hypothesis.

Definition 3. [cover context set] A *cover context set* CC is a set of contexts such that: for each ground irreducible context $c_{obs}[z_s] \in C_{obs}$, there exists $c[z_s] \in CC$ and a substitution θ such that $dom(\theta) = var(c)$ and $c\theta$ is a subcontext of c_{obs}.

A cover context set for the specification stack is $\{z_{nat}, top(z_{stack}), pop(z_{stack})\}$. The context $push(i, z_{stack})$ is not a cover context since $top(push(i, z_{stack}))$ and $pop(push(i, z_{stack}))$ are reducible. Note that usually there are infinitely many possible cover context sets. For instance, $\{z_{nat}, top(z_{stack}), top(pop(z_{stack})), pop(pop(z_{stack}))\}$ is also a cover context set.

In the following, we refine cover context sets so that to be able not only to prove behavioural properties, but also to disprove the non valid ones. We need first to introduce the following notions: A context c is *quasi ground reducible* if for all ground substitution τ such that $dom(\tau) = var(c)$, $c\tau$ is reducible. A term t is *strongly irreducible* if none of its non-variable subterms matches a left-hand side of a rule in R. A positive clause $C_{pos} \equiv \bigvee_{i=1}^{n} a_i = b_i$ is *strongly irreducible* if C_{pos} is not a tautology, and the maximal elements of $\{a_i, b_i\}$ w.r.t. $\prec$ are strongly irreducible by R.

Cover sets and cover context sets are fundamental for the correctness of our method. However, they cannot help us to disprove the non observationally valid clauses. For this purpose, we introduce a new notion of critical context sets and we use test sets defined in [7].

Definition 4 (test set, test substitution). A *test set* is a cover set which has the following additional properties: (i) the instance of a ground reducible term by a test substitution matches a left-hand side of R. (ii) if the instance of a positive clause C_{pos} by a test substitution σ is strongly irreducible, then $C_{pos}\sigma$ is not inductively valid w.r.t. R. A *test substitution* for a clause C instanciates all induction variables of C by terms taken from a given test set whose variables are renamed.

Definition 5 (critical context set, critical clausal context). A *critical context set* S is a cover context set such that for each positive clause C_{pos}, if $c[C_{pos}]\sigma$ is strongly irreducible where σ is a test substitution of C_{pos} and c is a clausal context of C_{pos}, then $C_{pos}\sigma$ is not observationally valid w.r.t. R. A *critical clausal context* for a clause C is a clausal context for C whose contexts belongs to S.

Test substitutions and critical context sets permit us to refute false conjectures by constructing a counterexample.

Definition 6 (provably inconsistent). Let R be a conditional rewriting system with observable preconditions. We say that $C \equiv \bigwedge_{i=1}^{n} a_i = b_i \Rightarrow \bigvee_{j=1}^{m} a'_j = b'_j$ is *provably inconsistent* if and only if there exists a test substitution σ and a clausal critical context c such that:

(i) for all i, $a_i\sigma = b_i\sigma$ is an inductive theorem w.r.t. R.

(ii) $c[\bigvee_{j=1}^{m} a'_j = b'_j]\sigma$ is strongly irreducible by R.

Provably inconsistent clauses are not observationally valid.

Theorem 7. *Let R be a conditional rewriting system with observable preconditions. Let C be a provably inconsistent clause. Then C is not observationally valid.*

5.1 Computation of test sets

The computation of test sets and test substitutions for conditional specifications is decidable if the axioms are sufficiently complete and the constructors are specified by a set of unconditional equations (see [12]). Unfortunately, no algorithm exists for the general case of conditional specifications. However, in [7], a procedure is described for computing test sets when the axioms are sufficiently complete over an arbitrary specification of constructors.

5.2 Computation of critical contexts

Let us first introduce the following lemma which gives us a useful characterization of critical context sets:

Lemma 8. *Let R be a conditional rewriting system. Let CC be a cover context set that has the following properties:*

(i) *any non-observable context in CC has variables at depth greater than or equal to $depth(R)$.*

(ii) *for each context $c[z_s] \in CC$, there exists an observable context c_{obs} such that $c_{obs}[c]$ is strongly irreducible.*

Then, CC is a critical context set for R.

Proof. Let C be a positive clause such that $c[C]\sigma$ is strongly irreducible, where σ is a test substitution of C and c is a critical clausal context of C. Let us prove that $C\sigma$ is not observationally valid. By (ii), there exists an observable clausal context c_{obs} such that $c_{obs}[c]$ is strongly irreducible. Now, using (i), we conclude that $c_{obs}[c[C]]\sigma$ is also strongly irreducible. Then, $c_{obs}[c[C]]\sigma$ is a provably inconsistent clause w.r.t. Definition 11 in [7]. By Theorem 12 in [7], $c_{obs}[c[C]]\sigma$ is not inductively valid. Thus, $R \not\models_{Obs} C\sigma$.

$CC_0 := \{c \in T(F, X) \mid |c| \leq depth(R), \quad c \in C_{obs} , \quad c$ is not quasi ground reducible, and does not contain any observable strict subcontext$\}$

$T_0 := \{c \in T(F, X) \mid |c| = depth(R), \quad c \notin C_{obs}, \quad c$ is not quasi ground reducible, c does not contain any observable subcontext, and all variables (including the context one) in c occur at $depth(R)\}$.

repeat
  $CC_{i+1} := CC_i \cup \{c \in T_i \mid \exists c_i \in CC_i$ such that $c_i[c]$ is not quasi ground reducible$\}$
  $T_{i+1} := T_i \setminus CC_{i+1}$
until $CC_{i+1} = CC_i$

output: CC_i

Fig. 2. Computation of Critical Contexts

Now, let us present our method for constructing such critical contexts. The idea of our procedure is the following: starting from the non quasi ground reducible observable contexts of depth smaller than or equal to $depth(R)$, we construct all contexts that can be embedded in one of those observable contexts, to give a non quasi ground reducible and observable context. It can be proved, by reduction to ground reducibility, that quasi ground reducibility is decidable too for equational systems and semi-decidable for conditional rewrite systems [11]. The following remark is also useful: given a context $c[z_s]$ of the form $f(t_1, \ldots, t_n)$ where f is a completely defined function and for all $i \in [1..n]$, t_i is a constructor term. If z_s does not appear at an induction position of f, then $c[z_s]$ is quasi ground reducible.

Theorem 9. *Let R be a rewriting system and CC be the result of the application of the procedure given in Figure 2. Then:*

- *CC is a cover context set for R.*
- *if R is equational and left-linear then CC is a critical context set for R.*

Proof. It is relatively easy to show that CC is a cover context set for R. Now, assume that R is equational and leftlinear and let us prove that CC is also a critical context set for R. By construction, any non-observable context in CC has variables at depth greater than or equal to $depth(R)$. Now, since R is equational, any non quasi ground reducible context is necessarily strongly irreducible. On the other hand, R is left-linear and the variables of non-observable context occur at $depth(R)$, then for each context $c[z_s] \in CC$, there exists i such that $c \in CC_i$, we can show that there exists an observable context c_{obs} such that $c_{obs}[c]$ is strongly irreducible. The proof is done by induction on i.

Example 10. Consider the Stack specification in Figure 1. We have $depth(R) = 1$, then:
$CC_0 = \{z_{nat}, top(z_{stack})\}$,
$T_0 = \{pop(z_{stack}), push(i, z_{stack})\}$.
$CC_1 = \{z_{nat}, top(z_{stack})\} \cup \{pop(z_{stack})\}$,
$CC = CC_1$ is a critical context set for R.

Example 11. Consider the List specification in Figure 3. We have: $depth(R) = 1$, then:
$CC_0 = \{z_{nat}, z_{bool}, in(x, z_{list})\}$,
$T_0 = \{union(z_{list}, x), insert(x, z_{list})\}$,
$CC_1 = CC_0 \cup \{union(z_{list}, x)\}$.
$CC = CC_1$ is a cover context set for R. In fact, $union(x, z_{list})$ is quasi ground reducible and $in(y, union(z_{list}, x))$ is not quasi ground reducible since $in(0, union(z_{list}, Nil))$ is irreducible, but $in(y, insert(x, z_{list}))$ is quasi ground reducible.

It is possible to compute critical context sets in the case where R is a conditional rewriting system. It is sufficient to apply our procedure given in Figure 2 to compute a cover context set CC, and then to check that for each non observable context $c \in CC$, there exists an observable context c_{obs} such that $c_{obs}[c]$ is strongly irreducible. In Example 11, we have $in(x, (union(z_{list}, y))$ is strongly irreducible, then we conclude that $CC = \{z_{nat}, z_{bool}, in(x, z_{list}), union(z_{list}, x)\}$ is a critical context set for R.

```
specification: LIST
sorts: nat, bool, list
observable sorts: nat, bool
constructors:
0:       →nat;
s:       nat →nat;
Nil:     →list;
insert: nat × list →list;
True:    →bool;
False:   →bool;
defined functions:
union: list × list → list;
in:      nat × list → bool;
eq:      nat × nat → bool;
axioms:
union(Nil, l) = l
union(insert(x, l), l1) = insert(x, union(l, l1))
in(x, Nil) = False
eq(x, y) = True => in(x, insert(y, l)) = True
eq(x, y) = False => in(x, insert(y, l)) = in(x, l)
eq(0, 0) = True
eq(0, s(x)) = False
eq(s(x), 0) = False
eq(s(x), s(y)) = eq(x, y)
```

Fig. 3. List specification

6 Inference system

The inference system we use (see Figure 4) is based on a set of transition rules applied to (E, H), where E is the set of conjectures to prove and H is the set of induction hypotheses. The initial set of conditional rules R is oriented with a well founded ordering. An *I-derivation* is a sequence of states: $(E_0, \emptyset) \vdash_I (E_1, H_1) \vdash_I \ldots (E_n, H_n) \vdash_I \ldots$. We say that an I-derivation is *fair* if the set of persistent clauses $(\cup_i \cap_{j \geq i} E_j)$ is empty. Context induction is performed implicitly by the **Generation** rule. An equation is selected in a clause and it is extended by critical contexts and test sets. These extensions are rewritten by R either by conditional rewriting or by case analysis. The resulting conjectures are collected in $\bigcup_{c, \sigma} E_{c, \sigma}$. **Case Simplification** illustrates the case reasoning: it simplifies a conjecture with conditional rules provided that the disjunction of their preconditions [2] is inductively valid in R.

Definition 12 (Case Analysis). Let R be a set of conditional rules and let $l \vee r$ be a clause. **Case Analysis**$(l[g\sigma]_u, r) = \{P_1\sigma \Rightarrow l[d_1\sigma]_u \vee r; \cdots; P_n\sigma \Rightarrow l[d_n\sigma]_u \vee r\}$ if $\forall i \in [1 \cdots n] : P_i \Rightarrow g \rightarrow d_i \in R$ and $R \models_{Ind} P_1\sigma \vee \cdots \vee P_n\sigma$.

---

[2] Recall that the preconditions of the axioms in R are assumed to be observable

The rule **Context subsumption** appeared to be very useful for manipulating non orientable conjectures.

An I-derivation *fails* when there exists a conjecture such that no rule can be applied to it. An I-derivation *succeeds* if all conjectures are proved.

Theorem 13 (correctness of successful I-derivations). *Let* $(E_0, \emptyset)$ $\vdash_I$ $(E_1, H_1) \vdash_I \ldots$ *be a fair I-derivation. If it succeeds then* $R \models_{Obs} E_0$.

Proof. The proof is done by contradiction. Suppose $R \not\models_{Obs} E_0$ and let $C \in \cup_i E_i$ be a minimal counterexample w.r.t. a well founded ordering on clauses extending $\succ$p. We can easily show, as in [8], that no inference rule can be applied to C. Hence C persists in the derivation contradicting the fairness hypothesis.

Theorem 14 (correctness of disproof). *Let* $(E_0, \emptyset) \vdash_I (E_1, H_1) \vdash_I \cdots$ *be an I-derivation. If there exists* j *such that* **Disproof** *is applied to* (E_j, H_j), *then* $R \not\models_{Obs} E_0$.

Proof. If there exists j such that **Disproof** is applied to (E_j, H_j), then by Theorem 7, we conclude that $R \not\models_{Obs} E_j$. Now, to prove that $R \not\models_{Obs} E_0$, it is sufficient to prove the following claim: Let $(E_j, H_j) \vdash_I (E_{j+1}, H_{j+1})$ be an I-derivation step. If $\forall i \leq j, R \models_{Obs} E_i$ then $R \models_{Obs} E_{j+1}$. If $(E_j, H_j) \vdash_I (E_{j+1}, H_{j+1})$ by a simplification rule, then the equations which are used for simplification occur in some E_k $(k \leq j)$ and therefore are observationally valid in R by assumption. Hence, E_{j+1} is observationally valid too in R. If $(E_j, H_j) \vdash_I (E_{j+1}, H_{j+1})$ by **Generation** on $C \in E_j$, every auxiliary equation which is used for rewriting an instance of C by a critical context c and a test substitution σ, is either in R or E_k $(k \leq j)$ and hence E_{j+1} is valid in R.

Now we consider boolean specifications. To be more specific, we assume there exists an observable sort *bool* with two free constructors $\{true, false\}$. The sort *bool* will be observable. Every rule in R is of type: $\bigwedge_{i=1}^{n} p_i = p'_i \Rightarrow s \rightarrow t$ where for all i in $[1 \cdots n]$, $p'_i \in \{true, false\}$. Conjectures will be *boolean clauses*, i.e. clauses whose negative literals are of type $\neg(p = p')$ where $p' \in \{true, false\}$. Let $f \in D$, a completely defined symbol in R. Then f is *strongly complete [7]* w.r.t R if for all the rules $p_i \Rightarrow f(t_1, \ldots, t_n) \rightarrow r_i$ whose left-hand sides are identical up to a renaming μ_i, we have $R \models_{Ind} \bigvee_{i=1}^{n} p_i \mu_i$. We say that R is *strongly complete* if for all $f \in D$, f is strongly complete w.r.t R.

Theorem 15 (refutational completeness). *Let* R *be a conditional rewrite system. Assume that* R *is ground convergent and strongly complete. Let* E_0 *be a set of boolean clauses. Then* $R \not\models_{Obs} E_0$ *iff all fair derivations issued from* $(E_0, \emptyset)$ *fail.*

Proof. The proof follows the line of the corresponding Theorem 6.5 in [6] that was given for the initial semantics.

Generation: $\dfrac{(E \cup \{l \vee r\}, H)}{(E \cup (\bigcup_{c,\sigma} E_{c,\sigma}), H \cup \{C\})}$

if $\begin{cases} \text{for all test substitution } \sigma \text{ and for all critical context } c: \\ \quad \text{either } c[l]\sigma \vee r\sigma \text{ is a tautology, then } E_{c,\sigma} = \emptyset \\ \quad \text{or } c[l]\sigma \rightarrow_R l', \text{ then } E_{c,\sigma} = \{l' \vee r\sigma\} \\ \quad \text{otherwise } E_{c,\sigma} = \textbf{Case Analysis}(c[l]\sigma, r\sigma) \end{cases}$

Case Simplification: $\dfrac{(E \cup \{l \vee r\}, H)}{(E \cup E', H)}$

if $E' = $ **Case Analysis**(l, r)

Simplification: $\dfrac{(E \cup \{(a = b) \vee r\}, H)}{(E \cup \{(a' = b) \vee r\}, H)}$

if $\begin{cases} a \rightarrow_R a', \text{ or} \\ a[v\lambda] \rightarrow_{H \cup E} a[w\lambda] \text{ by } v = w \text{ where } v \succ w \text{ and } (v\lambda \prec a \text{ or } w\lambda \prec b) \end{cases}$

Subsumption: $\dfrac{(E \cup \{C\}, H)}{(E, H)}$

if C is subsumed by a clause of $R \cup H \cup E$

Context Subsumption: $\dfrac{(E \cup \{C\}, H)}{(E, H)}$

if $\begin{cases} \text{there exists a clause } C' \in R \cup H \cup E \text{ and a clausal context } c \\ \text{such that } c[C'] \text{ subsumes } C \end{cases}$

Delete: $\dfrac{(E \cup \{C\}, H)}{(E, H)}$

if C is a tautology

Disproof: $\dfrac{(E \cup \{C\}, H)}{Disproof}$

if C is provably inconsistent

Fig. 4. Inference System I

7 Computer experiments

We have implemented these results in the Spike prover, written in Caml Light.

Example 16 (Stacks). We proved automatically that $push(top(S), pop(S)) = S$ is a behavioural property of the stack specification (see Figure 1). Note that this example fails with the approach of [4], since it is not possible to compute automatically a set of *crucial contexts*: if two stacks have the same top they are not necessarily equal. In the approach of [10], we have to introduce an auxiliary function $iterated\_pop :\ nat \times stack \rightarrow stack$ such that $iterated\_pop(n, s)$ iterates n times *pop*. This is easy because *pop* is unary. The function $iterated\_pop$ is defined by:

$$iterated\_pop(0, s) = s, \ iterated\_pop(n + 1, s) = iterated\_pop(n, pop(s))$$

Then, we have to prove the property for all contexts of the form $top(iterated\_pop(x, c[z_{stack}]))$. However, this schematization of contexts could be more complicated in case of a function of arity greater than two. So, this process seems to be not easy to automatize in general. In the approach of [14], this problem remains too.

Now, let us describe our proof. The prover computes first a test set for R and the induction positions of functions, which are necessary for inductive proofs. It also computes a critical context. These computation are done only once and before the beginning of the proof.

```
test set of R:
 -> elem = {0, s(x1)}
 -> stack = {Nil ; push(x1,x2)}

critical contexts of R:
 -> stack = {pop(x1)}
 -> elem = {x1, top(x1)}

induction positions of functions:
 -> top : [[1]]
 -> pop : [[1]]

E0 = {push(top(x1),pop(x1)) = x1}

Application of generation on:
    push(top(x1),pop(x1)) = x1 :
 1) Nil = pop(Nil) ;
 2) x2 = pop(push(x1,x2)) ;
 3) 0 = top(Nil) ;
 4) x1 = top(push(x1,x2))

E1 = {Nil = pop(Nil) ;
      x2 = pop(push(x1,x2)) ;
      0 = top(Nil) ;
      x1 = top(push(x1,x2))}
H1 = {push(top(x1),pop(x1)) = x1}

Delete  Nil = pop(Nil)
  it is subsumed by:pop(Nil) = Nil of R

Delete  x2 = pop(push(x1,x2))
  it is subsumed by:pop(push(x1,x2)) = x2 of R

Delete  0 = top(Nil)
  it is subsumed by:top(Nil) = 0 of R

Delete  x1 = top(push(x1,x2))
  it is subsumed by:top(push(x1,x2)) = x1 of R
```

```
E2 = {}
H2 = {push(top(x1),pop(x1)) = x1}
```

The initial conjectures are observationally valid in R

Example 17 (Lists). Consider now the specification *list* in Figure 3. The theorem
$insert(x1, insert(x1, x2)) = insert(x1, x2)$ is automatically proved.

```
test set of R:
 -> nat = {0 ; s(x1)}
 -> list = {Nil ; insert(x1,x2)}
 -> bool = {False ; True}

critical contexts of R:
 -> bool = {x1, in(x1,x2)}
 -> list = {x1, union(x1,x2)}

induction positions of functions:
 -> union : [[1]]
 -> in : [[2]]
 -> eq : [[1];[2]]

E0 = {insert(x1,insert(x1,x2)) = insert(x1,x2)}

Application of generation on:
    insert(x1,insert(x1,x2)) = insert(x1,x2) :
 1) eq(x3,x1) = True => True = in(x3,insert(x1,x2)) ;
 2) eq(x3,x1) = False => in(x3,insert(x1,x2)) = in(x3,insert(x1,x2)) ;
 3) eq(x3,x1) = False, eq(x3,x1) = True ;
 4) insert(x1,insert(x1,union(x2,x4))) = union(insert(x1,x2),x4)

Delete  eq(x3,x1) = False => in(x3,insert(x1,x2)) = in(x3,insert(x1,x2))

Delete  eq(x3,x1) = True => True = in(x3,insert(x1,x2))
 it is subsumed by:eq(x1,x2) = True => in(x1,insert(x2,x3)) = True of R

E1 = {eq(x3,x1) = False, eq(x3,x1) = True ;
        insert(x1,insert(x1,union(x2,x4))) = union(insert(x1,x2),x4)}
H1 = {insert(x1,insert(x1,x2)) = insert(x1,x2)}

Simplification of:
    insert(x1,insert(x1,union(x2,x4))) = union(insert(x1,x2),x4) by H1:
    insert(x1,union(x2,x4)) = union(insert(x1,x2),x4)

E2 = {eq(x3,x1) = False, eq(x3,x1) = True ;
        insert(x1,union(x2,x4)) = union(insert(x1,x2),x4)}
H2 = {insert(x1,insert(x1,x2)) = insert(x1,x2)}

Simplification of:
    insert(x1,union(x2,x4)) = union(insert(x1,x2),x4) by R:
    insert(x1,union(x2,x4)) = insert(x1,union(x2,x4))
```

```
E3 = {eq(x3,x1) = False, eq(x3,x1) = True ;
      insert(x1,union(x2,x4)) = insert(x1,union(x2,x4))}
H3 = {insert(x1,insert(x1,x2)) = insert(x1,x2)}

Delete  insert(x1,union(x2,x4)) = insert(x1,union(x2,x4))

Application of generation on:
    eq(x3,x1) = False, eq(x3,x1) = True :
 1) eq(0,0) = True, True = False ;
 2) eq(s(x1),0) = True, False = False ;
 3) eq(0,s(x1)) = True, False = False ;
 4) eq(s(x2),s(x1)) = True, eq(x2,x1) = False

Delete  eq(s(x1),0) = True, False = False

Delete  eq(0,s(x1)) = True, False = False

Delete  eq(0,0) = True, True = False
 it is subsumed by:eq(x1,x1) = True of R

Simplification of:
    eq(s(x2),s(x1)) = True, eq(x2,x1) = False by R:
    eq(x2,x1) = True, eq(x2,x1) = False

E4 = {eq(x2,x1) = True, eq(x2,x1) = False}
H4 = {eq(x3,x1) = False, eq(x3,x1) = True ;
      insert(x1,insert(x1,x2)) = insert(x1,x2)}

Delete  eq(x2,x1) = True, eq(x2,x1) = False
 it is subsumed by:eq(x3,x1) = False, eq(x3,x1) = True of H4

E5 = {}
H5 = {eq(x3,x1) = False, eq(x3,x1) = True ;

      insert(x1,insert(x1,x2)) = insert(x1,x2)}
```

The initial conjectures are observationally valid in R

In the same way we have proved the following conjectures:

$$insert(x, insert(y, l)) = insert(y, insert(x, l)) \quad and \quad union(l, l') = union(l', l)$$

8 Conclusion

We have presented an automatic procedure for proving observational properties in conditional specifications. The method relies on the construction of a set of *critical contexts* which enables to prove or disprove conjectures. Under reasonable hypotheses, we have shown that the procedure is refutational complete: each non observationally valid conjecture will be detected after a finite time.

A cover context w.r.t. our definition 3 garantees the soundness of our procedure. However, cover contexts computed by our procedure may contain unecessary contexts, as in Example 17 where $union(z_{list}, x)$ is useless for observations. We plan to refine our notion of cover and critical contexts in order to select only the needed contexts.

We also plan to extend the observation technique to terms and formulas.

References

1. B. Bauer and R. Hennicker. Proving the correctness of algebraic implementations by the ISAR system. In *DISCO'93*, volume 722 of *Lecture Notes in Computer Science*, pages 2–16. Springer-Verlag, 1993.
2. G. Bernot, M. Bidoit, and T. Knapik. Behavioural approaches to algebraic specifications: A comparative study. *Acta Informatica*, 31(7):651–671, 1994.
3. N. Berregeb, A. Bouhoula, and M. Rusinowitch. Observational proofs by implicit context induction. Technical Report 3151, INRIA, 1997.
4. M. Bidoit and R. Hennicker. How to prove observational theorems with LP. In U. Martin and J. Wing, editors, *Proc. of First International Workshop on Larch*. Springer-Verlag, 1992.
5. M. Bidoit and R. Hennicker. Behavioural theories and the proof of behavioural properties. *Theoretical Computer Science*, 165(1):3–55, 1996.
6. A. Bouhoula. Using Induction and Rewriting to Verify and Complete Parameterized Specifications. *Theoretical Computer Science*, 170(1-2):245–276, 1996.
7. A. Bouhoula. Automated theorem proving by test set induction. *Journal of Symbolic Computation*, 23(1):47–77, 1997.
8. A. Bouhoula and M. Rusinowitch. Implicit induction in conditional theories. *Journal of Automated Reasoning*, 14(2):189–235, 1995.
9. J. Guttag. *The specification and Application to Programming of Abstract Data Types*. PhD Thesis, University of Toronto, 1975.
10. R. Hennicker. Context induction: a proof principle for behavioural abstractions and algebraic implementations. *Formal Aspects of Computing*, 3(4):326–345, 1991.
11. S. Kaplan and M. Choquer. On the decidability of quasi-reducibility. *Bulletin of European Association for Theoretical Computer Science*, 28:32–34, February 1986.
12. E. Kounalis. Testing for the ground (co-)reducibility property in term rewriting systems. *Theoretical Computer Science*, 106:87–117, 1992.
13. O. Lysne. Extending Bachmair's method for proof by consistency to the final algebra. *Information Processing Letters*, 51:303–310, 1994.
14. G. Malcolm and J. Goguen. Proving correctness of refinement and implementation. Technical Monograph PRG-114, Oxford University Computing Laboratory, November 1994.
15. P. Padawitz. *Computing in Horn Clause Theories*. Springer-Verlag, 1988.
16. L. Puel. Proofs in the final algebra. IXth Colloquium on Trees in Algebra and Programming. Bordeaux, France, March 1984.
17. D.T. Sanella and A. Tarlecki. Towards formal development of ml programs: foundations and methodology. In J. Diaz and F. Orejas, editors, *TAPSOFT'89*, volume 352 of *Lecture Notes in Computer Science*, pages 375–389. Springer-Verlag, 1989.
18. M. Wirsing. Algebraic specifications. In J. van Leeuwen, A. Meyer, M. Nivat, M. Paterson, and D. Perrin, editors, *Handbook of Theoretical Computer Science*, volume B, chapter 13. Elsevier Science Publishers B. V. (North-Holland) and The MIT press, 1990.

Integrating AORTA with Model-Based Data Specification Languages

Steven Bradley[1], William Henderson[2], David Kendall[2], Adrian Robson[2]

[1] Department of Computer Science, Durham University, South Road, Durham, DH1 3LE, UK
[2] Department of Computing, University of Northumbria at Newcastle, Ellison Place, Newcastle upon Tyne, NE1 8ST, UK

Abstract. AORTA has been proposed as an implementable real-time algebra for concurrent systems where event times, rather than values of data, are critical. In this paper we discuss an extension to AORTA to include a formal data model, allowing integration with a variety of model-based data specification languages. An example is given using VDM with AORTA to define a time-critical system with important data attributes, and supporting software tools for AORTA and a simple imperative language are described.

1 Introduction

Although many timed formalisms exist, AORTA [6] (Application-Oriented Real-Time Algebra) is one of the few to consider how designs/specifications of concurrent systems can be implemented in a way that time behaviour can be guaranteed. Supporting tools exist which allow AORTA designs to be simulated, formally verified, and code to be generated [8]. One of the ideas behind the development of AORTA has been that formal methods are good for more than just proof: an unambiguously defined semantics allows early exercising of designs by simulation, and provides a basis for reliable code generation. Whilst proof remains an important aspect of any formal technique, we argue that it is not only the presentation of sound and complete proof theories or automatic verification algorithms which should influence the design of languages, but also the provision of facilities such as code generation and simulation.

AORTA only models formally the order and timing of events, and does not deal with data. Implementation details such as values to be passed during communication and the data transformations to be carried out during a given piece of computation are given as annotations to the AORTA design, in the form of fragments of C [5]. In this paper we examine the problem of introducing formal models of data into AORTA designs, and how this affects the notation, the semantics, the tool support and the development method. The approach given here is different from some other proposals [13, 20, 23, 25], in that rather than integrating with a particular formal specification language, integration within a relatively general framework (described in section 3) is suggested, which allows instantiations with model-based languages such as VDM [18] or Z [21], or with formally defined imperative languages. The formally specified data properties are given as annotations to the basic AORTA design (section 4), in much the same way that fragments of C code are, except that we give a formal semantics to the arrangement (section 5). An example using VDM and AORTA is given in section 6, and tool support for designs in a joint language is discussed in section 7, along with some methodological considerations. Finally, our conclusions are presented in section 8. First of all, though, we introduce the basic language of AORTA.

2 Background to AORTA

AORTA is a timed process algebra which can be used as a design language for communicating concurrent real-time systems. Its main novelty lies in its (semi-automatic) implementability, which is discussed in detail elsewhere [6]. A system is defined as a static parallel composition of processes, linked by explicit communication channels. In its description of processes, AORTA inherits some notation from CCS [19], but other ideas, such as communication channels, are borrowed from elsewhere. Within a (sequential) process, actions can be offered, which must be matched by a communicating partner before the process can proceed, and a choice may be offered between a number of actions. As in CCS, action prefix and choice (sometimes called summation) are represented by . and + respectively, with 0 for the null process which offers no actions. Recursion can be written using the same equational format as used in CCS (e.g. A = a.A), but all recursion must be guarded (i.e. all process names must appear inside an action prefix). The other constructs do not have analogues in CCS, and are concerned with including time information into the process description.

There are two constructs which are used to introduce time, and each of these has a deterministic and nondeterministic form. The first construct is a delay which causes the process to pause for the amount of time specified, during which time no actions are offered — time consuming operations such as computation are represented in this way. As precise times are not always known, the delay may be specified with an upper and lower bound, rather than a precise figure. A process which delays for precisely t time units before behaving like S is written [t]S, and if the delay is bounded by times $t1$ and $t2$ the process is written [t1,t2]S. The second construct is a time-out extension to summation, so that if none of the branches of the choice are taken up within the given time, control is transferred to another branch. Again, depending on how the time-out is implemented a precise figure for the time at which control is transferred may not be available, so an interval of possibilities can be given instead. A process S which times out to process T if no communication happens within time t is written S [t> T, and if the time is bounded by $t1$ and $t2$ it is written S [t1,t2> T. As data is not handled by the basic language of AORTA, a data-dependent branch is modelled as a nondeterministic choice between processes. Such a choice is written P++Q, and is similar to the nondeterministic choice $P \sqcap Q$ of CSP [17].

In summary, a sequential process may be constructed from action prefixes, summations (choices over prefixed processes), time delays, time-outs over choices, nondeterministic choices and guarded recursion. The syntax is summarised in Table 1. Each process has a behaviour in time which says which actions it is prepared to engage in, or in other words, at which of its gates it is prepared to engage in communication. Obviously, for communication to take place there has to be more than one process in the system — the composition of system from its component processes is kept separate from process definition in AORTA.

prefix	a.S
choice	S1 + S2
delay	[t]S
bounded delay	[t1,t2]S
time-out	(S1 + ... + Sn)[t>S
bounded time-out	(S1 + ... + Sn)[t1,t2>S
nondeterministic choice	S1 ++ S2
recursion	equational definition

Table 1. Summary of AORTA sequential process syntax

Parallel composition of processes in AORTA is defined statically, by listing the names of the processes, with | as a separator. Internal communication channels are also defined statically by giving the *connection set*, which lists pairs of gates of processes. Each gate may be connected only once, and a gate may not be connected to another gate of the same process. The parallel composition and connectivity within a system is easily represented graphically. A small example demonstrates most easily how process and system definition works in practice.

2.1 A Chemical Plant Controller Example

In this section we introduce a semi-realistic example, based on a chemical plant controller. The controller has to monitor and log temperatures within a reaction vessel, and respond to dangerously high temperatures by sounding an alarm. Two rates of sampling must be provided, to be selected by the plant operator, each of which has its own output format for a logging function. In order to ensure safety of the plant, the temperature must be sampled at least every two seconds, and if a reading lies outside the safety threshold the alarm must be sounded. This system is described in more detail in [4], and is extended in section 6 to include data information. More complex examples have also been defined in AORTA, including a car cruise controller [6] and a parallel development of part of an industrial submersible controller [5].

The design presented here involves two processes, one of which handles the actual conversion of the data, while the other is used to log the data, and to control the rate at which data is sampled. There are two internal connections, which are used to pass the converted data value, and to indicate a change in the required sampling rate. The graphical representation of this system is shown in figure 1.

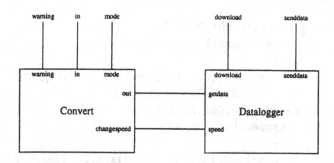

Fig. 1. Connectivity of the Chemical Plant Controller

The first of the two processes, Convert, accepts raw data on the gate in, and compares it with a threshold value. Depending on this comparison, the data conversion either takes place straight away, or is preceded by a warning signal. During the actual conversion, which takes place in the Convert2 part of the process, the calculation is done, and the result offered at the out gate, for connection to the Datalogger process. This output is timed out, to ensure that fresh data is always available, and that dangerously high input values are noticed within a reasonable time. As well as accepting data input, the Convert process allows the conversion mode to be changed, which in this case involves a signal to Datalogger, and the recalculation of a lookup table. Again, if no communication is available with the Datalogger process within about 1.5 seconds, control is returned to the main sampling loop. Changing mode during conversion is excluded by the choice (+) between in and mode.

```
Convert = in.(Convert2 ++ warning.Convert2)
        +
        mode.(changespeed.[0.3,0.4]Convert)[1.5,1.505>Convert
Convert2 = [0.001,0.004]
        (out.Convert)[1.5,1.505>Convert
```

The Datalogger process is fairly simple. Data is accepted on the getdata gate, which is then stored (requiring a computation delay). The normal sampling loop is driven by a time-out, which regularly requests new data. The period of this loop depends on the current mode of operation (it is either about 1.0 seconds or about 0.25 seconds), and this mode of operation can be changed by a speed message from the Convert process. As well as accepting mode change commands, the Datalogger process accepts requests for the downloading of the current data set to an external machine. In this case, the packet is constructed, and sent out via the senddata gate. This may take a considerable period of time, depending on the size of the packet and the nature of the communication link, and is represented by the communication delay associated with senddata in the connection set.

```
Datalogger = getdata.[0.001,0.015]
                (speed.Datalogger2
                +
                download.[0.5,1.0]senddata.Datalogger)
                   [1.00,1.005>Datalogger
Datalogger2 = getdata.[0.001,0.015]
                (speed.Datalogger)
                +
                download.[0.5,1.0]senddata.Datalogger2)
                   [0.25,0.255>Datalogger2
```

Having defined the individual processes, the full system is defined by the processes which run in parallel, along with connections, both internal and external. As well as providing a textual format for the data presented in Fig 1, communication delays are also associated with each communication channel.

```
(Convert | Datalogger)
<(Convert.changespeed,Datalogger.speed:0.001,0.003),
 (Convert.out,Datalogger.getdata:0.001,0.003),
 (Convert.in,EXTERNAL:0.001,0.003),
 (Convert.warning,EXTERNAL:0.001,0.003),
 (Convert.mode,EXTERNAL:0.001,0.003),
 (Datalogger.download,EXTERNAL:0.001,0.003),
 (Datalogger.senddata,EXTERNAL:0.5,10.0)>
```

3   Data Model Assumptions

Having described the basic language of AORTA, we can now describe the extensions to handle data. There are two main types of functional specification languages: model-based (such as Z [21], VDM-SL [18] and B [1]) and algebraic (such as ACT ONE [20] and OBJ [15]). In a model-based language, an abstract formal model of the data in the system is built, and operations are specified and described as transformations on that model. An algebraic approach does not require a complete model to be built, and operations are specified only in terms of each other. These two approaches are not entirely incompatible, as model-based specifications can be written in an algebraic style, and models can be built into an algebraic specification, but for the purposes of this paper the distinction is important,and we have chosen to use model-based languages. There are no pressing reasons for choosing one model-based language over another in our model, and in particular this work is equally applicable to Z, VDM, B, and formally defined imperative languages. Rather than choosing one of these languages arbitrarily, a general presentation is given here. Bowen and Hinchey, in their 'Ten Commandments of Formal Methods' [3] make the point that in industrial application of formal methods it is important to fit in with existing working practices. This point can be extended to the integration of formal methods, where integration with a variety of formal methods has the advantage that as little as possible extra effort has to be made in learning new notations. Therefore we feel that the loose coupling of AORTA with model-based specification languages, rather than a particular language, is a strong point. The specifics of how VDM can be used with AORTA are given with an example in section 6, and tool support for AORTA with a simple imperative language is described in section 7.

We now describe a fairly general framework for the description of model-based languages, and explain our assumptions. The basic model is that each process has a set of possible states, *States*, over which the variable Φ may range. The state Φ includes evaluations for a set of state variables. Each variable A has a set of values over which it may range, given by $values(A)$. Variables can be read using a projection $\Phi.A$, and may be updated using the standard notation $\Phi[A = v]$ where A is a variable name and $v \in values(A)$. Operations are represented using a three-place relation on states, so an operation Δ which can act on state Φ to give state Φ' is written

$$\Phi \overset{\Delta}{\Longrightarrow} \Phi'$$

The operation which changes nothing is then the identity relation on states Ξ, where

$$\Phi \overset{\Xi}{\Longrightarrow} \Phi$$

As well as accessing individual variables and performing operations on states, decisions have to be made based on the data state, which requires the definition of predicates on states, written $p(\Phi)$. Finally, we will need two distinguished state variables: $\mathcal{A}$, with $values(\mathcal{A}) = None = \{\bot\}$, and $\mathcal{T}$, with $values(\mathcal{T})$ as the time domain in use (positive reals or natural numbers).

4 Extension of Syntax

According to [6], the abstract syntax for AORTA sequential expressions is

$$S ::= \sum_{i \in I} a_i.S_i \mid [t]S \mid \sum_{i \in I} a_i.S_i \triangleright^t S \mid [t_1, t_2]S \mid \sum_{i \in I} a_i.S_i \triangleright^{t_2}_{t_1} S \mid \bigoplus_{i \in I} S_i \mid X$$

where t, t_1 and t_2 ($t_1 < t_2$) are time values taken from the time domain (either the positive reals or the naturals), a_i are gate names, and X is taken from a set of process names used for recursion. A system expression is written as a product of processes with a connection set K

$$P = \prod_{i \in I} S_i < K >$$

On the whole, the translation from concrete syntax to abstract syntax is straightforward, but some restrictions are imposed. Choice, with or without time-out, can only take place between communication events, otherwise parallel execution of computation within a single process is required, or a counterintuitive form of time nondeterminism must be adopted. $\sum$ is used to represent choice, and $\triangleright$ for time-outs. The syntax is extended for each of these constructs apart from recursion, so rather than give the whole new syntax at once, the extensions are dealt with in turn.

4.1 Communication

In the original abstract syntax, communication (and its extensions to choice and time-out) uses only gate names, reflecting the pure synchronisation model of the semantics [6]. Extending communication to include value-passing can be achieved by associating a different gate name with each data value to be offered or received (see [19]). While attractive from a theoretical point of view, as this requires only a little syntactic sugaring, it does raise some practical difficulties in implementation. Also, the abstract specification of data state transformation via computation is difficult to incorporate into this model.

The approach adopted here is more akin to that adopted by LOTOS, with its inclusion of the ACT ONE data language for value-passing [20]. Variable names can be attached to communications as input or output parameters, using a question mark for input and an exclamation mark for output. If a value is to be read from gate a into variable A, this is written $a?A.S$, and if the value held in the variable B is to be output on gate a, this is written $a!B.S$. In the general case a gate may have input and output, written $a?A!B.S$, so the abstract syntax form for choice is

$$\sum_{i \in I} a_i?A_i!B_i.S_i$$

If no data is associated with a communication then the input and output variables are both given as the distinguished variable A (which always has value $\perp$), so that $a.S$ is an abbreviation for $a?A!A.S$. Similarly, $a?B.S$ is an abbreviation for $a?B!A.S$ and $a!B.S$ is an abbreviation for $a?A!B.S$. The variable T is used to represent a perfect clock, and so cannot be used as a communication variable. Communications within a time-out are adapted in exactly the same way as for choice, giving the abstract syntax form

$$\sum_{i \in I} a_i?A_i!B_i.S_i \triangleright_{t_1}^{t_2} S$$

and a corresponding deterministic form.

4.2 Computation

Within AORTA, computations are represented only by a time delay, but during such delays a change of data state will usually take place. Operations which change state are represented by transformation functions Δ, which are attached to the time delay construct using braces. If an operation Δ takes between t_1 and t_2 time units to complete, this is represented by the abstract syntax form

$$[t_1, t_2\{\Delta\}]S$$

Some computations will require access to a real time clock, for time-stamping or time-averaging, so a special state variable $\mathcal{T}$ is used to represent a perfect clock. In practice, a physical clock will not be perfect, as it may run at the wrong speed, and may have its values discretised. This is modelled by defining a physical clock function on the perfect clock, which gives a set of values related to the perfect clock within some level of accuracy. During computations, time can only be accessed via the physical clock function.

4.3 Data dependent choice

Data dependent choice is represented as nondeterministic choice in AORTA, using the $\bigoplus_{i \in I} S_i$ notation. In order to give the conditions under which each branch of the choice is to be taken, a predicate on the state is attached to each, again using braces

$$\bigoplus_{i \in I} S_i\{p_i\}$$

Sometimes a degree of nondeterminism is helpful, so the predicates are allowed to overlap (i.e. there can be j and k such that $p_j^{-1}(true) \cap p_k^{-1}(true)$ is nonempty). There must, however, always be one predicate which is true (i.e. $\forall \Phi. \bigvee_{i \in I} p_i(\Phi)$), to ensure that some branch will be taken up.

Combining the extensions for communication, computation and data dependent choice gives the full abstract syntax for AORTA terms with data information

$$S ::= \sum_{i \in I} a_i ? A_i ! B_i . S_i \mid [t\{\Delta\}]S \mid \sum_{i \in I} a_i ? A_i ! B_i . S_i \triangleright^t S$$

$$\mid [t_1, t_2\{\Delta\}]S \mid \sum_{i \in I} a_i ? A_i ! B_i . S_i \triangleright^{t_2}_{t_1} S \mid \bigoplus_{i \in I} S_i\{p_i\} \mid X$$

where t, t_1 and t_2 ($t_1 < t_2$) are time values taken from the time domain (either the positive reals or the naturals), A_i and B_i are state variable names, Δ is a state transformation function, the p_i are predicates on the state, and X is taken from a set of process names used for recursion.

5 Enriched Semantics for AORTA

The semantics defined in [6] gives a stratified set of operational transition rules for defining a transition relation between AORTA terms. A similar approach is adopted here, except that the transition system is enriched with the data state.

An interleaving semantic model is used, with time transitions represented by $\xrightarrow{(t)}$ and action transitions (i.e. communications) represented by $\xrightarrow{a}$. A transition system *stratification* is a technique whereby transition rules with negative premises can be meaningfully included. By evaluating the transition system in layers, or strata, it can be shown that no transition's validity depends on its own negation, as circularities can be removed [16]. In our system, the lowest stratum contains transitions between sequential expressions, the second contains all internal system communications, and the third (and highest) contains system time transitions and external communications. By organising the transition system in this way, the negative premise for the system time delay rule given below can be consistently incorporated. This negative premise is essential to enforce maximal progress, or τ-urgency.

To define the first stratum, we have to consider an important subset of sequential expressions, known as the *regular* expressions, on which the semantics is defined (n.b. the semantics is undefined on non-regular expressions). Regular expressions have no nondeterminism or recursion before the next action, and can easily be syntactically characterised. A regular sequential expression is annotated with a data state Φ, written $S[\Phi]$, and a set of eight sequential expression transition rules (which are defined only on regular expressions) can be given. The full set of rules can be found elsewhere [7], but two example rules are given in figure 2, where we abbreviate the updating of the perfect clock using the definition $\Phi_{+t} \triangleq \Phi[\mathcal{T} = \Phi.\mathcal{T} + t]$ which changes the state only by adding t to the perfect clock variable. The semantics of data dependent choice

$$\overline{\sum_{i \in I} a_i.S_i \rhd^t S[\Phi] \xrightarrow{(t)} S[\Phi_{+t}]}$$

$$\frac{}{\sum_{i \in I} a_i.S_i \rhd^t S[\Phi] \xrightarrow{a_j?v!\Phi.B_j} [t\{\Xi\}]S_j'[\Phi[A_j = v]]} \quad \begin{array}{l} j \in I \\ S_j' \in Poss(S_j, \Phi[A_j = v]) \\ t \in delays(a_j) \\ v \in values(A_j) \end{array}$$

Fig. 2. Transition rules for sequential expressions with data

is not given by transition rules, but by the definition of the *Poss* function. Any AORTA term which starts with $\bigoplus_{i \in I} S_i$ is not regular, so has to be regularised when an action transition takes place. Without any data state information, the choice between branches is nondeterministic, but by attaching predicates to the branches, a data dependent choice can be made. The *Poss* function defines possible resolutions of nondeterminism which are used to regularise a process; again details can be found elsewhere [7]. There are three rules for system expressions, based on the transitions of sequential expressions, for internal communication, external communication, and time progress. The rule for time progress is

$$\frac{\forall i \in I.S_i[\Phi_i] \xrightarrow{(t)} S_i'[\Phi_i']}{\prod_{i \in I} S_i[\Phi_i] < K > \xrightarrow{(t)} \prod_{i \in I} S_i'[\Phi_i'] < K >} \forall t' < t. \prod_{i \in I} Age(S_i[\Phi_i], t') < K > \not\xrightarrow{\tau}$$

The negative premise $\not\xrightarrow{\tau}$ is used here to enforce the maximum progress principle, and a simple priority on communication — internal communication is preferred to external communication. A more sophisticated prioritisation can be achieved by making each communication dependent on all higher priority communications being impossible. To retain the consistency of the transition system, a more complex stratification must be used, with a different stratum for each priority level. The lowest priority level will always be for the time delay, so as to enforce the maximum progress principle. Within the rule for time progress, the function Age is used to represent the a process after a given amount of time has passed. More formally, we define

$$Age(E, t) = E' \iff E \xrightarrow{(t)} E'$$

In [6] a direct syntactic interpretation of Age is given, along with a theorem relating it to the definition just given, which indirectly demonstrates that Age is well-defined (i.e. it is a function).

6 An Example Using VDM

The chemical plant controller example of [4] is given here as an example of how data specifications can be built into AORTA. VDM is used as the specification language here, although other languages can equally well be used. Addressing the data model assumptions given in section 3 in turn, we first have to consider how the set of possible states of a process can be defined. In VDM this can be done by defining a composite type, including fields for each of the state variables of the process (including A and T). Invariants on the data type can be used to restrict the state space. The set of values for each state variable is defined by its type. Selectors are used to provide projections for individual variables, and the μ function gives an easy mechanism for updating:

$$\Phi[A = v] = \mu(\Phi, A \mapsto v)$$

Operations are simply VDM operations which take no argument and return no result, but have the process state as a writable external, and no (i.e **true**) precondition. The identity function on states Ξ is simply the operation

ID

ext wr s : *States*
post $s = \overleftarrow{s}$

Finally, predicates on states are defined simply as boolean valued functions on states (i.e. of type *States* → **B**).

To construct the set of (data) states for the Convert process, we use five state variables, including the perfect clock $\mathcal{T}$ and the dummy $\mathcal{A}$. There are two gates of the Convert process which carry data, namely in and out: the state variables associated with these gates are *input:Rawdata* and *output:Temp* respectively. A lookup table is used for the conversion, and this is stored in the state variable *table:Lookuptable*. With the time domain represented as the type *Time*, the composite type representing the state of Convert is given by

$$
\begin{array}{rcl}
Convert & :: & input \ : \ Rawdata \\
& & output \ : \ Temp \\
& & table \ : \ Lookuptable \\
& & \mathcal{T} \ : \ Time \\
& & \mathcal{A} \ : \ None
\end{array}
$$

Within Convert, there are two computations: the first converts raw data to a temperature, using a lookup table, and the second recalculates the lookup table for a different conversion mode. Assuming that we have the function *evaluate* then the conversion operation is defined as

DOCONVERSION

ext wr *conv* : *Convert*

post $conv = \mu(\overleftarrow{conv}, output \mapsto evaluate(\overleftarrow{input}, \overleftarrow{table}))$

Changing conversion mode depends on a function *newtable* which recalculates the lookup table, so the operation for changing mode is defined as

CHANGEMODE

ext wr *conv* : *Convert*

post $conv = \mu(\overleftarrow{conv}, table \mapsto newtable(\overleftarrow{table}))$

To specify the behaviour of nondeterministic choice, a predicate on the state must be attached to each branch of the choice. In the Convert process, the behaviour depends on whether the raw data value exceeds a threshold value; if so a warning signal must be sent. The predicates which we are interested in are

$convertdatahigh : Convert \rightarrow \mathbf{B}$

$convertdatahigh(conv) \ \triangleq \ input(conv) > threshold$

and a corresponding predicate *convertdataok* which assume that we have defined a total order > on *Rawdata* and that the value *threshold:Rawdata* is defined. Attaching these new data constructs to the Convert process gives the definition

```
Convert = in?input.
          (Convert2 {convertdataok} ++
```

```
                warning.Convert2 {convertdatahigh})
            +
            mode.(changespeed.
                    [0.3,0.4 {CHANGEMODE}]Convert)[1.5,1.505>Convert
Convert2 = [0.001,0.004 {DOCONVERSION}]
                    (out!output.Convert)[1.5,1.505>Convert
```

The Datalogger process has its own set of states, defined by the composite type

$$Datalogger :: \quad input : Temp$$
$$packet : Loggerpacket$$
$$history : (Temp \times Time)^*$$
$$T : Time$$
$$\mathcal{T} : Time$$
$$\mathcal{A} : None$$

Two of the variables, *input* and *packet* are used to carry data for communication on gates getdata and senddata, while *history* is used to record data with time stamps. The variable T is used for the physical clock, as well as the usual $\mathcal{T}$ and $\mathcal{A}$ variables. Two computations are associated with Datalogger, which correspond to adding a data item (with time stamp) to the store, and making up a data packet for downloading. To get the time stamp value from the clock, we require the function *possclocks* which returns the possible physical clock values at a given time. The data which is input from the getdata port is added to *history* with the operation

ADDDATA

ext wr $mk\text{-}Datalogger(h, i, p, t1, t2, a)$: $Datalogger$

post $t1 \in possclocks(t2) \wedge h = cons((t1, i), \overleftarrow{h}) \wedge t2 = \overleftarrow{t2}$

Finally, assuming the function *makepacket* we can define the operation

MAKEPACKET

ext wr $mk\text{-}Datalogger(i, p, h, t1, t2, a)$: $Datalogger$

post $p = makepacket(\overleftarrow{h}) \wedge h = [] \wedge t2 = \overleftarrow{t2}$

There are no nondeterministic choices in the Datalogger process, so the full version of the process, including data information, is

```
Datalogger = getdata?input.[0.01,0.015 {ADDDATA}]
                (speed.Datalogger2
                +
                download.[0.5,1.0 {MAKEPACKET}]
                        senddata!packet.Datalogger)
                    [1.00,1.005>Datalogger
Datalogger2 = getdata?input.[0.01,0.015 {ADDDATA}]
                (speed.Datalogger
```

```
        +
        download.[0.5,1.0 {MAKEPACKET}]
                    senddata!packet.Datalogger2)
        [0.25,0.255>Datalogger2
```

Having defined the individual processes, the system composition is given as before, using the | operator and a connection set, but with the addition of initial data states for each of the processes within the parallel composition.

7   Tool Support and Methodological Considerations

The emphasis of AORTA is on practicality, in that implementation and simulation issues have been considered alongside verification; designs written in the language can be represented purely in ASCII; implementations are based on generated C. One crucial aspect of a practical design method is the availability of supporting software tools, and research tools for graphical simulation, model-checking via graph generation, and code generation have been provided. These were all originally written for the basic language without a formal data model, where all computational aspects were represented by implementation fragments written in C.

In order to provide support for AORTA extended with a formal data model, some generalisation of the tool set was required. One possible approach would have been to choose a formal language for data, such as VDM, and to attempt a one-off integration of the AORTA tool set with some supporting tools for the data language. This would have the advantage that it might not require too much work, and could provide a fairly tight coupling, but would have the obvious disadvantages of inapplicability to other languages and tools. Instead a more general approach was adopted, whereby an abstract data language interface was specified, (based on the data model assumptions given in section 3) and the integration done at that level. In this way, integration with a new language or tool set involves providing an interpretation of the abstract notions of value, variable, state, computation, predicate and so on. The obvious advantage of this approach is in its flexibility, with the disadvantages that the tools which are to be integrated may need to be adapted to fit the interface provided.

The actual support which is provided for the data enriched language mostly falls into the area of simulation, which we introduced in section 1 as an important part of a formal method. For the basic language the tool set offers simulation as a technique for exercising the semantics, by choosing time and action transitions from a menu. Although this is helpful for a detailed exploration of the behaviour of a design, the more complete description given by a design with data allows a more dynamic simulation to be offered as well; one in which the processes of the design are simulated by concurrently executing threads, which communicate and evolve spontaneously in time. Put another way, we can now provide a direct interpreter for the combined language. The new support provides such a simulator, which allows any AORTA design annotated with formally specified data operations to be executed. Implementation code is provided as a separate annotation to the design, so that if the data formalism is supported by code generation, then the whole of the design (including data parts) can be used to generate complete implementation code directly.

Our initial experiment into providing a formal data language has used a simple formally defined imperative language with sequence, choice and iteration, and integer, boolean and enumerated data types. This language is substantially smaller than VDM, for example, but serves to demonstrate that a useful integration is possible. Furthermore, as the computation data relation is a function, direct interpretation is possible, and the language is explicit enough to allow direct code generation. In fact, this is just the sort of language that formal refinements from Z, B or VDM aim to produce, so it may be that two levels of data formalism should be provided: one for an abstract, possibly implicit, specification, and one for an explicit description, closely related to an implementation, and derived by a verified refinement from the specification. However, some approaches, such as that adopted by the IFAD VDM-Toolbox [11] are based on writing explicit specifications in the first place, and hence providing code generation and interpretation facilities directly. In such cases as these, direct integration with AORTA is possible, without the need for an intermediate language.

The discussion about whether implicit specification and refinement, or explicit specification and code generation is better is outside the scope of this paper, but we note that in order to satisfy our earlier criterion of integration with as wide a range of approaches as possible, we should be able to deal with both. This is possible because of a further level of generality built in to the tool support for AORTA, beyond that of a general data language. Not only is the actual type of data language with which designs can be annotated quite general, but the number and type of annotations themselves is general. For instance, for AORTA with the simple imperative language, annotations can be provided at each point in the syntax tree for the textual form of the data part, for its internal representation as a relation on states, or whatever, for the implementation code associated with it, and for information concerning the graphical presentation of the syntax. However, the notion of annotation is general, and the implementation of the tool set modularised such that the addition of new annotations, perhaps for a more abstract data specification, or perhaps for proofs of correctness, or perhaps for timing information about the code, is quite straightforward. Having provided different kinds of annotation, the tool then needs to be configured to say which will be used in code generation, which are to be used in simulation, and which in verification etc.

How then are such tools and languages to be used to develop systems? We suggest that early simulation is important, as it allows problems in the design to be detected before too much of the implementation detail is fixed. Similar arguments are given for the early application of specification and proof techniques during system development. The aim of this work is not necessarily to replace proof in system development, but rather to avoid wasted effort during proof by detecting and eliminating as many errors as possible by simulation, which can be thought of as high-level testing. With the addition of an interpretation for data two kinds of simulation are now possible. In the first, in which the processes evolve spontaneously, a design error may be detected and corrected immediately, or further, more detailed simulation, based on the semantics, may be required to locate the problem. Having satisfactorily tested the design, it may at this point be appropriate to attempt a formal correctness proof. Note that further work is required on proof techniques in a combined language (see section 8). Having verified the correctness of the design, further work will be required to produce the implementation. If code generation of data properties is not automatic then refinement to code, with proofs, will be required. Also, static analysis of code (possibly with user intervention) to extract timing information will we required, as inputs to the scheduling calculations, which are used to verify that the implementation timing will match that given in the design [4].

8 Conclusions

AORTA is a timed process algebra-based design language, so comparison might be made with other timed process algebras; however so many timed process algebras have been defined that even a cursory list of references would be too long for the scope of this paper, so the reader is referred elsewhere [9], and direct references given only for (a version of) Timed CCS [26], Timed CSP [22], and (a version of) Timed LOTOS [2]. At this level the main distinctive feature of AORTA is the ability to generate implementations about which timing guarantees can be made.

This paper has shown how it is possible to build a formal data model into AORTA and how tool support for simulation and implementation generation techniques and tools can be extended. Further work needs to be done on the use of model-checking techniques in association with data properties. One possible approach is to provide a (verified) refinement of the data associated with the state spaces, so that required data properties still hold, but that the state space is finite. Once the state space has been reduced to a finite size, data properties can be represented as propositions labelling timed graphs, so that model-checking of properties like 'The alarm will come on within 5 seconds of receiving a temperature reading above the safe limit' becomes possible. The abstraction to the trivial state space where all data information is ignored has been shown to be equivalent to the original semantics [9], so we can at least still perform simple model-checking with assurance of correctness.

Other research has covered some of the aspects of this work. MOSCA provides a formalism combining CCS, VDM and time, but without providing implementation techniques [25] whilst RAISE [24] and LOTOS [20, 27] provide data modelling in concurrent systems, with some implementation techniques, but no time. Work has also been done with timed extensions to LOTOS [2], which already has the data language ACT-ONE included, but in this case no implementation techniques are provided. A different kind of approach involves introducing time into data specification languages such as Z [10, 13, 14], with the closest work to ours being that by Fidge et al [12], which allows the timed refinement of concurrent systems, including reasoning about implementations by embedding scheduling theory into the Z model. This approach can only be described as 'different' to ours, with the relative merits and demerits associated with the two being the usual ones associated with refinement as opposed to code generation techniques. Also, most of their work has been associated with providing the proof theory (as would be expected for a refinement calculus), whereas our work has focussed on implementation aspects.

In summary, then, this paper has shown how a fairly general formal data model can be integrated syntactically and semantically into AORTA. Tool support for simulation and code generation has been discussed, and an example of using AORTA with VDM has been included. Proof support needs further work, although some suggestions have been made, so some may raise the question as to what purpose a formal semantics serves where no proof support is to be offered. In our introduction, we argued that formal methods and good for more than just proof, and we feel that this has been borne out by the provision of useful simulation tools, and also a clear statement of the necessary assumptions about the data model, which have formed the basis of tool support for the data-enriched language.

References

1. J-R Abrial. *The B-Book*. Cambridge University Press, 1996.
2. T Bolognesi and F Lucidi. LOTOS-like process algebras with urgent or timed interactions. In K R Parker and G A Rose, editors, *Formal Description Techniques IV, FORTE '91, Sydney*, pages 249–264. Elsevier, November 1991.
3. J P Bowen and M G Hinchey. Ten commandments of formal methods. *IEEE Software*, 28(4):56–63, April 1995.
4. S Bradley, W Henderson, D Kendall, and A Robson. A formally based hard real-time kernel. *Microprocessors and Microsystems*, 18(9):513–521, November 1994.
5. S Bradley, W Henderson, D Kendall, A Robson, and S Hawkes. A formal design and implementation method for real-time embedded systems. In P Milligan and K Kuchinski, editors, *22nd EUROMICRO Conference (EUROMICRO 96), Prague*, pages 77–84. IEEE, September 1996.
6. S Bradley, W D Henderson, D Kendall, and A P Robson. Application-Oriented Real-Time Algebra. *Software Engineering Journal*, 9(5):201–212, September 1994.
7. S Bradley, W D Henderson, D Kendall, and A P Robson. Modelling data in a real-time algebra. Technical Report NPC-TRS-95-1, Department of Computing, University of Northumbria, UK, 1995.
8. S Bradley, W D Henderson, D Kendall, and A P Robson. Validation, verification and implementation of timed protocols using AORTA. In Piotr Dembinski and Marek Sredniawa, editors, *Protocol Specification, Testing and Verification XV (PSTV '95), Warsaw*, pages 193–208. IFIP, North Holland, June 1995.
9. S P Bradley. *An Implementable Formal Language for Hard Real-Time Systems*. PhD thesis, Department of Computing, University of Northumbria, UK, October 1995.
10. A Coombes and J McDermid. Specifying temporal requirements for distributed real-time systems in Z. *Software Engineering Journal*, 8(5):273–283, September 1993.

11. René Elmstrøm, Peter Gorm Larsen, and Poul Bøgh Lassen. The IFAD VDM-SL Toolbox: A Practical Approach to Formal Specifications. *ACM Sigplan Notices*, 29(9):77–80, September 1994.

12. C Fidge, M Utting, P Kearney, and I Hayes. Integrating real-time scheduling theory and program refinement. In M-C Gaudel and J Woodcock, editors, *FME '96: Industrial Benefit and Advances in Formal Methods*, number 1051 in Lecture Notes in Computer Science, pages 327–346. FME, Springer, 1996.

13. C J Fidge. Specification and verification of real-time behaviour using Z and RTL. In J Vytopil, editor, *Formal techniques in real-time and fault-tolerant systems Second international symposium, Nijmegen, Lecture Notes in Computer Science 571*, pages 393–409. Springer-Verlag, 1992.

14. C J Fidge. Real-time refinement. In J C P Woodcock and P G Larsen, editors, *Formal Methods Europe '93: Industrial-Strength Formal Methods, Lecture Notes in Computer Science 670*, pages 314–331. Springer-Verlag, 1993.

15. J A Goguen and T Winkler. Introducing OBJ3. Technical Report SRI-CSL-88-9, SRI, August 1988.

16. J F Groote. Transition system specifications with negative premises. In J C M Baeten and J W Klop, editors, *CONCUR '90, Amsterdam, Lecture Notes in Computer Science 458*, pages 332–341. Springer-Verlag, 1990.

17. C A R Hoare. *Communicating Sequential Processes*. Prentice Hall, New York, 1985.

18. C B Jones. *Systematic software development using VDM*. Prentice Hall, New York, 1986.

19. R Milner. *Communication and Concurrency*. Prentice Hall, New York, 1989.

20. International Standards Organisation. *Informations processing systems - Open Systems Interconnection - LOTOS - A formal description technique based on the temporal ordering of observational behaviour*, volume ISO 8807. ISO, 1989-02-15 edition, 1989.

21. B Potter, J Sinclair, and D Till. *An Introduction to formal specification and Z*. Prentice Hall, New York, 1991.

22. S Schneider, J Davies, D M Jackson, G M Reed, J N Reed, and A W Roscoe. Timed CSP: Theory and practice. In J W de Bakker, C Huizing, W P de Roever, and G Rozenberg, editors, *Real-Time: Theory in Practice (REX workshop), Mook, Lecture Notes in Computer Science 600*, pages 640–675. Springer-Verlag, June 1991.

23. G Smith. A semantic integration of Object-Z and CSP for the specification of concurrent systems. In J Fitzgerald, C B Jones, and P Lucas, editors, *FME 97: Industrial Applications and Strengthened Foundations of Formal Methods*, volume 1313 of *Lecture Notes in Computer Science*, pages 62–81. FME, Springer, 1997.

24. The RAISE Language Group. *The RAISE Specification Language*. BCS Practicioner Series. Prentice Hall, 1992.

25. H Toetenel. VDM + CCS + Time = MOSCA. In *18th IFAC/IFIP Workshop on Real-Time Programming — WRTP '92, Bruges*. Pergamon Press, June 1992.

26. C Tofts. Timed concurrent processes. In *Semantics for Concurrency*, pages 281–294, 1990.

27. M van Sinderen, L Ferreira Pires, and C A Vissers. Protocol design and implementation using formal methods. *Computer Journal*, 35(5):478–491, 1992.

Specifying Safety-Critical Embedded Systems with Statecharts and Z: A Case Study

Robert Büssow[1], Robert Geisler[1], and Marcus Klar[2]

[1] Technische Universität Berlin, Institut für Kommunikations- und
Softwaretechnik Sekr. 6–1, Franklinstr. 28/29, D–10587 Berlin.
{buessow, geislerr}@cs.tu-berlin.de
[2] Fraunhofer-Institut für Software- und Systemtechnik ISST
Kurstr. 33, D–10117 Berlin. Marcus.Klar@isst.fhg.de

Abstract. In this paper we introduce a formal approach for the specification of safety-critical embedded systems. The specification formalisms Z and statecharts are integrated under a suitable structural model. The combined approach uses the advantages of the formalisms while avoiding their disadvantages. The different formalisms yield different, compatible views on the system: the functional view describing data and data-transformation, the reactive view, describing the system's reaction upon external stimuli, and the structural view, describing the components of the system and their interaction. The combination is discussed presenting parts of a case study: a traffic light control system. The case study is oriented at original planning documents. Besides its safety- and real-time-aspects, the case study is particularly interesting because structuring and reuse is of considerable importance in this example.

1 Introduction

Embedded systems are permanently increasing in size, complexity and responsibility. Failures of the control software can have disastrous consequences and, due to this, *safety* [18] of the software is becoming more and more important. In addition, embedded systems raise problems of concurrency, have to obey real-time requirements, and usually reside in a heterogeneous environment. This stresses the need of an adequate software specification technique and a suitable development method for large-scale (safety-critical) embedded systems. The used *specification formalisms* need to be comprehensive, expressive, and precise. We are using statecharts, an extension of finite automata, to describe reactive behaviors; because of its clear depiction of a system's reaction and states. For the data and data-transformations we are using the Z specification language because of its mathematical-like notation and expressiveness.

Instead of describing the whole system in one specification formalism, we use different formalisms to specify different aspects of the system, exploiting the advantages and avoiding the disadvantages of the particular formalisms; e.g. dynamic aspects like control flow can not be expressed very descriptive in Z, while the statecharts formalism provides only limited support for the description of data.

The *structural view* describes the components of the system and their relations with each other and their environment. Typically some variant of data flow diagrams [8] is used for this purpose. In the *dynamic view* the reaction of the system and its components to internal and external stimuli is specified. Such behavior can be described intuitively using state automata. The *functional view* describes data, data invariants and data transformations of the system and its components. The data transformations are controlled by the specification of the dynamic view. For the specification of the functional view, data type specification languages are an adequate tool.

The main emphasis of this work is the presentation of the case study—the specification of a traffic light system with statecharts and Z. The case study, the combination (called μSZ) as well as verification and validation techniques are investigated in detail in the ESPRESS project[1]. Methodological aspects of the ESPRESS project are presented in [11].

2 Specification Technique

We represent an embedded system as a collection of synchronous, communicating processes. Each process has a data space, an interface for the communication with other processes or the environment, and a statechart determining how it reacts upon external stimuli.

The description of a process is given by the specification of so called process classes. A process class describes a set of processes with common behavior. This description (a process-class) includes the structure of the process, i.e. its subprocesses, their communication relations, and the processes the specified process is linked to via associations. The description consists in its interface, its local variables, its dynamic behavior, its configuration, predicates and operations over its variables, as well as behavioral constraints. This combination is discussed in detail in [2], the different views are depicted in Figure 1.

The structure of a process is depicted in a so called *configuration* diagram. Processes communicate via shared variables and valued events. A process can have several interfaces called *ports* to read and write variables shared with other processes. In the configuration diagram, communication relations between processes are established by linking ports of different processes together. The structure and the interfaces of a process together are forming the *architectural* view of a process.

A process is storing, transforming, and exchanging data. This data is specified in the *functional* description of the process, using the Z language

[1] ESPRESS is a joint project of German industry and research institutes, funded by the German Bundesministerium für Bildung, Wissenschaft und Technologie (BMBF).

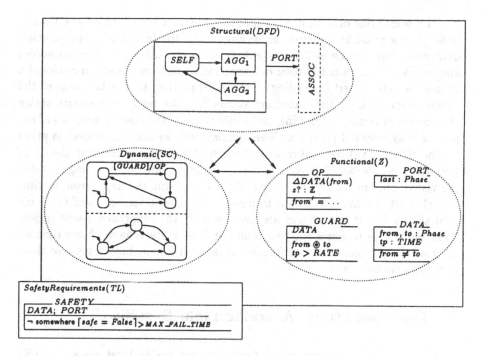

Fig. 1. The different Views on a Process

[21]. We distinguish local and shared data. The local data is described in so called *DATA*-schemas, whereas shared data is stored in *PORT*-schemas. Data transformation can be carried out via *operations*. In an *Op*-schema, the input-output relation of an operation is specified in Z.

The behavior of a process, i.e. the actions it performs during its lifetime, are subject to the statecharts [12] in the *dynamic view*. We are using the STATEMATE [13] tool to support the graphical languages used. Thus, for statecharts, the STATEMATE syntax and semantics [15,14] are adopted. The configurations are expressed with a subset of STATEMATE's *activity-charts*. Nevertheless, we specify the guards and actions of the statechart transitions in Z. The guards are predicates over a process's data space and the actions are operations over the data space.

Especially in the early development phases, it might not be possible or adequate to describe the process behavior in an operational manner, i.e. by using statecharts. Therefore, we express behavioral requirements (particularly safety requirements) in temporal logic. Here, we are using the logic introduced in [5]. These temporal requirements can later be "implemented" by a statechart. Thus, a process can as well include an abstract specification of behavioral constraints and requirements as a concrete implementation. It becomes a natural proof obligation in the development process to show that the implementation fulfills the constraints and requirements.

The semantics of a combined specification is a set of processes that is ordered in a tree-like structure according to the specification's configuration diagrams. The processes are connected via ports, allowing them to access and exchange the values of their external variables. The *static semantics* of a process is determined (according to the Z semantics) by the bindings of the process variables, by the statechart status (i.e. the set of statecharts states the process currently resides in), and recursively by the static semantics of the process's aggregated processes. The *dynamic semantics* of a process is given by the STATEMATE semantics described in [14]. The parallel statecharts of the processes are executed synchronously. Changes that occur during one step are visible only in the following step. We are applying the *asynchronous* time model of STATEMATE. We want to point out that the semantics of the basis formalisms Z and statecharts are preserved in the combined specification. This enables us to reuse existing tools for Z and Statecharts. Note that we do not aim at translating one formalism into the other, but rather use them in a supplemental way.

3 The Case Study: A Traffic Light System

In this case study we describe a fault tolerant traffic light system (TLS). The task of the TLS consists of (1) steering the signal heads[2] according to a given program (functionality), and (2) guaranteeing a safe signal situation on the junction, even in case of signal head failure (safety). To reduce complexity, this specification separates the functional and the safety aspects into different components. The means of structuring of the used specification formalism support this approach and allow a modular specification. A TLS has to comply to several norms and laws; for this case study the *German Road Traffic Law* and the German norms [9,10] are relevant. The requirements for a particular junction are given in the *planning documents*, made by an engineer's office. This specification is based on authentic planning documents of an existing junction.

The planning documents include the essential local informations for the traffic junction such as the road infrastructure, road markings, sidewalks, bike-ways, signing, signal heads, and detectors (see Figure 2). The street from north-east to south-west is the main road. The signal heads are numbered, the detectors (induction loops and pedestrian push buttons) are carrying numbers with a leading "D". The detectors are measuring the requirements of the road users. These requirements are influencing the control of the traffic light system, allowing to react in a flexible way on changing traffic volumes.

We model the signal heads of the TLS in Z as an enumeration type. The signal heads have different lamps, modeled as *Lamp*.

---

[2] A set of signal heads is a green, yellow, and red lamp or, for pedestrians, green and red lamps.

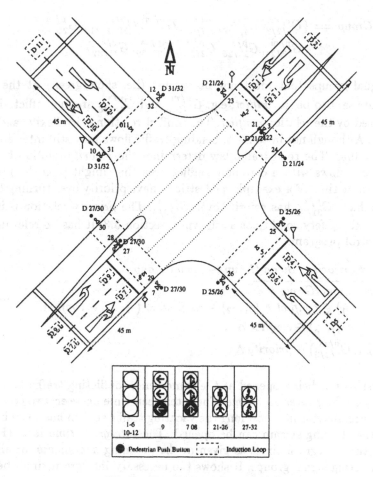

Fig. 2. The Signal Layout Plan

$$SignalHeads ::= Sh_1 \mid Sh_2 \mid Sh_3 \mid \ldots \mid Sh_{31} \mid Sh_{32}$$
$$Lamp \qquad ::= red \mid yellow \mid green$$

The signal heads that control the same traffic flows, are grouped together to *signal groups*. A signal group consists of a set of signal heads that, in absence of failure, indicate the same signal. In our traffic junction we have eleven signal groups (v denotes vehicle, p pedestrian, m the main road, and s the side road).

$$\begin{array}{|l}
G^{v/m}_{1/2/3},\, G^{v/s}_{4/5/6},\, G^{v/m}_{7/8},\, G^{v/m}_{9},\, G^{v/s}_{10/11/12} : \mathbb{P}\, SignalHeads \\
G^{p/m}_{21/22},\, G^{p/s}_{23/24},\, G^{p/m}_{25/26},\, G^{p/m}_{27/28},\, G^{p/m}_{29/30},\, G^{p/s}_{31/32} : \mathbb{P}\, SignalHeads \\
\hline
G^{v/m}_{1/2/3} = \{Sh_1, Sh_2, Sh_3\} \wedge \ldots \wedge G^{p/s}_{31/32} = \{Sh_{31}, Sh_{32}\}
\end{array}$$

$$SignalGroup == \{ G_{1/2/3}^{v/m}, G_{4/5/6}^{v/s}, G_{7/8}^{v/m}, G_9^{v/m}, G_{10/11/12}^{v/s}, G_{21/22}^{p/m},$$
$$G_{23/24}^{p/m}, G_{25/26}^{p/s}, G_{27/28}^{p/m}, G_{29/30}^{p/m}, G_{31/32}^{p/s} \}$$

Signal groups that must not be opened (i.e. show green) at the same time, are said to be in *conflict*, e.g. $G_{1/2/3}^{v/m}$ and $G_{4/5/6}^{v/s}$ are in conflict. This is expressed by the relation *conflict*. The conflict relation is irreflexive and symmetric. Although not in conflict, bending traffic flows may still interfere with non-bending. The road traffic law determines the *priority* relation between two traffic flows with a common conflict area that might pass the junction at the same time. For example, pedestrians have priority over turning traffic, e.g. we have $G_{31/32}^{p/s}$ has priority over $G_{1/2/3}^{v/m}$. The priority relation is important for the safety conditions as shown in section 3.3. It has no relevance for the control program.

$conflict, priority : SignalGroup \leftrightarrow SignalGroup$

$\forall s_1, s_2 : SignalGroup \bullet$
$\quad (s_1, s_1) \notin conflict \wedge (s_1, s_2) \in conflict \Leftrightarrow (s_2, s_1) \in conflict$
$(G_{1/2/3}^{v/m}, G_{4/5/6}^{v/s}) \in conflict \wedge \ldots$
$(G_{31/32}^{p/s}, G_{1/2/3}^{v/m}) \in priority \wedge \ldots$

Besides not being opened at the same time, conflicting traffic flows have to obey to their *intergreen time*. The intergreen time between two conflicting traffic streams specifies how long the vacating traffic stream has to be blocked until the starting stream can be opened. The *intergreen time table* (Fig. 3), shows the intergreen times as given in the planning documents for all pairs of conflicting signal groups. It shows the necessary intergreen times between starting (abscissa) and vacating (ordinate) traffic streams.

The intergreen time table is modeled in Z as a function that maps a pair of conflicting signal groups to its intergreen time. $IGT(grp_1, grp_2)$ denotes the time grp_1 has to be closed before grp_2 may be opened.

$| IGT : conflict \rightarrow TIME$

3.1 Structure of the Traffic Light Control System

We describe our system as a hierarchical set of interacting processes. The top level process is called *TRAFFIC_LIGHT_CONTROL*. Its configuration shows how it is divided into four aggregated processes as well as the interfaces between the processes and their environment. Here, the environment consists of the external traffic facilities, such as the signal heads and detectors of the system. The processes are connected via arrows that are labeled with port names. The processes communicate via the variables declared in their ports. These ports are specified in the process classes of the processes. In the

	1/2/3	4/5/6	7/8	9	10/11/12	21/22	23/24	25/26	27/28	29/30	31/32
1/2/3	×	5	-	4	7	4	4	7	8	8	6
4/5/6	7	×	4	5	-	5	5	4	8	8	7
7/8	-	6	×	-	5	8	8	7	5	5	-
9	7	5	-	×	6	-	-	-	4	4	9
10/11/12	6	-	5	4	×	8	8	8	6	6	4
21/22	6	3	1	-	2	×	-	-	-	-	-
23/24	6	3	1	-	2	-	×	-	-	-	-
25/26	8	10	9	-	8	-	-	×	-	-	-
27/28	1	1	6	6	2	-	-	-	×	-	-
29/30	1	1	6	6	2	-	-	-	-	×	-
31/32	9	8	-	8	10	-	-	-	-	-	×

Fig. 3. The Intergreen Time Table

following we give a short description of the four aggregates of the top-level process:

The *VEHICLE_ACTUATED_CONTROL* realizes the traffic control algorithm, i.e., it computes when the lamps of the signal heads are to be switched on or off and sends the relevant signals. The *SAFEGUARD* guarantees the safety of the traffic junction. If an unsafe signal indication occurs due to hardware or software failure, the safeguard has to take counter action. If, for example, a red light breaks, the safeguard and the suppression have to decide whether the resulting signal indication is still safe. If it is not, it has to take measures to reestablish a safe indication. If an unsafe signal indication is detected, the suppression tries to reestablish safety in, e.g. switching defective signal heads whereas the safe guard shuts off the entire TLS if an unsafe situation is imminent to last longer than 0.3 seconds. The safe guard is discussed in detail in section 3.3.

Signals that are sent by the control might interfere with measures taken by the *SAFEGUARD* while handling failures. Such signals are filtered out by the *SIGNAL_SUPPRESSION*. Moreover, the *SIGNAL_SUPPRESSION* suppresses all signals that would lead to an unsafe situation of the junction. By that, safety can be ensured independently of the *VEHICLE_ACTU-ATED_CONTROL*. The signals of the system's detectors (induction loops and pedestrian push buttons) are recorded and prepared for the control by the *DETECTOR_ACQUISITION*, because these detector values serve as parameters for the vehicle actuated control.

There are four interfaces between the traffic control system and the external traffic facilities: The signals, indicated to the road users, are transmitted via the port *ACTUAL_VALUES*. They are assumed to be measurable in a fail-safe way and can be always requested. The nominal values for signal heads are sent via the port *NOMINAL_VALUES*. The port *SENSOR_VALUES* serves to read the signals occurring at the detectors. The entire traffic light system can be shut off via the port *SHUT_OFF*. This transfers the system in a fail-safe state, if an error state can not be recovered by the signal suppression.

— *TRAFFIC_LIGHT_CONTROL* ———————————————

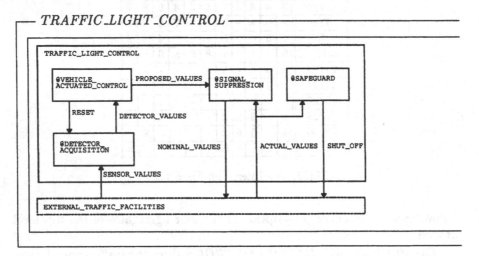

3.2 The Control Program

In the process class *VEHICLE_ACTUATED_CONTROL*, the control algorithm is specified. It switches between different phases. A phase can be characterized by the set of signal groups that are opened together during this phase. In many traffic light systems the order and duration of the phases is predefined (*fixed-time control*). Nevertheless, the control program, presented here, is driven by the actual traffic, measured by the induction loops and the pedestrian push buttons. It allows phase transitions between all phases. Note that the program has two rather unusual phases: in *phase0* all signal groups are closed and in *phase1* only the pedestrians have green. Obviously, groups that are in the same phase must not be in conflict.

$$phase0, phase1, phase2, phase3, phase4 : \mathbb{P}\ SignalGroup$$

$$
\begin{aligned}
&phase0 = \varnothing \\
&phase1 = \{\ G^{p/m}_{21/22},\ G^{p/m}_{23/24},\ G^{p/s}_{25/26},\ G^{p/m}_{27/28},\ G^{p/m}_{29/30},\ G^{p/s}_{31/32}\ \} \\
&phase2 = \{\ G^{v/m}_{7/8},\ G^{v/m}_{9}\ \} \\
&phase3 = \{\ G^{v/m}_{1/2/3},\ G^{v/m}_{7/8}\ \} \\
&phase4 = \{\ G^{v/s}_{4/5/6},\ G^{v/s}_{10/11/12}\}
\end{aligned}
$$

$$Phase == \{\ phase0, phase1, phase2, phase3, phase4\ \}$$

$| \forall p : Phase \bullet \forall grp_1, grp_2 : p \bullet (grp_1, grp_2) \notin conflict$

In the statechart[3] of the class *VEHICLE_ACTUATED_CONTROL*, the control is either in one of the five phases or a phase transition is performed.

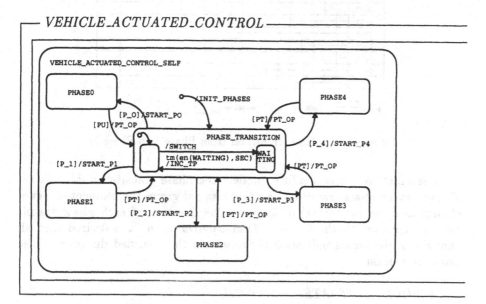

During a phase transition, the signal groups are switched according to the phase transition tables in the planning documents (Figure 4). The phase transition table denotes for each signal group the signaling over the time (measured in seconds). The traffic flows that are blocked in the new phase are closed and the flows that are to be opened are given green. The phase transition tables assure that the intergreen times are not violated during a phase transition.

In Figure 4, the phase transition table from phase 1 to phase 2 is shown. Initially, all pedestrian signal heads indicate green. One second after the beginning of the phase transition, signal group 27/28 is switched to red, three seconds later signal group 25/26 follows and so on.

The internal state variables of a process class are declared in a *DATA* schema. The variables *from* and *to* are used to record the actually desired phase transition. The variable *tp* of type *TIME* keeps track of the progress of the actual phase transition, i.e. the column of the phase transition table. The relation *Transition* describes the possible phase transitions, where (*phase0, phase1*) stands for the transition from phase 0 to phase 1.

---

[3] In the statechart, the transition labels are of the form [*cond*]/*action*, where *cond* is a condition specified in a Z schema or in STATEMATE syntax and *action* is a Z operation. The transition fires if the condition is true; the action is executed then.

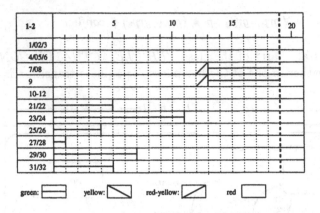

Fig. 4. The Phase Transition from Phase 1 to Phase 2

The function *TransitionTable* models the phase transition tables. It assigns to every phase transition and every signal group the moment of signal change and the new signal indication. The duration of each phase transition is expressed by the function *TransitionDuration*. It is desired that all changes in the signal indication occur within the specified duration of the phase transition.

VEHICLE_ACTUATED_CONTROL ───────────────

$DATA$ $PhaseTransition \cong [from, to : Phase; \ tp : TIME]$

$Transition : Phase \leftrightarrow Phase$

$\forall p : Phase \bullet (p, p) \notin Transition$

$TransitionTable : (Transition \times SignalGroup) \rightarrow (TIME \nrightarrow \mathbb{P} \, Lamp)$

$TransitionDuration : Transition \rightarrow TIME$

$\forall u : Transition; \ s : SignalGroup \bullet$
$\qquad \forall t : dom(TransitionTable(u, s)) \bullet t < TransitionDuration(u)$

$TransitionDuration((phase1, phase2)) = 19$

$\forall Gr : \{G^{v/m}_{1/2/3}, G^{v/s}_{4/5/6}, G^{v/s}_{10/11/12}\} \bullet$
$\qquad TransitionTable((phase1, phase2), Gr) = \varnothing$

$TransitionTable((phase1, phase2), G^{v/m}_{7/8}) =$
$\qquad \{12 \mapsto \{red, yellow\}, 13 \mapsto \{green\}\}$

$\ldots$

$TransitionTable((phase0, phase1), G^{p/s}_{31/32}) = \{5 \mapsto \{red\}\}$

3.3 The Safeguard

The safeguard guarantees the safety of the system. It works independently from the other parts and shuts the TLS off if an unsafe situation has been encountered. According to the norm DIN VDE 0832 [9], the TLS must not stay longer than 0.3 seconds in an unsafe situation. For the safeguard, firstly the requirements are specified using abstract temporal formulae. Then, these formulae are translated into more concrete, non-temporal predicates and a statechart. Here, we present three of the TLS's safety requirements. The signal heads sensor their own state, i.e. which bulbs are shining or not and make these values available to the safeguard. The safeguard reads these values through its port *ACTUAL_VALUES*. For the safety consideration, we assume that the actual values are supplied immediately (with no time delay). For the concrete implementation, this requirement can be weakened. If the TLS is to be shut off, the safeguard sets the variable *OFF* in the port *SHUT_OFF* to *True*.

We model the *actual* signal stage of the junction as a function, assigning to each set of signal heads the set of on-lamps. Based on the signaling situation, the signal groups are partitioned into *open* (i.e. showing green, yellow, etc.), *closed* (i.e. showing red), and *free* (i.e. are off). Note that normally signal heads of the same group should show the same signals, which might not be true in case of an defective signal heads. It might also happen that the green and red lights of one set of signal heads are on simultaneously. In these situations, the partition of the signal groups is quite intricate. Moreover the actual assessment sometimes changes with local regulations. We therefore omit a precise definition here.

 ┌─ *SAFEGUARD* ──
 │ ┌─ *PORT ACTUAL_VALUES* ──   ┌─ *PORT SHUT_OFF* ──────
 │ │ *actual* : *SignalHeads* $\to$ $\mathbb{P}$ *Lamp*   │ *OFF* : $\mathbb{B}$
 │ └──────────────────────────   └──────────────────────
 │
 │ ┌─ *GroupStates* ──────────   ┌─ *DATA SAFE* ─────────
 │ │ *ACTUAL_VALUES*   │ *safe* : $\mathbb{B}$
 │ │ *opened, closed, free* : $\mathbb{P}$ *SignalGroup*
 │ │ disjoint $\langle$ *opened, closed, free* $\rangle$
 │ │ ...
 │ └──────────────────────────   └──────────────────────
 │
 │ *MAX_FAIL_TIME* : *TIME*
 │ *SAMPLING_RATE* : *TIME*
 └──

Basing on the actual signal stage, the TLS has to judge whether the junction is in a safe situation or not. The safe guard introduces a predicate *safe* : $\mathbb{B}$, denoting whether the junction is in a safe situation in this particular state or not. In fact, the safety conditions presented here discriminate only states that are definitely not safe. We firstly define for each safety requirement the auxiliary schemas *Conflict_Abs*, *Priority_Abs*, and *ObeysIGT_Abs*. They are then used to formulate the safety requirement for the class *SAFEGUARD*.

We are using discrete interval logic to describe the safety requirements. A complete description of its syntax and semantics is beyond the scope of this paper. Here we only give a short introduction. The logic can be seen as a discrete variant of the Duration Calculus [7] adopted for Z. It is presented in [5]. $\lceil x = 0 \rceil$ denotes an interval where x equals zero all the time. By $\lceil x > 0 \rceil \frown \lceil x < 0 \rceil$ an interval is denoted, where x is greater zero in the beginning and is less than zero immediately afterwards. somewhere $\lceil x = 0 \rceil$ denotes an interval where for some sub-interval $x = 0$. The formula $\lceil x = 0 \rceil_{<t}$ describes an interval shorter than t, where x equals zero.

SAFEGUARD

DYNAMIC Conflict_Abs

GroupStates; SAFE

$\forall\, grp_1, grp_2 : Signalgroup \mid (grp_1, grp_2) \in conflict \,\bullet$
$\quad \neg\ \textsf{somewhere}\ \lceil grp_1 \in opened \wedge grp_2 \in opened \wedge safe = True \rceil$

DYNAMIC Priority_Abs

GroupStates; SAFE

$\forall\, grp_1, grp_2 : SignalGroup \mid (grp_1, grp_2) \in priority \,\bullet$
$\quad \neg\ \textsf{somewhere}\ (\lceil grp_1 \notin opened \wedge grp_2 \in opened \rceil \frown$
$\qquad\qquad \lceil grp_1 \in opened \wedge grp_2 \in opened \wedge safe = True \rceil)$

DYNAMIC ObeysIGT_Abs

ACTUAL_VALUES; GroupStates; SAFE

$\forall\, grp_1, grp_2 : SignalGroup \mid (grp_1, grp_2) \in conflict \,\bullet$
$\quad \neg\ \textsf{somewhere}\ (\lceil grp_1 \in opened \rceil \frown$
$\qquad\qquad \lceil true \rceil_{<IGT(grp_1, grp_2)} \frown \lceil grp_2 \in opened \wedge safe = True \rceil)$

The first safety requirement *Conflict_Abs* states that the junction is unsafe if two conflicting signal groups are opened at the same time, i.e., there is no sub-interval in which a conflicting pair of signal groups $((grp_1, grp_2) \in conflict)$ is opened and *safe = True*.

The second safety requirement *Priority_Abs* states that a prioritized signal group must not be opened while a signal group of lower priority is open. A group has priority over another one, if the two groups can be open simultaneously (i.e. are not in conflict), but their traffic flows interfere. This is, e.g., the case for bending vehicles and pedestrians. In this case the pedestrians have priority over the vehicles and the pedestrian flow must not be opened while the vehicles are already driving.

The third safety requirement *ObeysIGT_Abs* denotes that an opening signal group must obey to the intergreen time table, i.e., all conflicting signal groups have to be closed for at least their intergreen time before the group is opened.

If the TLS enters an unsafe situation the program has to react and reestablish safety within MAX_FAIL_TIME. We can now formulate the central safety requirement $Safety\_Abs$ for the TLS. Note that the actual value of MAX_FAIL_TIME depends on how fast the hardware can shut off the system, thus depends on the hardware environment the control software is embedded in. The $SAFEGUARD$ has to obey to the three safety conditions and there must not be any sub-interval with $safe = False$ for more than MAX_FAIL_TIME ($\lceil safe = False \rceil_{> MAX\_FAIL\_TIME}$). The behavior requirement for the $SAFEGUARD$ says that the TLS has to obey to $Safety\_Abs$ or has to be shut off. Note that $Conflict\_Abs$, $Priority\_Abs$, $ObeysIGT\_Abs$, and $Safety\_Abs$ are auxiliary schemas whereas a box labeled $PROPERTY$ denotes a direct requirement for the behavior of the class.

```
┌─ SAFEGUARD ─────────────────────────────────────────────
│ ┌─ DYNAMIC Safety_Abs ────────────────────────────────
│ │ GroupStates; SAFE
│ ├─────────────────────────────────────────────────────
│ │ Conflict_Abs ∧ ObeysIGT_Abs ∧ Priority_Abs
│ │ ¬ somewhere ⌈safe = False⌉_{> MAX_FAIL_TIME}
│ └─────────────────────────────────────────────────────
│ ┌─ PROPERTY DYNAMIC ──────────────────────────────────
│ │ GroupStates; SAFE
│ ├─────────────────────────────────────────────────────
│ │ Safety_Abs ∨ (Safety_Abs ⌢ ⌈OFF = True⌉)
│ └─────────────────────────────────────────────────────
└─────────────────────────────────────────────────────────
```

After having specified the requirements of the safeguard we can implement them. The safeguard needs to store the time when a signal group was closed and which signal groups have just been opened resp. closed. The function $blocking\_time$ assigns to each closed signal group the time it was closed. The set $last\_step\_opened$ holds all newly opened signal groups. Analogously, $last\_step\_closed$ holds all newly closed groups. The operation $UPDATE\_BLOCKING\_TIME$[4] updates these variables in $SAMPLING\_RATE$ intervals.

---

[4] Note that in this operation dom $blocking\_time$ is set of signal groups closed in the previous step, whereas $closed$ holds the current value. Therefore, $closed \setminus$ (dom $blocking\_time$) denotes the signal groups that were recently opened and are closed now. Correspondingly, $opened \cap$ (dom $blocking\_time$) denotes the signal groups that were closed in the last step and are opened now. $opened \lhd$ $blocking\_time$ restricts the domain of $blocking\_time$ to $opened$. Thus, the operation restricts $blocking\_time$ to the closed groups and adds the newly closed groups related to the current time $Time$.

┌─ SAFEGUARD ───
│ ┌─ DATA BlockingTime ────────────────────────────────────
│ │ $blocking\_time : SignalGroup \nrightarrow TIME$
│ │ $last\_step\_closed, last\_step\_opened : \mathbb{P}\ SignalGroup$
│ └──
│
│ ┌─ OP UPDATE_BLOCKING_TIME ──────────────────────────────
│ │ $\Delta BlockingTime$
│ │ $GroupStates$
│ ├──
│ │ $last\_step\_closed' = closed \setminus (\mathrm{dom}\ blocking\_time)$
│ │ $last\_step\_opened' = opened \cap (\mathrm{dom}\ blocking\_time)$
│ │ $blocking\_time' = (closed \lhd blocking\_time) \cup (last\_step\_closed' \times \{\ Time\ \})$
│ └──
│
│ ┌─ Conflict_Conc ──
│ │ $BlockingTime$
│ ├──
│ │ $\forall grp_1, grp_2 : SignalGroup \mid (grp_1, grp_2) \in conflict \bullet$
│ │ $\quad (grp_1 \in (\mathrm{dom}\ blocking\_time) \vee grp_2 \in (\mathrm{dom}\ blocking\_time))$
│ └──
│
│ ┌─ Priority_Conc ──
│ │ $BlockingTime$
│ ├──
│ │ $\forall grp_1, grp_2 : SignalGroup \mid (grp_1, grp_2) \in priority \bullet$
│ │ $\quad grp_1 \in last\_step\_opened \Rightarrow$
│ │ $\qquad (grp_2 \in \mathrm{dom}\ blocking\_time \vee grp_2 \in last\_step\_opened)$
│ └──
│
│ ┌─ ObeysIGT_Conc ──
│ │ $BlockingTime$
│ ├──
│ │ $\forall grp_1, grp_2 : SignalGroup \mid (grp_1, grp_2) \in conflict \bullet$
│ │ $\quad grp_1 \notin (\mathrm{dom}\ blocking\_time)$
│ │ $\qquad \Rightarrow (blocking\_time(grp_2) + IGT(grp_2, grp_1) < Time)$
│ └──
│
│ $SAFESITUATION \cong Conflict\_Conc \wedge Priority\_Conc \wedge ObeysIGT\_Conc$
│
│
└──

With these data values we can translate the temporal requirements into operational predicates that can be used in the statechart. We translate *Conflict_Abs* into *Conflict_Conc*, *Priority_Abs* into *Priority_Conc*, and *Obeys-*

IGT_Abs into $ObeysIGT\_Conc$. $Priority\_Conc$ says that for a group that has just been opened ($grp_1 \in last\_step\_opened$) all other groups it has priority over (($grp_1, grp_2) \in priority$) must be either closed or also just been opened.

The statechart implements the reactive behavior of the safeguard. It resides in the state SAFE if $SAFESITUATION$ is true and switches to UNSAFE otherwise. If it stays in UNSAFE for $MAX\_DELAY\_TIME - SAMPLING\_RATE$ it shuts the system off.[5] Meanwhile, it periodical reads the actual values sent by the external facilities and updates $blocking\_time$ and $last\_step\_opened$ accordingly. The statechart has to implement the behavior constraint of the process, i.e. the set of observable runs it defines has to be a subset of the set defined by the behavior constraint. Here, we have to prove that $in(SAFE) \Rightarrow (safe = True)$, where $in(SAFE)$ denotes that the statechart state $SAFE$ is active.

4 Conclusion

In this paper we have presented a combination of formal specification techniques with a well-known structuring technique that has been successfully applied in software engineering. We are using Z and statecharts as basis formalisms for expressing the functional and reactive behavior of embedded systems. Both formalisms have found broad acceptance in the research area as well as in industry. The presented combination exploits the advantages of each formalism. Note that in this approach the semantics of the basic formalisms are preserved, which is very important for tool reuse. In contrast, in [22,6] the STATEMATE semantics were not preserved.

The usage of Z as language for the description of the functional aspects has turned out to be superior to e.g. the STATEMATE data description language [15], especially for the formulation of data invariants and safety requirements, and for the rather complex data-items as the phase transition table. The dynamic behavior of a process could be modeled very naturally with statecharts. Its graphical nature (in contrast to other process description languages and combinations of specification languages like [17,19,1,20,16]) provides a good overview over the different states and possible state transitions of a process. The architectural view was described by data flow diagrams. Here, a more powerful notation would have been helpful, supporting genericity in order to reuse components as well as collections of processes.

Supplementing Z with temporal logic and an adequate satisfaction relation for statecharts and temporal logic is still subject to further research. Nevertheless, we believe that the case study shows impressively the advantage of this approach. Within the ESPRESS project, work on the development of tools to support the presented technique and method is investigated. This includes type-checking, execution of Z specifications, and verification and

---

[5] $tm(E, T)$ is true T seconds after event E occured. $en(UNSAFE)$ denotes the event that state UNSAFE was entered.

validation of combined specifications. With that, it should be possible to simulate and analyze the model extensively.

With the formalization of safety requirements we were able to discover ambiguities and unprecise formulations in the natural language specification. We believe that the precise formulation of safety requirements in an early development phase will turn out to be very helpful to increase the developer's understanding of the problem, avoiding misconceptions and design errors caused by ambiguous or incomplete requirements.

The applicability of our approach has been demonstrated in a case-study where a traffic light system has been specified [3,4]. Even if only parts of the case study could be presented here (the entire specification contains over 70 pages), we found the division of a system into different views and the formulation of explicit safety requirements convincing for the specification of safety-critical embedded systems.

References

1. G. Berry and G. Gonthier. The ESTEREL synchronous programming language: design, semantics, implementation. *Science of Computer Programming*, 19:87–152, 1992.
2. R. Büssow, H. Dörr, R. Geisler, W. Grieskamp, and M. Klar. μSZ – Ein Ansatz zur systematischen Verbindung von Z und Statecharts. Technical Report 96-32, Technische Universität Berlin, Feb. 1996.
3. R. Büssow, R. Geisler, M. Klar, and S. Mann. Spezifikation einer Lichtsignalanlagen-Steuerung mit μSZ. Technical Report 97-13, Technische Universität Berlin, 1997.
4. R. Büssow, R. Geisler, and M.Klar. Spezifikation eingebetteter Steuerungssysteme mit Z und Statecharts. In *Tagungsband zur 5. Fachtagung Entwurf komplexer Automatisierungssysteme*. TU Braunschweig, 1997.
5. R. Büssow and W. Grieskamp. Combinig Z and temporal interval logics for the formalization of properties and behaviors of embedded systems. In R. K. Shyamasundar and K. Ueda, editors, *Advances in Computing Science – Asian '97*, volume 1345 of *LNCS*, pages 46–56. Springer-Verlag, 1997.
6. R. Büssow and M. Weber. A steam-boiler control specification using statecharts and Z. In *Formal Methods for Industrial Applications: Specifying and Programming the Steam Boiler Control*, volume 1165 of *LNCS*. Springer, 1996.
7. Z. Chaochen, C. A. R. Hoare, and A. P. Ravn. A calculus of durations. *Information Processing Letters*, 40(5):269–276, 1991.
8. T. DeMarco. *Structured analysis and system specification*. Yourdon Press, Engelwood Cliffs, NY, USA, 1978.
9. Deutsche Elektrotechnische Kommission im DIN und VDE (DKE). DIN Norm VDE 0832 - Strassenverkehrs-Signalanlagen (SVA), 1990.
10. Forschungsgesellschaft für Strassen- und Verkehrswesen. Richtlinien für Lichtsignalanlagen - RiLSA, 1992.
11. W. Grieskamp, M. Heisel, and H. Dörr. Specifying safety-critical embedded systems with statecharts and Z: An agenda for cyclic software components. accepted for publication at ETAPS'98, 1998.

12. D. Harel. Statecharts: A visual formalism for complex systems. *Science of Computer Programming*, 8(3):231–274, June 1987.
13. D. Harel, H. Lachover, A. Naamad, A. Pnueli, M. Politi, R. Sherman, A. Shtull-Trauring, and M. Trakhtenbrot. Statemate: A working environment for the development of complex reactive systems. *IEEE Transactions on Software Engineering*, 16 No. 4, Apr. 1990.
14. D. Harel and A. Naamad. The statemate semantics of statecharts. Technical report, The Weizmann Institute of Science, Oct. 1995.
15. D. Harel and M. Politi. Modeling reactive systems with statecharts: The statemate approach. i-Logix Inc, Three Riverside Drive, Andover, MA 01810, USA, June 1996. Part No. D-1100-43, 6/96.
16. M. Heisel and C. Sühl. Combining Z and Real-Time CSP for the development of safety-critical systems. In *Proceedings 15th International Conference on Computer Safety, Reliability and Security*. Springer, 1996.
17. C. Hoare. *Communicating Sequential Processes*. Prentice Hall, Eaglewood Cliffs, N.J., 1985.
18. N. Leveson. *Safeware – System Safety and Computers*. Addison Wesley, 1995.
19. LOTOS - A formal description technique based on temporal ordering of observational behaviour. Information Processing Systems - Open Systems Interconnection **ISO DIS 8807**, jul. 1987. (ISO/TC 97/SC 21 N).
20. G. Smith. A semantic integration of Object-Z and CSP for the specification of concurrent systems. In *Proceedings of FME'97: Industrial Benefits of Formal Methods*, Graz, Austria, September 1997. Springer-Verlag.
21. J. M. Spivey. *The Z Notation: A Reference Manual*. Prentice Hall International Series in Computer Science, 2nd edition, 1992.
22. M. Weber. Combining statecharts and Z for the desgin of safety-critical control systems. In *Industrial Benefits and Advances in Formal Methods*, volume 1051 of *LNCS*, pages 307–326. Springer, 1996.

Specifying Embedded Systems
with Statecharts and Z:
An Agenda for Cyclic Software Components

Wolfgang Grieskamp[1], Maritta Heisel[2], and Heiko Dörr[3]

[1] Technische Universität Berlin, Institut für Kommunikations- und Softwaretechnik, Sekr. FR5-13, Franklinstr. 28/29, D-10587 Berlin, Germany, email: wg@cs.tu-berlin.de
[2] Otto-von-Guericke-Universität Magdeburg, Fakultät für Informatik, Institut für Verteilte Systeme, D-39016 Magdeburg, Germany, email: heisel@cs.uni-magdeburg.de
[3] Daimler-Benz AG, Forschung Systemtechnik, Alt-Moabit 96a, D-10569 Berlin, Germany, email: Heiko.Doerr@DBAG.Bln.DaimlerBenz.com

Abstract. The application of formal techniques can contribute much to the quality of software, which is of utmost importance for safety-critical embedded systems. These techniques, however, are not easy to apply. In particular, methodological guidance is often unsatisfactory. We address this problem by the concept of an *agenda*. An agenda is a list of activities to be performed for solving a task in software engineering. Agendas used to support the application of formal specification techniques provide detailed guidance for specifiers, templates of the used specification language that only need to be instantiated, and application independent validation criteria. We apply the agenda approach to a particular class of embedded safety-critical systems, the formal specification of which has been investigated in the case-studies of the German ESPRESS project during the last two years.

1 Introduction

Every software-based system potentially benefits from the application of formal techniques. For the development of mission or even safety-critical embedded systems, however, their use is of particular advantage, because the potential damage operators and developers have to envisage in case of malfunction may be much worse than the additional costs of applying formal techniques in system development.

A major drawback of formal techniques is that they are not easy to apply for the average software engineer. Besides the facts that users of formal techniques need an appropriate education and have to deal with lots of details, they are often left alone with a mere formalism without any guidance on how to use it. Hence, *methodological support* is a key issue to bring formal techniques into practice.

Methodological support for specification development must be abstract enough to cover a significant range of applications, but also detailed enough

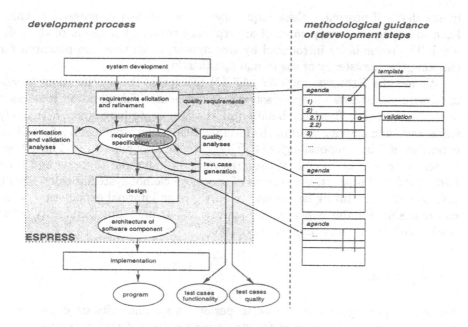

Fig. 1. Basic ESPRESS process model

to provide real guidance to developers. *Agendas,* as introduced in [9,10], provide a concept for representing methodological process knowledge for particular software architectures on a relatively fine-grained level of detail.

In this paper, we demonstrate the application of the concept of agendas to a particular class of embedded safety-critical systems. The architecture we study is that of a *cyclic software component* – a piece of software in a technical system which is triggered in regular time intervals by its environment to compute output values (usually commands to some actuators) from given input values (usually sensor values), and an internal state. The agenda we represent for this architecture is condensed from experiences with case studies performed in the ESPRESS project during the last two years[1].

Figure 1 shows the basic ESPRESS process model. The agenda presented in this paper guides the development of a requirements specification. Such a requirements specification is further validated and serves as a basis for safety analyses, test case generation, and software design.

Our agenda for cyclic software components elaborates on two particular aspects of embedded systems, motivated by the demands of the ESPRESS application context. First, special care is taken to accurately develop the embedding of the software in its surrounding technical system. Second, *quality requirements* such as high-level or safety-related conditions which have to be guaranteed by the software are treated systematically. The general ESPRESS methodology re-

---

[1] The ESPRESS project is a cooperation of industry and research institutes funded by the German ministry BMBF ("Förderschwerpunkt Softwaretechnologie").

quires that – if possible – these requirements are specified as *properties*, which have to be logical *consequences* of an explicitly constructed model of the software. The redundancy introduced by this approach increases the potential for checking the consistency of the formal specification.

We use the ESPRESS notation μSZ [2] to express the specifications developed with our agenda for cyclic software components. This notation provides a semantically well-defined combination of the Statemate languages [7] (namely statecharts and activity charts), the formal specification language Z [16], and an extension of Z by temporal logics [4]. The Statemate languages and Z have been chosen for ESPRESS because of their relevance in industrial contexts and their fairly good tool support. For reasons of space, we cannot systematically explain μSZ and its constituting languages; we only give an informal explanation of the constructs used in this paper as they appear, and assume some familiarity of the reader with the Z and Statemate languages.

2 Agendas

An agenda gives guidance on how to perform a specific software development activity. Agendas can be used for structuring quite different activities in different contexts. We have set up and used agendas that support requirements engineering, specification acquisition, software design using architectural styles, and developing code from specifications [8]. Agendas are especially suitable to support the application of formal techniques in software engineering.

An agenda is a list of steps to be performed when carrying out some task in the context of software engineering. The result of the task will be a document expressed in a certain language. Agendas contain informal descriptions of the steps. With each step, *templates* of the language in which the result of the task is expressed are associated. The templates are instantiated when the step is performed. The steps listed in an agenda may depend on each other. Usually, they will have to be repeated to achieve the goal, similar to the general process proposed by the spiral model of software engineering. Agendas are presented as tables, see Fig. 3 on page 5. Agendas may be nested, and we call the "supersteps" *stages* (see, e.g., Fig. 2 on the following page).

Agendas are not only a means to guide software development activities. They also support quality assurance because the steps of an agenda may have validation conditions associated with them. These validation conditions state necessary conditions that the artifact must fulfill in order to serve its purpose properly. When formal techniques are applied, some of the validation conditions can be expressed and proven in a formal way. Since the validation conditions that can be stated in an agenda are necessarily application independent, the developed artifact should be further validated with respect to application dependent needs.

Working with agendas proceeds as follows: first, the software engineer selects an appropriate agenda for the task at hand. Usually, several agendas will be available for the same development activity, which capture different approaches to perform the activity. This first step requires a basic understanding of the problem to be solved. Once the appropriate agenda is selected, the further procedure is fixed to a large extent. Each step of the agenda must be performed, in an order that respects the dependencies of steps. The informal description of the step informs the software engineer about the purpose of the step. The templates associated with the step provide the software engineer with patterns that can just be filled in (which nevertheless requires creativity) or modified according to the needs of the application at hand. The result of each step is a concrete expression of the language that is used to express the artifact. If validation conditions are associated with a step, they should be checked immediately to avoid unnecessary dead ends in the development. When all steps of the agenda have been performed, a product has been developed that can be guaranteed to fulfill certain application-independent quality criteria. This product should then be subject to further validation, taking the specific application into account.

Agendas cannot replace creativity, but they can tell the software engineer what needs to be done and help avoid omissions and inconsistencies. Their advantage lies in an improvement of the quality of the developed products and in the possibility for reusing the knowledge incorporated in an agenda.

3 Agenda for Cyclic Software Components

Stage
1 Context embedding
2 Quality requirements
3 Model construction

Fig. 2. Stages of the agenda for cyclic software components

The agenda for cyclic software components consists of three stages, which are shown in Fig. 2. Stage 1 must be performed first; Stage 2 and 3 can be performed independently of each other. Each of the stages is performed following a sub-agenda, as described below. As a running example, we use an *intelligent cruise control* system, which serves to automatically adjust the speed of a vehicle according to the driver's request. In addition to this conventional cruise control functionality, our version uses a sensor to detect a vehicle driving ahead, and adjusts the speed to maintain a certain safety distance. This example is extracted from one of the internal ESPRESS case studies, and modified for our illustration purposes.

Stage 1: Context embedding

Embedded software is characterized by the fact that the interfaces to the environment are not standardized to a degree as it is nowadays common for software running on e.g. workstations. Hence, a developer should take special care to model the *context embedding* of the software. In ESPRESS, the context definition also serves as a starting point for a simulation of the software, using the Statemate tool. The sub-agenda for context embedding is shown in Fig. 3 on the following page.

Step 1.1: Specify technical interfaces. The technical interfaces of an embedded software component are usually determined during system design, and

Step	Validation Conditions
1.1 Specify technical interfaces: — *TechnicalDefs* —————————————— [...] ... | ... — *TechnicalSensors* ——— — *TechnicalActuators* —— *TechnicalDefs* *TechnicalDefs* — PORT $S1$ —— — PORT $A1$ ——	o ranges of values of sensors and actuators are consistent with the technical specifications of the interfaces o errors of sensors and actuators are taken into account ⊢ invariants are consistent
1.2 Design and specify logical interfaces and their mapping to technical ones: — *LogicalDefs* —————————————— ... — *LogicalSensors* ——— — *MapLS1* ——— *LogicalDefs* *LogicalSensors*; ... — PORT $LS1$ —— — *BEHAVIOR* —— ... ... — *LogicalActuators* ——— — *MapLA1* ———	o errors of technical sensors are taken into account ⊢ invariants are consistent ⊢ mappings are unique ⊢ mappings are total
1.3 Derive software/context information flow and cycle control: — *Context* ——————————————— *TechnicalSensors*; *TechnicalActuators* *LogicalSensors*; *LogicalActuators* 	*no conditions*

Fig. 3. Steps of Stage 1: context embedding

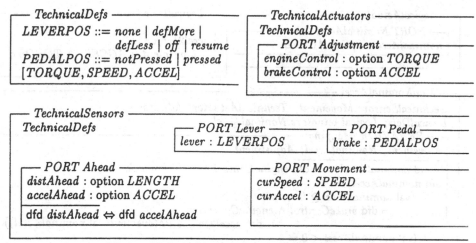

Fig. 4. Technical interfaces of the cruise control

cannot be modified by the software developer. Since their characteristics and capabilities may have significant influence on the further development, the first step of context embedding is to describe the technical interfaces in the modeling language.

Figure 3 on the page before gives templates for describing technical interfaces in our modeling language μSZ. The structuring entities of μSZ are *process classes* (the outer boxes in the figure, e.g., *TechnicalDefs*), which are containers for sets of plain Z declarations, of schema definitions, and of Statemate statecharts and activity charts. The schema definitions inside a class may have assigned certain *roles*. For example, the role of schema definitions introduced with the keyword *PORT* is to describe data variables that can be shared by a process with its environment. Interpreted standalone, *PORT* schemata do not differ from plain Z schemata. However, they contribute to the semantics of an entire process class, defining the variables belonging to the shared data state of instances of the class.

For Step **1.1**, the agenda in Fig. 3 suggests to collect the technical interfaces in process classes called *TechnicalSensors* and *TechnicalActuators*, respectively, which contain sets of *PORT* schemata. The types and constants used to define these ports are collected in a third process class, *TechnicalDefs*, which is included by the other classes. The inclusion of process classes can be interpreted as textual expansion.

The validation conditions associated with Step **1.1** first require the developer to carefully check whether the types defined to model the values of sensors and actuators really capture the technical properties of the technical sensors and actuators. The second validation condition suggests to define appropriate error values for the types. Finally, all invariants must be satisfiable, i.e., there must exist legal states of the system ports. Note that validation conditions marked with "o" are informal, whereas validation conditions marked with "⊢" are formal and hence can be checked with appropriate tool support.

```
┌─ LogicalActuators ──────────────────    ┌─ LogicalDefs ──────────────────────────
│ ┌─ PORT NominalAccel ─────────────       │
│ │ nominalAccel : option ACCEL            │  accel2torque :
│ └──────────────────────────────          │     Movement × ACCEL → TORQUE
└────────────────────────────────────      └────────────────────────────────────────
```

```
┌─ MapNominalAccel ─────────────────────────────────────────────────────────────────
│ TechnicalSensors.Movement;  TechnicalActuators.Adjustment
│ LogicalDefs;  LogicalActuators.NonimalAccel
│ ┌─ BEHAVIOR Mapping ──────────────────────────────────────────────────────────────
│ │ Movement;  NominalAccel;  Adjustment
│ │ ┌────────────────────────────────────────────────────────────────────────────────
│ │ │ ¬ dfd nominalAccel ⇒ ¬ dfd engineControl ∧ ¬ dfd brakeControl
│ │ │ dfd nominalAccel ⇒
│ │ │     (val nominalAccel ≥ 0 ⇒
│ │ │         ¬ dfd brakeControl ∧ engineControl =
│ │ │                             def accel2torque(θMovement, val nominalAccel))
│ │ │ ∧ (val nominalAccel < 0 ⇒
│ │ │         ¬ dfd engineControl ∧ brakeControl = nominalAccel)
│ │ └────────────────────────────────────────────────────────────────────────────────
└───────────────────────────────────────────────────────────────────────────────────
```

Fig. 5. Logical interfaces of the cruise control

Cruise Control. Fig. 4 on the preceding page shows how we apply Step **1.1** to the specification of the cruise control. The port *Lever* describes the driver's control lever, which can be used to turn off the cruise control, to increase or decrease the requested speed, to turn off the cruise control, and to resume its operation. The port *Pedal* models the brake pedal, the port *Ahead* the distance and relative acceleration with respect to a vehicle driving ahead, and the port *Movement* provides information about the current speed and acceleration of the vehicle. The port *Adjustment* describes the output of the cruise control, which consists of an engine torque and a (negative) acceleration for controlling the brake. Variables declared as x : option A carry values of A which may be available or not; we use dfd x to indicate whether the value of the optional variable x is available, val x to refer to that value (if it is defined), and def v to construct a defined value from v. If, e.g., the value of the sensor *distAhead* is not defined, then no vehicle driving ahead is detected, and if the actuator *engineTorque* is not defined, then the cruise control does not affect the engine.

For reasons of space, we cannot present the full specification of the technical interfaces of the cruise control system. Hence, we cannot check the validation conditions in detail. Let us just note that the only given invariant, dfd *distAhead* ⇔ dfd *accelAhead*, is indeed consistent, and that – for reasons of simplicity – we assume to have perfect sensors without errors in this example.

Step 1.2: Design and specify logical interfaces. Apart from being non-standardized, the technical interfaces of an embedded software component may be also on a relatively low technical level, which hinders a problem-oriented specification. It may therefore be useful to introduce *abstractions* of the technical interfaces, which is achieved by defining *logical interfaces*.

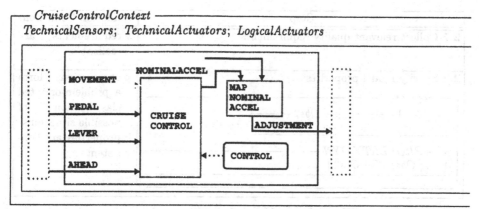

Fig. 6. Activity chart of the cruise control context

The values of sensors and actuators of a logical interface should be totally and uniquely defined by the technical values (see validation conditions associated with this step). In the simplest case, this mapping can be defined by a conversion function which maps a technical sensor to a logical sensor or a logical actuator to a technical actuator, respectively. In more complex situations, the mapping may require an internal state, for example if a logical sensor accumulates the values of a technical one. In any case, we define the mapping by a dedicated process class that describes the conversion by a property schema or by a state-chart (in the template of Fig. 3 on page 5, these classes are called *MapLS*1 and *MapLA*1, respectively). These process classes are instantiated as sub-processes of the overall process modeling the system context, as will be seen in the next step.

The first validation condition associated with Step **1.2** suggests to apply fault tolerance techniques, e.g., consistency checks on sensor values and feedback control to check if actuator commands have been executed appropriately.

Cruise Control. We introduce a logical actuator *nominalAccel*, which abstracts from the two quite technical values *engineControl* and *brakeControl* given in the output port *Adjustment*, as sketched in Fig. 5 on the preceding page. The process class *MapNominalAccel* performs the mapping of the logical to the technical actuators. A schema introduced with the role *BEHAVIOR* describes an invariant which holds whenever a process is running.

Proving the last two validation conditions amounts to proving that the function *accel2torque* defined in the class *LogicalDefs* is indeed a total function.

Step 1.3: Derive software/context information flow. The description of the technical interfaces, the logical interfaces, and their mapping induces an activity chart, which is derived from the template given for Step **1.3** in Fig. 3 on page 5. The activity charts of Statemate used in μSZ combine the descriptions of information flow, of instantiation of sub-processes from process classes (rectangular boxes), and of behavior described by statecharts (rounded boxes). In Fig. 3, the overall description of the system's behavior aggregates a sub-process *Software*, as well as sub-processes for mapping technical to logical interfaces. The

Step	Validation Conditions
2.1 Collect relevant quality requirements	o requirements are realizable
2.2 Specify model properties: ┌─ *Software* ─────────────── ┌─ *Obs1* ──── ┌─ *Obs2* ──── ... │ ... │ ... ┌─ *PROPERTY DYN* ─────── ...⌈ *Obs1* ⌉ ⁀ ⌈ *Obs2* ⌉ ...	o observations form a problem-oriented classification of possible situations ⊢ properties are consistent

Fig. 7. Steps of Stage 2: quality requirements

information flows between these processes are labeled with ports, and semantically describe visibility of shared variables between processes. The aggregation of the statechart *Control* and the dotted lines are only for documentation purposes; they indicate that *Control* schedules the activity of the sub-process *Software*.

The scheduler defined by *Control* applies to any cyclic software component developed using this agenda, and is quite simple. It assumes that the software, once running, reads the sensors, computes the actuators, and then suspends itself. The scheduler thus periodically resumes the software in intervals of a certain cycle time. Notationally, Statemate's mechanism for suspending and resuming processes (processes are also called *activities* in Statemate) is used. The Statemate action sd ! (SOFTWARE) stands for suspending a process, rs ! (SOFTWARE) for resuming, and the condition hg(SOFTWARE) tests whether a process is "hanging", that is suspended. The event tm(en(RUN),CYCLETIME) appears *cycleTime* time units after the state RUN has been entered, where en stands for "entered", and tm stands for "timeout". Because the result of Step **1.3** can be derived schematically from the parts of the specification defined in Steps **1.1** and **1.2**, there are no validation conditions associated with this step.

Cruise Control. Fig. 6 on the preceding page shows the result of Step **1.3**. We only need to draw the activity chart (where the information flows are already induced by Steps **1.1** and **1.2**); the statechart *Control* can be taken as is from the template in Fig. 3 on page 5. Only *Software* is renamed to *CruiseControl*.

Stage 2: Quality requirements

The systems we study have to fulfill certain *quality requirements*. Typical examples are safety requirements, but also high-level requirements from earlier development phases may be transferred to the software development phase. A common characteristic of quality requirements is that they only address certain *selected aspects* to be realized by the software – these aspects are important enough to be emphasized explicitly in the specification. Technically, quality requirements are formulated as *model properties*, which have to be logical consequences of the model of the software as it is constructed in Stage 3. With model properties, redundancy is deliberately introduced in the specification. This contributes to the potential for checking consistency by deduction, model checking, and systematic testing. Figure 7 on the preceding page describes the agenda for treating quality requirements.

Step 2.1: Collect relevant quality requirements. The quality requirements are usually defined during system design. In this step, the ones that are relevant for the software component under development are collected and documented.

Cruise Control. A few of the quality requirements are the following:

- *Activity.* The cruise control is allowed to adjust speed only if the driver has activated it through the control lever, and did not deactivate it since then.
- *Asymptotic String Stability.* If several vehicles using the cruise control drive in a queue, a sudden change of the speed of one of them must lead to changes of speed of the the following vehicles which fade away along the queue.

Because cruise control systems are already on the market, these requirements are well understood and known to be realizable with our technical interfaces. Hence, the validation condition associated with this step is fulfilled.

Step 2.2: Specify model properties. It is not realistic to demand that all quality requirements be specified formally as model properties. For example, the property of string stability cannot be expressed easily, because it would require to formalize aspects of the mathematics of control theory[2]. However, where it is possible, the quality requirements should be expressed as model properties, to be treated automatically in a review stage later on.

Our modeling language allows us to formalize properties as *temporal observations* of the sensors and actuators of the technical and logical interfaces. The logic used for this purpose is based on *discrete temporal interval logic*, including real-time constraints [4]. The modifier *DYN* in a schema declaration (possibly in conjunction with roles such as *PORT* or *PROPERTY*) signals that the schema uses temporal logic.

A useful guideline for specifying the model properties is to first introduce abstractions of common situations observable on the interfaces. In the template of Fig. 7 on the page before, these are introduced by the schemata *Obs*1, *Obs*2, and applied in the temporal formula of the dynamic property box.

The first (informal) validation condition suggests that the model properties be oriented on a classification of the relevant situations of the observable behavior of the system, whereas the second validation condition is an obvious consistency requirement.

Cruise Control. In Fig. 8 on the following page, we define schemata for observing the situations where the driver activates and deactivates the cruise control, and where the cruise control produces an output value to adjust speed. These schemata are used to formalize one of the quality requirements, namely the safety-condition "Activity". Intuitively, the temporal formula given in the property-box *Activity* can be interpreted as a kind of regular expression: the

---

[2] In fact, notions of control theory could be expressed in Z, but ESPRESS does not aim at these goals.

```
┌─ CruiseControl ────────────────────────────────────────────────────┐
│ TechnicalSensors; LogicalActuators                                   │
│ ┌─ Activating ──────────┐ ┌─ Deactivating ──────────┐ ┌─ Adjusting ──────────┐ │
│ │ Lever                 │ │ Lever; Brake            │ │ NominalAccel         │ │
│ │ ─────────────────     │ │ ─────────────────────── │ │ ──────────────────── │ │
│ │ lever = defMore       │ │ lever = off             │ │ dfd nominalAccel     │ │
│ │   ∨ lever = defLess    │ │   ∨ brake = pressed      │ │                      │ │
│ └───────────────────────┘ └─────────────────────────┘ └──────────────────────┘ │
│ ┌─ PROPERTY DYN Activity ─────────────────────────────────────────┐ │
│ │ Lever; Brake; NominalAccel                                       │ │
│ │ ──────────────────────────────────────────────────────────────  │ │
│ │ repeat (⌈¬ Adjusting⌉ ⌢ ⌈ Activating ∧ ¬ Adjusting⌉ ⌢ ⌈¬ Deactivating⌉) │ │
│ └──────────────────────────────────────────────────────────────────┘ │
└─────────────────────────────────────────────────────────────────────┘
```

Fig. 8. Model properties of the cruise control

admissible traces of the behavior of the cruise control repeatedly consists of an interval where adjustment of speed is not performed, followed by an interval where the driver activates the cruise control (adjustment of speed still does not take place), followed by an interval where the driver continuously does not deactivate the cruise control. Thereby, the temporal predicate $\lceil p \rceil$ holds for those finite or infinite intervals where the predicate p holds in each state. Note that we do not say anything about whether the cruise control actually *ever* adjusts speed; we just say when it should *not* do so. This is typical for specifying model properties, where we are only interested in selected aspects of the software.

Stage 3: Model construction

In this stage, we construct a model for the cyclic software component under consideration. There are several strategies for doing so, which depend on the problem to solve. Here we consider two variants: model construction by functional decomposition, and model construction by partitioning behavior into operational modes.

Variant 3a: Model construction by functional decomposition The problem to solve by the cyclic software component might be more adequately solved by decomposing it into subproblems, instead of giving a monolithic solution. The reasons for this may be that the problem is to large to be tackled in a monolithical way, that a decomposition follows naturally from the structure of the problem, or that existing components should be integrated into the design.

For a cyclic software component which computes output values from input values and internal state, a decomposition is naturally achieved in a *functional* style, based on information flow between the subcomponents (Fig. 9 on the next page). This is also the approach the Statemate tool supports best.

Step 3a.1: Design functional decomposition using an activity chart. Guidelines on how to perform a functional decomposition depend on the application. A useful approach is data-oriented, and considers intermediate values to be computed by the subcomponents. If we reuse existing components, these intermediate values are naturally their output interfaces. However, in general, decomposition is a problem that requires creativity. Hence our agenda suggests

Step	Validation Conditions
3a.1 Design functional decomposition: — *Software* ———————————————— *InternalInterfaces* 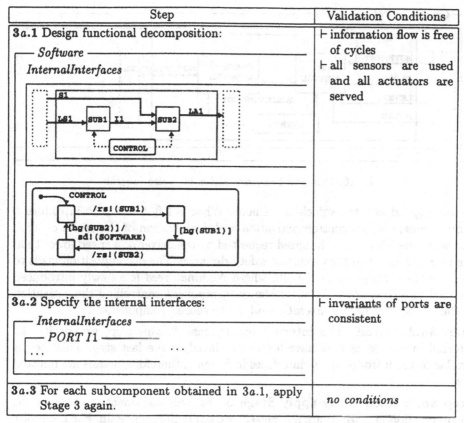	⊢ information flow is free of cycles ⊢ all sensors are used and all actuators are served
3a.2 Specify the internal interfaces: — *InternalInterfaces* ———————————————— — *PORT I1* —————————	⊢ invariants of ports are consistent
3a.3 For each subcomponent obtained in 3a.1, apply Stage 3 again.	*no conditions*

Fig. 9. Steps of Stage 3, Variant *a*: model construction by functional decomposition

to first design the *principle* information flow between subcomponents by drawing an activity chart. The precise specification of the intermediate interfaces themselves is postponed unitl the next step[3].

Once a information flow between the subcomponents has been defined, the data dependencies canonically induce a scheduling as described by the statechart *Control* of the template for Step **3a.1** in Fig. 9. Each subcomponent is treated similarly to a cyclic-software component: once it is resumed, it is expected to compute its output values and then to suspend itself. The scheduler activates the subcomponents one after the other in the order induced by the information flow.

The validation conditions associated with this step ensure that the component eventually produces an output if the subcomponents do so, and that all sensors and actuators are actually used by the system.

Cruise Control. We assume that we can reuse an existing component that implements a speed adjustment: it calculates a nominal acceleration from a given

---

[3] This differs from the order used in Stage 1, where we first specified the interfaces, and then the information flow; but there the exact definition of the interfaces had been given by the environment.

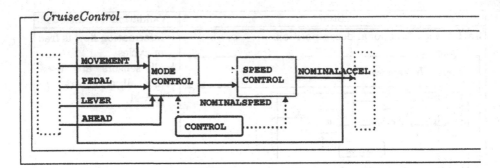

Fig. 10. Functional decomposition of cruise control

nominal speed and the vehicle movement. What is left to do is to introduce a subcomponent which controls activation and deactivation of the cruise control, and which decides to use the speed requested by the driver or a speed lower than the nominal speed to keep a certain safety distance. The decomposition leads to the activity chart given in Fig. 10, where *NominalSpeed* is a newly introduced internal interface, *ModeControl* is the subcomponent controlling the activation of the cruise control, and *SpeedControl* is the reused component.

Step 3a.2: Specify the internal interfaces. In this step, we specify the internal interfaces as they have been introduced in the last step. This step is similar to the introduction of interfaces in Stage 1; therefore, details are omitted here.

Step 3a.3: Recursively apply Stage 3. For subcomponents yielded by the decomposition and which are not reused, we apply Stage 3 again. For the cruise control, this applies to the subcomponent *ModeControl*, which we specify using a different sub-agenda, shown in Fig. 11 on the following page.

Variant 3b: Model construction by mode-based design The problem to solve by the software component might be adequately modeled by introducing *operational modes* for the software component (such as passive, active, emergency, etc.). A cyclic computation then triggers transitions between the operational modes. The agenda in Fig. 11 on the next page describes how to proceed for this modeling technique.

Step 3b.1: Define modes by initial statechart. In this step we introduce the different operational modes of the software component. Technically, this is done by defining an initial statechart (without transitions), where states or combinations of parallel states represent modes. We introduce this chart before the internal data (next step), because we might want to specify invariants on the data that depend on the current operational mode.

The initial statechart contains a so-called static reaction (en(M1) or en(M2)/sd!(SOFTWARE)) which suspends the software whenever a mode is entered, signaling to the environment that the computation of the current cycle has been finished. A static reaction in Statemate is syntactically similar to a transition label guard/action; semantically, its action is executed whenever the guard becomes true.

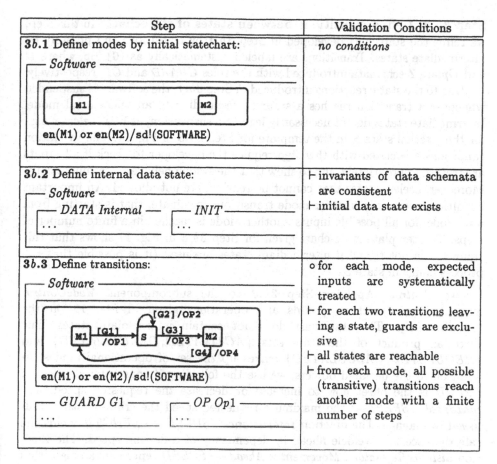

Step	Validation Conditions
3b.1 Define modes by initial statechart: *Software* M1 M2 en(M1) or en(M2)/sd!(SOFTWARE)	*no conditions*
3b.2 Define internal data state: *Software* — *DATA Internal* — — *INIT* —	⊢ invariants of data schemata are consistent ⊢ initial data state exists
3b.3 Define transitions: *Software* M1 [G1]/OP1 → s → [G3]/OP3 → M2, [G2]/OP2, [G4]/OP4 en(M1) or en(M2)/sd!(SOFTWARE) — *GUARD G1* — — *OP Op1* —	○ for each mode, expected inputs are systematically treated ⊢ for each two transitions leaving a state, guards are exclusive ⊢ all states are reachable ⊢ from each mode, all possible (transitive) transitions reach another mode with a finite number of steps

Fig. 11. Steps of Stage 3, Variant *b*: model construction by mode-based design

— *ModeControl* —
— *DATA Request* —
requestedSpeed : option *SPEED*

— *INIT* —
Request
¬ dfd *requestedSpeed*

Fig. 12. Internal data of the *ModeControl* subcomponent of the cruise control

Cruise Control. The complete statechart with transitions as it is obtained in Step **3b.3** is given in Fig. 13 on page 16, and will be explained there.

Step 3b.2: Define internal data state. Internal data is introduced in μSZ by a schema with the *DATA* role, its initialization by a schema with the *INIT* role. The validation conditions associated with this step stem from the recommended Z methodology [17].

Cruise Control. In Fig. 12, the internal data of the subcomponent *ModeControl* is defined. It declares a variable *requestedSpeed*, whose value (if defined) describes the nominal speed which the last time has been requested by the driver. Initially, *requestedSpeed* is undefined.

Step 3b.3: Define transitions between states of statechart. In this step, we refine the statechart developed in Step **3b.1** by transitions and possibly by intermediate states. Transitions are labeled systematically as [G]/Op, where G and Op are Z schemata introduced with the roles *GUARD* and *OP*, respectively.

Due to the static reactions introduced in Step **3b.1**, the software is suspended whenever a transition reaches a state corresponding to an operational mode. Intermediate states do not necessarily lead to a suspension, as it is the case, e.g., for the internal state S in the template for Step **3b.3** in Fig. 11. The validation conditions associated with this step require the developer to check if all inputs are treated appropriately, and to show that the system behaves deterministically. Moreover, useless states that cannot be reached are not allowed. An important condition to check is whether mode transitions terminate, that is starting from any mode, for all possible inputs another mode is reached in a finite number of steps. The template state-chart given for Step **3b.3** in Fig. 11 shows that this condition is not trivial if intermediate states are used (it is possible that the process hangs in state S).

Cruise Control. Applying Step **3b.3** to the subcomponent *ModeControl* leads to the statechart, guards and operations given in Fig. 13 on the following page. The statechart does not contain intermediate states. The cartesian product of the state sets $\{ACTIVATED, DEACTIVATED\}$ and $\{REQUESTED, CALCULATED\}$ makes up the set of operational modes. In addition to the declared objects, we use the following Z constants: *stepSpeed* : *SPEED* is the offset how to increase or decrease the requested speed, and *maxSpeed* : *SPEED* is the maximum requested speed the cruise control is allowed to manage. The function *safeDistance* : *SPEED* $\longrightarrow$ *LENGTH* yields the safe distance to a vehicle ahead in dependency of a driving speed. The function *distanceRegulator* : *Movement* $\times$ *Ahead* $\longrightarrow$ *SPEED* represents an algorithm calculating a nominal speed from the movement of the vehicle and information about a vehicle ahead.

4 Conclusions

We have demonstrated that the agenda approach supports the systematic development of requirement specifications for high quality embedded systems on a non-trivial level of detail which gives substantial guidance to developers. As already noted, agendas are not intended to replace creativity and do not aim at completely automating development processes. Hence, in the first steps of an agenda, high-level decisions have to be taken. The validation conditions associated with the early steps of an agenda are mostly informal, encouraging developers to carefully re-consider their decisions, see e.g. Step 1.1 of the agenda of Fig. 3. Later steps in an agenda, on the other hand, often have validation conditions associated with them that can be formally expressed and proven. The reason is that in the later steps consistency conditions between the various parts of the specification that are already developed can be stated. Step 1.2 of the agenda shown in Fig. 3 is an example. Finally, some steps of an agenda

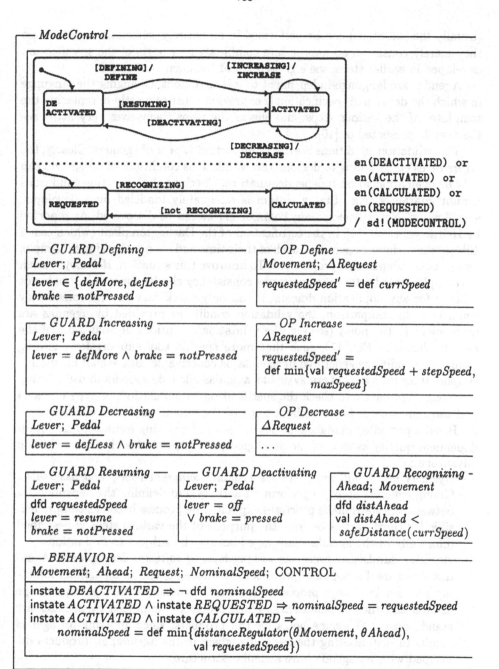

Fig. 13. Modes and transitions of the *ModeControl* subcomponent of the cruise control

(usually the last steps) can be performed in an entirely schematic way, because they merely consist in an appropriate combination of parts of the specification developed in earlier steps, see e.g. Step 1.3 of the agenda of Fig. 3.

Agendas are language-independent to a large extent. Changing the language in which the developed specification is expressed consists mostly in replacing the templates of the various steps, and effects the steps themselves very little, see the agenda presented in [10].

The validation conditions are a very important aspect of agendas. Clearly, the errors revealed by failing to demonstrate validations conditions of an agenda can only be of an application-independent nature. Checking the validation conditions cannot guarantee, e.g., that a system is adequately modeled by a developed specification. Nevertheless, many common errors can be discovered. As reported by Heitmeyer et al. [11], in the certification of the Darlington plant (which cost $ 40M), "the reviewers spent too much of their time and energy checking for simple, application-independent properties." To improve this situation, Heitmeyer et al. have implemented a tool that performs consistency checks. Since this tool is not tailored for any application domain, it can only check very general consistency conditions. In comparison, the validation conditions provided by agendas are much more to the point (see e.g. the validation conditions of Step 3.b.3 of the agenda shown in Fig. 11), such that more specific tool support for checking validation conditions generated by agendas is conceivable. But even if no specific support tools for agendas are available, agendas allow developers to use existing tools, e.g., Statemate to check the specification by simulation, or type checkers and theorem provers for Z to check some of the formal validation conditions.

Besides providing guidance for developers and ensuring some application independent quality aspects of the developed product, agendas offer the following advantages:

- *Agendas make software processes explicit, comprehensible, and assessable.* Giving concrete steps to perform an activity and defining the dependencies between the steps make processes explicit. The process becomes comprehensible for third parties because the purpose of the various steps is described informally in the agenda. Thus, agendas may be subject to evaluation.
- *Agendas standardize processes and products of software development.* Agendas structure development processes. The development of an artifact following an agenda always proceeds in a way consistent with the steps of the agenda and their dependencies. Thus, processes supported by agendas are standardized. The same holds for the products: since applying an agenda results in instantiating the templates given in the agenda, all products developed with an agenda have a similar structure.
- *Agendas support maintenance and evolution of the developed artifacts.* Understanding a document developed by another person is less difficult when the document was developed following an agenda than without such information. Each part of the document can be traced back to a step in the agenda, which reveals its purpose. To change the document, the agenda can be "replayed". The agenda helps focus attention on the parts that actually are subject to change.

– *Agendas are a promising starting point for sophisticated machine support.* They can form the basis of a process-centered software engineering environment (PSEE) [6]. Such a tool would lead its users through the process described by the agenda.

For these reasons, agendas play a central role in the ESPRESS methodology.

Related Work. Recently, efforts have been made to support re-use of special kinds of software development knowledge: *Design patterns* [5] have had much success in object-oriented software construction. They represent frequently used ways to combine classes or associate objects to achieve a certain purpose. Furthermore, in the field of software architecture [14], *architectural styles* have been defined that capture frequently used design principles for software systems. In contrast to these, the general concept of an agenda is not specialized to a programming paradigm such as object-orientedness or an activity such as software design, as is the case for design patterns and architectural styles. Apart from the fact that these concepts are more specialized in their application than agendas, the main difference is that design patterns and architectural styles do not describe *processes* but *products.*

Agendas have much in common with approaches to software process modeling [12]. The difference is that software process modeling techniques cover a wider range of activities, e.g., management activities, whereas with agendas we always develop a document, and we do not take roles of developers etc. into account. Agendas concentrate more on technical activities in software engineering. On the other hand, software process modeling does not place so much emphasis on validation issues as agendas do.

Related to our aim to provide methodological support for applying formal techniques is the work of Souquières and Lévy [15]. They support specification acquisition with *development operators* that reduce *tasks* to subtasks. However, development operators do not provide means for validation conditions.

Astesiano and Reggio [1] also emphasize the importance of method when using formal techniques. In the "method pattern" they set up for formal specification, agendas correspond to *guidelines.*

Future Work. In ESPRESS, we are currently working an agendas supporting further activities of the general development process as shown in Fig. 1 on page 2. We already have a first version of an agenda for the activity of safety analyses, which is based on common techniques such as FTA (failure-tree analysis) and SHARD (software hazard analysis and resolution design). We are working on an agenda for the verification and validation analyses, which captures the process how to check model properties. Verification is based on deduction techniques being developed in ESPRESS [13, 4], and on an adaption of existing model checking techniques. How the testing process is described by an agenda is a topic of ongoing research. Another important task is to support software design with agendas, where the starting point is a requirements specification as developed in this paper.

Cyclic software components, though important in practice, are indeed a rather simple software architecture. We are currently working on an extension of our agenda for this architecture to certain kinds of event-triggered software components, which are also studied in the case studies of ESPRESS [3]. We expect to reuse significant parts of the given agenda, in particular from Stage 1, context embedding, and Stage 2, quality requirements.

Acknowledgments. Many results and ideas presented in this paper stem from the broader context of the ESPRESS project and the work of its many collaborators in Berlin. We would especially like to thank Mirco Conrad and Eckard Lehmann for their work on the cruise control case study, and Thomas Santen for his comments on a draft of this paper.

References

1. E. Astesiano and G. Reggio. Formalism and Method. In M. Bidoit and M. Dauchet, editors, *Proc. TAPSOFT'97*, LNCS 1214, pages 93–114. Springer-Verlag, 1997.
2. R. Büssow, H. Dörr, R. Geisler, W. Grieskamp, and M. Klar. μSZ – ein Ansatz zur systematischen Verbindung von Z und Statecharts. Technical Report TR 96-32, Technische Universität Berlin, 1996.
3. R. Büssow, R. Geisler, and M. Klar. Specifying safety-critical embedded systems with statecharts and Z: a case study. this volume, 1997.
4. Robert Büssow and Wolfgang Grieskamp. Combinig Z and temporal interval logics for the formalization of properties and behaviors of embedded systems. In R. K. Shyamasundar and K. Ueda, editors, *Advances in Computing Science – Asian '97*, volume 1345 of *LNCS*, pages 46–56. Springer-Verlag, 1997.
5. E. Gamma, R. Helm, R. Johnson, and Vlissides. J. *Design Patterns – Elements of Reusable Object-Oriented Software*. Addison Wesley, Reading, 1995.
6. P. Garg and M. Jazayeri. Process-centered software engineering environments: A grand tour. In A. Fuggetta and A. Wolf, editors, *Software Process*, number 4 in Trends in Software, chapter 2, pages 25–52. Wiley, 1996.
7. D. Harel, H. Lachover, A. Naamad, A. Pnueli, M. Politi, R. Sherman, A. Shtull-Trauring, and M. Trakhtenbrot. Statemate: A working environment for the development of complex reactive systems. *IEEE TSE*, 16 No. 4, April 1990.
8. M. Heisel. *Methodology and Machine Support for the Application of Formal Techniques in Software Engineering*. Habilitation Thesis, TU Berlin, 1997.
9. M. Heisel and C. Sühl. Methodological support for formally specifying safety-critical software. In P. Daniel, editor, *Proceedings 16th International Conference on Computer Safety, Reliability and Security (SAFECOMP)*, pages 295–308. Springer-Verlag London, 1997.
10. Maritta Heisel. Agendas – a concept to guide software development activites. In *Proc. Systems Implementation 2000*, 1998. to appear.
11. C. Heitmeyer, R. Jeffords, and B. Lebaw. Automated consistency checking of requirements specifications. *ACM Transactions on Software Engineering and Methodology*, 5(3):231–261, July 1996.
12. K. Huff. Software process modelling. In A. Fuggetta and A. Wolf, editors, *Software Process*, number 4 in Trends in Software, chapter 2, pages 1–24. Wiley, 1996.
13. Kolyang, T. Santen, and B. Wolff. A structure preserving encoding of Z in Isabelle/HOL. In J. von Wright, J. Grundy, and J. Harrison, editors, *Theorem Proving in Higher-Order Logics*, LNCS 1125. Springer-Verlag, 1996.
14. M. Shaw and D. Garlan. *Software Architecture*. IEEE Computer Society Press, Los Alamitos, 1996.
15. Jeanine Souquières and Nicole Lévy. Description of specification developments. In *Proc. of Requirements Engineering '93*, pages 216–223, 1993.
16. J.M. Spivey. *The Z Notation – A Reference Manual*. Prentice Hall, 1992.
17. J. B. Wordsworth. *Software Development with Z*. Addison-Wesley, 1992.

Algebra Transformation Systems and their Composition

Martin Große–Rhode *

Dipartimento di Informatica, Università degli Studi di Pisa,
Corso Italia, 40, I – 56125 Pisa, Italia, email: mgr@di.unipi.it

Abstract. Algebra transformation systems are introduced as formal models of components of open distributed systems. They are given by a transition graph modelling the control flow and partial algebras and method expressions modelling the data states and their transformations. According to this two–level structure they cover both labelled transition systems and rule based specification approaches, corresponding to information, computation and engineering viewpoint models. Different composition operations for algebra transformation systems are investigated. Limits and colimits model parallel and sequential composition of components, signature morphisms yield appropriate syntactical support for such compositions. The most important compositionality properties known from algebraic specification, like colimits of signatures and amalgamation of models, also hold for the framework of algebra transformation systems.

1 Introduction

Algebra transformation systems are introduced as formal models of components in open distributed systems in order to support multiple viewpoint modelling. The background for their development has been the reference model for open distributed systems RM–ODP, introduced as ISO–standard / ITU–recommendation [ODP]. One of the main features of RM–ODP is the introduction of five designated *viewpoints* as structuring means for design and specification of distributed systems. Viewpoints allow the separation of different aspects of a system, such that specifications can be restricted to the parts that are relevant for some specific use. The five viewpoints defined in RM–ODP are *enterprise, information, computation, engineering*, and *technology* viewpoint. With the approach of algebra transformation systems especially the information, computation, and engineering viewpoints are supported. That means the information model, the computational model, and the infrastructure needed to realize the services of the system in a distributed environment could be modelled formally as algebra transformation systems.

* This work has been partially supported by the EEC TMR network GETGRATS (General Theory of Graph Transformation Systems), contract number ERB-FMRX-CT960061.

As specification languages for these viewpoints RM–ODP recommends, beyond others, Z for the information viewpoint and LOTOS for computation and engineering viewpoints. In Z *static*, *invariant*, and *dynamic* schemata for the specification of designated states, state invariants, and state transformations respectively can be given, corresponding to the requirements of an information viewpoint specification language. LOTOS supports the specification of the interaction of computation objects at interfaces, corresponding to computational and engineering viewpoint resp.

The purpose of the algebra transformation system approach is to deliver a formal semantical approach that covers both specification approaches explicated by Z and LOTOS. That means, the rule based approach with internally structured states and their transformation underlying Z, as well as the approach via the temporal ordering of observable actions underlying LOTOS shall be integrated. One of the main advantages of such an integration is the possibility to embed both kinds of models into one framework to compare them and check their consistency.

An algebra transformation system is given by two levels. The first one, called the transition graph, models the reactive behaviour of the system, that is, its temporal ordering of actions. Associated with each *control state* of this level is a *data state* on the second level that models the information available in this state. The transitions of control states are accordingly labelled with sets of *method expressions* on the second level, that indicate which methods have been applied for this data state transformation and how they have been applied.

The second main purpose of this paper is to introduce composition operations for algebra transformation systems, that allow to model different kinds of compositions of components. According to their two–level structure these composition operations are inherited from composition operations for labelled transition systems on the one hand, and abstract data types on the other hand. Parallel composition of labelled transition systems for instance is modelled by limits, such as products (see [WN95]), whereas composition of abstract data types is given by colimits (see e.g. [BG77,EM85]). This duality is reflected for algebra transformation systems in the definition of the corresponding morphisms, where the two levels are mapped in opposite order. In this way the right composition operations are put together for the two levels. Beyond parallel composition, with appropriate synchronization mechanisms, sequential composition is investigated. This is particularly important for the definition of control structures for rule based specifications, which are usually encoded into the states. However, an explicit modelling of the control flow as in algebra transformation systems, independently of the information represented in the data states, is much more appropriate and supports clear and manageable specifications much better. Sequential composition is given by colimits of the transition graphs (i.e. the control structure) with identities on the data states; passing the control flow from one component to another should not change the underlying data state.

The paper is organized as follows. In the next section the category of algebra transformation systems is introduced. Then composition in the sense discussed above is introduced, i.e. limits and colimits are defined. In section 4 signature morphisms are defined and their support for composition operations is discussed. For all definitions and constructions small examples are given to show how they work and how they can be used for applications. Further examples can be found in [Gro97], where also a methodology for the presentation of transformation systems is discussed. Finally in section 5 a short summary and a comparison with other approaches are given, and further questions are discussed. Full proofs of the propositions and theorems of sections 2 and 3 of this paper can be found in [Gro97].

2 The Category of Transformation Systems

As discussed above an algebra transformation system is given by two levels, the transition graph modelling the control flow, and the data states and method expressions representing the information available in the states and transitions. The data states of an algebra transformation system are given by partial algebras to a common partial equational specification. A signature for partial algebras is a usual algebraic signature $SIG = (S, OP)$, given by a set S of sort names and a family $OP = (OP_{w,s})_{w \in S^*, s \in S}$ of operation symbols indexed by their arities. As usual an operation symbol $op \in OP_{w,s}$ is denoted $op : w \to s$. The semantical difference to total algebras is that an operation symbol $op : w \to s$ is interpreted as a *partial* function $op^A : A_{s_1} \times \cdots \times A_{s_n} \dashrightarrow A_s$ (if $w = s_1 \ldots s_n$), given by a domain of definition $dom(op^A) \subseteq A_{s_1} \times \cdots \times A_{s_n}$ and a total mapping $dom(op^A) \to A_s$. Homomorphisms of partial $SPEC$-algebras are given by families of total functions that preserve the domains of definition of the operations, and operation application. An equation $t = t'$ is satisfied by a partial algebra A if both terms t and t' can be evaluated (are defined) in A, and yield the same value. Satisfaction of a conditional equation $r = r' \Rightarrow t = t'$ is defined as usual: whenever the premise $r = r'$ is satisfied, then also the conclusion $t = t'$ must be satisfied. The interpretation of equations also yields the definedness predicate for terms t, denoted $t \downarrow$, given by $t \downarrow$ iff $t = t$. A signature SIG with a set CE of conditional equations is called a partial equational specification $SPEC$. The category of partial $SPEC$-algebras and homomorphisms is denoted $PAlg(SPEC)$, its class of objects $|PAlg(SPEC)|$. (For further details see [Rei87,CGW95].)

Partial algebras have been chosen for two reasons. Firstly they comprise first order structures, since predicates can be modelled by partial functions to a singleton set. Of course they are more general than first order structures because of the partial functions. Secondly, partiality allows to model the difference between declaration and instantiation (resp. initialization) of syntactic entities in a natural way, because terms to a signature need not be interpreted in all partial algebras to this signature. Especially in the context of dynamically changing states this feature is very appropriate.

Method names are added to the data state specification, like operation symbols, as names with arities that determine the number and type of the parameters they require. However, methods do not have an output sort, they do only change the state. Data outputs have to be modelled by data type functions whose value can be determined by the actual state, according to the conditional equations in the data type specification.

Definition 1 (Transformation Signature). A *transformation signature* $T\Sigma = (SPEC, M)$ is given by a partial equational specification $SPEC = (S, OP, CE)$ and a *method signature* $M = (M_w)_{w \in S^*}$. A method name $m \in M_w$ is denoted $m : w$ for short.

Transitions are labelled by sets of method expressions that contain the names of the methods that have been applied, and corresponding lists of parameters from the actual state.

Definition 2 (Method Expression). Given a transformation signature $T\Sigma = (SPEC, M)$ the set $ME_{T\Sigma}$ of *method expressions* is defined by

$$ME_{T\Sigma} = \bigcup_{A \in |PAlg(SPEC)|} ME_{T\Sigma}(A) ,$$

where the components $ME_{T\Sigma}(A)$, $A \in |PAlg(SPEC)|$, are defined by

$$ME_{T\Sigma}(A) = \{m(a) \mid m \in M_w, a \in A_w\} .$$

As prerequisite for the definition of transformation systems let me shortly fix the formal structure of *sets of method expressions*. The powersets $\mathcal{P}(ME_{T\Sigma}(A))$ with inclusions as morphisms are categories. These are indexed by the functor

$$\mathcal{P}(ME_{T\Sigma}(\_)) : PAlg(SPEC) \to \mathbf{Cat}.$$

It is defined on a $SPEC$–homomorphism $h : A \to B$ as the direct image, i.e.

$$\mathcal{P}(ME_{T\Sigma}(h))(K) = \{m(h(a)) \mid m(a) \in K\} \subseteq ME_{T\Sigma}(B)$$

for all $K \subseteq ME_{T\Sigma}(A)$. Obviously $\mathcal{P}(ME_{T\Sigma}(h))$ and $\mathcal{P}(ME_{T\Sigma}(\_))$ are functors. This indexing induces, via the appropriate Grothendieck construction, the flat category denoted $\mathcal{P}(ME_{T\Sigma})$, whose objects are pairs (A, K), with $A \in |PAlg(SPEC)|$ and $K \subseteq ME_{T\Sigma}(A)$, and whose morphisms are pairs $(h, \subseteq) : (A, K) \to (B, L)$, where $h : A \to B$ is a $SPEC$–homomorphism such that $\mathcal{P}(ME_{T\Sigma}(h))(K) \subseteq L$. Overloading notation a bit both the functor $\mathcal{P}(ME_{T\Sigma}(h))$ and the morphism $(h, \subseteq)$ will be denoted by h in the sequel.

Beyond the data states (= partial $SPEC$–algebras) and the method expressions an algebra transformation system comprises the control flow. It is modelled by a directed graph of control states and transitions, and it may have loops and multiple edges. This graph is formally given by sets of states and transitions, and functions src and tar that assign source and target states to the transitions. The data states and sets of method expressions are then formally modelled as labels of control states and transitions.

Definition 3 (Transformation System). Let $T\Sigma = (SPEC, M)$ be a transformation signature. A $T\Sigma$–*transformation system* $\mathcal{A} = (TG_{\mathcal{A}}, lab_{\mathcal{A}})$ is given by a transition graph

$$TG_{\mathcal{A}} = (\mathcal{S}, \mathcal{T}, src, tar) \text{ with } src, tar : \mathcal{T} \to \mathcal{S},$$

and a pair of functions

$$lab_{\mathcal{A}} = (lab_{\mathcal{S}} : \mathcal{S} \to |PAlg(SPEC)|, lab_{\mathcal{T}} : \mathcal{T} \to \mathcal{P}(ME_{T\Sigma})),$$

such that

$$lab_{\mathcal{T}}(l) \subseteq ME_{T\Sigma}(lab_{\mathcal{S}}(src(l)))$$

for all $l \in \mathcal{T}$, i.e. the parameters are always taken from the actual source state.

The two labelling functions support the methodological separation between control flow and data transformation level. The first one is completely independent from the transformation signature, which will be used later on in the definition of the forgetful functor. Note that a transition may be labelled by the empty set, which allows to model data state transformations induced by the environment.

A transition $l \in \mathcal{T}$ with $src(l) = s$ and $tar(l) = t$ will be denoted $l : s \to t$. Moreover both $l \in \mathcal{T}$ and the triple $l : s \to t$ will be called transition. Correspondingly $\mathcal{T}$ is called the *transition relation*. The labels of states and transitions will also be indicated by capital letters, i.e. $lab_{\mathcal{S}}(s) = S$ and $lab_{\mathcal{T}}(l) = L$ for states $s \in \mathcal{S}$ and transitions $l \in \mathcal{T}$. The condition that parameters are always taken from the actual state in the definition above thus reads: $L \subseteq ME_{T\Sigma}(S)$ for all $l : s \to t \in \mathcal{T}$.

Example 4. Consider as running example the following signature of a program that increments the value of a program variable by a given positive natural number.

A specification **nat** of the natural numbers is extended by a sort *prog_var* of program variables and a partial function ! that assigns — in each state — the actual values to the program variables. Furthermore a variable name p is introduced and a method *inc* to increment the value of a variable by a given amount.

> **prog = nat +**
>   **sorts**   prog_var
>   **opns**   !: prog_var $\to$ nat
>   p: $\to$ prog_var
>   **meths** inc: prog_var, nat

A **prog**–transformation system that models the expected behaviour is defined as follows. Let **prog–data** be the partial equational specification given by **prog** without the method name *inc*, and X_n for some $n \in \mathbb{N}$ be the partial **prog–data–algebra** defined by

$$X_n|_{\mathbf{nat}} = \mathbb{N}, \ (X_n)_{prog\_var} = \{X\}, \ p^{X_n} = X, \ !^{X_n}(X) = n,$$

i.e. X_n is the state in which X has the value n. Then a **prog–transformation** system $\mathcal{X} = (TG_{\mathcal{X}}, lab_{\mathcal{X}})$ can be defined by

control states	$S_{\mathcal{X}} = \mathbb{N}$
data states	$lab_S(n) = X_n$
transitions	$T_{\mathcal{X}} = \{(k : n \to n + k) \mid k > 0\}$
method expressions	$lab_T(k : n \to n + k) = \{inc(X, k)\}$

This model contains as labelled paths all sequences of method applications.

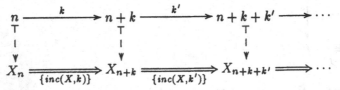

In order to model a control flow that stops after each single step the control flow information has to be refined. E.g. the control states are extended by marks *start* and *stop*, and each transition leads from a *start*–state to a corresponding *stop*–state.

control states	$S = \mathbb{N} \times \{start, stop\}$
data states	$lab_S(n, start) = lab_S(n, stop) = X_n$
transitions	$T = \{k : (n, start) \to (n + k, stop) \mid k > 0\}$
method expressions	$lab_T(k : (n, start) \to (n + k, stop)) = \{inc(X, k)\}$

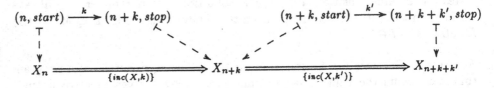

In both examples the method *inc* induces a function, that assigns to each data state X_n and all parameters X and k in X_n a successor state X_{n+k}. In general methods need neither be total nor deterministic, that is, they correspond to relations rather than functions.

As mentioned in the introduction morphisms of transformation systems are defined in such a way that appropriate composition operations are supported. Composition of data states is modelled by colimits in the category of partial algebras. This models the superposition of data states w.r.t. some shared parts. (Thus also the communication on the data state level is given by sharing.) A coproduct of two partial *SPEC*–algebras A and B for example can roughly be described as follows. The carrier sets of $A + B$ are the unions of the (renamed) carriers of A and B, where the term generated elements are identified and the non generated parts are united disjointly. The operations of $A + B$ are given by the corresponding unions of the operations of A and B, provided they coincide on the intersections of their domains in $A + B$, and their union still satisfies the axioms. (Otherwise the carriers may collapse.) Thus coproduct is disjoint union with sharing of term generated parts.

On the other level, parallel composition of transition graphs, like parallel composition of labelled transitions systems, is given by limits. Products correspond to pure parallel composition, pullbacks correspond to parallel composition with synchronization between the parts, induced by actions that both components must perform during the same step. Since parallel composition of components should be supported for the case that both components act on different parts of a data state, possibly overlapping in basic types or the part they synchronize upon, limits of the transition graph part should be combined with colimits on the data state part. That means, the two levels of a morphism of transformation systems must have opposite direction. [1]

Definition 5 (Transformation System Morphism). Let $\mathcal{A} = (TG_A, lab_A)$ and $\mathcal{A}' = (TG_{A'}, lab_{A'})$ be $T\Sigma$-transformation systems. A $T\Sigma$-*morphism* $h = (h_{TG}, (h_s)_{s \in S}) : \mathcal{A} \to \mathcal{A}'$ is given by a graph homomorphism

$$h_{TG} : TG_A \to TG_{A'},$$

and a family of $SPEC$-homomorphisms

$$(h_s : S' \to S)_{s \in S} \quad (\text{with } s' = h_{TG}(s)),$$

such that

$$h_s(L') \subseteq L \quad (\text{with } l' = h_{TG}(l))$$

for all $l : s \to t \in T$.

Proposition 6. $T\Sigma$-*transformation systems and morphisms form a category, called* $\mathbf{TS}(T\Sigma)$, *for each transformation signature* $T\Sigma$.

---

[1] An analogy for these opposite directions can be seen in the duality of algebraic specification of data types and coalgebraic specification of dynamic systems. Initial algebras are the designated, typical and generated models of an algebraic specification, final coalgebras play the corresponding role for dynamic systems.

3 Composition by Limits and Colimits

A limit $\mathcal{A}$ of a diagram of transformation systems $\mathcal{A}^i$ and morphisms $h : \mathcal{A}^i \to \mathcal{A}^j$ is constructed as follows. First the limit $TG_{\mathcal{A}}$ of the transition graphs $TG_{\mathcal{A}^i}$ and graph morphisms $h_{TG} : TG_{\mathcal{A}^i} \to TG_{\mathcal{A}^j}$ is constructed. Thus a transition $l : s \to t$ in $\mathcal{A}$ is given by a family of transitions $l^i : s^i \to t^i$ in $\mathcal{A}^i$ with $h_{TG}(l^i : s^i \to t^i) = l^j : s^j \to t^j$ for all $h : \mathcal{A}^i \to \mathcal{A}^j$ in the diagram. For any state s in $TG_{\mathcal{A}}$ the data state S is then given by the colimit of all data states S^i of the control states $s^i = \pi^i_{TG}(s)$ and the data state homomorphisms $h_{s^i} : S^j \to S^i$ with $h_{TG}(s^i) = s^j$. The label L of a transition $l : s \to t$ in $TG_{\mathcal{A}}$ is obtained in the same way as a colimit in $\mathcal{P}(ME_{T\Sigma})$.

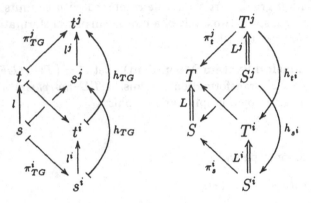

Since both the categories of graphs and partial algebras have limits and colimits, the dual construction yields colimits of algebra transformation systems. Thus we obtain

Theorem 7. $\mathbf{TS}(T\Sigma)$ *is complete and cocomplete.*

Example 8 (Parallel Composition). As an example for the parallel composition of transformation systems via limits consider the following extension of the transformation signature **prog** and the **prog**–transformation system $\mathcal{X}$ in example 4. First the signature is extended to a transformation signature **p,q–prog** by a second program variable $q: \to prog\_var$. Then two **p,q–prog**–transformation models $\mathcal{Y}$ and $\mathcal{Z}$ are constructed similarly to the **prog**–model $\mathcal{X}$. Each has access to one of the two program variables and increments it using the method *inc*. The corresponding data states Y_n and Z_m for $n, m \in \mathbb{N}$ are given by

$$Y_n|_{\mathbf{nat}} = Z_m|_{\mathbf{nat}} = \mathbb{N}, (Y_n)_{prog\_var} = \{Y\}, (Z_m)_{prog\_var} = \{Z\},$$

$$p^{Y_n} = Y, q^{Y_n} \text{ is undefined}, !^{Y_n}(Y) = n,$$

$$p^{Z_m} \text{ is undefined}, q^{Z_m} = Z, !^{Z_m}(Z) = m .$$

The transition graphs of $\mathcal{Y}$ and $\mathcal{Z}$ are defined like the one of $\mathcal{X}$, extended by *idle* transitions $0 : n \to n$ labelled by the empty set. This allows to model *independent* transformations in the product constructed below. The other labels are defined accordingly.

	$\mathcal{Y}$	$\mathcal{Z}$
control states	$\mathbb{N}$	$\mathbb{N}$
data states	$n \mapsto Y_n$	$m \mapsto Z_m$
transitions	$\{(k : n \to n + k) \mid k \geq 0\}$	$\{(l : m \to m + l) \mid l \geq 0\}$
method exp.'s	$k \mapsto \begin{cases} \{inc(Y, k)\} & \text{if } k > 0 \\ \emptyset & \text{if } k = 0 \end{cases}$	$l \mapsto \begin{cases} \{inc(Z, l)\} & \text{if } l > 0 \\ \emptyset & \text{if } l = 0 \end{cases}$

According to the general construction of limits discussed above the product $\mathcal{Y} \times \mathcal{Z}$ is given by the products of the transition graphs of $\mathcal{Y}$ and $\mathcal{Z}$, for each control state the coproduct of the component data states, and for each transition the union of the sets of method expressions labelling the component transitions. Explicitly this means $\mathcal{Y} \times \mathcal{Z}$ is given by

$$S_{\mathcal{Y} \times \mathcal{Z}} = \mathbb{N} \times \mathbb{N}$$

$$lab_{\mathcal{Y} \times \mathcal{Z}}(n, m) = Y_n + Z_m$$

$$\mathcal{T}_{\mathcal{Y} \times \mathcal{Z}} = \{(k, l) : (n, m) \to (n + k, m + l)) \mid k, l \geq 0\}$$

$$lab_{\mathcal{Y} \times \mathcal{Z}}((k, l) : (n, m) \to (n + k, m + l))) =$$

$$= \begin{cases} \{inc(Y, k), inc(Z, l)\} & \text{if } k > 0, l > 0 \\ \{inc(Y, k)\} & \text{if } k > 0, l = 0 \\ \{inc(Z, l)\} & \text{if } k = 0, l > 0 \\ \emptyset & \text{if } k = 0, l = 0 \end{cases}$$

where the partial **prog–data–algebras** $Y_n + Z_m$ are given by

$$Y_n + Z_m|_{\mathbf{nat}} = \mathbb{N}, \ (Y_n + Z_m)_{prog\_var} = \{X, Y\},$$

$$p^{Y_n + Z_m} = Y, q^{Y_n + Z_m} = Z,$$

$$!^{Y_n + Z_m}(Y) = n, !^{Y_n + Z_m}(Z) = m,$$

i.e. $Y_n + Z_m$ is the state in which Y has the value n and Z has the value m .

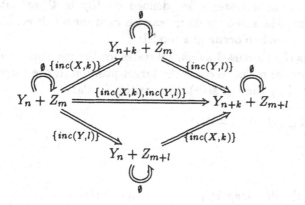

Example 9 (Sequential Composition). In this example colimits are used for the sequential composition of transformation systems. A mutable list of data items with list cursor on a given set of data shall be modelled, and a method to delete the n'th element of this list. This *delete*-method is put together by a *move*-method that moves the cursor to the right place and an *erase*-method that erases the actual element of the list.

The list is defined in each state by a partial function *next:data* $\rightarrow$ *data*, the list cursor by a pointer to natural numbers. The position n of the element that shall be deleted is given to the system as parameter of the *move* and *delete* methods.

> **list = nat + data +**
>   **opns**   next: data $\rightarrow$ data
>   cursor: $\rightarrow$ nat
>   **meths** erase:
>   move, delete: nat

The data states are represented by two lists corresponding to the parts of the list before the cursor and the remainder. These lists $l, r \in A^*$ shall satisfy the side condition that their concatenation lr has no repetitions in order to define a partial function *next*. Each such pair $(l, r) \in A^* \times A^*$ then defines a partial **list-data** algebra $S(l, r)$ by

$$S(l, r)|_{\textbf{nat}} = \mathbb{N}, \; S(l, r)_{\textbf{data}} = A,$$

$$next^{S(l,r)}(a_i) = a_{i+1} \text{ if } lr = a_1 \ldots a_m$$

$$cursor^{S(l,r)} = length(l) + 1 \; .$$

Now three **list**-transformation systems are defined on top of these data states, one for each method. The same signature can be used for all three, because not all method names need to occur in a model.

Move : The pairs of lists (l, r) are used as control states for the *move* method, together with a natural number n that records the target position. If the target is reached this is represented by the tag $st(n)$; the position is *stable*.

$$S^{move} = A^* \times A^* \times (\mathbb{N} \cup \{st(n) \mid n \in \mathbb{N}\})$$

$$lab_S(l, r, \eta) = S(l, r)$$

$\mathcal{T}^{move}$ is defined by

$$
\begin{array}{llll}
(l, xr', n) & \rightarrow (lx, r', n) & \text{iff} & length(l) + 1 < n \leq length(lxr') \\
(l, r, n) & \rightarrow (\epsilon, lr, n) & \text{iff} & n \leq length(l) \\
(l, r, n) & \rightarrow (l, r, st(n)) & \text{iff} & length(l) + 1 = n
\end{array}
$$

All these transitions are labelled $\{move(n)\}$, i.e. the index n in the abstract state representation is the parameter of the method until it reaches its target.

Erase : Since the erasion of the actual list element requires exactly one step the marks *start* and *stop* are used again in the state representation.

$$\mathcal{S}^{erase} = A^* \times A^* \times \{start, stop\}$$

$$lab_{\mathcal{S}^{erase}}(l, r, s) = S(l, r)$$

The transition relation is given by the transitions

$$(l, xr', start) \to (l, r', stop)$$

all labelled $\{erase\}$.

Delete : Now *move* and *erase* are put together to implement the *delete* method. For that purpose define the connecting **list–transformation model** $\mathcal{C}$ that contains all pairs of control states of *move* and *erase* that are to be connected, and no transitions. Note that the data states of connected control states are identical.

$$\mathcal{S}_{\mathcal{C}} = \{((l, r, st(n)), (l, r, start)) \mid l, r \in A^*, n \in \mathbb{N}\}$$

$$lab((l, r, st(n)), (l, r, start)) = S(l, r)$$

$$\mathcal{T}_{\mathcal{C}} = \emptyset$$

The transformation system morphisms from $\mathcal{C}$ to the *move* and *erase* models are given by the projections of $\mathcal{S}_{\mathcal{C}}$ to $\mathcal{S}^{move}$ and $\mathcal{S}^{erase}$ resp., and the identity data state homomorphisms. Due to the pushout construction of graphs the pushout of this diagram of transformation systems identifies all pairs of control states $(l, r, st(n)), (l, r, start)$. That means, when *move* has reached its target, *erase* starts, and performs one step in which it erases the actual ($= n$'th) list element.

4 Composition by Signature Morphisms

The two program models in example 8 that update different variables could be defined w.r.t. a common signature, because partial algebras make it possible to leave parts of the signature uninterpreted. In general a signature can always be chosen large enough to be suitable for a given set of partial algebras in this way. The same holds for method names, because they need not necessarily occur in any transition label set. Thus formally local signatures and signature morphisms would not be necessary. However, restricting the signatures to the parts that are actually accessed yields a much better overall structure of the specification. It documents independence of methods and supports local modelling. Moreover signature morphisms can be used to rename components and put them together in different ways. Instead of equality of names, that might always be considered as accidental, categorical composition techniques always require morphisms to make explicit the connections between the components. All items from different components that are not explicitly related are considered as being different.

Definition 10 (Transformation Signature Morphism). Let $T\Sigma = (SPEC, M)$ and $T\Sigma' = (SPEC', M')$ be transformation signatures. A *transformation signature morphism* $\sigma = (\sigma_{SPEC}, \sigma_M) : T\Sigma \to T\Sigma'$ is given by a specification morphism $\sigma_{SPEC} : SPEC \to SPEC'$ and a family of functions $\sigma_M = (\sigma_{M,w} : M_w \to M'_{\sigma_{SPEC}(w)})_{w \in S^*}$, where S is the set of sorts of $SPEC$.

Transformation signatures and transformation signature morphisms define the category **TransSig** .

Since signatures and signature morphisms for algebra transformation systems formally coincide with signatures and signature morphisms for partial algebras we immediately obtain the following constructions, that are the basis for the subsequent compositionality results.

Proposition 11. *The category TransSig is cocomplete.*

The forgetful functor of transformation systems induced by a transformation signature morphism leaves the transition graphs unchanged. (Recall that the transition graphs are independent of the transformation signatures.) The data states are replaced by their restrictions according to the forgetful functor of partial algebras, and the sets of method expressions are replaced by the (renamed) subsets of method names corresponding to the smaller set of method names.

Definition 12 (Forgetful Functor). Given a transformation signature morphism $\sigma = (\sigma_{SPEC}, \sigma_M) : T\Sigma \to T\Sigma'$ the *forgetful functor* $V_\sigma : \mathbf{TS}(T\Sigma') \to \mathbf{TS}(T\Sigma)$ is defined as follows.

1. Let $A' = (TG_{A'}, lab_{A'}) \in \mathbf{TS}(T\Sigma')$.
   Then $V_\sigma(A') =: A = (TG_A, lab_A) \in \mathbf{TS}(T\Sigma)$ is defined by
   - $TG_A = TG_{A'}$
   - $lab_S(s) = V_{\sigma_{SPEC}}(lab_{S'}(s))$
       where $V_{\sigma_{SPEC}} : PAlg(SPEC') \to PAlg(SPEC)$ is the forgetful
       functor induced by $\sigma_{SPEC} : SPEC \to SPEC'$,
   - $lab_T(l : s \to t) = \{m(a) \in ME_{T\Sigma} \mid \sigma_M(m)(a) \in lab_{T'}(l : s \to t)\}$
2. Let $h' = (h'_{TG}, (h'_{s'})_{s' \in S_{A'}}) : A' \to B'$ in $\mathbf{TS}(T\Sigma')$.
   Then $V_\sigma(h') =: h = (h_{TG}, (h_s)_{s \in S_A}) : V_\sigma(A') \to V_\sigma(B')$ is defined by
   - $h_{TG} = h'_{TG}$
   - $h_s : lab_{V_\sigma(B')}(h_{TG}(s)) \to lab_{V_\sigma(A')}(s) =$
     $= V_{\sigma_{SPEC}}(h_s : lab_{B'}(h'_{TG}(s)) \to lab_{A'}(s))$

It is easily checked that V_σ is well defined.

Definition 13 (Model Functor). The *model functor Mod* : **TransSig** $\to$ **Cat**^{op} is defined by $Mod(T\Sigma) = \mathbf{TS}(T\Sigma)$ and $Mod(\sigma) = V_\sigma$.

Since the forgetful functor for algebra transformation systems is given by the identity on transition graphs and algebraic forgetful functors on data states, the *amalgamation property*, known from algebraic specification, carries over to algebra transformation systems. That means, given a pushout of transformation signatures its model category is the pullback of the model categories of the components.

Theorem 14 (Amalgamation). *Mod preserves pushouts.*

This property guarantees the existence and uniqueness of amalgamated sum of algebra transformation systems and morphisms. If $\sigma_1 : T\Sigma_0 \to T\Sigma_1$ and $\sigma_2 : T\Sigma_0 \to T\Sigma_2$ are transformation signature morphisms and $\bar{\sigma}_1 : T\Sigma_1 \to T\Sigma_3$ and $\bar{\sigma}_2 : T\Sigma_2 \to T\Sigma_3$ is their pushout, then for each pair of transformation systems $A_1 \in \mathbf{TS}(T\Sigma_1)$ and $A_2 \in \mathbf{TS}(T\Sigma_2)$ with $V_{\sigma_1}(A_1) = V_{\sigma_2}(A_2)$ there is a $T\Sigma_3$-transformation system $A_3 = A_1 +_{A_0} A_2 \in \mathbf{TS}(T\Sigma_3)$, where $A_0 = V_{\sigma_1}(A_1)$, such that $V_{\bar{\sigma}_1}(A_3) = A_1$ and $V_{\bar{\sigma}_2}(A_3) = A_2$. Moreover A_3 is uniquely determined by this property. The same amalgamation property holds for morphisms. The model $A_3 = A_1 +_{A_0} A_2$ is called the *amalgamated sum* of A_1 and A_2.

Let's finally combine the signature morphisms for the data transformation level with morphisms of transition graphs in order to obtain the appropriate composition operations for both levels together. For that purpose the appropriate Grothendieck category has to be taken. (Cf. the construction of sets of method expressions above.) In this case it is given by

$$\begin{aligned}
\textit{objects} \quad & (T\Sigma, A), \quad \text{with } A \in |\mathbf{TS}(T\Sigma)| \\
\textit{morphisms} \quad & m = (\sigma, h) : (T\Sigma, A) \to (T\Sigma', A')
\end{aligned}$$

$$\begin{aligned}
& \text{with } \sigma : T\Sigma' \to T\Sigma \text{ in } \mathbf{TransSig} \\
& \text{and } h : V_\sigma(A) \to A' \text{ in } \mathbf{TS}(T\Sigma')
\end{aligned}$$

Note how the opposite direction of transition graph morphisms and data state morphisms is reflected in the direction of the algebraic specification morphisms.

Pullbacks in this category are given by pullbacks of transition graphs, and for each control state s the amalgamated data state $S = S_2 +_{S_0} S_1$, where the $s_i = \pi_i(s), i = 0, 1, 2$, are the projections of s in the components. The method expressions are the corresponding amalgamations (= unions of renamed sets of method expression).

Example 15. With signature morphisms and the Grothendieck morphisms, the construction of the parallel composition $\mathcal{Y} \times \mathcal{Z}$ in example 8 can be reformulated in such a way, that the independence of the two incrementation processes is documented already on the syntactical level. That means, the models $\mathcal{Y}$ and $\mathcal{Z}$ can be reconstructed as models to a signature that contains only one program variable — the variable the model has access to — and their product can be reconstructed as a corresponding pullback.

According to the definition of Grothendieck morphisms first an appropriate pushout diagram of transformation signatures has to be given:

$$\begin{array}{ccc}
\mathbf{prog\_0} & \longrightarrow & \mathbf{prog} \\
\downarrow & & \downarrow \\
\mathbf{prog} & \longrightarrow & \mathbf{p, q - prog}
\end{array}$$

Here **prog** is defined as in example 4, introducing the only program variable and the incrementation method. **prog_0** is **prog** without the program variable p, and the morphisms are inclusions. Then the transformation signature **p,q–prog** of example 8, together with the inclusion morphisms, is a pushout of this diagram. There are two copies of the program variable, because it is not shared in **prog_0**.

Now let $\mathcal{X}'$ be given by the **prog**–transformation system $\mathcal{X}$ defined in example 4, extended by idle transitions as in example 8. Obviously $\mathcal{X}'$ coincides with the restrictions to **prog** of $\mathcal{Y}$ and $\mathcal{Z}$. The image $V(\mathcal{X}')$ under the forgetful functor V induced by the inclusion **prog_0** $\rightarrow$ **prog** is the same as $\mathcal{X}'$, except that in the data states $V(X_n)$ the program variable X is no longer designated by the constant p.

In order to obtain the product of the transition graph of $\mathcal{X}'$ with itself as a pullback, it must be connected by graph morphisms to the terminal graph, that consists of one node and one edge.

Finally the sharing of the data states must be expressed by appropriate amalgamations. The natural numbers shall be shared, whereas the sets of program variables and the label sets of method expressions shall be united disjointly. All this is obtained by the **prog_0**-transformation system $\mathbb{1}$, given by the one node–one edge–transition graph, data state $\mathbb{N}$ with empty set of program variables, and empty set of method expressions for the transition. Then there is a Grothendieck morphism $\mathcal{X}' \rightarrow \mathbb{1}$ given by the transition signature inclusion **prog_0** $\rightarrow$ **prog** , the unique morphism of transition graphs $TG_{\mathcal{X}'} \rightarrow TG_{\mathbb{1}}$, data state injections $(\mathbb{N}, \emptyset) \rightarrow V(X_n)$ for all $n \in \mathbb{N}$, and inclusions of sets of method expressions $\emptyset \rightarrow \{inc(X, k)\}$.

Since $TG_{\mathbb{1}}$ is a terminal graph the pullback of $TG_{\mathcal{X}'} \rightarrow TG_{\mathbb{1}}$ with itself is the product $TG_{\mathcal{X}'} \times TG_{\mathcal{X}'}$. Data states are the amalgamations $X_n X'_m :=$ $X_n +_{(\mathbb{N}, \emptyset)} X_m$, that contain two copies of X, i.e. $p^{X_n X'_m} = X$ and $q^{X_n X'_m} = X'$, with values $!^{X_n X'_m}(X) = n$ and $!^{X_n X'_m}(X') = m$ respectively. The sets of method expressions are given by the disjoint unions of the corresponding sets of method expressions of the components. Thus the pullback of $\mathcal{X}' \rightarrow \mathbb{1}$ with itself is the desired parallel composition of $\mathcal{X}'$ with a copy of itself, that manipulates the copy q of p .

5 Conclusion

In this paper I have introduced the two layered structures of algebra transformation systems, their morphisms and their composition by limits, colimits, and signature morphisms. This framework belongs to the *algebras–as–states* approach to the specification of dynamic systems, whose foremost representative are the abstract state machines, formerly called evolving algebras (see [Gur94]). A formalisation of evolving algebras has been presented in [DG94], where however algebraic specifications are considered as algebraic programs, and consistency conditions become part of the definition of the semantics. A very general abstract mathematical model within this approach, D–oids, has been presented in [AZ95]. It introduces a model theory for dynamic systems, parameterized by the underlying static framework for values and state algebras. Specification means, i.e. sentences and satisfaction for D–oids are introduced in [Zuc96]. There, however, methods are total functions, which is problematic for the modelling of non–deterministic systems, and identities are modelled by a tracking map, which might be in conflict with the data signature. However, there are no composition operations for D–oids, and the technique developed here cannot be applied directly, because signatures are used in a very different way. The idea to use signature morphisms to compose specifications of concurrent systems has been adapted from [FM92]. There temporal logic theories are introduced as specification units and specification morphisms as interconnections. Due to the temporal logic approach one temporal structure for all models had to be fixed, in this case discrete linear time, as opposed to the arbitrary transition graphs of algebra transformation systems.

Labelled transition systems can be embedded into the framework of algebra transformation systems, taking the transition system as transition graph, empty data states (over the empty signature), and the labels as method expressions. Models of Z–specifications and graph transformation systems can be embedded as the other extreme case, where the control states do not contain additional information. I.e. the transition graph is the graph of all reachable data states (= data models in Z, supposed they are (first order) partial algebras, graphs in graph transformation systems). In Z the signature of the data states is given explicitly, signatures for graphs would introduce sorts for nodes and edges, and functions *src* and *tar* for sources and targets of edges. More elaborated graph structures can be defined accordingly.

Partial algebras have been chosen as specification framework for the data states for the reasons discussed above. However, it is easy to see that the approach is (rather) institution independent concerning the data state models. The only requirement used in this paper has been that data state models have carrier sets from which the parameters can be chosen, i.e. the model theory is *concrete* (see [BT96]), and that the model categories have limits and colimits. In this way *institution independent transformation systems* can be defined.

What is left open in this paper are the development of a syntax to represent or specify the transition graphs, and axioms for the description of transformation systems, i.e. the logical part of the institution. First results concerning such axioms are presented in [Gro96], where the *descriptive* and the *constructive* meanings of *replacement rules* for (a class of) partial algebras are investigated. The constructive interpretation of a rule describes how a successor state can be constructed from a given state and parameters, its descriptive meaning is a pre/post condition for a method.

The first point is left open because process languages can be used to present the transition graphs, or regular expressions for instance. A more detailed investigation however would have to take into account also the possible mutual relationships between control states and data states. There should be means for instance to state that a method can (cannot) be applied if the data state satisfies a certain condition, like being *stable* for instance. (A state is stable if all admissible method applications yield isomorphic states.) Furthermore a *diagram language* should be developed that allows to specify diagrams of connected components. Ideally such a language should also support dynamic evolution of diagrams, i.e. creation, deletion, and reconfiguration of components. Some ideas concerning static diagram languages have been presented in [Fia97].

References

[AZ95]   E. Astesiano and E. Zucca. D-oids: A model for dynamic data types. *Math. Struct. in Comp. Sci.*, 5(2):257–282, 1995.

[BG77]   R. M. Burstall and J. A. Goguen. Putting theories together to make specifications. In *Proc. Int. Conf. Artificial Intelligence*, 1977.

[BT96]   M. Bidoit and A. Tarlecki. Behavioural satisfaction and equivalence in concrete model categories. In *Proc. CAAP'96*, Springer LNCS 1059. 1996.

[CGW95]   I. Claßen, M. Große-Rhode, and U. Wolter. Categorical concepts for parameterized partial specifications. *Math. Struct. in Comp. Science*, 5(2):153–188, 1995.

[DG94]   P. Dauchy and M.C. Gaudel. Algebraic specifications with implicit states. *Tech. Report, Univ. Paris Sud*, 1994.

[EM85]   H. Ehrig and B. Mahr. *Fundamentals of Algebraic Specification 1: Equations and Initial Semantics*, volume 6 of *EATCS Monographs on Theoretical Computer Science*. Springer, Berlin, 1985.

[FM92]   J. Fiadeiro and T. Maibaum. Temporal theories as modularisation units for concurrent system specifications. *Formal Aspects of Computing*, 4(3):239–272, 1992.

[Fia97]   J.L. Fiadeiro. Algebraic semantics of coordination. Talk given at the 12th Workshop on Algebraic Development Techniques, Tarquinia, Italy, 1997.

[GB92]   J. A. Goguen and R. M. Burstall. Institutions: Abstract Model Theory for Specification and Programming. *Journals of the ACM*, 39(1):95–146, January 1992.

[Gro96]   M. Große-Rhode. First steps towards an institution of algebra replacement systems. Technical Report 96-44, Technische Universität Berlin, 1996. Also available under http://tfs.cs.tu-berlin.de/~ mgr.

[Gro97]   M. Große-Rhode. Sequential and parallel algebra transformation systems and their composition. Technical Report 97-07, Università di Roma *La Sapienza*, Dip. Scienze dell'Informazione, 1997. Also available under http://tfs.cs.tu-berlin.de/~ mgr.

[Gur94]   Y. Gurevich. Evolving algebra 1993. In E. Börger, editor, *Specification and Validation Methods*. Oxford University Press, 1994.

[ODP]   ISO/IEC International Standard 10746, ITU–T Recommendation X.901–X.904: Reference model of open distributed processing – Parts 1–4.

[Rei87]   H. Reichel. *Initial Computability, Algebraic Specifications, and Partial Algebras*. Oxford University Press, Oxford, 1987.

[WN95]   G. Winskel and M. Nielson. Models for concurrency. In *Handbook of Logic in Computer Science*. Oxford University Press, 1995.

[Zuc96]   E. Zucca. From static to dynamic abstract data–types. In W.Penczek and A. Szałas, editors, *Mathematical Foundations of Computer Science 1996*, volume 1113 of *Lecture Notes in Computer Science*, pages 579–590. Springer Verlag, 1996.

Navigation Expressions in Object-Oriented Modelling

Ali Hamie, John Howse, Stuart Kent
Division of Computing,
University of Brighton, Lewes Rd., Brighton, UK.
http://www.biro.brighton.ac.uk/index.html
biro@brighton.ac.uk[1]

Abstract. In component-based development, object-oriented modelling notations such as UML are being proposed as a way of providing richer specifications of components. Much more so than in bespoke software development, this requires a high level of precision coupled with sufficient expressive power. Expressive power is delivered by adding textual annotations, such as invariants, pre & post conditions, to diagrams. Navigation expressions, which identify collections of objects by navigating associations, are central to making such annotations precise. We give a semantics to navigation expressions as they are used in recently proposed extensions to object-oriented modelling notations *in widespread use by practitioners*. The semantics is given using Larch (essentially FOPL), which makes it as accessible as possible while enabling some support for reasoning. The semantics helps to clarify some subtle issues to do with navigation expressions, including the meaning of navigating across collections (sets, bags and sequences) as opposed to just single objects, and the use of filters on collections within expressions.

1 Introduction

Modern object-oriented modelling notations, such as UML [19], [7], are based on graphical notations for expressing a wide variety of concepts which are relevant to a problem domain. While these notations are intuitive and easy to understand by users, they lack expressive power. Kent [15] shows that in order to write some constraints on the behaviour of a system it is necessary to step outside the diagrams and write them textually. Navigation expressions are critical to making these textual languages precise, which we argue is essential to enable the current advance of software engineering towards component-based development. Semantics of such languages, hence navigation expressions, will be required to (a) check the integrity of the language and (b) support the development of CASE tools.

For bespoke software development, it is possible in many cases to get by with informal, imprecise annotations. This is because models are often discarded at the end of a development, because short-term economic pressure mitigates against them being maintained and kept up to date as the code is developed and tested: Why spend a lot of time making these models precise if they are only going to be thrown away? Of course, putting the effort into making them more precise and then maintaining them would likely pay off in the long term, as precision early in the development cycle is likely to lead to cleaner designs and code and less need for testing. As documentation such models can be invaluable, as they avoid implementation detail, allowing maintainers to uncover the essence of the software design more quickly.

---

1. This research is partially funded by the UK EPSRC under grant number GR/K67304

In component-based development (CBD), however, the requirement for precision cannot be so lightly discarded. Object-oriented modelling notations are being proposed (e.g. [18], [1]) as an approach to documenting component interfaces in a more accessible and more detailed form than is the case in CBD technologies such as Microsoft's COM, the Object Management Group's (OMG) CORBA and SunSoft's Java Beans, which rely upon a list of operations with their signatures, accompanied with some informal, though not necessarily informative, descriptions. The need for precision and formality when using these notations, both diagrams and text, for CBD is elaborated in [18] and [16]. Precise, expressive specifications are required to facilitate searching and matching of components and component assembly. Precision is essential for the automation of these processes. A user of a component will require a certificate giving her confidence that the component does what is claimed. This is especially important when components are "black box", where the design and implementation is not supplied. Confidence in certificates will only be achieved if appropriate techniques are used. This means, for example, the use of precise models at all levels of the construction process, enabling the implementation to be traced back to the specification and conformance of the implementation against the specification to be checked. In other words a rigorous approach to refinement should be supported.

CBD also increases the importance of specification models. Components must be described in business (requirements) oriented terms rather than implementation oriented terms, as the focus is always on using the component rather than on how it works. Indeed, often there may be a considerable mismatch between the specification and implementation. Combined with a need for precision and expressiveness, this has led to the extension of diagrammatic notations such as UML with a precise textual language for expressing pre/post conditions and invariants, where the latter allow modellers to abstract away from implementation detail. Syntropy [4] extends OMT [17] with a Z-like textual language for adding invariants to class diagrams and annotating transitions on state diagrams with pre/post conditions. Catalysis [5], [6] does something very similar for UML, adopting an arguably simpler and more usable approach. The Catalysis and Syntropy notations have now been superseded with the Object Constraint Language (OCL) which has recently become part of the UML standard.

Semantics work [2], [3], [8] for OO modelling notations in widespread use, such as OMT or UML, is generally restricted to capturing the meaning of those notations, so navigation expressions are not considered, as they are not officially part of those notations at least as far as their use in pre/post conditions and invariants are concerned. The semantics of the extensions is at best rigorous. For example in [4] the semantics comprises six pages of informal text interleaved with examples.[1] The semantics given for Catalysis in [5] and [6] is similarly informal. A key result of this paper is to check this intuitive semantics. One specific result is to show that the introduction of so-called "flat sets" in the semantics, as suggested in [6], is not necessary.

The focus of this paper, then, is on the use of navigation expressions in writing invariants, pre and post conditions in UML extended with a precise textual language. As the work in this paper was completed before the publication of OCL in the UML 1.1. standard, we use the textual language of Catalysis, one of its immediate predecessors. However, the

---

1. Recently, a semantics has been given for a part of Syntropy ([2]) but only cursory coverage of navigation expressions is given.

work is applicable to any precise textual language which uses navigation expressions. Indeed, since the original submission of this paper we have been using the work presented here as a basis for the semantics of OCL [14].

The semantics is characterised in terms of the Larch Shared language (LSL) [11] which is essentially a syntax for writing and composing theories in many-sorted first order predicate logic with equality. This follows a well-rehearsed approach to semantics, dating back at least to Burstall and Goguen [9], whereby specifications are given a semantics in terms of (compositions of) theories of some logic.

Larch is a mature language which comes with a toolset including a sophisticated proof assistant. The choice of Larch was motivated by the desire not to be engaged in the design of logics and reasoning systems, but instead to focus on elaborating the meaning of the modelling notations themselves in a way that is widely accessible. It was also chosen because it supports a compositional approach to semantics [13].

Section 2 is an informal introduction to navigation in object-oriented modelling. Section 3 establishes the semantic framework by giving a semantics to class diagrams and associations. Section 4 defines the semantics of navigation expressions, considering in turn the use of navigation expressions in invariants, the semantics of filters, the use of navigation expressions in pre and post conditions, and the semantics of navigation expressions considering navigation over collections other than sets, in particular sequences and bags. Section 5 defines the general mapping of class diagrams in UML and terms in the Catalysis textual language to expressions in Larch.

2 Navigation in Object Oriented Modelling

In order to understand what is meant by navigation in object oriented modelling, it is necessary first to understand what is an object oriented model, which essentially comprises two parts:

- a generic model, which is made up of a collection of diagrams and textual annotations modelling the general behaviour of a system, usually a software system;
- one or more specific models, each a collection of diagrams illustrating specific examples of system behaviour.

In UML, the language of choice for this paper, the class diagram is central to any generic model. An example of this for a simple course scheduling system is given in Figure 1. This is a system for scheduling *presentations* of *courses* to a collection of *students*, with *instructors* who must be *qualified for* the course in question. As this is a specification model, the boxes are interpreted as types or interfaces, rather than classes, as they carry no implementation information. A full description of the notation can be found in [19] or [7]. The diagram is best explained by giving an example of (part of) a specific model. Figure 2 is an object diagram depicting an example state of the system at a particular point in time. It includes objects, depicted by boxes, and links. For this to be a specific model of the generic model described in part by Figure 1, the types of objects, indicated by :Type, must be of a type mentioned in the class diagram, and the links must correspond to (appropriately labelled) associations. Furthermore, the number of links between objects must obey the cardinality constraints imposed by the class diagram. For example, the latter states that a course may have zero, one or many qualified instructors (shown by a * appearing at the end labelled *qualified* of the association between Course and Instructor). This is clearly

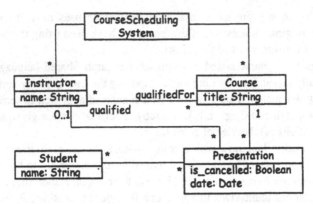

Figure 1: Class diagram for a course scheduling system

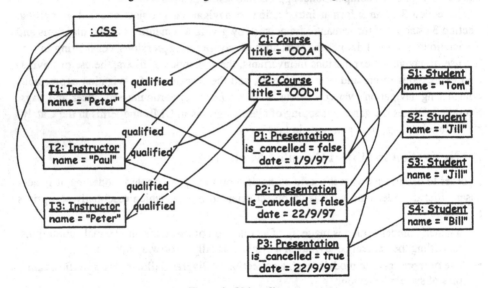

Figure 2: Object diagram

the case in the object diagram. It also states that a presentation may have at most one instructor: there are two presentations each linked to exactly one instructor and one with no link to an instructor. And so on. Objects on an object diagram may be given an explicit identity, to make it easy to refer to them in any explanation. Here, I1, I2, etc. are object identities. The only object without an identity is the one of type CSS (short for Course-SchedulingSystem). Values of attributes may also be shown on an object diagram and these should, of course, correspond to the attribute declarations in the class diagram. Thus the class diagram may be thought of as defining a set of object diagrams, namely the ones which are consistent in the way described. It identifies the types of object allowed in the system, and, via associations, the kind and number of links. It also identifies attributes that objects can have with their return types.

Navigation in OO modelling means following links from one object to locate another object. It is possible to navigate across many links, or navigate from a collection to a collection. *Navigation expressions* allow us to write in generic models constraints on the behaviour of objects identified by navigating from the object or objects which are the focus of the constraint. At the specification level, the expressions appear in invariants, pre and post conditions. Examples of these will be given later; for this section we'll just consider basic navigation expressions in isolation.

In order to write a navigation expression we must start with an object of known type and we must have a way of referring to that object. Given the object type Course, a declaration as c:Course means that c is a variable that can refer to an object taken from the set of objects conforming to type Course. Here, the type name is used to represent the set of objects in the model that conforms to the type. A navigation expression is written using ".", an attribute or role name, and an optional parameter list. Given this declaration, the expression c.title represents the value of the attribute title for the object represented by c, namely, the title of course c. In this case the navigation expression yields a value of type String, which means that it is not possible to navigate any further. For example, if the variable c is assigned to the object C1 in the object diagram then the meaning of the expression c.title is the string "OOA".

Given the declaration i:Instructor, the expression i.qualifiedFor denotes the set of courses associated with instructor i. If the variable i is assigned to the object I2 then the meaning of the expression i.qualifiedFor is the set {C1, C2} consisting of C1 and C2. If the value of a navigation expression is another object or set of objects then we could navigate on to their attributes. In this case, the value of the expression i.qualifiedFor is a set of objects; any subsequent navigation must be applied to each member of the set and the result is a set constructed from the set of objects located. For example, the expression i.qualifiedFor.title yields a set of strings, namely {"OOA", "OOD"}. In this case the attribute title is applied to the set i.qualifiedFor (using the "." operator) and the result is a set whose members are the results of applying title to the members of i.qualifiedFor.

In Syntropy, Catalysis and now OCL is the idea of navigating across collections. For example, the expression i.qualifiedFor.presentations represents the set whose members are all the Presentation objects which can be got by traversing qualifiedFor and presentations. This is obtained by evaluating the expression i.qualifiedFor yielding a set of Course objects, then by navigating from each member of this set using presentations, to obtain a set of sets of Presentation objects. The resulting set is the union of these sets. Thus if i is I2 then i.qualifiedFor.presentations is the set {P1,P2,P3}, whereas if i is I1, the set is {P1,P2}, i.e. the presentations associated with course C1 only.

Another navigation expression which may occur is s[pred], where s is a set and pred is a boolean predicate. This expression denotes the set of members in the set s for which the predicate pred is true. That is, the set s is *filtered* using the predicate pred. In Figure 1, the expression c.presentations is the set of presentations for a course c. The expression c.presentations[is_cancelled] is the set of all presentations of course c, for which is_cancelled is true, i.e. the set of cancelled presentations. For example, if c is assigned to the object C2 then the meaning of the expression c.presentations[is_cancelled] is the singleton set {P3}.

The above describes navigation solely in terms of sets. More generally, navigation may occur over collections, including bags and sequences. This is discussed more fully in Section 4.4. Another extension of navigation expressions, as described, is to use them to constrain operation invocations, for example on state diagrams or sequence diagrams. This is similar to the way in which navigation expressions are used in OO programming, and is not the focus of this paper.

3 Interpreting Class Diagrams

As explained in the introduction, we use the *Larch Shared Language* (LSL) [11] to illustrate how object types, associations, and navigation expressions are incorporated into structured specification. LSL uses specification modules, called *traits*, to describe abstract data types and theories. Traits are presented in the following form:

SpecName(*parameters*) : **trait**
   includes
         existing specification modules to be used
   introduces
         function signatures are listed here
   asserts
         axioms are listed here

SpecName is the name of the specification module or trait (not the name of a sort). Following the name, is the list of *sorts* and *operators* that form the parameters of the trait. The *includes* section lists other traits on which the specification is built. The *introduces* section lists a set of *operators* (function identifiers) together with their *signatures* (the sorts of their domain and ranges). Overloading of operators is allowed in LSL. All operators used in a trait must be declared so that *terms* can be sort-checked in the same way as function calls are type-checked in programming languages. The *asserts* section lists the axioms that constrain the operators expressed in first-order predicate logic with equality. An equation consists of two terms of the same sort, separated by "==". If one term of an equation is "true" then the equation can be abbreviated to just the other term. When using LSL, it is assumed that a basic axiomatisation of Boolean algebra is part of every trait. This axiomatisation includes the sort Bool, the truth values true and false, the logical connectives "∧", "∨", "⇒" and "¬".

3.1 Object Types

An object type is a description of a set of objects in terms of properties and behaviour they all share. In our formalisation, an object type is associated with an LSL basic sort consisting of elements that uniquely represent objects (instances) of the type, which can be thought of as object identifiers. The attributes of an object type are formalised as functions with the appropriate signatures.

The object type *Course* in Figure 1 is interpreted as a basic sort denoted by Course, namely a sort of object identifiers. The attribute title[1] is interpreted as a function title with signature title : Course → String, which is added to the specification for object type *Course*. The type String is interpreted as the sort of strings String. The definition of attribute functions varies with the system states, so no additional constraints are required.

According to the above description, the specification of the object type *Course* has only two sorts: Course and String. The only function is the attribute function title on Course. Hence, the simple specification given in Figure 3 is derived.

---

1. Alternatively, we can represent an attribute as a value of the sort of finite maps, e.g.
title : Map[Course, String]

Object-Type-Course: **trait**
    includes
        Type-String
    introduces
        title: Course → String

Figure 3: specification of object type *Course* with attribute title

The trait Type-String specifies the sort of strings String, which is available in the Larch HandBook of specification modules [11]. Any constraints on the attribute title are expressed as axioms on the function title in the *asserts* section of the trait. In a very similar way we interpret the other object types for the course administration system.

3.2 Associations

We now extend the interpretation of object types and attributes given in the previous section to include binary associations. We interpret associations between object types as two related mappings that map an object of one type to the set of associated objects of another (or the same) type. These mappings are specified in a way that is independent of the structure of types they associate. Thus we have a generic Larch theory for associations that can be renamed to specify each particular association in the model.

The many-many association between Instructor and Course (Figure 1) has two role names qualified and qualifiedFor. Intuitively, the role name qualifiedFor of the association is a mapping that maps an object i of type Instructor to a set of objects of type Course that are associated with i. In some navigation expressions the role name qualifiedFor is also used to map a set of instructors to a set of courses. In our formalisation, this association would be represented as two mappings qualified and qualifiedFor with the following signatures:

$$qualified : Set[Course] \rightarrow Set[Instructor]$$

$$qualifiedFor : Set[Instructor] \rightarrow Set[Course]$$

where Set[Course] and Set[Instructor] are the power sorts of Course and Instructor respectively. By choosing power sorts for the domains and ranges of these mappings, we have a uniform treatment of associations which simplifies the formalisation and provides generic theory for associations. The case where navigation is from a single object is subsumed with the general case where the set is a singleton containing that object. In addition, the corresponding mappings that map single objects can be defined in terms of those that map sets of objects (see later). A similar approach for formalising associations as two related mappings is presented in [10].

The two mappings qualified and qualifiedFor satisfy the axioms:

$$qualified(\{\}) == \{\}$$
$$qualifiedFor(\{\}) == \{\}$$

$$qualified(s \cup s') == qualified(s) \cup qualified(s')$$

$$qualifiedFor(s \cup s') == qualifiedFor(s) \cup qualifiedFor(s')$$

The operation $\cup$ is the union operation on sets, and $\{\}$ is the empty set. These axioms imply that these functions are completely determined by their values at singleton sets.

In order to represent the association, these functions must also be related. This relationship is expressed by the following axiom:

$$c \in \text{qualifiedFor}(\{i\}) == i \in \text{qualified}(\{c\})$$

Intuitively, this axiom asserts that if instructor i is qualified to teach course c, then i must be included in the set of instructors qualified to teach c.

The corresponding functions that operate on single objects may be constructed from those whose domains are power sorts as follows:

$$\text{qualified}(c) == \text{qualified}(\{c\})$$

$$\text{qualifiedFor}(i) == \text{qualifiedFor}(\{i\})$$

Semantically, navigating from a single object is equivalent to navigating from a singleton set containing that object. Note that we are overloading the function names which is allowed by LSL.[1]

A trait for the association between **Instructor** and **Course** is presented in Figure 4.

Association-qualified-qualifiedFor: **trait**
   includes
      Set(Instructor), Set(Course)
   introduces
      qualified : Set[Course] → Set[Instructor]
      qualified : Course → Set[Instructor]
      qualifiedFor : Set[Instructor] → Set[Course]
      qualifiedFor : Instructor → Set[Course]
   asserts
      ∀i:Instructor, c:Course, s,s':Set[Course], t, t' : Set[Instructor]
      qualified({}) == {}
      qualifiedFor({}) == {}
      c ∈ qualifiedFor({i}) == i ∈ qualified({c})
      qualified(c) == qualified({c})
      qualifiedFor(i) == qualifiedFor({i})

Figure 4: Specification of the association between Instructor and Course

Multiplicity constraints on roles can be interpreted quite easily in terms of the mappings that represent them by imposing a limit on the cardinality of the obtained sets. For further details and for the generic traits of types and associations the reader is referred to [12] and [13].

4 Interpreting Navigation Expressions

In this section we extend the object type, attributes, and association semantics given in the previous section to include navigation expressions. Navigation expressions are actually interpreted as terms (or expressions) over the signatures of object types and associations specifications.

4.1 Invariants

We start with simple expressions. The expression c.title represents the title of the course denoted by c. In our language this expression is interpreted as title(c) that is, the operator "." is interpreted as the application operator. Parameterised attributes can also be interpreted in a similar way.

---

1. An alternative way is to define the functions that operate on sets in terms of those that operate of single elements as:
    qualified({}) == {}
    qualified(insert(c, s)) == qualified(c) ∪ qualified(s)
where { } denotes the empty set, insert(c, s) denotes the set obtained by adding c to the set s.

An expression with a role name such as *i.qualifiedFor* is interpreted as qualifiedFor(i) or equivalently qualifiedFor({i}). When a navigation expression yields another object or a set of objects, then it is possible to navigate on to their attributes. In the case where the result is a set of objects, any subsequent navigation must be applied to each member of the set and the result is a set of values constructed from the attributes of each of the objects located. For example, the expression *i.qualifiedFor.title* yields a set of strings. In this case the attribute *title* is applied to the set *i.qualifiedFor* (using the "." operator) and the result is a set whose members are the results of applying *title* to the members of *i.qualifiedFor*. It is clear that we cannot interpret this expression as title(qualifiedFor(i)) since the attribute *title* is interpreted as a function that operate on single objects. What we need is to define a function that takes a set as argument and returns a set obtained by applying *title* to each member of the argument set. For this, we introduce the function $mapSet_{title}$ with the signature: $mapSet_{title}$: Set[Course] → Set[String] satisfying the axioms:

$$mapSet_{title}(\{\}) = \{\}$$
$$mapSet_{title}(insert(c, s)) = insert(title(c), mapSet_{title}(s))$$

Function symbols can be overloaded, so we can use *title* instead of $mapSet_{title}$. Now the expression *i.qualifiedFor.title* is interpreted simply as title(qualifiedFor(i)).

The expression *i.qualifiedFor.presentations* represents the set whose members are all the objects of **Presentation** which can be obtained by evaluating the expression *i.qualifiedFor* yielding a set of *Course*'s objects, and then by navigating from each member of this set using **presentations** to obtain a set of sets of **Presentation**'s objects. Taking the union of these sets we obtain the resulting set. This expression is interpreted as presentations(qualifiedFor(i)).

4.2 Filters

Navigation expressions of the form *s[pred]*, where *s* is a set and *pred* is a boolean predicate, denotes the set of members in the set *s* for which the predicate *pred* is true. That is, the set *s* is filtered using the predicate *pred*. In Figure 1, the expression *c.presentations* is the set of presentations for a course *c*. The expression *c.presentations[is_cancelled]* is the set of all presentations of course *c*, for which *is_cancelled* is true, i.e. the set of cancelled presentations. Formally, the attribute *is_cancelled* is represented by the function: is_cancelled : Presentation → Bool. Now, we define a function filter with the signature: filter : Set[Presentation] → Set[Presentation] satisfying the axioms:

```
filter({}) = {}
filter(insert(p, s)) = if is_cancelled(p) then insert(p, filter(s))
                       else filter(s)
```

Intuitively, filter(s) returns the elements of *s* that satisfy the predicate is_cancelled. This can be easily generalised to predicates with several arguments.

The navigation expression *c.presentations[is_cancelled]* is interpreted as filter(presentations(c)). The expression *c.presentations[is_cancelled].students* represents the set of students associated with the cancelled presentations for course *c* and is interpreted as `students(filter(presentations(c)))`, where `students` is the interpretation of the default role name **students**.

4.3 Pre and Post Conditions

So far we have interpreted object types, associations and navigation expressions statically. However, when specifying actions or operations on an object type it is necessary to refer to the values of an attribute (say) before and after the action is executed. In some modelling notations $\bar{f}$, old(f) are used to refer to the value of attribute f before the action is executed and f is used to refer to the value after the execution. In our formalisation, we introduce a sort Σ to represent the system states. Attributes of a given object type are interpreted as functions with additional argument for the system states. For example, the attribute **title** is now interpreted as a function `title` with the signature: $\texttt{title} : \texttt{Course}, \Sigma \rightarrow \texttt{String}$ where the expression $\texttt{title}(c, \sigma)$ is the title of the course c in the state σ. If σ and σ' are the states before and after an action is executed respectively, then $\texttt{title}(c, \sigma)$ and $\texttt{title}(c, \sigma')$ is the title of course c before and after this action is executed respectively.

Associations are also interpreted as two related functions as in the previous section, with an additional argument for the system state. The trait that specifies the association between **Instructor** and **Course** is given in Figure 5.

Association-qualified-qualifiedFor: **trait**
  includes
    Set(Instructor), Set(Course)
  introduces
    qualified : Set[Course], $\Sigma \rightarrow$ Set[Instructor]
    qualified : Course, $\Sigma \rightarrow$ Set[Instructor]
    qualifiedFor : Set[Instructor], $\Sigma \rightarrow$ Set[Course]
    qualifiedFor : Instructor, $\Sigma \rightarrow$ Set[Course]
  asserts
    $\forall$i:Instructor, c:Course, s,s':Set[Course], t, t' : Set[Instructor], σ:Σ
    qualified({}, σ) $==$ {}
    qualifiedFor({}, σ) $==$ {}
    qualified(s $\cup$ s', σ) $==$ qualified(s, σ) $\cup$ qualified(s', σ)
    qualifiedFor(t $\cup$ t', σ) $==$ qualifiedFor(t, σ) $\cup$ qualifiedFor(t', σ)
    c $\in$ qualifiedFor({i}, σ) $==$ i $\in$ qualified({c}, σ)
    qualified(c, σ) $==$ qualified({c}, σ)
    qualifiedFor(i, σ) $==$ qualifiedFor({i}, σ)

Figure 5: Specification of the association between Instructor and Course

The interpretation of navigation expressions in this case is very similar to the interpretation given in the previous section where a new state parameter is added to the functions interpreting navigation expressions. For example, Figure 6 gives the specification of an action *assignInstructor* in terms of *pre/post* conditions. The navigation expressions in the *pre* and *post* conditions are interpreted as the following expressions respectively:

$$(\texttt{instructor}(p, \sigma) = \{\}) \wedge (\texttt{course}(p, \sigma) \subseteq \texttt{qualifiedFor}(i, \sigma))$$

$$\texttt{instructor}(p, \sigma') = \{i\}$$

where σ and σ' are the states before and after the action is executed respectively.

4.4 Navigation Expressions Involving Bags and Sequences

In some cases s.f, where s is a set and f is an attribute, could be interpreted as a bag (rather than a set) of values (e.g., as in Syntropy). To use the same notation could lead to ambigu-

assignInstructor(p : Presentation, i : Instructor)	-- assigns instructor 'i' to give presentation 'p'	
<u>pre:</u> p.instructor = nil	-- an instructor is not already assigned	
∧ p.course ∈ i.qualifiedFor	-- the instructor is qualified to give the course	
<u>post:</u> p.instructor = i	-- 'i' is assigned to give presentation 'p'	

Figure 6: A partial specification of action assignInstructor

ity. For this reason we propose to use the notation $s._{bag}f$ for expressions with bags as results. To interpret such expressions we define a mapping mapSet_f that maps sets into bags using the function representing the attribute f. This mapping has the following signature $\text{mapSet}_f : \text{Set[A]} \rightarrow \text{Bag[A]}$, where Bag[A] is the sort of bags of A's elements, and satisfies the following axioms:

$$\text{mapSet}_f(\{\}) == \text{nil}$$
$$\text{mapSet}_f(\text{insert}(e, s)) == \text{insert}(f(e), \text{mapSet}_f(s))$$

where nil represents the empty bag and the function f represents the attribute f. The expression $s._{bag}f$ is interpreted as $\text{mapSet}_f(s)$ where s interprets the set s. In a similar way we interpret expressions $s._{seq}f$ yielding sequences as results.[1]

In most cases navigating an association yields a set. However, some associations have constraints that specify the order of objects obtained. For instance, we can use constraints to specify a sequence, a bag or a sort order.

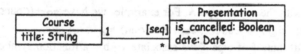

Figure 7: Association with sequence constraint

Figure 7 shows a modified association between the types **Course** and **Presentation** with a constraint that specifies a sequence indicated by the annotation [seq]. This means that navigating from an object of type **Course** via the association yields a sequence of objects of type **Presentation**. Formally, we interpret the role name **presentations** as a function with the signature[2]:presentations : Course → Seq[Presentation], where Seq[Presentation] is the sort of sequences with elements from the sort Presentation.

The relationship between the two functions course and presentations is expressed by the following axiom:

$$p \in \text{presentations}(c) == c \in \text{course}(p)$$

where the ∈ used on the left of the equation is the membership function on sequences.

The expression **c.presentations.is_cancelled** is the sequence of results obtained by applying the attribute **is_cancelled** to every member of the sequence **c.presentations**. To interpret this expression, we define the function mapSeq with the signature: mapSeq : Seq[Presentation] → Seq[Bool] and satisfying the axioms:

$$\text{mapSeq}(\text{nil}) == \text{nil}$$
$$\text{mapSeq}(\text{insert}(p, s)) == \text{insert}(\text{is\_cancelled}(p), \text{mapSeq}(s))$$

---

1.   An alternative approach would be to interpret expressions of the form $s.f$ as yielding sequences, and then using appropriate coercion functions to obtain sets or bags as results.
2.   An alternative way is to represent sequences as totally ordered sets

where `nil` denotes the empty sequence and `insert(p, s)` is the sequence obtained by adding the element p to the sequence s.

Associations with constraints that specify bags are interpreted in a similar way.

4.5 Subtyping and Navigation

Subtyping is a special relationship between two object types, known as the *is-a* relationship. An assertion that type B is a subtype of type A implies that objects that conform to type B inherit all the attributes and associations of the supertype A, and can be used in contexts where objects of type A are expected. Navigation expressions involving subtypes are interpreted in exactly the same way we interpret expressions involving supertypes. To do this we must provide an interpretation of the subtype, its attributes and associations. See [12] for details.

5 The Denotation Mappings

In interpreting the type diagrams of a model we associate with any object type name A a sort in Larch of all possible object identities that conform to the type, denoted by A. Let Type be the set of types given in a type diagram of a modelling notation. We assume that the set Type includes object types (*mutable*) and value types (*immutable*). Let Sort be the set of sorts in LSL. We define a mapping that associates with every type in the modelling notation a sort in Larch: $sort : Type \rightarrow Sort$ by $sort(A) =_{def} A$. That is, $sort(A)$ is the sort associated with the object type A. For example, we have $sort(Course) =_{def} Course$, $sort(Instructor) =_{def} Instructor$, $sort(Boolean) =_{def} Bool$, etc..

For each attribute f of type T we associate with it a function symbol denoted by f. Let Attributes be the set of attributes of an object type A, and let Functions be the set of function symbols in LSL, then we define: $Fun : Attributes \rightarrow Functions$ where $Fun(f:T) =_{def} f : A, \Sigma \rightarrow T$. If the type A has a parameterised attribute $g(S):T$ of type T, then we have: $Fun(g(S):T) =_{def} g : A, S, \Sigma \rightarrow T$.

Let Associations be the set of association symbols in the type diagram, then for association roles we define a similar mapping: $Fun : Associations \rightarrow Functions$ where $Fun(r:set[B]) =_{def} r : set[A], \Sigma \rightarrow set[B]$.

In a similar way we deal with parameterised association roles. The table in Figure 8 summarizes the above mappings.

Modelling Notation	Description	LSL
A	object type (mutable)	A (sort of object identities)
T	value type (immutable)	T (sort of values)
f : T	attribute of type T, for object type A	$f : A, \Sigma \rightarrow T$
g(S) : T	parameterised attribute of type T, for object type A	$g : A, S, \Sigma \rightarrow T$
r : set[B]	association role with set result for object type A	$r : Set[A], \Sigma \rightarrow Set[B]$
r (S) : set[B]	parameterised association role with set result	$r : Set[A], S, \Sigma \rightarrow Set[B]$
r : B	association role with single result for type A	$r : Set[A], \Sigma \rightarrow Set[B]$
r (S) : B	parameterised association role with single result	$r : Set[A], S, \Sigma \rightarrow Set[B]$

Figure 8: Mappings of types, attributes and associations

We now define a mapping that maps navigation expressions to LSL expressions based on the above mappings. Let NExpressions the set of navigation expressions and LExpressions be the set of LSL expressions. We define L : NExpressions → LExpressions. The definition of L is given in Figure 9. The interpretation of a navigation expression as given by L is given at a moment in time corresponding to a system state σ. In this definition variables are mapped into variables in LSL, and expressions of the form a.f are mapped to f(a, σ). Expressions of the form s.f, where s is a set and f is an attribute, are mapped to mapSet$_f$(s, σ), where s is the interpretation of the set expression s, i.e. L(s) = s, which satisfies the following axioms:

```
mapSet_f({}, σ) == {}
mapSet_f(insert(a, s), σ) == insert(f(a, σ), mapSet_f(s, σ))
```

Expressions of the form s.r where r (r : Set[B]) is an association role are mapped to r(s, σ), where s is the interpretation of the set expression s, i.e. L(s) = s. Note that in this case we obtain a set rather than a set of sets because of the interpretation of association roles is different from the interpretation of attributes. If on the other hand we treat association roles as attributes, then the expression r(s, σ) yields a set of sets obtained by applying the function r to each element of the set s. However, in order to obtain the desired result namely a set of objects of type B, the obtained set of sets need to be flattened by taking the union of all its elements. Therefore, it is always necessary to distinguish between association roles and attributes when interpreting navigation expressions. In Catalysis [5], [6] where an association is considered to be a pair of related attributes, a notion of *flat* sets is introduced when navigating via association roles, which does not seem to be strictly necessary in our formalisation.

Filter expressions of the form s[p] where s is a set and p is a boolean predicate are mapped to filter$_p$(s, σ), where s is the interpretation of the set expression s, i.e. L(s) = s, which satisfies the following axioms:

```
filter_p({}, σ) == {}
filter_p(insert(p, s), σ) == if p(a, σ) then insert(a, filter_p(s, σ)) else
                             filter_p(s, σ)
```

Other value expressions such as sets, boolean values, sequences, bags can be mapped directly since value types can be specified algebraically.

NExpressions	Description	LExpressions
a	variable	a (variable)
a.f	a variable, f attribute of type T	f(a, σ)
s.f	s set, f attribute of type T	mapSet$_f$(s, σ), where (L(s) = s)
a.r	a variable, r association role	r(a, σ)
s.r	s set, r association role	r(s, σ), where (L(s) = s)
s[p]	s set, p boolean predicate	filter$_p$(s, σ), where (L(s) = s)

Figure 9: Definition of the mapping L

6 Conclusions

A semantics has been provided for navigation expressions, which are essential to making object-oriented modelling notations precise. The semantics is given as theories in the Larch Shared Language, and a systematic mapping from class diagrams, with accompanying textual language, to Larch expressions has been defined. The semantics covers the use of navigation expressions in invariants, pre and post conditions, and handles not only navigation across single objects but also navigation across collections of objects, including sets, sequences and bags. Filters within navigation expressions have also been considered.

This work provides the basis for a semantics for UML incorporating OCL. Since this paper was originally submitted, this work has been further developed towards a semantics for OCL [14]. This will pave the way for giving a semantics to state diagrams, which state diagrammatically some of what otherwise can be said using class diagrams and pre/post conditions, and sequence diagrams. These will involve extending the semantics to deal with navigation expressions used to refer to operation invocations (This is the way navigation expressions are used in programming, and is similar to those expressions whose final segment is an attribute.). The semantics can also be used as a basis for the semantics of "Constraint Diagrams" in [15] which allow invariants and pre/post conditions to be visualised diagrammatically.

In the short term, the main purpose of the semantics work is to clarify concepts and refine notation. In the medium to long term we are interested in using it to develop CASE tools which are able, for example, to check the integrity of models and check conformance between models. This needs specific semantic support, so for example, we are currently working out the semantics of refinement in the OO/UML setting, that is checking the conformance of design and implementation models against specification models; and working on a compositional semantics [13], to support assembly of components through their specifications.

Acknowledgements

We gratefully acknowledge the support of the UK EPSRC under grant number GR/K67304. We thank Richard Mitchell and Franco Civello for their helpful comments.

References

1. Allen, P.: Components and Objects. Available at http://www.selectst.com/download (1997)

2. Bicarregui, J., Lano, K., Maibaum, T.S.E.: Objects, Associations and Subsystems: a hierarchical approach to encapsulation. Proceedings of ECOOP'97, LNCS Series, Springer-Verlag (1997)

3. Bordeau, H., Cheng, B.: A Formal Semantics for Object Model Diagrams. IEEE Transactions on Software Engineering, Vol. 21, No. 10 (1995)

4. Cook, S., Daniels, J.: Designing Object Systems: Object-Oriented Modelling with Syntropy. Prentice Hall (1994)

5. D'Souza, D., Wills, A.: Extending Fusion: practical rigor and refinement. R. Malan et al., OO Development at Work, Prentice Hall (1996)

6. D'Souza, D., Wills, A.: Objects, Components and Frameworks with UML: The Catalysis Approach. Addison-Wesley, to appear 1998. Draft and other related material available at http://www.trireme.com/catalysis

7. Fowler, M., Scott, K.: UML Distilled. Addison-Wesley (1997)

8. France, R., Bruel, J., Larrondo-Petrie, M., Shroff., M.: Exploring The Semantics of UML Type Structures with Z. Proceedings of International Workshop on Formal Methods for Object-based Distributed Systems (FMOODS), Chapman and Hall (1997)

9. Burstall R., Goguen J.: Putting theories together to make specifications. In Reddy R. (ed.) Proc. IJCAI 77, (1977) 1045-1058.

10. Graham, I., Bischof, J., Henderson-Sellers, B.: Associations considered a bad thing. Journal of Object-Oriented Programming, SIGS Publications, February (1997)

11. Guttag, J., Horning, J.: Larch: Languages and Tools for Formal Specifications. Springer-Verlag (1993)

12. Hamie, A., Howse, J.: Interpreting Syntropy in Larch. Technical Report ITCM97/C1, University of Brighton (1997)

13. Hamie, A., Howse, J., Kent, S.: Compositional Semantics of Object-Oriented Modelling Notations. Evans, A. and Lano, K., Making Object-Oriented Methods more Rigorous, LNCS Series, Springer Verlag, to appear (1998)

14. Hamie, A., Kent, S., Howse J.: A Semantics for OCL, submitted to ECOOP98 (1997)

15. Kent, S.: Constraint Diagrams: Visualising Invariants in Object-Oriented Models. Procs. of OOPSLA97, ACM Press, to appear (1997)

16. Kent, S., Lauder, A.: Rigorous Techniques in Component-Based Development. Evans, A. and Lano, K.: Making Object-Oriented Methods more Rigorous, LNCS Series, Springer Verlag, to appear (1998)

17. Rumbaugh, J., Blaha, M., Premerali, W., Eddy, F, Lorensen, W.: Object-Oriented Modelling and Design. Prentice Hall (1991)

18. Short, K.: Component Based Development and Object Modeling. Available from http://www.cool.sterling.com/cbd (1997)

19. UML Consortium: The Unified Modeling Language Version 1.1. Available from http://www.rational.com (1997)

Compositional Verification of Reactive Systems Specified by Graph Transformation[*]

Reiko Heckel[1]

Dipartimento di Informatika, Università degli Studi di Pisa,
Corso Italia, 40, I - 56125 Pisa, Italia, e-mail: reiko@di.unipi.it

Abstract. A loose semantics for graph transformation rules which has been developed recently is used in this paper for the compositional verification of specifications. The main conceptual tool here is the notion of *view*, that is, an incomplete specification describing only a certain aspect of the overall system. A view anticipates the (potential) behavior of the complete system by its loose semantics. This ensures that properties of the view are inherited by the complete system.

Based on this result one may verify temporal properties by decomposing a specification into several views, analyzing them separately, and deriving the desired property from properties shown for the views.

1 Introduction

One of the most challenging problems in specifying reactive systems is the complexity of the development and verification of large specifications. An important approach to solve this problem is the separation of different aspects or *views*. They may be used to split a team of developers into subgroups specifying only that aspect of a system which is later responsible for a certain task or is seen and used by a certain type of user. In the software engineering field, this view-oriented approach is known by the notion of viewpoints (cf. e.g., [FKN+92]).

Reactive systems in the sense of [MP92] are distinguished by the complex interaction between the system and its environment (as opposed to classical programs which basically transform input to output). They include concurrent, object-oriented, or distributed systems like operating systems, process control systems, seat reservation systems, etc., typically consisting of several components which can be seen as reactive systems themselves.

Probably, the most natural representation of such a system is a *graph*, where nodes represent components (objects, processes, ...) and edges communication links. If the system's topology is dynamic (since e.g., components are created and deleted) some sort of *graph transformation* has to be performed. Among the

---

[*] Research supported by the TMR network GETGRATS and the ESPRIT BRWG APPLIGRAPH.

various possibilities of specifying the transformation of graphs, I prefer a rule-based approach which exploits the visual character of the graph representation for describing transformations. In particular, the "algebraic, Double Pushout (DPO) approach" is applied [EPS73,CMR$^+$97], which owes its name to the basic construction of a direct derivation step: This is modeled indeed by two gluing diagrams (i.e., pushouts) in the category of graphs and total graph morphisms.

In [EHTE97] a specification technique based on graph transformations has been presented which supports a view-based development approach. Since each view specifies only a part of the operations, it may be that a view operation is executed in parallel with operations of other views. Thus, a view operation specifies only what *at least* has to happen on a system's state, but it allows also additional effects which may be caused by the environment. In this sense, the semantics of a view is a loose one, in contrast to the semantics of the complete specification. A loose operational semantics for graph transformation rules, called *graph transitions* as opposed to direct derivations, has been developed in [HEWC97b] and used in [EHTE97] as the semantics of views.

Here, this loose semantics is exploited for compositional reasoning about reactive systems. The hope is that a meaningful decomposition of a specification into views reduces the complexity of the verification and, which seems equally important, that it allows to concentrate on the verification of the most important (e.g., safety-critical) aspects.

The general idea of compositionality through loose semantics can be traced back to several sources. In the area of algebraic specification a class of algebras forms the loose semantics of an incomplete specification, as opposed to a single (initial) algebra associated to a complete specification. Extending a specification (e.g., by adding equations) reduces its class of models [EM85]. Similar to the present approach is [MP92], where a loose interpretation of assignments in a shared variable languages (allowing for unspecified change of values) is used for compositional proofs of temporal properties.

The approach here is to verify temporal properties of a big specification by decomposing it into views and analyzing them separately. Then, the properties of the big specification are derived from properties of the views. The verification of properties of views is not addressed in this paper. The main technical result shows the correctness of this compositional verification approach, that is, temporal properties of the views remain valid in the complete specification. The technique is applied to a small case study specifying an algorithm for mutual exclusion and deadlock detection in a distributed system with dynamic topology.

2 Specifying a Distributed Algorithm with Graph Transformation Rules

The following specification of a distributed mutual exclusion (MUTEX) algorithm shall illustrate the expressive power of rule-based graph transformation and serves as running example throughout the paper. The ideas are standard in distributed computing and have been communicated to me through [Sch94].

Along with this specification the basic notions of the algebraic DPO approach to graph transformation [EPS73,CMR+97] are introduced.

Distributed MUTEX algorithms are used in (distributed) operating systems and data base systems. Their task is to ensure that a resource is never used by more than one process at a time. However, each request of a process for a resource must eventually be granted. Here the main problem is to prevent processes from running into a deadlock.

Graph transformation rules are used for specifying a MUTEX algorithm with deadlock detection for a variable number of processes and resources. The specification is presented in three views, the *system view* (SYS) specifying the creation and deletion of processes and resources, the *token ring view* (TR) ensuring mutual exclusion, and the *distributed deadlock detection view* (DDD) detecting and announcing deadlocks. All views share a common graph signature specifying the structure of system states. They use disjoint sets of graph transformation rules for describing the evolution of the system.

A *graph signature* is an algebraic signature $GS = \langle S, OP \rangle$ having only unary operation symbols $op : s \to s'$.[1] GS-Algebras and -homomorphisms are called *graphs* and *graph morphisms*, respectively.[2] The category of graphs and graph morphisms for a signature GS is denoted by $\mathcal{G}r(GS)$. In the MUTEX specification *type graphs* (in the sense of e.g., [HCEL96]) are used as a more intuitive, graphical notation for signatures.

Fig. 1. Type graph of *MUTEX* (left) and deadlock state (right)

Example 1. The type graph of the MUTEX specification is shown in the left of Figure 1. It may be read like an entity/relationship schema specifying the node and edge types which may occur in graphs modeling system states. *Processes* are drawn as black nodes and *resources* as light boxes. An edge from a process to a resource models a *request*. A solid edge in the opposite direction shows that the resource is currently *held_by* the process. A dashed edge from a resource to a process asks the process to *release* the resource.

The token ring is a cyclic list of processes, where an edge between two processes points to the *next* process. For each resource there is a *token*, represented

---

[1] Some basic notions of universal algebra are assumed, like *signature Sig*, *Sig-algebra A* and *Sig-homomorphism h : A → B*, *subsignature Sig' ⊆ Sig*, and *Sig'-reduct* $(A)_{Sig'}$ and $(h)_{Sig'}$, see e.g., [EM85].

[2] Graphs of this kind have been mainly used in the algebraic single-pushout approach under the name of *graph structures* [Löw93]. They include, beside ordinary graphs, also more general kinds of structures like hyper-graphs or higher-order graphs.

by an edge with a white flag, which is passed from process to process along the ring. If a process wants to use a resource, it waits for the corresponding token. Mutual exclusion is ensured because there is only one token for each resource in the system. The distributed deadlock detection uses *blocked* messages in order to detect cyclic dependencies. They are represented by edges with a black flag from a resource to a process.

The graph signature $GS_{MUTEX} = \langle S, OP \rangle$ has as sorts the nodes and edges of the type graph, i.e., the node sorts P and R and the edge sorts $request, held\_by, release, next, token$, and $blocked$. The operations of the signature are the obvious *source* and *target* assignments from edge sorts to node sorts, like $source : request \rightarrow P$ and $target : request \rightarrow R$. A graph over this signature is shown in the right of Figure 1. It represents a system state with two processes and two resources, where each process requests one resource while holding the other one, i.e., both processes are deadlocked.

Graph transformation rules (or productions) according to the DPO approach are specified by spans of injective graph morphisms $sp = (L \xleftarrow{l} K \xrightarrow{r} R)$, called *production spans*. The *left-hand side* L and the *right-hand side* R represent pre and postconditions, i.e., items which have to be present before and after the application. The *interface graph* K specifies the objects which are required and preserved, that is, the "intersection" of L and R.

Example 2. The rules of the MUTEX specification are given in Figure 2. In the upper part, the SYS-rules are shown modeling the operations *new* and *kill(p)* for inserting and removing processes to and from the ring, and the operations *mount* and *unmount(r)* for creating a resource with a token, and deleting it. The interface graph K is omitted. It can be reconstructed from the graphical layout of productions: Items that appear in the same position in the left- and right-hand side are usually preserved and belong to the interface.

The complete representation of the production *new* is given by the top span of the left diagram in Figure 3 which shows an application modeling the insertion of a new process in the ring. Given the match $m : L \rightarrow G$ which maps the processes 1 and 2 to the process in G and the edge in between to the loop, the application consists of two steps: The objects of G matched by $L - l(K)$ are removed which leads to the graph D without loop. Then, the objects of $R - r(K)$ are added to D leading to the derived graph H. Notice that the application deletes and creates exactly what is specified by the production: There is an *implicit frame condition* ensuring that everything that is not rewritten explicitly by the production is left unchanged.

The gluing of L and D over K is again the given graph G, i.e., the left-hand square (1) of d forms a so-called *pushout complement*. Only in this case the application is permitted. Similarly, the derived graph H is the gluing of D and R over K, which creates the right-hand side pushout square (2). The resulting *double-pushout (DPO) diagram* d represents the transformation of G into H, denoted $G \xRightarrow{d} H$. Since this diagram is symmetric, it can also be read from

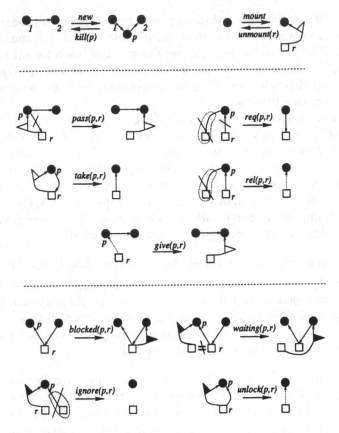

Fig. 2. The MUTEX-productions of the SYS-, TR- and DDD-view (from top to bottom).

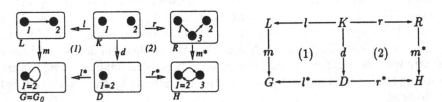

Fig. 3. A sample direct DPO derivation using *new* (left), and a generic double-pushout (resp., double-pullback) diagram *d* (right).

right to left, as *inverse transformation*. The corresponding *inverse production span* is $sp^{-1} = (R \xleftarrow{r} K \xrightarrow{l} L)$.

The existence of the pushout complement (1), and hence of a direct derivation[3] $G \xRightarrow{d} H$, is characterized by the *gluing conditions*: The *dangling condition* ensures that the structure D obtained by removing from G all objects to be deleted is indeed a graph, that is, no edges are left "dangling" without source or target node. The *identification condition* states that objects from the left-hand side may only be identified by the match if they also belong to the interface (and are thus preserved).

Example 3. The TR-rules are shown in the middle of Figure 2, where $pass(p, r)$ describes that a process having the token may pass it to the next process in the ring, provided that it does not have a request on the corresponding resource. This *negative application condition* is visualized by the crossed-out *request* edge from the process to the resource, see [HHT96] for a formalization of this concept. If a process wants to use a resource, it may generate a request. This is modeled by the rule $req(p, r)$, which is only applicable if the process does not have any requests yet, and if the particular resource is not used already by this process. If a process receives a token and there *is* a request for the resource, the process will chose the rule $take(p, r)$ replacing the token and the request by a *held_by* edge from the resource to the process. When it has finished its task, the process may release its resource and give the token to the next process using $rel(p, r)$ and $give(p, r)$. This will happen only when there are no pending requests, which is modeled by a negative application condition at $rel(p, r)$.

The algorithm for distributed deadlock detection specified by the DDD-rules in the lower part is a variant of [CMH83]: In a graph representing a state, a deadlock is represented as a cycle of *request* and *held_by* edges. In order to detect such cycles in a distributed way, a process holding a resource requested by another process will use the rule $blocked(p, r)$ to send a *blocked*-message to that process. If this process itself blocks another one, he will use the $waiting(p, r)$ rule to pass this message on. The inequation in this rule, which is also a negative application condition in the sense of [HHT96], ensures that resource r is not the original one. If the process does not hold any resource, it deletes the message with $ignore(p, r)$.

Thanks to the mutual exclusion, each resource is held by only one processes. Hence, if the message arrives at a process who holds the original resource, this is the original sender of the message. The deadlock thus detected is broken by the $unlock(p, r)$ rule which replaces the *held_by* edge and the *blocked* message with a *release* edge, asking the TR-view to give the token to the next process.

3 Temporal Specification of Graph Transition Systems

Graph transition systems are labeled transition systems whose states are graphs. In [HEWC97a] they are defined for a *graph grammar* (i.e., a set of productions

---

[3] The pushout (2) always exists since the category of graphs over GS is cocomplete.

with a start graph) using coalgebraic techniques. Following [GR97] in this section graph transition systems are defined for a *signature*, independently of their generation by productions. Like in [HEWC97a] a temporal logic is developed for specifying graph transition systems axiomatically.

The common base for graph transition systems, temporal formulas, and graph transition specifications (in the next section) are *graph transition signatures*:

Definition 4 (graph transition signature). A *graph transition signature* $GTSig = \langle GS, C, P, Q \rangle$ consists of a graph signature GS, a *global context graph* C over GS, and two families of sets $P = (P_w)_{w \in S^*}$ and $Q = (Q_w)_{w \in S^*}$ of *production names* and *state formula symbols*. For $p \in P_v$ and $q \in Q_w$ I write $p : v$ and $q : w$.

Given an S-indexed family of sets $A = (A_s)_{s \in S}$, the set of *transition expressions over* A is defined by $\mathcal{TE}_P(A) = \{p(a) | p : w, a \in A_w\}$. Similarly, the set of *state formulas over* A is defined by $\mathcal{SF}_Q(A) = \{q(a) | q : w, a \in A_w\}$.

Example 5. The graph transition signature of the MUTEX algorithm is $GTSig_{MUTEX} = \langle GS_{MUTEX}, C_{MUTEX}, P_{SYS} \cup P_{TR} \cup P_{DDD}, Q_{MUTEX} \rangle$ where

- GS_{MUTEX} is the graph signature introduced in Example 1
- $C_{MUTEX} = \langle (C_s)_{s \in S}, (op^C)_{op \in OP} \rangle$ is a "complete graph structure" of size $\mathbb{N}$, that is, $C_s = \mathbb{N}$ for all node sorts s and $C_{s'} = \mathbb{N} \times \mathbb{N} \times \mathbb{N}$ for all edge sorts s'. The *source* and *target* mappings from node to edge sorts are given, respectively, by the first and third projection. Hence C_{MUTEX} has for each node type all natural numbers as nodes, and for each edge type the set of natural numbers as edges between every pair of nodes.
- $P_{SYS} = \{new, kill : P, mount, unmount : R\}$,
  $P_{TR} = \{pass : PR, req : PR, take : PR, rel : PR, give : PR\}$, and
  $P_{DDD} = \{blocked : PR, waiting : PR, ignore : PR, unlock : PR\}$.
- $Q_{MUTEX} = \{no\_request : PR, no\_request : P, not\_held\_by : RP, \ldots\}$

The global context graph C provides a common name space for the states, formally represented as injective graph morphisms $g : G \to C$. The set of all states is denoted by S_C. Transitions are labeled by sets of transition expressions representing parallel transitions. For evaluating temporal formulas, a valuation $\mathcal{V}$ of state formulas over C is assumed.

Definition 6 (graph transition system). A *graph transition system* over a signature $GTSig = \langle GS, C, P, Q \rangle$ is a triple $GTSys = \langle \mathcal{V}, \rightsquigarrow, \mathcal{R} \rangle$ where

- $\mathcal{V} : \mathcal{SF}_Q(C) \to \mathcal{P}(S_C)$ is a *valuation* assigning to each state formula $q(c)$ over C a class $\mathcal{V}(q(c))$ of states (at which $q(c)$ is assumed to be true)
- $\rightsquigarrow \subseteq S \times \mathcal{P}_f(\mathcal{TE}_P(C)) \times S$ is a labeled transition relation[4], where $\langle g, L, h \rangle \in \rightsquigarrow$ is denoted by $g \overset{L}{\rightsquigarrow} h$.
- $\mathcal{R}$ is a class of *runs*, i.e., infinite sequences $\rho : g_0 g_1 g_2 \ldots$ of states over C such that for all $i \in \mathbb{N}$ there exists a transition $g_i \overset{L_i}{\rightsquigarrow} g_{i+1}$.

---

[4] For a set A, $\mathcal{P}_f(A)$ denotes the set of finite subsets of A.

Graph transition systems can be specified axiomatically (via their runs) by temporal logic formulas. Assume in the following definitions a graph transition signature $GTSig = \langle GS, C, P, Q \rangle$.

Definition 7 (temporal formulas). Given a family of sets of variables $X = (X_s)_{s \in S}$, the syntax of *temporal formulas over* X has the form

$$\Phi ::= q(x) \mid \neg\Phi \mid \Phi_1 \wedge \Phi_2 \mid \exists y.\Phi \mid \Diamond\Phi$$

where $q(x)$ is a state formula over X, and $y \in X$ is a variable. A *temporal formula with variables* is a pair $X : \Phi$ where Φ is a temporal formula over X. The set of all such formulas is $T\mathcal{F}_{GTSig}$.

Here, $\Diamond$ is the usual *sometime* operator of temporal logic. The *always* operator is defined by: $\Box\Phi$ iff $\neg\Diamond\neg\Phi$. The usual definitions are applied for the propositional operators $T, F, \vee$, and $\Longrightarrow$, and for the universal quantification $\forall$.

Satisfaction of temporal formulas is defined for a *temporal model* $M = \langle GTSys, ass \rangle$ over $GTSig$ consisting of a graph transition system $GTSys = \langle \mathcal{V}, \rightsquigarrow, \mathcal{R} \rangle$ over $GTSig$, and an *assignment* $ass : X \to C$.

Definition 8 (satisfaction). Let $M = \langle GTSys, ass \rangle$ be a temporal model. The satisfaction of temporal formulas $X : \Phi \in T\mathcal{F}_{GTSig}$ by runs $\rho \in \mathcal{R}$ is defined inductively as follows:[5]

- $\rho \models_M q(x)$ iff $\rho(0) \in \mathcal{V}(q(ass(x)))$
- $\rho \models_M \neg\Phi$ iff $\rho \not\models_M \Phi$,
- $\rho \models_M \Phi_1 \wedge \Phi_2$ iff $\rho \models_M \Phi_1$ and $\rho \models_M \Phi_2$,
- $\rho \models_M \exists y.\Phi$ iff there is an assignment ass' s.t. $ass'(x) = ass(x)$ for all variables $x \neq y$ and $\rho \models_{\langle GTSys, ass' \rangle} \Phi$
- $\rho \models_M \Diamond\Phi$ iff there is $k \in \mathbb{N}$ such that $\rho_k \models_M \Phi$.

The model M satisfies $X : \Phi$, written $\models_M X : \Phi$, if $\rho \models_M \Phi$ for all runs $\rho \in \mathcal{R}$. A transition system $GTSys$ satisfies $X : \Phi$, written $\models_{GTSys} X : \Phi$, if $\models_M X : \Phi$ for all models $M = \langle GTSys, ass \rangle$.

Example 9. The temporal specification of the MUTEX algorithm consists of the *safety property MUTEX-safe*: $\Box[held\_by(r, p_1) \wedge held\_by(r, p_2) \Longrightarrow p_1 = p_2]$ which states that a resource must not be held by two different processes, and the *liveness property MUTEX-live*: $\Box[requests(p, r) \Longrightarrow \Diamond held\_by(r, p)]$ saying that each request will eventually be served. The set of state formulas is extended by equations and edge predicates, like $edge\_sort : node\_sort_1 \ node\_sort_2$, with the obvious interpretations.

The MUTEX liveness property is decomposed according to the different tasks performed by the TR- and the DDD-view. The latter has to announce all permanent deadlocks by a *release* edge, that is, *DDD-live* reads:

$$\Box[deadlocked(p_1) \Longrightarrow \exists p_2, r. \ path(p_1, p_2) \wedge \Diamond[release(r, p_2) \vee \neg deadlocked(p_1)]]$$

---

[5] $\rho(i) = g_i$ denotes the ith state and $\rho_i = g_i g_{i+1} \ldots$ the ith suffix of ρ.

Here $path(p_1, p_2)$ is true in a state if the processes p_1 and p_2 are connected by a path of *request* and *held_by* edges, and *deadlocked(p)* is equivalent to $path(p, p)$. Notice that the *release* edge may point to any process in the deadlock cycle.

The liveness property of the TR-view is that each request will eventually be served, provided that deadlocks are always detected and the number of processes is bounded, i.e., *TR-live* : $\Box bounded(n) \wedge$ *DDD-live* $\Longrightarrow$ *MUTEX-live*. Here *bounded(n)* is true in a state if the number of P nodes does not exceed n.

4 A Loose Semantics for Graph Productions

A graph transition system (or rather its transition relation) can be specified constructively by a set of graph productions (plus a set of initial states and some additional constraints). One can ask if this specification is *correct* w.r.t. a certain temporal formula by checking the validity of this formula in the transition system. If the specification is incomplete like the DDD-view which describes only a particular aspect of the MUTEX algorithm, the closed behavior of this view given by the classical DPO interpretation is rather poor. Starting for example with the deadlock state in Figure 1 on the right, the DDD-productions could (at most) replace two *held_by* edges by *release* edges, and stop. Properties verified for this transition system are obviously not very interesting and of little use for the verification of the MUTEX algorithm.

One way out is, of course, to verify the DDD-view in the context of the SYS- and TR-view, but this would contradict the aim of compositional verification. The solution I propose in this paper is a loose semantics of graph productions which anticipates the effects of applying them in a bigger context. So-called *graph transitions* will ensure that an application preserves, deletes, and adds at least as much as it is specified by the productions, but it permits also additional effects which may be caused, in the example, by concurrent application of the SYS- and TR-productions. Thus the implicit frame condition is dropped. Instead, *explicit frame conditions* are introduced which protect only particular parts of the graphs from unspecified changes.

Definition 10 (graph transition). A *sequential graph transition* is defined by replacing the double-pushout diagram of direct derivations with a *double-pullback (DPB) diagram*, that is, a diagram d like in the right of Figure 3 where (1) and (2) are pullbacks. This diagram represents a transition from G to H with production span $sp = (L \longleftarrow K \longrightarrow R)$ and bottom span $t = (G \longleftarrow D \longrightarrow H)$, denoted by $G \overset{d}{\leadsto} H$.

The *parallel production span* $Par(Sp)$ of a finite set Sp of production spans $sp = (L_{sp} \longleftarrow K_{sp} \longrightarrow R_{sp})$ is constructed as component-wise disjoint union (coproduct)

$$Par(Sp) = \sum_{sp \in Sp} L_{sp} \overset{l}{\longleftarrow} \sum_{sp \in Sp} K_{sp} \overset{r}{\longrightarrow} \sum_{sp \in Sp} R_{sp}$$

A graph transition using a parallel production span is called *parallel graph transition*.

Each pushout in $\mathcal{G}r(GS)$ where two opposite morphisms are injective is also a pullback. Hence, graph transitions generalize direct derivations defined by double-pushouts. From an operational point of view a span $G \xleftarrow{l^*} D \xrightarrow{r^*} H$ represents a transition where $G - l^*(D)$ is deleted, $l^*(D) \subseteq G$ is preserved as $r^*(D) \subseteq H$, and $H - r^*(D)$ is newly created. Then, referring to the right diagram of Figure 3:

- Commutativity of (1) and (2) ensures that the image of K in G is preserved in D and H, i.e., $m(l(K)) \subseteq l^*(D)$ and $m^*(r(K)) \subseteq r^*(D)$.
- Pullback property of (1) ensures that at least every image of $L - l(K)$ in G is deleted, i.e., $m(L - l(K)) \cap l^*(D) = \emptyset$.
- Pullback property of (2) ensures that at least every image of $R - r(K)$ in H is newly created, i.e., $m^*(R - r(K)) \cap r^*(D) = \emptyset$.

Example 11. A sample graph transition is shown in the left of Figure 4. It applies the TR-production $take(p, r)$ replacing a request and the corresponding token by a *held_by* edge. Meanwhile, another process is inserted in the ring, which is not specified by the production but permitted by the loose semantics. In fact, none of the two squares is a pushout: The given graph G adds to the gluing of L and D a *next* loop which is "spontaneously deleted", and in the derived graph H, an additional process with two *next* edges has been "spontaneously created". This effect could be obtained by applying production *new* in parallel.

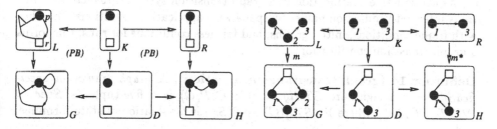

Fig. 4. A sample graph transition (left) and a graph transition not satisfying the dangling condition (right).

It is worth stressing that graph transitions may not only have additional effects but are also more likely to exist than DPO derivations. In general, the match m of a DPB diagram may satisfy neither the identification nor the dangling condition of the corresponding production, and so does the comatch m^*. Consider for example the transition in the right of Figure 4, using the SYS-production $kill(p)$, where the match does not satisfy the dangling condition: Process 2 is removed from the ring while still holding the resource. Here deleting the dangling *held_by* edge is an unspecified effect. Symmetrically, it would be possible to attach edges to newly created processes (for example in the inverse transition).

Motivated by these observations *safe* transitions are introduced:

Definition 12 (safe transitions). A graph transition $G \overset{d}{\leadsto} H$ like in the right of Figure 3 is *safe* if m satisfies the gluing conditions w.r.t. $sp = (L \longleftarrow K \longrightarrow R)$, and m^* satisfies the gluing conditions w.r.t. $sp^{-1} = (R \longleftarrow K \longrightarrow L)$.

In the following all transitions are assumed to be safe.

Hence, a safe graph transition exists if and only if there is also a direct DPO derivation with the same match.

In order to ensure that, e.g., processes and resources are only created and deleted by SYS-productions, one may declare certain sorts as *input* and/or *output* sorts. Only elements of such sorts may be spontaneously created and deleted. Sorts that are neither input nor output are called *private* since they are protected from the influence of the environment.

Definition 13 (explicit frame condition). An *explicit frame condition* over GS is a pair of sets $FC = \langle IS, OS \rangle$ of input and output sorts $IS, OS \subseteq S$. Denote by $\overline{IS}$ $(\overline{OS})$ the biggest subsignature of GS not containing input (output) sorts. Then, a graph transition $G \overset{d}{\leadsto} H$ *respects* IS (OS) if the reduct of the left-hand side (right-hand side) pullback square of d to $\overline{IS}$ $(\overline{OS})$ is a pushout.[6]

If all sorts are private (that is, $FC = \langle \emptyset, \emptyset \rangle$), transitions are reduced to direct derivations. In this way, the classical DPO interpretation of productions becomes a special case of the loose one.

As constructive specification of a graph transition system, *production definitions* interpret production names by spans with application conditions. Together with frame conditions, initial graphs, and fairness conditions for runs, this forms a graph transition specification.

Definition 14 (graph transition specification). A *graph transition specification* over a signature $GTSig = \langle GS, C, P, Q \rangle$ is a five-tuple $GTSpec = \langle \mathcal{V}, \mathcal{PD}, FC, I, F \rangle$ where $\mathcal{V} : \mathcal{SF}_Q(C) \to \mathcal{P}(S_C)$ is a valuation of state formulas, and

- $\mathcal{PD}$ is a set of *production definitions* of the form $p(a) : sp$ **if** AC, where $sp = (L \longleftarrow K \longrightarrow R)$ is a production span, $p(a) \in \mathcal{TE}_P(L)$ is a transition expression over L, and $AC \subseteq \mathcal{SF}_Q(L)$ is a set of state formulas over L representing application conditions.
- $FC = \langle IS, OS \rangle$ is a frame condition
- $I \subseteq S_C$ is a set of *initial states*
- $F = \langle weak, strong \rangle$ is a *fairness condition*[7] where $weak, strong \subseteq \mathcal{TE}_P(C)$

---

[6] Here, the reduct is extended from graphs and graph morphisms to diagrams in $\mathcal{G}r(GS)$. This is possible because it forms a functor, called *forgetful functor* in [EM85]. It follows from the component-wise construction of pullbacks and pushouts in $\mathcal{G}r(GS)$ that their reduct is a pullback or pushout again. Hence, it preserves direct derivations as well as transitions.

[7] In [MP92] weak and strong fairness are called *justice* and *fairness*, respectively.

Example 15. The graph transition specification $MUTEX = \langle V_{MUTEX},$ $PD_{SYS} \cup PD_{TR} \cup PD_{DDD}, FC_{MUTEX}, I_{MUTEX}, F_{MUTEX}\rangle$ is given by

- the obvious valuation V_{MUTEX} of state formula symbols, e.g., $g : G \to C \in$ $V_{MUTEX}(no\_request(p, r))$ iff there is no *request* edge from p to r in $g(G)$.
- PD_{SYS}, PD_{TR}, and PD_{DDD} are given, respectively, by the productions in the upper, middle and lower part of Figure 2. The second TR-production, e.g., leads to the definition $req(p, r)$: sp_{req} if $\{no\_request(p), not\_held\_by(r, p)\}$.
- $FC_{MUTEX} = \langle \emptyset, \emptyset \rangle$ that is, the specification is considered as complete.
- I_{MUTEX} is the set of all states $g : G_0 \to C$ where G_0 is the graph in the left of Figure 3, which is put in all possible naming contexts.
- $F_{MUTEX} = \langle weak, strong \rangle$ where $weak = T\mathcal{E}_{P_{TR} \cup P_{DDD}}(C)$ and $strong = T\mathcal{E}_{\{rel:PR, unlock:PR\}}(C)$

A transition expression $p(c) \in T\mathcal{E}_P(C)$ is *enabled* by a state g if there is a transition $g \overset{L}{\rightsquigarrow} h$ with $p(c) \in L$. Then, a run $\rho : g_0 g_1 g_2 \ldots$ satisfies the fairness condition $F = \langle weak, strong \rangle$ if

Weak Fairness: For all $p(c) \in weak$ and $k \in \mathbb{N}$: if for an $i \geq k$, g_i enables $p(c)$, then there exists $n \geq k$ such that $g_n \overset{L}{\rightsquigarrow} g_{n+1}$ with $p(c) \in L$.
Strong Fairness: For all $p(c) \in strong$ and $k \in \mathbb{N}$: if there exist infinitely many $i \geq k$ where g_i enables $p(c)$, then there exist infinitely many $n \geq k$ such that $g_n \overset{L}{\rightsquigarrow} g_{n+1}$ with $p(c) \in L$.

Hence, the weak fairness condition of F_{MUTEX} above says that a TR- or DDD-transition which is continuously enabled must eventually take place. The strong fairness condition implies that transitions using $rel : PR$ or $unlock : PR$ which are enabled infinitely many times, must be taken infinitely often.

Each graph transition specification generates a transition systems:

Definition 16 (generated transition system, correctness). The transition specification $GTSpec = \langle V, PD, FC, I, F \rangle$ over $GTSig$ *generates* the transition system $TS(GTSpec) = \langle V, \rightsquigarrow, \mathcal{R} \rangle$ where

- $g \overset{L}{\rightsquigarrow} h$ holds for two states $g : G \to C$ and $h : H \to C$ iff there exists a parallel graph transition $G \overset{d}{\rightsquigarrow} H$ respecting FC with
  - production span $Par(Sp(L))$ where

$$Sp(L) = \{sp | p(c) \in L \land p(a) : sp \text{ if } AC \in PD\}$$

  is the set of all production spans for production names in L
  - bottom span $t = (G \longleftarrow D \longrightarrow H)$ given by the pullback of g and h modeling the "intersection" D of G and H in C,
  such that $c = g \circ m \circ in_{sp}(a)$[8] for all $p(c) \in L$ with $p(a) : sp$ if AC, i.e., the formal parameter a is mapped to the actual parameter c, and the application conditions are satisfied, that is, $g \in V(q(g \circ m \circ in_{sp}(b)))$ for all $q(b) \in AC$.

---

[8] Here, m is the match of the DPB diagram d, and in_{sp} the embedding of the left-hand side of sp in the parallel production span.

– each run $\rho : g_0 g_1 g_2 \ldots$ in $\mathcal{R}$ starts in an initial state $(g_0 \in I)$ and satisfies the fairness conditions F.

The transition specification $GTSpec$ is *correct w.r.t.* $X : \Phi$ iff $\models_{TS(GTSpec)} X : \Phi$.

5 Compositional Verification of System Properties

This section formalizes the concept of a view on a specification. The idea is to ensure that the behavior of the overall specification is permitted by the view's loose semantics.

Definition 17 (view on a specification). Let $GTSig = \langle GS, C, P, Q \rangle$ and $GTSig = \langle GS, C, P_0, Q_0 \rangle$ be graph transition signatures such that $P_0 \subseteq P$ and $Q_0 \subseteq Q$. Then, a graph transition specification $GTSpec_0 = \langle V_0, PD_0, FC_0, I_0, F_0 \rangle$ over $GTSig_0$ is a *view of* $GTSpec = \langle V, PD, FC, I, F \rangle$ over $GTSig$, written $GTSpec_0 \subseteq GTSpec$, iff $V_0 = V|_{SF_{Q_0}(C)}, PD_0 \subseteq PD, FC \subseteq FC_0, I \subseteq I_0$ and $F_0 \subseteq F$, such that for each *hidden production name* $p \in P \setminus P_0$ with definition $p(a) : (L \xleftarrow{l} K \xrightarrow{r} R)$ if AC, the reduct of l and r to non-input and non-output sorts, $(l)_{\overline{IS_0}}$ and $(r)_{\overline{OS_0}}$, respectively, yields isomorphisms.

Both transition specifications have the same graph signature GS and context graph C, that is, their generated transition systems have the same set of states. All input (output) sorts in $GTSpec$ are also input (output) sorts in the view. Hence, the frame conditions in $GTSpec$ are stronger, which means that $GTSpec$ is the more complete specification and effects that are covered by the loose semantics of $GTSpec_0$ are explicitly specified in $GTSpec$. On the other hand, each production of $GTSpec$ which is hidden from the view must not have effects on its private sorts since for those the view is assumed to be complete.

A view of $GTSpec$ can be induced by choosing a suitable subset of production names P_0 together with a frame condition FC_0. This choice is *valid* if the five-tuple $GTSpec_0 = \langle V|_{SF_{Q_0}(C)}, PD_0, FC_0, I, F_0 \rangle$ where $PD_0 = \{p(a) : sp$ if $AC \in PD | p \in P_0\}$ and $F_0 = \langle weak \cap TE_{P_0}(C), strong \cap TE_{P_0}(C) \rangle$ for $F = \langle weak, strong \rangle$ is indeed a view of $GTSpec$.

Example 18. The DDD-view of the $MUTEX$ specification is induced by the DDD-productions with the private sort *blocked*. The TR-view is given by all TR-productions and the frame condition $IS = \{P, R, next, token, blocked, release\}$ and $OS = IS \setminus \{release\}$.

Semantically, $GTSpec_0 \subseteq GTSpec$ implies that every run in $GTSpec$ is also a run in $GTSpec_0$, or vice versa, the extension of a specification leads to a restricted behavior.

Proposition 19 (restriction of behavior). *Let* $GTSpec_0$ *and* $GTSpec$ *be transition specifications such that* $GTSpec_0 \subseteq GTSpec$, $TS(GTSpec) = \langle V, \rightsquigarrow, \mathcal{R} \rangle$, *and* $TS(GTSpec_0) = \langle V_0, \rightsquigarrow_0, \mathcal{R}_0 \rangle$. *Then,* $\mathcal{R} \subseteq \mathcal{R}_0$.

Proof. A sequence of states ρ is a run in $GTSpec$ iff each pair of consecutive states g, h is related by $g \overset{L}{\rightsquigarrow} h$ (i), ρ starts in an initial state (ii), and it satisfies the fairness conditions (iii). In this case, ρ is also a run in $GTSpec_0$: For (i), $g \overset{L}{\rightsquigarrow} h$ implies $g \overset{L'}{\rightsquigarrow}_0 h$ where $L' = \{p(c) \in L | p \in P_0\}$, because $\mathcal{PD}_0 \subseteq \mathcal{PD}$. If (the parallel graph transition generating) $g \overset{L}{\rightsquigarrow} h$ respects FC, then it also respects the weaker condition FC_0. In this case, also $g \overset{L'}{\rightsquigarrow}_0 h$ respects FC_0 since the hidden productions in $P \setminus P_0$ do not create anything of non-input sort or delete anything of non-output sort, which concludes the proof of (i).

By assumption, $I \subseteq I_0$, that is if $\rho(0) \in I$ then $\rho(0) \in I_0$ implying (ii). For (iii), $F_0 \subseteq F$ that is, the fairness condition is weakened. A state g enables a transition expression $p(c)$ in $TS(GTSpec_0)$ if and only if it enables $p(c)$ in $TS(GTSpec)$. This follows from the fact that, on the one hand, $g \overset{L}{\rightsquigarrow} h$ implies $g \overset{L'}{\rightsquigarrow}_0 h$, as shown above. On the other hand, $g \overset{L'}{\rightsquigarrow}_0 h$ implies $g \overset{L}{\rightsquigarrow} k$, for some state $k \in S_C$ because, by default, all transitions are safe, and strengthening the frame conditions does not disable safe transitions. □

This result is based on the notion of (safe) graph transition which anticipates the additional effects of the rules in the bigger specification. The main theoretical result of this paper follows from the definition of correctness and the proposition above.

Theorem 20 (correctness of compositional verification). *Let $GTSpec_0$ and $GTSpec$ be graph transition specifications such that $GTSpec_0 \subseteq GTSpec$, and $X : \Phi \in \mathcal{TF}_{GTSig_0}$ be a temporal formula such that $GTSpec_0$ is correct w.r.t. $X : \Phi$. Then, also $GTSpec$ is correct w.r.t. $X : \Phi$.*

This allows to verify the properties of the MUTEX specification in a compositional way, by analyzing its views separately and deriving the MUTEX properties from the properties the views:

Example 21. For safety properties, the decomposition of the specification depends on the property to be shown. In order to prove *MUTEX-safe*, the stronger *consistency condition* □ *MUTEX-cc* is established, where *MUTEX-cc* is satisfied in a state $g : G \to C$ iff for each resource $r \in g(G)$ there is a unique *token* edge t with $source(t) = r$, or a unique *held_by* edge h with $source(h) = r$, or a unique *release* edge e with $source(e) = r$. This property is verified for the view induced by the production names $\{mount, unmount : R, pass : PR, take : PR, rel : PR, give : PR, unlock : PR\}$ with private sorts $\{R, held\_by, token, release\}$, i.e., all other sorts are input and output sorts. This is obviously a view of *MUTEX* since all the productions not mentioned do not affect the private sorts. Moreover, it is correct w.r.t. *MUTEX-cc*. In fact, the initial graphs satisfy the constraint and, since the relevant sorts are private and the condition is not violated by the productions of the view, the constraint is preserved by all transitions. By Theorem 20 one concludes that the complete specification *MUTEX* is correct w.r.t. *MUTEX-cc* and hence w.r.t. *MUTEX-safe*.

Another basic consistency condition is the integrity of the ring structure. Here, *ring-cc* shall be satisfied by a state g if its *next* edges form a cycle containing all processes of the state. For proving $\Box$ *ring-cc* let's pick up the view given by $P_0 = \{new, kill : P\}$ with private sorts $\{P, next\}$. Again, the chosen productions are the only ones affecting the private sorts, and it is similarly easy to see that the view is correct. Hence, also *MUTEX* is correct w.r.t. $\Box$ *ring-cc*.

It is worth mentioning here that most of the requirements checked so far can be verified automatically: Given the production names and frame conditions, it is ease to test if they induce a valid view, and for verifying that the productions preserve certain consistency conditions, a procedure has been developed in [HW95].

The more difficult task is presented by the verification of liveness properties. Here, *MUTEX-live* has been decomposed into the local properties *DDD-live* and *TR-live*. Since the focus is on the composition of properties rather than on their verification for views, I do not present a proof of the correctness of *DDD* and *TR*. Notice, however, that the consistency properties above have to be assumed.

Like safety properties, also the liveness properties *DDD-live* and *TR-live* carry over to the global system by Theorem 20. Combining them one obtains $\Box bounded(n) \Longrightarrow MUTEX\text{-}live$, that is, the boundedness of the system is left as an assumption for the schedule of SYS-productions.

6 Conclusion

In this paper I introduced graph transitions as a loose semantics of productions. By formalizing the notion of view I provided conceptual tools for compositional verification, and proved their correctness. An example showed the usefulness of the approach for specifying reactive systems and verifying their properties.

This notion of view is not very flexible yet since it does not allow the renaming of types or the extension of productions. It is not difficult, however, to generalize the concepts and results to some sort of specification morphisms, like the view relations in [EHTE97] or GTS morphisms in [HCEL96]. These papers also consider the problem of composing specifications.

A topic of ongoing work is the verification of views w.r.t. temporal properties. First results have been presented in [GHK] using graphical constraints [HW95] in order to define the evaluation of state formulas.

Acknowledgments Thanks to Martin Große-Rhode for helpful discussions and careful reading of the draft, and to Manuel Koch and Fabio Gadducci for joint work on temporal logic for graph transformation.

References

[CMH83]   K.M. Chandy, J. Misra, and L.M. Haas. Distributed deadlock detection. *ACM Transactions on Computer Systems*, 1:144–156, May 1983.

[CMR+97] A. Corradini, U. Montanari, F. Rossi, H. Ehrig, R. Heckel, and M. Löwe. Algebraic approaches to graph transformation I: Basic concepts and double pushout approach. In G. Rozenberg, editor, *Handbook of Graph Grammars and Computing by Graph transformation, Volume 1: Foundations.* World Scientific, 1997.

[EHTE97] G. Engels, R. Heckel, G. Taentzer, and H. Ehrig. A view-oriented approach to system modelling based on graph transformation. In *Proc. of ESEC/FSE'97, Zürich,* Springer LNCS 1301, 1997. Extended version to appear in *International Journal of Software Engineering and Knowledge Engineering,* 1998.

[EM85] H. Ehrig and B. Mahr. *Fundamentals of Algebraic Specification 1: Equations and Initial Semantics,* volume 6 of *EATCS Monographs on Theoretical Computer Science.* Springer Verlag, Berlin, 1985.

[EPS73] H. Ehrig, M. Pfender, and H.J. Schneider. Graph grammars: an algebraic approach. In *14th Annual IEEE Symposium on Switching and Automata Theory,* pages 167–180. IEEE, 1973.

[FKN+92] A. Finkelstein, J. Kramer, B. Nuseibeh, M. Goedicke, and L. Finkelstein. Viewpoints: A framework for integrating multiple perspectives in system development. *International Journal of Software Engineering and Knowledge Engineering,* 2(1):31–58, March 1992.

[GHK] F. Gadducci, R. Heckel, and M. Koch. Combining graph transformations with temporal logic. In *First TMR GETGRATS Workshop, Bordeaux, October 1997.*

[GR97] M. Große-Rhode. Algebra transformation systems and their composition. In this volume.

[HCEL96] R. Heckel, A. Corradini, H. Ehrig, and M. Löwe. Horizontal and vertical structuring of typed graph transformation systems. *Math. Struc. in Comp. Science,* 6(6):613–648, 1996. Also Techn. Rep. 96-22, TU Berlin.

[HEWC97a] R. Heckel, H. Ehrig, U. Wolter, and A. Corradini. Integrating the specification techniques of graph transformation and temporal logic. In *Proc. of MFCS'97, Bratislava,* Springer LNCS 1295, 1997.

[HEWC97b] R. Heckel, H. Ehrig, U. Wolter, and A. Corradini. Loose semantics and constraints for graph transformation systems. Techn. Rep. 97-07, TU Berlin, 1997. http://www.cs.tu-berlin.de/cs/ifb/TechnBerichteListe.html.

[HHT96] A. Habel, R. Heckel, and G. Taentzer. Graph grammars with negative application conditions. *Fundamenta Informaticae,* 26(3,4), 1996.

[HW95] R. Heckel and A. Wagner. Ensuring consistency of conditional graph grammars – a constructive approach. *Proc. of SEGRAGRA'95 "Graph Rewriting and Computation",* Electronic Notes of TCS, 2, 1995. http://www.elsevier.nl/locate/entcs/volume2.html.

[Löw93] M. Löwe. Algebraic approach to single-pushout graph transformation. *TCS,* 109:181–224, 1993.

[MP92] Zohar Manna and Amir Pnueli. *The Temporal Logic of Reactive and Concurrent Systems, Specification.* Springer-Verlag, 1992.

[Sch94] Enno Scholz. Verteilte Betriebssysteme. Seminar notes at the graduate college "Communication-based Systems", TU Berlin, 1994.

Reflections on the Design
of a Specification Language

Stefan Kahrs* and Donald Sannella**

Laboratory for Foundations of Computer Science, University of Edinburgh,
Edinburgh EH9 3JZ

Abstract. We reflect on our experiences from work on the design and
semantic underpinnings of Extended ML, a specification language which
supports the specification and formal development of Standard ML programs. Our aim is to isolate problems and issues that are intrinsic to
the general enterprise of designing a specification language for use with
a given programming language. Consequently the lessons learned go far
beyond our original aim of designing a specification language for ML.

1 Introduction

There are many different approaches to the problem of producing correct software systems in a given programming language. One line of attack involves the
use of a specification language that is tailor-made to specifying and verifying
properties of programs written in that particular programming language. This
typically involves the use of a logical language that is appropriate for writing
assertions about entities arising in programs written in that programming language. Some examples are: Anna [LvH+87] for use with Ada; Larch [GH93]
adapted to the programming language in question via use of an appropriate
"interface language", e.g. Larch/C++ [Lea96]; and our favourite, Extended ML
[KST97] for use with Standard ML. Closely related is work on logics for reasoning about programs written in particular programming languages, e.g. Haskell
[Tho93]. Although most of the details of this enterprise are specific to the particular programming language at hand, certain problems and issues are common
to all programming languages or to a class of languages.

In this paper, we reflect on our experiences from work on the design and
semantic underpinnings of Extended ML with emphasis on some of the more
general lessons learned. The topics we cover range from the very general to the
somewhat specific: Sect. 4 on the relationship between models of programs and
models of specifications applies to any programming language; Sect. 5 on adding
logical formulae to a language with a Hindley-Milner (implicitly polymorphic)

* Now at Computing Laboratory, University of Kent, Canterbury CT2 7NF. E-mail
  smk@ukc.ac.uk. This research was supported by EPSRC grant GR/K63795.
** E-mail dts@dcs.ed.ac.uk. This research was supported by EPSRC grant
  GR/K63795, an EPSRC Advanced Fellowship, an SOEID/RSE Support Research
  Fellowship and the EC-funded FIREworks working group.

type system is relevant to any programming language having such a type system; most of Sect. 6 on indistinguishability is relevant mainly to ML and fragments of ML. We begin with a brief description of Extended ML to provide some context for the rest of the paper.

2 Extended ML in brief

Extended ML (EML) is a wide-spectrum language for the specification and development of modular Standard ML (SML) programs. "Wide-spectrum" means that it encompasses both specifications and programs, as well as hybrids between the two. These hybrids arise as the intermediate stages of the process that turns a formal specification into a concrete program that implements it.

EML was conceived in the mid-1980s [ST85], combining ideas from algebraic specification and the then rapidly evolving functional programming language ML. Once ML was standardised and given a formal semantics in 1990 [MTH90], a project was set up to do the same with EML, resulting in its formal definition in 1994 [KST94].

We are not going to describe the features of EML in any but the most superficial detail. See [KST97] for more details and a gentle but thorough introduction to the EML semantics. A programmer-oriented introduction is [San91].

We can roughly describe EML as an extension of SML (minus some of its imperative features) with the following specification features:

- placeholders for expressions, type expressions, and *structure*[1] expressions; these are used to express incomplete programs, which are useful entities during program development
- axioms in structures; these are used to narrow down the possible choices for replacing placeholders
- axioms in *signatures*[1]; these demand and/or export properties of the implementing structure
- first-order logic with equality as the language for axioms.

This is a gross simplification and we shall have to expand on some of this later on. The definition of EML [KST94] is an extension of the definition of SML [MTH90] by (among other things) a definition of the meaning of axioms and what it means for a structure to satisfy the axioms in a signature.

3 Fundamental principles

Suppose we are given a programming language P and the task of designing a specification language S suitable for the specification and development of P-programs.

---

[1] "Structure" is ML-speak for module, "signature" for module interface.

Is this always possible? Which features should S contain, which primitives, which logical connectives? Equally importantly: which features should S *not* contain? To a certain extent one can answer these questions generically.

Different specification languages have different aims. Near one extreme would be a specification language that is intended as a formal notation for documenting programs, or as a vehicle for requirements capture, with no way to verify with any degree of formality that a given program satisfies a given specification. Then there is no need to make a formal connection between P and S, and indeed S may be appropriate for a range of programming languages. Near the opposite extreme would be specification languages like EML where a central aim is to enable proofs about specifications, and proofs that a given program satisfies a given specification. Here a formal connection between P and S is essential to establish the soundness of inference rules used in proofs that connect P-programs and S-specifications. Our concern in this paper is with specification languages of the latter kind.

Given that aim, it is not possible to come up with a meaningful specification language for P unless P has a formal semantics. Without a formal semantics for P we are not certain what P-programs are supposed to do, making it impossible to establish reliably any property of any P-program or to prove interesting relationships between P-programs and S-specifications. Unfortunately, this requirement rules out most present-day programming languages.

The design of S is constrained by the properties of the semantics of P. For example, the properties of P-programs we can express in S should not transcend the properties we can establish from the formal semantics of P. This is closely related to the reason why we need a formal semantics for P in the first place.

For instance, the dynamic semantics of SML [MTH90] defines the result of evaluating an expression in a particular environment and a given state. But it does not specify the required time and space resources for such an evaluation. The size of the derivation of the evaluation judgement (built from instances of the rules of the semantics) indicates the required resources *in a naive evaluation model*, but this information is unreliable — SML compilers are not forced to stick to the evaluation model implicitly suggested by the SML semantics and hardly any of them do so. This means that any specification language for SML should abstain from specifying the efficiency and/or complexity of a program.

One may object: people do reason about the efficiency of SML programs, don't they? But if compilers are allowed to modify the performance of a program by optimising it (which in some cases may even slow it down) then the observed performance becomes compiler-dependent. In other words: efficiency is a property of the machine program the compiler chooses to realize a source program, rather than a property of source programs themselves. When we reason about the efficiency of programs we assume that the compiler is not clever enough to significantly depart from the naive evaluation model given by the operational semantics. There is no formal justification for such an assumption.

If P is a typed language, it is natural to exploit its type system both to coordinate the required link with S and to provide the basis of a type system for S. Although the utility of a type system for specifications as such is a matter of some debate — see e.g. [LP97] — we can hardly avoid mentioning types in S when asserting properties of typed programs in P. For example, when specifying the behaviour of a function $f : t \to t'$ it is often necessary to quantify over the values of type t. Apart from this, there is also the important design issue of making P-programmers feel "at home" when writing S-specifications. It therefore seems desirable that the type system for S be as close as possible to the type system for P. When, as in the case of EML, P is a subset of S, the type system of S should be a *conservative* extension of the type system of P: a P-expression e has a P-type t in S iff e has type t in P.

4 Models of programs vs. models of specifications

The semantics of the programming language P will assign *models* to programs of P. For each P-program p, its model $[\![p]\!]$ will contain some assortment of mathematical objects modelling the components of p, including (for example) the functions defined by p.

Any specification language S needs a semantics which defines the meaning $[\![s]\!]$ of each S-specification s. This is a necessary basis for specification-based proof: proof that a given program satisfies a given specification; proof that one specification is a *refinement* of another; or proof that all programs satisfying a given specification will satisfy a given property. When we design a specification language S for use with a programming language P, it is natural to define the meaning of an S-specification as the class of all P-models (i.e. models of well-formed P-programs) having the indicated components and satisfying the requirements spelled out in the specification (see e.g. [ST97]). This enables us to say that a P-program p satisfies an S-specification s exactly when the model of p is in the class of models determined by s: $[\![p]\!] \in [\![s]\!]$.

The expressiveness of P dictates the structure of models of P-programs. For instance, if P provides constructs for defining non-deterministic functions, models of P-programs containing such functions will need to model them using something more exotic than ordinary set-theoretic functions. Even if P does not provide such constructs, provided P is sufficiently expressive (that is: unless it is extremely inexpressive), functions in P-programs cannot be modelled by arbitrary set-theoretic functions. For example, the untyped λ-calculus requires a domain D of values such that $D \cong D \to D$; here $D \to D$ cannot be the whole function space (since $D \cong D \to D$ implies $|D| = |D \to D| = |D|^{|D|}$ i.e. $|D| = 1$) so it is taken to be the space of *continuous* functions [Gun92]. Another source of restrictions on models of P-programs is the desire to reflect more accurately the constraints that P imposes. For instance, no matter what P is, no P-program will contain definitions of non-computable functions and so it would be natural to take only *computable* functions in P-models. In SML, each function is modelled as a *closure* which contains the expression used in defining the function, so we get only the SML-expressible functions [MTH90]. Of course, all of these are computable, but not all computable functions of a given type are SML-expressible [Kah96].

Putting these together (the decision to interpret S-specifications using classes of P-models and the imposition of computability and other restrictions on P-models) leads to a possible problem, as the following example from [ST96] illustrates.

Example 1. Let φ_{equiv} be a sentence which asserts that `equiv`(n,m) = `true` iff the Turing machines with Gödel numbers n and m compute the same partial function (this is expressible in first-order logic with equality, since the equivalence of TMs is arithmetical [Rog67]). Now consider the following specification:

> *local val* `equiv : nat * nat -> bool`
>   *axiom* φ_{equiv}
> *in val* `opt : nat -> nat`
>   *axiom forall* `n:nat => equiv(opt(n),n) = true`
> *end*

This specifies an optimizing function `opt` transforming TMs to equivalent TMs. (Axioms could be added to require that the output of `opt` is at least as efficient as its input.) If functions in P-models are required to be computable (and the semantics of specifications is compositional with models of *local s in s' end* obtained by forgetting the s-components of models of s; s') then this specification will have *no* models because there is no computable function `equiv` satisfying φ_{equiv}. Yet there *are* computable functions `opt` having the required property, for instance the identity function on **nat**. Thus this specification disallows P-programs that provide exactly the required functionality. □

The example is expressed in terms of Gödel encodings of Turing machines where its practical utility may not be apparent, but exactly the same example could be phrased in terms of program fragments in a real programming language and a specification like the one above (and exhibiting exactly the same problem) could then appear as part of the specification of an optimizing compiler or program transformation system.

Here are three ways around this problem:

1. Treat local functions differently from "exported" functions, allowing them to be non-computable. Programs are not required to implement local functions in specifications anyway.
2. Relax the computability requirement on all functions.
3. Prohibit local functions in specifications.

The second solution seems simpler than the first because it is uniform. This is the approach taken by EML, where each function is modelled as an *EML-expressible* closure — still a closure, but where the expression in the closure is allowed to include "logical" constructs such as universal and existential quantifiers rather than being expressible using just the constructs of SML [KST94,KST97]. The third solution is unattractive since it sacrifices a great deal of expressive power.

Relaxing conditions on models needs to be done with care. Restrictions needed to ensure that models exist are still required (see the discussion of the untyped λ-calculus above). And there is a "logical" limit on expressibility: provided S extends Peano arithmetic, Gödel's fixpoint theorem can be applied to show that if satisfaction of the closed formulae of S can be defined in S itself (e.g. as a total function of type `formula -> bool`), then S is necessarily inconsistent.[2] It appears that any attempt to define EML satisfaction in EML yields a function that fails to terminate in some cases.

5 Parametricity

The kernel type system of most functional programming languages these days is Hindley-Milner polymorphism [Mil78], i.e. shallow, implicit polymorphism. ("Shallow", means that all type quantifiers occur outermost; "implicit" means that type abstraction and application are syntactically suppressed.) SML needs some modifications to cope soundly with imperative features, but we can ignore this for the moment.

The implicitness of type abstraction and type application strongly limits the options for possible extensions of the type system, should an extension be required to accommodate the specification logic: type inference and type checking for System F are undecidable [Wel94], as is type inference for Hindley-Milner polymorphism with the addition of proper polymorphic recursion [KTU93].

5.1 Prerequisites for implicit polymorphism

Why do we get away with implicit polymorphism? That is, why are we satisfied with the particular choices of type abstraction and type application selected by the type inference algorithm?

There are two fundamental reasons why this is so:

1. There is a best possible choice — and the type inference algorithm picks it.
2. Whatever choice is made, the outcome of evaluation is not affected.

The mentioned best possible choice is the so-called "principal" or "most general" type. The principal type subsumes all other possible types, in a technical sense which we can ignore here. In a certain sense, choosing the principal type is like[3] making no choice at all, leaving all options open.

The second reason is much more important.

Since type applications are implicit, the types inferred for expressions by the type inference algorithm are to a certain degree arbitrary. Consider the inference rule for type-checking function application:

$$\frac{\Gamma \vdash e_1 : \sigma \to \tau \qquad \Gamma \vdash e_2 : \sigma}{\Gamma \vdash e_1\,e_2 : \tau}$$

[2] Thanks to Martin Hofmann for this observation.

[3] There are a couple of involved technical reasons why this is not quite true for SML, even after the 1997 revision [MTHM97]. For our purposes this is a side-issue.

When we infer the type of an application term $e_1\ e_2$, the rule requires that the argument type of the function e_1 and the type of the actual parameter e_2 agree — these are the two occurrences of σ in the premise of the rule. The type inference algorithm makes sure that this is the case, but this does not necessarily completely determine the type σ, since it is possible that different types have this property. We would not want these arbitrary choices to influence the computation in any way.

Other arbitrary choices arise when type variables are implicitly abstracted at declaration level. *All* type variables are abstracted that can possibly be abstracted (i.e. those in the type that do not occur free in the context), and the order of abstraction is arbitrary. Again, these arbitrary choices should not influence the computation.

There are several (related) ways of capturing this idea, e.g. Reynolds' notion of *parametricity* [Rey83] and Wadler's *theorems for free* [Wad89]. Essentially, type quantification can be manipulated in this implicit manner because types do not interfere with computation in System F.

More concretely, one can view type inference as a process that inserts *type conversion* functions, in addition to type abstractions and applications, whenever necessary to generate an explicitly typed program. Parametricity requires that these conversions are isomorphisms; this may not be the case — see [Cos92] — but for purposes of evaluation, verification and analysis of programs it is sufficient if they *behave* like isomorphisms: in other words, the function that converts back and forth should be *indistinguishable* from the identity function. (An informal understanding of indistinguishability will suffice for now. See Sect. 6.1 below for a definition.)

From what we have already seen, it should be clear that we need isomorphisms $\forall\alpha.\forall\beta.\ \tau \cong \forall\beta.\forall\alpha.\ \tau$ since we abstract type variables in an arbitrary order, and $\forall\alpha.\ \tau \cong \tau$ (if $\alpha \notin \mathrm{FV}(\tau)$) since we only abstract type variables that occur. There are more such requirements[4], but these two are sufficient to make our points.

It is not difficult to formulate the required isomorphisms in System F. We will write $\Lambda\alpha.t$ and $t[\tau]$ to denote type abstraction and type application on term level, respectively.

We can express the commutativity isomorphism (in both directions) by

$$\iota = \lambda x : (\forall\alpha.\forall\beta.\tau).\Lambda\gamma.\Lambda\delta.x[\delta][\gamma]$$

It is easy to check that $\iota \circ \iota$ is $\beta\eta$-convertible[5] to the identity function, and so ι is an isomorphism. More problematic is the conversion between τ and $\forall\alpha.\tau$ (with

---

[4] Another one is $\forall\alpha.\ (\tau_1 \times \tau_2) \cong (\forall\alpha.\ \tau_1) \times (\forall\alpha.\ \tau_2)$ which is needed since SML supports simultaneous declarations.

[5] To be precise, for call-by-value languages such as SML we need to restrict $\beta\eta$-conversion to *values*, as in Moggi's λ_c-calculus [SW96]. Under this restriction, we can reasonably assume that $\beta\eta$-convertible expressions are indistinguishable, even when the language is extended.

$\alpha \notin \mathrm{FV}(\tau)$). The required maps are

$$\iota_1 = \lambda x : \tau . \Lambda \alpha . x \qquad \iota_2 = \lambda x : (\forall \alpha . \tau) . x[1]$$

where **1** is the unit type (or any other chosen type). Again, $\iota_2 \circ \iota_1$ can easily be seen to be $\beta\eta$-convertible to the identity. However, while $\iota_1 \circ \iota_2$ is $\beta\eta$-convertible to $\lambda x : (\forall \alpha . \tau) . \Lambda \beta . x[1]$, it is not convertible to the identity function. We therefore require that $\lambda x : (\forall \alpha . \tau) . \Lambda \beta . x[1]$ is indistinguishable from the identity function whenever α is not free in τ. In this case, the required property can be proven in an extension of System F with "Axiom C" from [LMS93]. Turning this back into English: if the type of a term t does not depend on the type parameter then neither should the value of t itself be affected by it.

Extensions of the purely functional sublanguage with other features should preserve the property that $\iota_1 \circ \iota_2$ is indistinguishable from the identity function. This requirement applies to various forms of language extension including an extension with logical formulae or imperative features.

5.2 Assessing the logic

Quantification over values in a typed language P is itself necessarily typed, i.e. we quantify over values of a particular type. For example, if we specify the **reverse** function for lists then we are not concerned with what it would do if applied to numbers or functions — the type system of P is supposed to prevent that.

There is a problem with typed quantification which arises from the fact that the truth value of a formula may depend on the type of quantification. The simplest example is the following:

> *forall* x:t => false

This formula is **false**, *unless* t is an empty type, in which case it is **true**. In EML, we view a type as empty if it has no values. There are indeed empty types in SML and EML, e.g. **datatype t = C of t**.

The example is perhaps unconvincing, first because in languages with lazy evaluation one would normally regard $\perp$ as inhabiting any type, and second because it resembles the empty-sort problem in algebraic specification [GM85,PW84] which can be dealt with by banning empty sorts altogether, considering that their usefulness for specification and programming is rather limited. However, the problem goes deeper than that; consider the following EML formula:

> *forall* (x,y:t) => x == y

(Here, == is EML logical equality, see Sect. 6.) Again, this formula is **true** if t is an empty type, but it is also **true** if t is a singleton type, like **unit**. In general, first order logic with equality allows one to distinguish finite types from infinite types and also finite types of different cardinality.

The above example shows that the problem already appears for universally quantified equations. Here is another example of the same thing, which relies on the use of a function:

forall (xs: t list) => rev xs == xs

If **rev** is ordinary list reversal then this formula implicitly specifies the same property as the previous one: x==hd[x,y]==hd(rev[y,x])==hd[y,x]==y.

These examples show that the truth value of a logical formula can depend on the type of quantification. Indirectly, this means that its truth value can depend on the assignment of types to type variables, and therefore formulae for which this assignment can vary may have varying truth values. Since the type of a formula is just **bool**, the addition of typed quantification breaks the required isomorphism between **bool** and ∀α.**bool**.

After making this observation it should not come as a surprise to observe that implicit polymorphism has some rather uneasy interactions with formulae. These do not occur often; in EML one has to employ the available forms of explicit polymorphism to contrive unpleasant examples. Here is one:

type 'a dummy = bool
val b:'a dummy = *forall* (x,y:'a) => x==y

The variable b is bound to a boolean value, but is it **true** or **false**? Morally, this should depend on the type application at each instance of b, being **true** iff the argument type has at most one element. But type application is implicit in ML and in this case we cannot reconstruct what the type argument is as it is not retained by our implicit conversion ι_2.

The problem is aggravated by the identification of formulae and boolean expressions. As a consequence of this identification, formulae can appear within arbitrary expressions, exporting the observed type dependency to values of all types.

Of course, one can argue that in view of the evident type-dependency of the logic one should abandon implicit polymorphism and make all type abstractions and applications explicit. There are just two problems with this: firstly, implicit polymorphism is such a successful design feature because it combines the benefits of a strong type system (soundness) with the benefits of an untyped language (you do not have to write types); secondly, an explicitly typed wide-spectrum language would co-exist rather uneasily with an associated implicitly typed programming language.

EML sidesteps the problem of type-dependency by giving type-dependent expressions in axioms *no* value, and taking an *arbitrary* choice from among the possible values of type-dependent expressions that are not within axioms. The solution for axioms is satisfactory because we are concerned only with whether axioms are *satisfied* or not, and when an axiom has no value it is regarded as not being satisfied. The solution for type-dependent expressions outside axioms is less satisfactory but it seems adequate for practical purposes since this situation is very rarely encountered.

5.3 Imperative features

At this point it is perhaps worth pointing out that the addition of logical features is not the only language extension that sits uneasily with implicit polymorphism.

It is well known that imperative features such as references endanger the soundness of a polymorphic type system [Dam85,Tof88,Wri95]. What is perhaps less well-known is that the associated problems can largely be attributed to the *implicitness* of the polymorphism. One of the proposals in Xavier Leroy's thesis [Ler92] to circumvent the known soundness problems with polymorphic references is to make type abstraction explicit. Technically, this is achieved by having two different kinds of `let`-binding, a polymorphic one and a monomorphic one; whenever a `let`-bound variable is used which originates from a polymorphic `let` then we have an implicit type application which — in Leroy's suggested semantics — forces a new evaluation of the associated expression. In other words, Leroy only makes the type abstraction explicit; for his purposes he does not need to know the type parameter of the type application, the fact that there is *some* type application is sufficient.

The key to Leroy's idea is that type abstractions are treated as value abstractions — the evaluation of the body of the abstraction is delayed until a parameter is provided. The problem that this circumvents is again the fact that $\iota_1 \circ \iota_2$ is not indistinguishable from the identity function in System F extended with references. But this time it *is* $\beta\eta$-convertible to the identity function if η-conversion is unrestricted, which shows that unrestricted η-conversion is unsound in the presence of side-effects. There is a difference between passing t and $\Lambda\alpha.t[\alpha]$ as a parameter: for t we generate references once, for $\Lambda\alpha.t[\alpha]$ we generate references at each type application separately.

6 Logical equality and indistinguishability

The concept of equality is much underestimated in mainstream mathematics. The general attitude seems to be: what could be simpler than that? Consequently, equality is viewed as a primitive concept in set theory, in universal algebra, and thus in algebraic specification. In type theory, equality is no longer a primitive concept, and some type theories even have more than one notion of equality.

Considering the origins of EML in algebraic specification, it should not come as a surprise that the EML logic contains $t{==}u$ (so-called *logical equality*) as one form of atomic formulae. Logical equality is defined using the notion of *indistinguishability* in order to make it extensional on function types [KST97]. Some problems that arise with the use of indistinguishability are discussed in the rest of this section.

6.1 Indistinguishability

Two expressions exp_1 and exp_2 of type τ are indistinguishable if and only if for any context $C[\,]$ of type `unit` with a hole of type τ we have that the evaluation of $C[exp_1]$ terminates iff the evaluation of $C[exp_2]$ terminates (cf. e.g. [Ong95]). One can always distinguish "genuinely" different values (such as 0 and 1, or `true` and `false`) in this way.

The choice of unit as the result type for the distinguishing contexts is somewhat arbitrary, except that expressions of type unit are *only* distinguished by their termination behaviour. An obvious alternative would be bool and distinguishing contexts returning true and false, respectively. If $C[exp_1] = $ true and $C[exp_2] = $ false then there is obviously a context C' that distinguishes exp_1 and exp_2 in the above sense. However, with this choice we would not even be able to distinguish the totally undefined function undef from any other function. This would make indistinguishability non-transitive since we would have $f==$undef$==g$ for any two functions f, g having the same type. But in a system like the typed λ-calculus where evaluation always terminates, this choice is perfectly reasonable.

Indistinguishability is a difficult relationship. Clearly, it is not decidable, but worse than that, it is neither semi-decidable nor co-semi-decidable. The theory of β-conversion (for untyped λ-calculus) is not recursive either, but at least it is r.e. and so there is a complete proof system that enables us to establish β-convertibility whenever it holds. With typed λ-calculi (without general recursion) we typically have that indistinguishability is co-r.e., because we can enumerate the distinguishing contexts and evaluation always terminates,[6] but not r.e., because equality in the fully abstract model is undecidable; thus, we can at least have a proof system to *refute* indistinguishability in that setting.

For a system like SML where termination is not guaranteed, we have the worst of both worlds: indistinguishability is defined in terms of distinguishing contexts (which we can enumerate), but even if the context $C[\ ]$ is given, comparing the termination behaviour of $C[exp_1]$ and $C[exp_2]$ requires a solution to the halting problem, in general.

Proposition 1. Indistinguishability for SML is neither semi-decidable nor co-semi-decidable.

Proof. Suppose that indistinguishability were co-semi-decidable, i.e. that distinguishability were semi-decidable. Then we would be able to decide the halting problem for any program t by comparing the constant c with the expression $(t; c)$ (which computes t, throws it away and then returns c). This solves the halting problem for t, because we can distinguish c from $(t; c)$ iff t fails to halt: if t fails to halt then the semi-decision procedure would terminate; so we just have to run the evaluation of t in parallel and wait to see which process terminates first.

Suppose that indistinguishability were semi-decidable. A similar argument applies, where we compare t with a looping program. □

The above argument can easily be adapted to languages other than SML.

Proposition 1 says that whatever proof system we may come up with to support formal proofs and/or refutations of indistinguishability, it will be incomplete in the strong sense that there will be indistinguishable expressions which the system will fail to certify as indistinguishable as well as distinguishable expressions which it will fail to distinguish.

---

[6] Since evaluation always terminates, here we define indistinguishability via contexts of type bool returning true or false.

6.2 Indistinguishability in the presence of impure features

The computational sublanguage of EML is not quite a "pure" functional programming language. Although references and input/output were omitted, exceptions were retained in the hope that they would not upset reasoning about programs too much. This hope turned out to be misplaced.

One aspect of ML exceptions can be expressed by so-called *names*. Names can be generated using a **new** function, and names can be compared for equality where separately-generated names are not equal. The type of names can be implemented in SML in various ways: using references (e.g. via **unit ref** and the equality of references, or an **abstype** with a local counter); or just via exceptions:

```
abstype name = A of exn * (exn -> bool)
with fun new f = let exception X
                 in f(A(X,fn X=>true| z=> false))
                 end
     fun eq(A(_,f),A(e,_)) = f e
end
```

As type of **new** we have (name->'a)->'a which exactly corresponds to the idea that **new** is a variable binder, i.e. we write **new** (fn x=>a) for the expression a with the new name x.

Reasoning about indistinguishability of programs containing names is notoriously difficult [PS93], to the point where for certain "obviously" equivalent expressions, no syntactic method of establishing indistinguishability is known. So, this is already bad news. What makes the situation worse is that the very presence of names affects indistinguishability of ordinary applicative programs:

Example 2. Consider the functions g1 and g2, defined as follows:

```
fun g1 f x = (f x, f x)
fun g2 f x = let val z=f x in (z,z) end
```

The functions g1 and g2 are clearly indistinguishable in a purely applicative call-by-value language.[7] However, in the presence of names we can write the function C which distinguishes them: C g1 is **false** while C g2 is **true**.

```
fun C g = eq(g new (fn x=>x))
```

□

Notice that the result of post-composing g1 or g2 with either the first or second projection is indistinguishable (even in the presence of names) from ordinary function application. If follows that pairing is not a categorical product.

In EML we do not have names as a primitive; we have exceptions which — as we have seen — are expressive enough to encode names. However, they are

---

[7] In our examples, we nonchalantly claim the indistinguishability of particular expressions in certain sublanguages of SML without proof. One could establish these formally by using and combining techniques from the literature, e.g. applicative bisimulations [Abr90] and applicative equivalences [PS93].

more expressive than names, in the sense that the presence of exceptions allows even more applicative programs to be distinguished than names do.

Example 3. Consider the functions andl and andr, defined as follows:

```
fun andl a b () = if a() then b() else false
fun andr a b () = if b() then a() else false
```

The functions andl and andr are indistinguishable in applicative contexts and remain indistinguishable if we have names at our disposal. However, in the presence of exceptions we can write the function C which distinguishes them: C andr is false and C andl is true.

```
exception A
fun nothing() = raise A
fun ff() = false

fun C a = a nothing ff () handle _ => true
```
□

If we further add references and/or input/output then even more applicative programs can be distinguished. Here is an example of two functions that are indistinguishable in the presence of exceptions but distinguishable by references.

Example 4. Consider the functions r1 and r2, defined as follows:

```
fun r1 g x = (g x; g x)
fun r2 g x = g x
```

The functions r1 and r2 are indistinguishable in the absence of references: if g x fails to terminate or raises an exception e then so will both r1 g x and r2 g x; otherwise the resulting values could only differ in freshly generated exception names, but then these sets of names are isomorphic. But the following function C distinguishes them: C r1 is 3 and C r2 is 2.

```
fun C r =
    let val x = ref 1
        fun g y = y := !y + 1
    in r g x; !x
    end
```
□

Fans of pure functional languages might be feeling smug at this point, since all our problems appear to be caused by just the features that are absent in pure languages. But this reaction misses an important point, since it is well-known that *monads* can be used to model imperative features within pure functional languages [Mog89], [PW93]. It follows that all the problems of reasoning about these features are already present in the applicative world.

Example 5. Consider the following definition of a "clock" monad:

```
type 'a clock = int -> 'a
fun unit x = fn _ => x
infix >>=
fun x >>= f = fn n => f (x n)(n+1)
```

This is not a monad in the categorical sense since the coherence laws do not hold, but for our purposes this does not matter. It is simply a program fragment which we could write if we were inclined to do so. The idea is to view the integer parameter of `clock` as the current time, so that each expression in the monad world can access the current time, while function application (>>=) makes time advance, because the result of application is interpreted one clock tick after the interpretation of the argument. One can use `clock` to simulate names as follows:

```
abstype name = A of int
with fun new f = f o A
     fun eq(A n,A m) = unit (m=n)
end
```

Now `new` and `eq` do not return `name` and `bool` but `name clock` and `bool clock`, respectively. We can now translate Example 2 into this setting:

```
fun g1' f x = f x >>= (fn r => f x >>= (fn s => unit (r,s)))
fun g2' f x = f x >>= (fn z => unit (z,z))
fun C' g = (g new (fn x=>x) >>= eq) 0
```

The functions `g1'` and `g2'` are the monadic translations of `g1` and `g2`, respectively. If the corresponding monad were the identity monad — with `unit` the identity function and `>>=` being reverse function application — then they would be identical to the original versions `g1` and `g2`. But in the clock monad, the function `C'` distinguishes `g1'` from `g2'`.   □

The lesson we can learn from this is the following: if indistinguishability is such a difficult relationship in the presence of names that we have to resort to denotational methods to prove it, then it is just as difficult in the absence of names — we still need denotational methods. The only difference is that names pull the problem a few grades down the type hierarchy, making it omnipresent. But if we were looking for a *general* method to prove indistinguishability, one that operates on all types, then sticking to a pure language does not avoid the inherent problem. Indistinguishability is difficult!

Moreover it is a rather volatile relation: any additional features[8] chosen by an SML implementor for the library of his or her implementation may affect indistinguishability. As one of our earlier examples has shown, the indistinguishability relations of SML and EML differ because SML has references which can be used to distinguish otherwise equivalent applicative programs while these are absent in EML. Thus, SML programs developed in the EML formalism may only be partially correct in the sense that equivalences required in the specification which hold in the absence of references may fail to hold in their presence.

---

[8] A particularly nasty example would be an access to "system time", as this immediately makes any program optimisation invalid.

7 Conclusion

The design of EML unmasked more problems and issues than we have been able to cover above. We have concentrated on those that are of more general interest, and that are relatively easy to explain. One class of interesting issues that are rather difficult to explain in the space available involve SML's *module* language, concerning e.g. the interpretation of module interfaces and the treatment of module components that are not exposed by the interface. All of the issues discussed above pertain to SML's *core* language for defining the components of modules (types, values, etc.).

Some of the problems discussed above arose from our attempt to combine specification features with programming features *in a single language*. It is unclear to us whether all of the problems mentioned will arise if the specification and programming languages are decoupled as they are in the Larch "two-tiered" approach [GH93]. Our feeling is that the same problems, or some of them, may well re-emerge in a different form, but we have no concrete evidence for this assertion. Direct comparisons are difficult because the preliminary work on Larch/ML in [WRZ93] was (to the best of our knowledge) never followed up.

Prior to 1990, work on EML (by the second author and Andrzej Tarlecki) focussed on the use of ML-style modules in specification and formal development. The features of SML's core language and the specification constructs required at that level were viewed as one possible instantiation of this general picture [ST86]. Only when we looked at these features in excruciating detail while working on the semantics of EML did we discover problems like those described above. This makes us skeptical of attempts to connect specifications and programs on an informal level without reference to formal definitions of both languages. Even if the aim is not formal proofs of correctness, programming languages are complicated enough that there are bound to be hidden problems. Undertaking the detailed analysis that is required when writing a semantics appears to be the best way of exposing these.

Acknowledgements:

Our special thanks to Andrzej Tarlecki for long and productive collaboration on all aspects of EML and related topics, including some of the specific issues discussed above. Thanks to Michel Bidoit for useful comments on a draft.

References

[Abr90] S. Abramsky. The lazy lambda calculus. In D. Turner, editor, *Research Topics in Functional Programming*, pages 65–116. Addison-Wesley, 1990.

[Cos92] R. di Cosmo. Type isomorphisms in a type-assignment framework. In *Proc. 19th ACM Symp. on Principles of Programming Languages*, pages 200–210, 1992.

[Dam85] L. Damas. *Type Assignment in Programming Languages*. PhD thesis, University of Edinburgh, 1985.

[GM85]   J. Goguen and J. Meseguer. Completeness of many-sorted equational logic. *Houston Journal of Mathematics*, 38:173–198, 1985.

[Gun92]   C. Gunter. *Semantics of Programming Languages*. MIT Press, 1992.

[GH93]   J. Guttag and J. Horning. *Larch: Languages and Tools for Formal Specification*. Springer, 1993.

[Kah96]   S. Kahrs. Limits of ML-definability. In *Proceedings of PLILP'96*, volume 1140 of *Lecture Notes in Computer Science*, pages 17–31. Springer, 1996.

[KST94]   S. Kahrs, D. Sannella, and A. Tarlecki. The definition of Extended ML. Technical Report ECS-LFCS-94-300, University of Edinburgh, 1994.

[KST97]   S. Kahrs, D. Sannella, and A. Tarlecki. The definition of Extended ML: A gentle introduction. *Theoretical Computer Science*, 173(2):445–484, 1997.

[KTU93]   A. Kfoury, J. Tiuryn, and P. Urzyczyn. Type reconstruction in the presence of polymorphic recursion. *ACM Transactions on Programming Languages and Systems*, 15(2):290–311, 1993.

[LP97]   L. Lamport and L. Paulson. Should your specification language be typed? Technical Report 425, University of Cambridge, Computer Lab, 1997.

[Lea96]   G. Leavens. An overview of Larch/C++: Behavioral specifications for C++ modules. In H. Kilov and W. Harvey, editors, *Object-Oriented Behavorial Specifications*, pages 121–142. Kluwer Academic, 1996.

[Ler92]   X. Leroy. Polymorphic typing of an algorithmic language. Rapports de Recherche No. 1778, INRIA, 1992.

[LMS93]   G. Longo, K. Milsted, and S. Soloviev. The genericity theorem and parametricity in the polymorphic λ-calculus. *Theoretical Computer Science*, 121:323–349, 1993.

[LvH+87]   D. Luckham, F. von Henke, B. Krieg-Brückner, and O. Owe. *Anna, a Language for Annotating Ada Programs: Reference Manual*, volume 260 of *Lecture Notes in Computer Science*. Springer, 1987.

[Mil78]   R. Milner. A theory of type polymorphism in programming. *Journal of Computer and System Sciences*, 17:348–375, 1978.

[MTH90]   R. Milner, M. Tofte, and R. Harper. *The Definition of Standard ML*. MIT Press, 1990.

[MTHM97]   R. Milner, M. Tofte, R. Harper, and D. MacQueen. *The Definition of Standard ML (Revised)*. MIT Press, 1997.

[Mog89]   E. Moggi. Computational lambda-calculus and monads. In *Proc. 4th IEEE Symp. on Logic in Computer Science*, pages 14–23, 1989.

[Ong95]   C.-H. L. Ong. Correspondence between operational and denotational semantics: The full abstraction problem for PCF. In S. Abramsky, D. Gabbay, and T. Maibaum, editors, *Handbook of Logic in Computer Science, Vol. 4*, pages 269–356. Oxford Univ. Press, 1995.

[PW84]   P. Padawitz and M. Wirsing. Completeness of many-sorted equational logic revisited. *EATCS Bulletin*, 24:88–94, 1984.

[PW93]   S. Peyton Jones and P. Wadler. Imperative functional programming. In *Proc. 20th Symp. on Principles of Programming Languages*, pages 71–84, 1993.

[PS93]   A. Pitts and I. Stark. Observable properties of higher order functions that dynamically create local names, or: What's new? In *Proc. 18th Intl. Symp. on Mathematical Foundations of Computer Science*, volume 711 of *Lecture Notes in Computer Science*, pages 122–141. Springer, 1993.

[Rey83]   J. Reynolds. Types, abstraction, and parametric polymorphism. In R.E.A. Mason, editor, *Information Processing '83*, pages 513–523, 1983.

[Rog67] H. Rogers. *Theory of Recursive Functions and Effective Computability*. McGraw-Hill, 1967.

[SW96]   A. Sabry and P. Wadler. A reflection on call-by-value. In *Proc. Intl. Conf. on Functional Programming*, 1996.

[San91] D. Sannella. Formal program development in Extended ML for the working programmer. In *Proc. 3rd BCS/FACS Workshop on Refinement*, Workshops in Computing, pages 99–130. Springer, 1991.

[ST85]   D. Sannella and A. Tarlecki. Program specification and development in Standard ML. In *Proc. 12th ACM Symp. on Principles of Programming Languages*, pages 67–77, 1985.

[ST86]   D. Sannella and A. Tarlecki. Extended ML: An institution-independent framework for formal program development. In *Proc. Workshop on Category Theory and Computer Programming*, volume 240 of *Lecture Notes in Computer Science*, pages 364–389. Springer, 1986.

[ST96]   D. Sannella and A. Tarlecki. Mind the gap! Abstract versus concrete models of specifications. In *Proc. 21st Intl. Symp. on Mathematical Foundations of Computer Science*, volume 1113 of *Lecture Notes in Computer Science*, pages 114–134. Springer, 1996.

[ST97]   D. Sannella and A. Tarlecki. Essential concepts of algebraic specification and program development. *Formal Aspects of Computing*, 9:229–269, 1997.

[Tho93] S. Thompson. Formulating Haskell. In *Proc. Workshop on Functional Programming*, Workshops in Computing. Springer, 1993.

[Tof88] M. Tofte. *Operational Semantics and Polymorphic Type Inference*. PhD thesis, University of Edinburgh, 1988.

[Wad89] P. Wadler. Theorems for free! In *Proc. 4th ACM Conf. on Functional Programming Languages and Computer Architecture*, pages 347–359, 1989.

[Wel94] J. Wells. Typability and type-checking in the second-order λ-calculus are equivalent and undecidable. In *Proc. 9th IEEE Symp. on Logic in Computer Science*, pages 176–185, 1994.

[WRZ93] J. Wing, E. Rollins, and A. Zaremski. Thoughts on a Larch/ML and a new application for LP. In *Proc. 1st Intl. Workshop on Larch*, Workshops in Computing, pages 297–312. Springer, 1993.

[Wri95] A. Wright. Simple imperative polymorphism. *LISP and Symbolic Computation*, 8(4):343–365, 1995.

Constructs, Concepts and Criteria for Reuse in Concurrent Object-Oriented Languages

Ulrike Lechner

Institute for Media and Communications Management
University of St. Gallen
CH–9000 St. Gallen, Switzerland
email: Ulrike.Lechner@mcm.unisg.ch

Abstract. For reuse in concurrent object-oriented languages we present a set of *reuse constructs*. We give *criteria* for relations between classes that can be implemented by those reuse constructs, characterize the properties inherited via the constructs and explore that we have not only constructs but *concepts* for reuse.
We demonstrate the concepts and constructs with the object-oriented concurrent language Maude. We employ the μ-calculus to reason about these specifications and (bi)simulation relations parameterized with Galois connections to model reuse.
Keywords: Reuse, Object orientation, Concurrency, Rewriting, Maude, μ-calculus, Abstract Interpretation, Inheritance Anomaly.

1 Introduction

Reusability is considered to be one of the distinguishing advantages of object orientation. However, Matsuoka and Yonezawa demonstrated in their seminal paper on the inheritance anomaly that reuse in object-oriented concurrent languages is hardly feasible with inheritance alone [MY93].

To facilitate reuse in object-oriented concurrent languages more precisely in a particular language Maude we have developed a set of *reuse constructs* and we demonstrated that this set of reuse constructs is powerful enough to circumvent the inheritance anomaly [LLNW96].

However, reuse of code alone is not satisfactory, in particular, not at the level of a specification language, where *inheritance of properties* must have preference over mere *reuse of code*. We characterize the classes of properties that are inherited via our reuse constructs. We employ the modal μ-calculus [Koz83,Bra92] to reason about Maude specifications and we employ property preserving mappings, namely (bi-)simulation relations parameterized with Galois connections [LGS+95], for relations between classes and to characterize the properties that are inherited via the reuse relations.

We go one step further and give criteria for reuse relations, i.e., *criteria*, according to which classes can be implemented with a reuse relation. The scenario, we have in mind is object-oriented analysis and design of which establishing an appropriate class hierarchy is an essential part [WK96,BJR98]. In sequential object-oriented languages, the information stored inside the classes together with the methods determine possible reuse relation [HP92]. The more concurrency a language admits, the more the behavior of classes becomes relevant in reuse and for relations between classes. We provide with our relations between classes of algebras criteria about which classes can be in a "reuse relation".

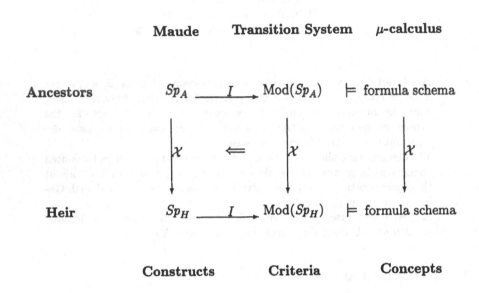

$$\begin{array}{ccc} \textbf{Maude} & \textbf{Transition System} & \mu\textbf{-calculus} \end{array}$$

$$\textbf{Ancestors} \qquad Sp_A \xrightarrow{\ \ I\ \ } \mathrm{Mod}(Sp_A) \ \models \ \text{formula schema}$$

$$\textbf{Heir} \qquad Sp_H \xrightarrow{\ \ I\ \ } \mathrm{Mod}(Sp_H) \ \models \ \text{formula schema}$$

$$\begin{array}{ccc} \textbf{Constructs} & \textbf{Criteria} & \textbf{Concepts} \end{array}$$

Let us explain this diagram. $\mathcal{X}$ is one of the three reuse relations. Note that we are able to have more than one ancestor. We have three different levels at which we explore reuse. The first level is our specification language, Maude with its reuse constructs. Maude specifications can be interpreted and the semantics of Maude specifications are classes of algebras. For those classes of algebras, we develop relations, which can be implemented as reuse constructs at the level of Maude. The second level, which we consider in this paper, is thus the semantic level of transition systems. The third level is the μ-calculus. Properties of objects can be phrased in the μ-calculus and we can prove whether those properties hold for a transition system [Lec97]. We characterize the classes of properties that are inherited via our reuse constructs.

This paper is organized as follows. We introduce in Sect. 2 our specification language Maude and in Sect. 3 our constructs for reuse. In Sect. 4, we give a brief introduction to the μ-calculus and the formula schemata. Sect. 5 contains the framework of property-preserving mappings. In Sect. 6, we explore the criteria for reuse and in Sect. 7 we characterize the properties that are inherited. Sect. 8 contains an example. We give a brief overview of related work in Sect. 9 and conclude our results in Sect. 10.

2 Maude

This section provides a brief introduction to our specification language, Maude [Mes96]. Note, that we employ the notation implemented in the CafeObj System [FN96]. E.g., [Mes96,Lec97] provide a more detailed introduction to Maude.

Maude [Mes96] has two parts: one which defines the basic data types using order-sorted equational specification and another which specifies states (so-called *configurations*) and state changes.

In the state-dependent part of Maude one writes object-oriented specifications consisting of an import list, a number of class declarations, message declarations, equations and transition rules. An *object* of a class is represented by a term comprising an object identifier (of sort ObjectId), a class identifier and a set of attributes with their values; e.g., < B : BdBuffer | cont = C, max = M > represents an object of class BdBuffer with identifier B and attributes cont and max with values C and M, respectively. A *message* is a term of sort Message (in mixfix notation) that consists of the message's name, the identifiers of the objects the message is addressed to and, possibly, parameters; e.g., the term (put E into B) is a message. A *configuration* (of sort ACZ-Configuration) is a multiset of objects and messages. Multiset union is denoted by juxtaposition. *State changes* are specified by *transition rules* (keyword rl or crl).

As an example of a specification let us give the specification of bounded buffers and explain it subsequently. The specification EXT-ACZ-CONFIGURATION specifies the basic data types of objects, messages and configurations (for a formal definition see [Mes96,Lec97]). The empty state, i.e., the element of sort ACZ-CONFIGURATION is denoted by acz-empty. LIST specifies the sort List of finite sequences together with a juxtaposition operation where adding an element E to a list C on the left is written E C and a list consisting of a list and a single element is written C E. NAT contains the specification of natural numbers (Nat) and the sort NzNat for natural numbers strictly greater than zero.

```
module BD-BUFFER {
  import {
    protecting (NAT)
    protecting (LIST)
    protecting (EXT-ACZ-CONFIGURATION) }

  signature {
    class BdBuffer {
      max  : NzNat
      cont : List }

      op get _ replyto _  : ObjectId ObjectId -> Message
      op to _ answer is _ : ObjectId Elem -> Message
      op put _ into _     : Elem ObjectId -> Message }

  axioms {
```

```
    vars B R  : ObjectId
    var  E    : Elem
    var  C    : List
    var  M    : NzNat
    var  ATTS : Attributes

crl [P]: (put E into B)
          < B : BdBuffer | cont = C,   max = M, ATTS >
      =>  < B : BdBuffer | cont = E C, max = M, ATTS >
          if length(C) < M .

rl  [G]: (get B replyto R)
          < B : BdBuffer | cont = C E, max = M, ATTS >
      => < B : BdBuffer | cont = C  , max = M, ATTS >
          (to R answer is E) . } }
```

The class BdBuffer has two attributes, max is the capacity of a bounded buffer and cont stores the buffered elements. The variable ATTS collects—according to the syntax supported by the CafeObj system [FN96]—attributes not mentioned in a rule or additional attributes particular to heirs of BdBuffer.

A bounded buffer may react to two messages: put and get. Put stores an element in the buffer, get removes the oldest element being stored in the buffer and sends it to a "receiver". The transition rule with rule label P says that an object of class BdBuffer can react to a put message only if the actual number of objects being stored, length(C) is smaller than the capacity max. Sending a get message triggers not only a state change of buffer B but also initiates an answer message to R which contains the result (an element). Note, that a get is only accepted if the buffer is not empty, i.e., if attribute cont contains a structure C E indicating that there is at least one element part of the list.

Generally speaking, transition rules specify *explicit, asynchronous communication* via message passing: if a message is part of a configuration, a state transition may happen and new (answer) messages waiting to be processed in subsequent state transitions may be created as part of the resulting configuration (in the specification given above only one new message is generated). We could also have more than one object at the left-hand side of a transition rule and specify thereby a synchronous state transition of several objects [Lec97].

The matching itself is done by a Rewriting Calculus. Examples for rewriting calculi can be found in [Mes92,Mes96,Lec97,LLNW96]. Note, that we consider in contrast to [Mes96] labeled transition systems, whose labels are the messages triggering a state transition.

A specification comprises thus a signature, a set of equations and a set of transition rules. Later, we use the notation $Sp = (\Sigma, E, T)$ for Maude specifications. The signature itself consists of a set of sorts, a subsort relation and a set of operators and is written as $\Sigma = (S, \leq, OP)$.

3 Reuse Constructs for Maude

We have developed a set of three reuse constructs for Maude: (1) Maude's inheritance relation, (2) subconfiguration and (3) message algebra. We explain the constructs briefly and give a typical example for each of them. Sect. 8 contains the specification code.

According to *Maude's inheritance relation* [Mes96], an heir inherits all attributes, all equations and all transition rules from all its ancestors. Thus, an heir reacts at least in all situations in which one of its ancestors was able to react to a message. A typical example for the use of inheritance is a bounded buffer that reacts to more messages than BdBuffer.

The construct of *subconfiguration* is dual to inheritance [LLNW96]. It allows to restrict the ability of a class encapsulated in a subconfiguration to react to messages. A typical example is a bounded buffer which is implemented by reusing an unbounded buffer. The unbounded buffer, providing the facilities to store elements is encapsulated inside a bounded buffer that restricts the messages that come into contact with the unbounded buffer [Lec97].

The concept of *message algebra* is particular to Maude [LLNW96]. We specify message combinators and their semantics that allows us to construct composed messages from atomic messages. A typical example is a get2 message implemented as a sequential composition of two get messages. The semantics of the sequential composition, provides (1) non-interference and (2) that a get2 message is accepted if and only if both its get messages can be accepted in sequence. Moreover, we ensure by the semantics of the message combinator that the answer messages are arranged properly such that they can be transformed into an answer containing two elements in proper order. Note, that the message combinators and their semantics is subject to a Maude specification and thus, this concept gives us a large amount of freedom and expressivity.

Note, that we employ equations and not only transition rules alone. Thus, transformations of the state, necessary for implementing a get2 message by a sequential composition of two get messages, or by modeling the migration of messages into and out from subconfigurations does not involve additional "administrative" transitions.

4 The μ-calculus

The μ-calculus is used to reason about state transition systems at a property-oriented level [Koz83,Bra92]. The language of μ-formulas, denoted by $\mathcal{L}_\mu$, is constructed from atomic propositions, conjunction and disjunction, modal connectives and fixpoint operators according to the following grammar. Let the set T be non-empty (but possibly infinite).

$$p ::= \text{tt} \mid \text{ff} \mid \neg p \mid \text{``}o\text{''} \mid \text{``}m\text{''}$$
$$\phi ::= p \mid (\wedge i : i \in T : \phi_i) \mid (\vee i : i \in T : \phi_i) \mid (\exists x \in T : \phi) \mid (\forall x \in T : \phi)$$
$$\mid \langle L \rangle \phi \mid [L]\phi \mid (\nu X.\phi) \mid (\mu X.\phi)$$

o, respectively m, is a term over a signature Σ representing an object respectively a message. The double quotes around an object or message represent the proposition "this object exists" or "this message exists". E.g., state C satisfies "< B1 : BdBuffer | max = 1 >" if one of its elements is an object with object identifier B1 belonging to class BdBuffer (which includes all subclasses of BdBuffer) whose value of attribute max is equal to 1.

L is a set of labels. $[L]\phi$ and $\langle L\rangle\phi$ are the labeled modal connectives. Intuitively, $[L]\phi$ holds if ϕ holds immediately after all transitions with labels in L. Dually, $\langle L\rangle\phi$ holds if there is a transition with a label in L such that ϕ holds immediately afterwards. We use $\langle-\rangle$ and $[-]$ as abbreviations for modal connectives with the label set of all possible labels.

ν is the *greatest fixpoint* operator used, typically, for invariant (safety, "always") properties. μ is the *least fixpoint* operator used, typically, for variant (liveness, "sometime") properties.

We are interested in the truth of formulas in a structure (A, R) which is a model of a Maude specification. Let us introduce some notation. Let v be a valuation and I be an interpretation function which indicates in which structure formulas are interpreted. $|\phi|_{(A,R),I}\, v$ denotes all elements of A, for which ϕ holds under valuation v and under an interpretation $I : \mathcal{L}_\mu \to (A, R)$.

We introduce a set of formula schemata describing the behavior of classes.

Definition 1 (Formula schemata). Let C be a class and atts resp. atts' denote the attributes with their values of class C. Let $SI(<$ B : C | $atts_i$ $>)$, $\phi_i(<$ B : C | $atts_i$ $>)$ and $\psi_i(<$ B : C | $atts_i$ $>)$ be propositions on the state of an object B of class C. SI is the state invariant of class C. Let a_i be a message and let p be variables in the formulas with the range P. We define five formula schemata by closed μ-formulas for a class C with n methods:

$Persistence(B) = (\nu X.(\forall p \in P :$
$\quad$ "< B : C >" $\Rightarrow [-]($ "< B : C >" $\wedge X)))$
$State(B) = (\nu X.(\forall p \in P :$
$\quad SI($ "< B : C | atts >" $) \Rightarrow [-](SI($ "< B : C | atts' >" $) \wedge X)))$
$Synchronization(B) = (\wedge i : 1 \leq i \leq n : (\forall p \in P :$
$\quad$ "m_i" $\wedge$ "< B : C | atts >" $\wedge \psi_i(<$ B : C | atts $>) \wedge \langle m_i\rangle tt))$
$StateChange(B) = (\nu X.(\forall p \in P : (\wedge i : 1 \leq i \leq n :$
$\quad$ "< B : C | atts >" $\wedge SI(<$ B : C | atts $>) \wedge \psi_i(<$ B : C | atts $>)$
$\quad \Rightarrow [m_i](\phi_i(<$ B : C | $atts_i'$ $>) \wedge X))))$
$AnswerMessages(B) = (\nu X.(\forall p \in P : (\wedge i : 1 \leq i \leq n :$
$\quad$ "< B : C | atts >" $\wedge SI(<$ B : C | atts $>) \wedge \psi_i(<$ B : C | atts $>)$
$\quad \Rightarrow [m_i]($ "a_i" $\wedge X))))$

Each of the formula schemata reflects one particular notion of the object model of Maude. *Persistence* describes that objects do not disappear, *State* that a state invariant holds, *Synchronization* under which circumstances an object reacts to a message, *AnswerMessages* gives the messages created as a result of a state transition of an object and *StateChange* describes the changes in the state of an object.

5 Property Preserving Mappings

The property-preserving mappings we employ to relate transition systems comprise (1) Galois connections as a relation between (sets of) states and (2) (bi)simulation relations parameterized with Galois connections as a relation between transition systems, whose states are in Galois connection. We rely on [LGS+95] for notation and formal framework.

Let us introduce some abbreviations and notation: $\overline{X}$ is the complement of X in the domain of X. Id^Q is the identity function on a set Q. The dual of a function α is $\widetilde{\alpha}$, defined by $\widetilde{\alpha}(X) =_{\text{def}} \overline{\alpha(\overline{X})}$. Let Q be a set of states, $X \subseteq Q$, L a set of labels and R a relation; the set of predecessors in a labeled transition relation R by transitions with a label in the label set L is represented by $pre(R)(L)(X)$, the set of successors respectively by $post$. Let S_1, S_2 be two sets of configurations: $S_1 \uplus S_2 =_{\text{def}} \{C_1\ C_2 \mid C_1 \in S_1, C_2 \in S_2\}$. (Remember that the multiset union of configurations is written $C_1\ C_2$.)

A Galois connection is a relation between sets, which is determined by two functions α and γ. As the names of the two functions suggest, we refer to them as the abstraction and concretion function, respectively.

Definition 2 (Galois connection). Let Q_1 and Q_2 be two sets. A *Galois connection* (α, γ), from $\wp(Q_1)$ to $\wp(Q_2)$ is a pair of continuous functions $\alpha : \wp(Q_1) \to \wp(Q_2)$, $\gamma : \wp(Q_2) \to \wp(Q_1)$ such that $Id^{Q_1} \subseteq \gamma \circ \alpha$ and $\alpha \circ \gamma \subseteq Id^{Q_2}$.

Note, that α distributes over union of sets, i.e., $\alpha(S_1 \cup S_2) = \alpha(S_1) \cup \alpha(S_2)$.

Galois connections provide the formal framework for relating sets of states. Let us now define a simulation relation between transition systems whose states are in a Galois connection.

Definition 3 ($\sqsubseteq_{(\alpha,\gamma)}$ and $\simeq_{(\alpha,\gamma)}$). Let $S_1 = (Q_1, R_1)$ and $S_2 = (Q_2, R_2)$ be two transition systems, L_1 the set of labels of S_1 and (α, γ) a Galois connection from $\wp(Q_1)$ to $\wp(Q_2)$. S_2 is an (α, γ)-*simulation* of S_1, written $S_1 \sqsubseteq_{(\alpha,\gamma)} S_2$, if and only if, for any $L \subseteq L_1$, $\alpha \circ pre(R_1)(L) \circ \gamma \subseteq pre(R_2)(\alpha(L))$.

S_1 and S_2 are (α, γ)-*bisimilar*, written $S_1 \simeq_{(\alpha,\gamma)} S_2$, if and only if, S_1 (α, γ)-simulates S_2 and S_2 $(\widetilde{\gamma}, \widetilde{\alpha})$-simulates S_1, i.e., $S_1 \sqsubseteq_{(\alpha,\gamma)} S_2$ and $S_2 \sqsubseteq_{(\widetilde{\gamma},\widetilde{\alpha})} S_1$.

Note, that a Σ-homomorphism $f : A_1 \to A_2$, more precisely, its extension to sets, which we also denote by f, is an abstraction function and induces a simulation relation $A_1 \sqsubseteq_{(f,f^{-1})} A_2$ [LGS+95,Lec97]. Note that a (simulation) relation $\rho \subseteq A_1 \times A_2$ induces a simulation relation $A_1 \sqsubseteq_{(post(\rho),\widetilde{pre}(\rho))} A_2$ [LGS+95,Lec97].

Preservation of a formula by a function α means that, if a formula holds for a set of states, then it holds for the image of this set under α as well. Let (A_1, R_1) and (A_2, R_2) be two transition systems, $\phi \in \mathcal{L}_\mu$ a formula, and $I : \mathcal{L}_\mu \to \wp(A_1)$ an interpretation function. f *preserves* ϕ for I iff for $q \in Q_1$, $q \in |\phi|_{(A_1,R_1),I}\ v$ implies $f(q) \subseteq |\phi|_{(A_2,R_2),f \circ I}\ f(v)$. A function f is *consistent* with an interpretation function I if, for all formulas ϕ, $f(\overline{I(\phi)}) \cap f(I(\phi)) = \emptyset$.

Theorem 4 (Preservation of properties). *Let (A_1, R_1) and (A_2, R_2) be two transition systems. Let $I_1 : \mathcal{L}_\mu \to A_1$ and $I_2 : \mathcal{L}_\mu \to A_2$ be two interpretation functions.*

1. *If $(A_1, R_1) \sqsubseteq_{(\alpha,\gamma)} (A_2, R_2)$ then α preserves $[\,]$-free, positive formulas, and if α is consistent with I_1, then α preserves $[\,]$-free formulas.*
2. *If $(A_1, R_1) \sqsubseteq_{(\alpha,\gamma)} (A_2, R_2)$ then $\tilde{\gamma}$ preserves $\langle\,\rangle$-free positive formulas for I_2 and, if $\tilde{\gamma}$ is consistent with I_2, then $\tilde{\gamma}$ preserves $\langle\,\rangle$-free formulas.*
3. *If $(A_1, R_1) \simeq_{(\alpha,\gamma)} (A_2, R_2)$ then α preserves positive formulas for I_1 and, if α is consistent with I_1, then α preserves all formulas for I_1.*

Proof. Proof by induction on the size of formulas. See [LGS+95] or [Lec97].

6 Criteria for Reuse

Let us sketch briefly our design scenario and the role of our results for the object-oriented specification of distributed systems. In object-oriented design, the class hierarchy has to be established with the reuse relations between the different classes. We provide via our relations information about criteria which classes are similar so that they can be implemented via a reuse relation. The formal basis for "similarity" is the property preserving relation introduced in Sect. 5.

The design of the class hierarchy is the first phase: only in the second phase a system is modeled as a collection of objects. Thus, the properties (and possibly proofs) whose inheritability one is interested in are properties of single classes. We are interested in the inheritability of the instances of the formula schemata of Def. 1.

In the following, we define relations between classes of algebras, which can be implemented by reuse relations. The relations consist of two parts: (1) a relation between the algebras and (2) a relation between transition systems. Common to the three criteria for reuse is also the function fl (an abbreviation for filter), which abstracts from the structures of the heir and relates ancestor states (terms of sort ACZ-Configuration) to heir states. Note that we consider only specifications with coherent order-sorted signatures [HN96].

Definition 5 (Common basis for reuse criteria). We consider an "ancestor" specification $Sp_A = (\Sigma_A, E_A, T_A)$ with $\Sigma_A = (S_A, \leq_A, OP_A)$ and a "heir" specification $Sp_H = (\Sigma_H, E_H, T_H)$ with $\Sigma_H = (S_H, \leq_H, OP_H)$. Σ_A and Σ_H are coherent order-sorted signatures. Let $\sigma : \Sigma_A \to \Sigma_H$ be the canonical injection.

Let $fl \subseteq \Sigma_H \times \Sigma_A$ be given by

$$fl(D_1 D_2) = fl(D_1) \uplus fl(D_2)$$
$$fl(\texttt{acz-empty}) = \texttt{acz-empty}$$
$$fl(\texttt{<}O\texttt{:}Cl\{a = v\}\texttt{>}) = \{\texttt{<}O : Cl\{a = w\}\texttt{>}|w \in fl(v)\} \quad \text{for } C \in \Sigma_A, C \not\leq_H C_H$$
$$fl(\texttt{<}O\texttt{:}Cl\{a = v\}\texttt{>}) = \texttt{acz-empty} \quad \text{for } C \in \Sigma_H \backslash \Sigma_A, C \not\leq_H C_H$$
$$fl(m(p_1 \ldots p_n)) = m(fl(p_1) \ldots fl(p_n)) \quad \text{for } m \in \Sigma_A$$
$$fl(m(p_1 \ldots p_n)) = \texttt{acz-empty} \quad \text{for } m \in \Sigma_H \backslash \Sigma_A$$
$$fl(v) = v \quad \text{for } v : s, s \not\leq Cf$$

Let us motivate the common basis for the reuse relations. Common to the reuse relations is that we require that the heir specification has at least the sorts and function symbols of the ancestor. We ensure this by the existence of a canonical embedding $\sigma : \Sigma_A \to \Sigma_H$ and we require that the reduct of a Sp_H-algebra is a Sp_A-algebra, i.e., $H|_\sigma = A$ for some $(A, R) \in Mod(Sp_H)$.

We apply fl to abstract from the new classes and relations and to relate ancestor and heir configurations of the transition systems.

In Maude, an heir inherits from its ancestor the implementation of the state and the ability to react to messages. Thus, in order to establish inheritance one needs a relation in which the heir acts and reacts if the ancestors act and react. This is captured by a simulation relation.

Definition 6 (Inheritance Criterion). Let Def. 5 be included. Let C_{A_i} for $1 \leq i \leq n$ be classes in Σ_A and C_H a class in Σ_H. Sp_H is an *heir of* Sp_A via $C_H \leq_H C_{A_1}, \ldots, C_{A_n}$ if

$$(\forall (H, S) \in Mod(Sp_H) : (\exists (A, R) \in Mod(Sp_A) :$$
$$H|_\sigma = A \wedge (A, R) \sqsubseteq_{(pre(fl), \widetilde{post}(fl))} (H, S)))$$

where for $C_{H'} \leq_H C_H$
$$fl(<O : C_{H'} \mid atts>) = \{< O : C_{A_i} \mid atts_{A_i} > \mid$$
$$(\forall a = w \in atts, a \text{ attribute of } C_{A_i}, v \in fl(w) : a = v \in atts_{A_i})\}$$

Let us explain and motivate this inheritance relation. We relate in the simulation relation modeling inheritance those states whose parts belonging to the ancestor specification are equal. Function fl provides this abstraction for the heir configurations and induces a simulation relation on states.

The abstraction filters the "new observations", which are particular to the heir specification, while the reduct excludes "new elements". This difference in the treatment of the inheritance relation reflects the difference in the construction in algebras and observation in transition systems. fl links the two concepts by abstracting in a way such that behaviorally equal configurations, which are constructed differently, are related in the inheritance relation. Maude's object model is the reason why we cannot abstract from the values and consider only the sorts, since the values of the attributes determine whether and how an object reacts to a message. Thus, we cannot extend the domain of basic values.

Our second construct and concept for reuse is subconfiguration. Subconfiguration are a means to restrict the ability of the reused classes to act and react. Thus, subconfiguration and accordingly the simulation relation and the criterion are dual to inheritance.

Definition 7 (Subconfiguration Criterion). Let Def. 5 be included. Let Σ_A comprise the classes C_{A_i} for $1 \leq i \leq n$ and let C_H with attribute a be a class in Σ_H. Sp_H is an *heir by subconfiguration via* (C_H Subconfiguration of $C_{A_1} \ldots C_{A_n}$) of Sp_A if

$$(\forall (H, S) \in Mod(Sp_H) : (\exists (A, R) \in Mod(Sp_A) :$$
$$H|_\sigma = A \wedge (H, S) \sqsubseteq_{(post(fl), \widetilde{pre}(fl))} (A, R)))$$

where for $C_{H'} \leq_H C_H$
$$\text{fl}(<O : C_{H'} \mid atts>) = \; < O : C_{A_i} \mid atts_{A_i} > \mid$$
$$(\forall a = w \in atts, a \text{ attribute of } C_{A_i}, v \in \text{fl}(w) : a = v \in atts_{A_i})\}$$

The criterion for reusability via subconfiguration is that an object of class C_H can be replaced by a number of objects of class $C_{A_1} \ldots C_{A_n}$ and that this increases the number of possible transitions. Hereby, the values of the respective attributes of the ancestor(s) and the heir are identical. When two specifications for which the criterion holds are implemented by reuse we replace a "normal" value of an attribute (of class C_H) by an object of the reused class (C_{A_i}).

The third reuse construct and concept is the message algebra with which new message combinators together with their semantics, i.e., the way composed messages are being processed, are specified. A message combinator such as, e.g., sequential composition, does not affect the state changes triggered by these single messages. Maude provides us with the flexibility to combine less benign message combinators that allow us to manipulate the states of the objects in a way which cannot be achieved by processing (uncomposed) messages with the rules of the rewriting calculus. Such message combinators alter the properties of the objects involved in an arbitrary way. We are not interested in such a kind of reuse, which we consider to be dangerous, and we restrict the reuse relation "via message combinator" to message combinators which compose messages and transitions only.

Definition 8 (Message Algebra Criterion). Let Def. 5 be included. Let op_i be message combinators for $1 \leq i \leq n$ such that $op_i : \text{Message}^i \text{-> Message} \in \Sigma_H$.
Sp_H *inherits via* m_H *combined from* $m_0 op_1 \ldots op_n m_n$ *from* Sp_A *if*

$$(\forall (H, S) \in Mod(Sp_H) : (\exists (A, R) \in Mod(Sp_A), \text{f} \subseteq H \times A :$$
$$H|_\sigma = A$$
$$\wedge (H, S) \simeq_{(post(\text{f}), \widetilde{pre}(\text{f}))} (A, R)$$
$$\wedge (H, S) \sqsubseteq_{(post(\text{fl}), \widetilde{pre}(\text{fl}))} (A, R)))$$

where $\text{fl}(D) \supseteq \text{f}(D)$ and
$\text{fl}(m_H(p)) = \text{fl}(m_1(p_1)) \ldots \text{fl}(m_n(p_n))$ for $p_i \subseteq p$.

Let us motivate this relation. We have two different relations, a simulation and a bisimulation relation, to model the inheritance relation via message algebras. Function fl relates states of the ancestor and the heir specification, provided they consist of the same objects and the same messages, regardless of whether they are composed in the reusing specification.

The simulation relation abstracts from the message combinators and relates all states with the same objects and the same messages, regardless of whether they are part of a composed message or whether they are "simply" part of the configuration.

The bisimulation relation relates—like the simulation relation—states, which consist of the same objects and messages. But, in contrast to a simulation relation, it also takes into account that the composed messages are accepted, provided the state of the reused specification accepts the uncomposed messages.

Naturally, for this relation there is no purely syntactical criterion like for the simulation relation and thus, we only know that the bisimulation relation is a subset of the simulation relation.

7 Inheritance of Properties

Up to now we have considered reuse at the syntactical level with constructs and at the semantical level with criteria. Constructs and criteria, Maude and transition systems have all a quite operational "flavor". Now, we reason about these reuse relations and the objects and classes at the more property-oriented level of the μ-calculus and characterize the properties preserved by simulation and bisimulation relations modeling the reuse relations.

Proposition 9 (Inheritance of Properties). *Let Sp_A and Sp_H be two specifications, such that Sp_H inherits via $\mathcal{X}$ from Sp_A where $\mathcal{X}$ is one of the three reuse relations and $\rho_{(\mathcal{X},\mathcal{X}')}$ the criterion. Choose $(A, R) \in Mod(Sp_A)$ and $(H, S) \in Mod(Sp_A)$ such that $(A, R)\rho_{(\mathcal{X},\mathcal{X}')}(H, S)$.*

A property ϕ is called inheritable via $\mathcal{X}$ if $C \in |\phi|_{(A,R),I_A} \Rightarrow D \in |\phi|_{(A,R),I_H}$ for all $C \in A$, $D \in H$, $C\rho_{(\mathcal{X},\mathcal{X}')}D$. Then, the properties inheritable via the reuse relations are marked by $\sqrt{}$:

	Persistence	State	Synchronization	Answer-Messages	State-Change
Inheritance			$\sqrt{}$		
Subconfiguration	$\sqrt{}$	$\sqrt{}$		$\sqrt{}$	$\sqrt{}$
MessageAlgebra ($\sqsubseteq$)	$\sqrt{}$	$\sqrt{}$		$\sqrt{}$	$\sqrt{}$
MessageAlgebra ($\simeq$)	$\sqrt{}$	$\sqrt{}$	$\sqrt{}$	$\sqrt{}$	$\sqrt{}$

Proof. (Sketch) *Persistence, State, AnswerMessages* and *StateChange* are $\langle \rangle$-free formulas, which are preserved by simulation relations, more precisely by the consistent dual of a concretion function. Inheritance and the simulation relation modeling reuse via Message Algebra are modeled by a simulation relation employing a Galois connection with a consistent concretion function.

Synchronization is a [ ]-free, positive formula, which is preserved by simulation and bisimulation relations, as defined by Inheritance and Message Algebra.

The proof can be found in [Lec97].

Naturally, one cannot expect to inherit all properties, and, probably all proofs when reusing code. The correspondence between the operational paradigm with Maude and the transition system on the one hand and the property-oriented paradigm with μ-calculus on the other hand shows that we have not only constructs for a language but concepts which work at different levels of abstraction.

We are interested in properties for single classes, more precisely in the instances of the formula schemata. The reason for this is that those properties are the ones that are of interest in establishing the class hierarchy. More complex properties, e.g., involving many objects of different classes are more of interest, when a system is composed from different objects in a later phase in the design.

8 An Example: Buffer, BdBuffer and BdBuffer2

Let us sketch the scenario of our example first. Assume we would like to have three buffers with different properties (0) an unbounded buffer, (1) a bounded buffer like BdBuffer of Sect. 2 (2) a bounded buffer BdBuffer2 that accepts put, get as well as get2, a message that triggers a retrieval of two elements from the bounded buffer.

Assume that we have finished the phase in the design where we have identified the classes, the objects and the messages and assume we have given the system as a Maude specification, which contains now three different, not related descriptions of the three buffers. Assume furthermore, that we would like to start with the specification of the unbounded buffer (maybe because it is implemented in the standard library) and implement the other two buffers by reusing this specification.

The specification BUFFER containing a class Buffer is the starting point.

```
module BUFFER {
  import {
    protecting (LIST)
    protecting (EXT-ACZ-CONFIGURATION) }

  signature {
    class Buffer { cont : List }

    op get _ replyto _    : ObjectId ObjectId -> Message
    op to _ answer is _   : ObjectId Elem -> Message
    op put _ into _       : Elem ObjectId -> Message }

  axioms {
    vars B R   : ObjectId
    var  E     : Elem
    var  C     : List
    var  ATTS  : Attributes

  rl [P]: (put E into B)
          < B : Buffer | cont = C   , ATTS >
      =>  < B : Buffer | cont = E C, ATTS > .

  rl [G]: (get B replyto R)
          < B : Buffer | cont = C E, ATTS >
      => < B : Buffer | cont = C,    ATTS >
          (to R answer is E) . } }
```

First, we implement BdBuffer (as it is given in Sect. 2) by reusing Buffer. Since the bounded buffer is more restricted to acting and to reacting than the buffer, we employ subconfiguration for reuse. We establish the relation by:

fl(< B : BdBuffer | max = M, cont = C, ATTS >) =
                    < B : Buffer | cont = C, ATTS >

We have to check that BDBUFFER simulates BUFFER. Thus, class BdBuffer can be implemented by reusing Buffer, more precisely, the value of attribute cont of BdBuffer can be replaced by an object of class Buffer. The reuse relation is BdBuffer cont : Subconfiguration of Buffer.

Let us deal with the second task, namely to implement a class BdBuffer2, which accepts put, get and get2. First we apply inheritance to let BdBuffer2 inherit put and get from BdBuffer. Hereby, fl is given by

fl(< B : BdBuffer2 | ATTS >) = < B : BdBuffer | ATTS >

Since we do not give the original specification of BdBuffer2 here, we have to assume that BdBuffer2 and BdBuffer are in the appropriate relation.

The second step is to implement get2 by subconfiguration as a sequential composition of two get messages. Assume we have a message algebra, called MSG-ALGEBRA, containing the following fragments of a specification, describing the message combinator for sequential composition ; ; and its semantics in rule Seq:

```
op _ ;; _ : Message Message -> Message
vars m1 m2 n1 n2 : Message
vars c1 c2 d1 d2 h : ACZ-Configuration

crl [Seq]   (m1;;m2) c1 c2 => d1 d2 (n1;;n2)
                if (m1 c1 ==> d1 h n1) and (m2 c2 h ==> d2 n2) .
```

Then fl relates all configurations containing a get2 to configurations containing two get messages. Again, one has to check whether the appropriate simulation relations can be established. Critical here is that get2 does not provide the possibility to reach states, that are not reachable by two get messages.

Finally, we give the specification of the three buffers with their reuse relations.

```
module ALL-BUFFERS {
  import {
    protecting (BUFFER)
    protecting (MSG-ALGEBRA) }

  signature {
    class BdBuffer {                    -- A new bounded buffer
      max  : NzNat                      -- Capacity
      cont : ACZ-Configuration }        -- Encapsulating a buffer

    class BdBuffer2 [BdBuffer] { }       -- BdBuffer2 inherits
                                         -- from BdBuffer
```

```
     op get2 _ replyto _        : ObjectId ObjectId  -> Message
     op to _ answer is _ and _ : ObjectId Elem Elem -> Message }

axioms {
  vars B R      : ObjectId
  vars E E1 E2 : Elem
  var  C        : List
  var  M        : NzNat
  vars ATTS A  : Attributes

ceq [P]: (put E into B)
          < B : BdBuffer |
               ( cont = < B : Buffer | cont = C, A > ), ATTS >
     = < B : BdBuffer | ( max = M ),
               ( cont = < B : Buffer | cont = C, A >
                          (put E into B) ),  ATTS >
          if length(C) < M .

eq [G]: (get B replyto R)
          < B : BdBuffer | ( max = M ),
             ( cont = < B : Buffer | cont = C E, A > ), ATTS >
     = < B : BdBuffer | ( max = M ),
             ( cont = < B : Buffer | cont = C E, A >
                          (get B replyto R) ), ATTS > .

eq [A]: < B : BdBuffer | ( max = M ),
             ( cont = < B : Buffer | A >
                          (to R answer is E) ), ATTS >
     = < B : BdBuffer | ( max = M ),
             ( cont = < B : Buffer | A > ), ATTS >
          (to R answer is E) .

eq [E2]: (get2 B replyto R)
          < B : BdBuffer2 | ATTS >
     = ((get B replyto R);;(get B replyto R))
          < B : BdBuffer2 | ATTS > .

eq [A2]: (to R answer is E1 and E2)
          = (to R answer is E);;(to R answer is E) . } }
```

Let us discuss this specification. In this example, the specification is not shorter than the original specification, containing the three entirely different specification with 7 rules (1 rule for each of the three buffers to implement get, 1 for each buffer for put, and 1 rule to implement get2). However, one can imagine to applying schemata, in particular, for rules describing the migration into and out of subconfigurations. This would make our reuse concepts more effective in terms of length of code. However, establishing the class hierarchy at this abstract level of Maude is much easier than at the concrete level of a programming language, and it is more concise than it would be based on a semi-formal design notation only.

9 Related Work

Object-oriented concurrent language deal differently with the inheritance anomaly [MY93]. Languages as, e.g., $\pi o\beta\lambda$ [Jon93], do not provide inheritance at all. Other languages separate the methods from the synchronization code that decides which methods are accepted [DH97] and/or provide sophisticated constructs to reuse the synchronization code [Frø92].

The formal framework of property-preserving simulation relations [MPW93] stems from abstract interpretation [CC78,LGS$^+$95,Bru93,SMC96]. Relations between classes that are based on the behavior respectively (behavioral) subtyping are [Ame90,HP92,PS94,Vas94]. Roles and views [AB91,ABGO93] could be expressed within our framework as well. Bisimulation relations are employed in [Jac96] as the abstraction from the constructive, algebraic, intra-object to the behavioral, coalgebraic view.

We restrict ourselves to the world of formal specifications and start with the criteria at a point in the design process where objects and classes are already specified in Maude. [WK96] integrates Maude and semi-formal object-oriented design notations.

10 Concluding Remarks

We have established a link from reuse at the syntactic level of Maude and the reuse constructs, to reuse at the semantic level and reuse at the property-oriented level. We distinguish three kinds of reuse: (1) via inheritance, (2) via subconfiguration and (3) via message algebra.

In [LLNW96], we have already explored the power of these reuse constructs. Together they are *powerful* enough to circumvent the inheritance anomaly. The upshot of our work is that the are also *safe* kinds of reuse, since we can reflect the syntactic reuse at the semantic level by an operation on the classes of algebras, which are the model of our specifications. This suggests that we do not only have constructs but concepts that work independent from the language and from the level of abstraction. Thus, our means of reuse are *adequate* both for the property-oriented level of a specification language, when one would like to achieve presumably not reuse of specification text but reuse of properties and for the concrete level of a programming language with a class hierarchy reflecting ideas and concepts and not mere reuse of code.

Acknowledgments

We are indebted to Christian Lengauer and Martin Wirsing for their support and for many fruitful discussions.

We would like to thank the anonymous referees for their helpful comments and detailed suggestions.

Funding was granted by the Grundlagenforschungsfonds of the University of St. Gallen.

Part of this work war carried out while Ulrike Lechner was a member of the Lehrstuhl für Programmierung, Fakultät für Mathematik und Informatik, Universität Passau. During that time, funding was granted by the Deutsche Forschungsgemeinschaft (Project OSIDRIS) and travel support by the ARC and the DFG.

References

[AB91]   S. Abiteboul and A. Bonner. Objects and views. In *Proc. ACM SIGMOD Conference on the Management of Data*, pages 238–247. ACM, 1991.

[ABGO93]   A. Albano, R. Bergamini, G. Ghelli, and R. Orsini. An object data model with roles. In *Proc. 19th International Conference on Very Large Databases (VLDB'93)*, pages 39–51, Dublin, Ireland, 1993.

[Ame90]   P. America. Designing an object-oriented programming language with behavioural subtyping. In J.W. de Bakker, W.P. de Roever, and G. Rozenberg, editors, *Proc. REX/FOOLS Workshop*, Lecture Notes in Computer Science 489, pages 60–90. Springer-Verlag, 1990.

[BJR98]   G. Booch, I. Jacobson, and J. Rumbaugh. *Unified Modeling Language User Guide*. Addison-Wesley, 1998.

[Bra92]   J.C. Bradfield. *Verifying Temporal Properties of Systems*. Birkhäuser, 1992.

[Bru93]   G. Bruns. A practical technique for process abstraction. In E. Best, editor, *4th Int. Conf. on Concurrency Theory (CONCUR'93)*, Lecture Notes in Computer Science 715, pages 37–49. Springer-Verlag, 1993.

[CC78]   P. Cousot and R. Cousot. Static determination of dynamic properties of recursive procedures. In E.J. Neuhold, editor, *Proc. 2nd IFIP TC-2 Working Conf. on Formal Description of Programming Concepts*, pages 237–277. North-Holland, August 1978.

[DH97]   G. Denker and P. Hartel. TROLL – An Object Oriented Formal Method for Distributed Information System Design: Syntax and Pragmatics (Version 3.0). Technical Report Informatik-Bericht 97–03, TU Braunschweig, 1997.

[FN96]   K. Futatsugi and A. Nakagawa. An overview of Cafe project. In *First CafeOBJ workshop, Yokohama, Japan*, 1996. Available at: http://ldl-www.jaist.ac.jp:8080/cafeobj/abstracts/ocp.html.

[Frø92]   S. Frølund. Inheritance of synchronisation constraints in concurrent object-oriented programming languages. In O. Lehrmann Madsen, editor, *European Conf. on Object-Oriented Programming (ECOOP'92)*, Lecture Notes in Computer Science 615, pages 185–196. Springer-Verlag, 1992.

[HN96]   A.E. Haxthausen and F. Nickl. Pushouts of order-sorted algebraic specifications. In M. Wirsing and M. Nivat, editors, *Algebraic Methodology and Software Technology (AMAST 96)*, Lecture Notes in Computer Science 1101, pages 132–147. Springer-Verlag, 1996.

[HP92]   M. Hofmann and B.C. Pierce. An abstract view of objects and subtyping. Technical Report ECS-LFCS-92-226, August, 1992.

[Jac96]   B. Jacobs. Inheritance and cofree constructions. In P. Cointe, editor, *European Conf. on Object-Oriented Programming (ECOOP'96)*, Lecture Notes in Computer Science 1098, pages 210–231. Springer-Verlag, 1996.

[Jon93]   C.B. Jones. Reasoning about Interference in an Object-Based Design Method. In J.C.P. Woodcock and P.G. Larsen, editors, *Industrial-Strength Formal Methods (FME'93)*, Lecture Notes in Computer Science 670, pages 1–18. Springer-Verlag, 1993.

[Koz83]   D. Kozen. Results on the propositional mu-calculus. *Theoretical Computer Science*, 27:333–354, 1983.

[Lec97]   U. Lechner. *Object-Oriented Specification of Distributed Systems*. PhD thesis, University of Passau, 1997. Technical Report: MIP-9717. Available at: www.mcm.unisg.ch/~ulechner or www.fmi.uni-passau.de/~lechner.

[LGS+95]   C. Loiseaux, A. Graf, J. Sifakis, A. Bouajjani, and S. Bensalem. Property preserving abstraction for the verification of concurrent systems. *Formal Methods in System Design*, 6(1):11–45, 1995.

[LLNW96]   U. Lechner, C. Lengauer, F. Nickl, and M. Wirsing. (Objects + Concurrency) & Reusability – A Proposal to Circumvent the Inheritance Anomaly. In *European Conf. on Object-Oriented Programming (ECOOP'96)*, Lecture Notes in Computer Science 1098, pages 232–248. Springer-Verlag, 1996.

[Mes92]   J. Meseguer. Conditional rewriting as a unified model of concurrency. *Theoretical Computer Science*, 96(1):73–155, 1992.

[Mes96]   J. Meseguer. Rewriting logic as a semantic framework for concurrency: a progress report. In U. Montanari and V. Sassone, editors, *7th Int. Conf. on Concurrency Theory (CONCUR'96)*, Lecture Notes in Computer Science 1119, pages 331–372. Springer-Verlag, 1996.

[MPW93]   R. Milner, J. Parrow, and D. Walker. Modal logics for mobile processes. *Theoretical Computer Science*, 25:267–310, 1993.

[MY93]   S. Matsuoka and A. Yonezawa. Analysis of inheritance anomaly in concurrent object-oriented languages. In G. Agha, P. Wegner, and A. Yonezawa, editors, *Research Directions in Concurrent Object-Oriented Programming*, pages 107–150. MIT Press, 1993.

[PS94]   J. Palsberg and M.I. Schwartzbach. *Object-Oriented Type Systems*. Wiley, 1994.

[SMC96]   B. Steffen, T. Margaria, and A. Claßen. Heterogeneous analysis and verification for distributed systems. *SOFTWARE: Concepts and Tools*, 17:13–25, 1996.

[Vas94]   V.T. Vasconcelos. Typed concurrent objects. In M. Tokoro and R. Pareschi, editors, *European Conf. on Object Oriented Programming (ECOOP'94)*, Lecture Notes in Computer Science 821, pages 100–117. Springer-Verlag, 1994.

[WK96]   M. Wirsing and A. Knapp. A formal approach to object-oriented software engineering. *Electronic Notes in Theoretical Computer Science*, 4:321–359, 1996. Proc. First International Workshop on Rewriting Logic and its Applications.

Backtracking-Free Design Planning
by Automatic Synthesis in METAFrame

Tiziana Margaria   Bernhard Steffen

Universität Passau* (D)   Universität Dortmund** (D)

Abstract. We present an environment supporting the flexible and application-specific construction of design plans, which avoids the insurgence of unsuccessful design plans at design time, and is thus backtracking-free. During a planning phase the collection of all complete, executable design plans is automatically synthesized on the basis of simple constraint-like specifications and the library of available tools. The designer's choice of the best alternative is eased by a user friendly graphical interface and by hypertext support for the generation and management of plans, as illustrated along a user session. Example application field is the generation of design plans in a CAD environment for hardware design.

1 Motivation

To master the complexity and variety of system-level design, flexible environments are required, which efficiently support reuse, 'design in the large' strategies and teamwork. In particular, a rich collection of design tools with different application profiles is needed to allow an application-specific treatment of complex design tasks. We focus here on a concrete application domain, and consider the functionality of CAD Frameworks. Themselves large and complex software systems, frameworks like e.g. NELSIS [17], CADLAB [10], or the Jessi CAD Framework [11] have succeeded to provide VLSI designers with sophisticated and user friendly project management wrt. data and design execution flow. As such, they are widely used, mainly to enforce standard design plans, i.e. predefined successions of activities (e.g. synthesis, verification, simulation, test pattern generation, and - at the physical design level - placement, routing, binding, etc...) which are carried out to get from a circuit specification through many successive design steps to the corresponding layout masks for physical realization on chips.

CAD frameworks are good at enforcing a prescribed plan of design activities, but they still offer little support for advanced, application-specific synthesis of design plans involving a *flexible use and combination* of available tools. Flexibility is however increasingly needed, since projects become larger, tool functionalities

---

* Fakultät für Mathematik und Informatik, Universität Passau, Innstr. 33, D-94032 Passau (Germany), `tiziana@fmi.uni-passau.de`
** Lehrstuhl für Programmiersysteme, Universität Dortmund, GB IV, Baroper Str. 301, D-44221 Dortmund (Germany), `steffen@cs.uni-dortmund.de`

more complex, and therefore standard plans need to be increasingly complemented or substituted by ad-hoc design planning on a case by case basis.

Related Work. Some flexibilization of tool management was first offered by design environments like ULYSSES [3], ADAM [8] and later Cadweld [4]. In these systems, tools are either directly chosen according to hardwired criteria or they are dynamically proposed at design-time according to the remaining design task. Hercules [1, 7] and recent versions of NELSIS [18] enhance these methods to a workflow management which captures both tool and design management aspects. However, as a consequence of their implicit treatment of design planning, *during* design execution, all these systems detect unsuccessful design attempts only *after* some unsuccessful design step has already been concretely carried out. This requires complex and expensive backtrackings to undo wrong runtime planning decisions. Since in hardware design tool executions typically generate huge amounts of data[1], the files containing intermediate and previous results are usually destroyed after carrying out successive design steps. Therefore the amount of work wasted through backtracking is increased by the frequent need of 'undoing' many more steps, in order to start the redesign from a data consistent point. Here the frameworks' data management functionality helps in keeping track of data completeness and consistency (design plan recovery), but it would be much more efficient to avoid backtrackings at all.

Our Contribution. With CAP-METAFrame we propose the introduction of a Computer-Aided Planning phase *prior* to design execution, where design plans are generated from loose formal descriptions of the desired design tasks. Our approach to the synthesis of (linear) design plans from goal-oriented specifications is novel in its intent and its solution. Intuitively, our synthesis procedure can be regarded as a mechanism to explore the future development of plans *prior* to any execution, in a depth that allows designers to detect traps early enough to avoid backtracking. The generation of the collection of complete, executable design plans on the basis of simple but powerful constraint-like specifications (given in a temporal logic) and of the library of available CAD tools is completely automatic. Once the set of solutions is available, they can be investigated and executed. Of course this feature comes at the price of some structural restrictions on the side of the considered plans. However, linearity is no vital constraint and concurrency could be dealt with along the lines of a serialization (i.e. interleaving) semantics.

The distinctive feature of our specifications is their *global* character, i.e., in our context, their ability to express required *interdependencies* between tools (like orderings, precedences, eventualities, and conditional occurrences) when striving to solve a complex task. Exactly such interdependencies are responsible

[1] To give an idea, the now popular Binary Decision Diagrams were initially devised for use in hardware design, to cope with the huge state spaces of gate-level circuit descriptions.

for the expensive backtrackings at design time, since they cannot be captured by formalisms describing properties of single tools, and thus cannot be taken into account while proposing tools "on the fly" as in the common local approaches.

More concretely, constraints in the logic capture the following significant classes of *global* properties:

- general ordering properties, like *this design step must be executed some time before this other*,
- abstract liveness properties, like *a certain design step is required to be executed eventually*, and
- abstract safety properties, like *two certain design steps must never be executed simultaneously*.

Being implemented on top of METAFrame, a general purpose environment for the systematic and structured computer aided generation of application-specific complex objects from collections of reusable components, CAP-METAFrame additionally supports the flexible tool integration into a CAD environment. Moreover its hypertext system, graphical user interface and local checking routines provide a strong basis for *local* design decisions. Thus the formalism behind the global planning can be introduced *incrementally* with CAP-METAFrame: if no formal constraints are used, local design decision are supported, however, the more constraints are used the better is the automatic support [14]. In fact, playing with the synthesis algorithm by successively strengthening and loosing specifications, its feedback via the solution graph is a good guidance even during the requirement engineering phase [2] (cf. Sec. 5).

The next section will give an overview of METAFrame, Section 3 presents the synthesis component, Section 4 defines our specification language SLTL, and Sections 5 and 6 illustrate the computer-aided synthesis of design plans.

2   The METAFrame Environment

METAFrame [15] is a *meta-level framework* designed to offer a sophisticated support for the systematic and structured computer aided generation of application-specific complex objects from collections of reusable components. Special care has been taken in the design of an intuitive specification language, of a user-friendly graphical interface, of a hypertext based navigation and documentation tool, and in the automation of the synthesis process (our planner).

This application-independent core is complemented by application-specific libraries of components, which constitute the objects of the synthesis. The principle of separating the component implementation from its description is systematically enforced: for each application we have a distinct meta-data repository containing a logical view of the components, comprising information which includes what shown in [4] (basically, a collection of module signatures and classification keywords), but also links to a rich documentation. This information is accessible via hypertext. Components' implementations and their documentation are available in different repositories. This organization offers a maximum of flexibility since the synthesis core is independent of the direct physical availability of the tools and can work on a library including *virtual* components.

METAFrame [15] has been successfully used since 1995 both in-house, e.g. for the construction of heterogenous analysis and verification algorithms [13], but also in several joint projects with industrial partners (Siemens Nixdorf Munich [16, 14], Siemens AG, Telemedia-Bertelsmann, and the Springer Verlag [12]).

3 Synthesizing Plans in CAP-METAFrame

The novelty of our approach consists of introducing a declarative specification layer, which is used for the construction of the desired plans according to *global properties* guaranteeing executability, tool compatibility, and other consistency conditions. Accordingly, CAP-METAFrame can be regarded as a global planner where

- the **Repository** contains a collection of basic reusable components which are considered as atomic on this level. Components include elementary CAD tools, but also transformation components to bridge the gap between different representations or I/O formats.
- **Design Tasks** are (combinations of) instantiated reusable components available in the repository, where instantiation means that multifunctional tools are separately configured for each specific function.
- **Specifications** of design plans express constraints of admissible plans. They may be input in a domain level formulation, which is automatically translated into a *temporal logic*, SLTL (see Section 4).
- **Synthesized plans** are hierarchically structured: design plans are themselves considered as (complex) design tasks on a higher level of the design hierarchy. Plans are directly executable, as they are written in a high-level programming language for the combination of complex component programs, which may even be written in different programming languages.

Figure 1 illustrates the interplay of the CAP-METAFrame components during the synthesis process. Given a design-plan specification, our system synthesizes a graph representing the set of all, all minimal or all shortest tool compositions satisfying the specification, which can be built on the basis of the underlying repository. Each path is a design plan consistent with the specification. Proposed tool compositions may differ in the techniques they use, their application profiles, and, because of the potential looseness of specifications, in their overall behaviour. This overview allows designers to choose their most appropriate design on the basis of a complete graphical description of all possibilities offered by the underlying library of tools. Whereas global aspects of this collection are represented in form of a graph, we rely on hypertext support for 1) the investigation of the characteristics of single tools and data structures, 2) information on

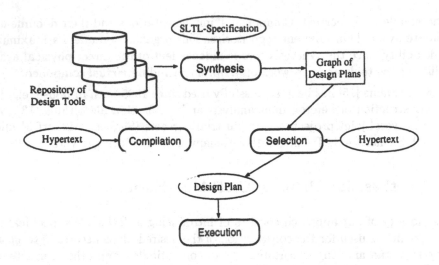

Fig. 1. The METAFrame Design Plan Synthesis Process

the current state of the tool repository, and 3) the classification scheme (called taxonomy) characterizing the application profile of each available tool.

Besides proposing the set of all successful plans, our system also provides diagnostic information highlighting the reason of failure of other plans. We will illustrate the features of our tool in Section 5 along the lines of the motivating example for Cadweld [4]. This allows a direct comparison with the most similar approach. A more detailed discussion of related work can be found in [1, 13].

Our synthesis component works by model construction roughly along the lines of [9]. In general *global constraints* lead to an exponential worst-case complexity, which is not surprising for a global search problem. However, as confirmed by our experience in a joint project with Siemens Nixdorf, typical specifications consist of a number of well-defined subgoals which must be met successively. These subgoals can be treated independently. Together with our limitation to linear design plans, i.e., plans which only require sequential compositions of tools, this leads to a good performance in practice. General compositions require user interaction for treating branches and joins, as described in Section 6 for the synthesis-based design plan editor.

Advanced data and project management features offered by object oriented CAD frameworks as NELSIS or Cadweld, or the task management of Hercules are orthogonal and could be integrated too.

4   The Metalevel Specification Language

Plans are generated by the synthesis component of METAFrame by determining the set of solutions to specifications given in terms of global and local constraints. These constraints can uniformly and elegantly be formulated within the temporal logic SLTL (Semantic Linear-Time Temporal Logic), which combines *type*,

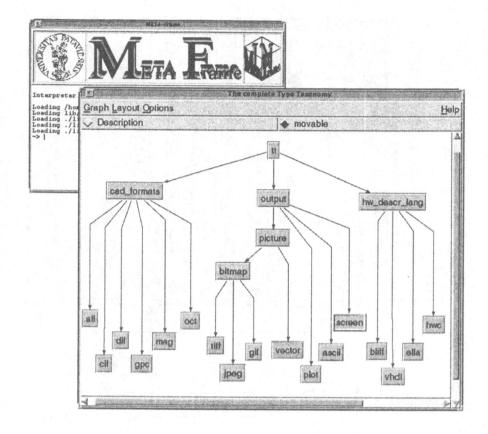

Fig. 2. Main Window and Type Taxonomy

module, and *ordering* constraints to a specification language with a coherent semantics. Given an SLTL specification, all legal (design task) compositions satisfying these constraints are synthesized.

CAD tools and algorithms are seen as transformations that take an input and produce the corresponding output. Thus they can abstractly be described as a triple (*input-type*, `operation`, *output-type*). There can be more than one input/output combination for an operation, thus allowing polymorphism[2].

Our goal is the specification and automatic synthesis of *legal plans*, i.e. of executable finite sequences of design tasks realizable within the underlying library. Two tasks can be sequentially combined iff they are *neighbours*, i.e. the output type of the first is compatible with the input type of the second. Legal plans are simply sequential compositions of successively neighbouring design tasks.

A core issue is the abstract characterization of the tools and algorithms available in the library. Each of them has an associated abstract description in terms

---

[2] Each combination can be seen as a separate design task, i.e. an instantiation of the functionality of the tool.

194

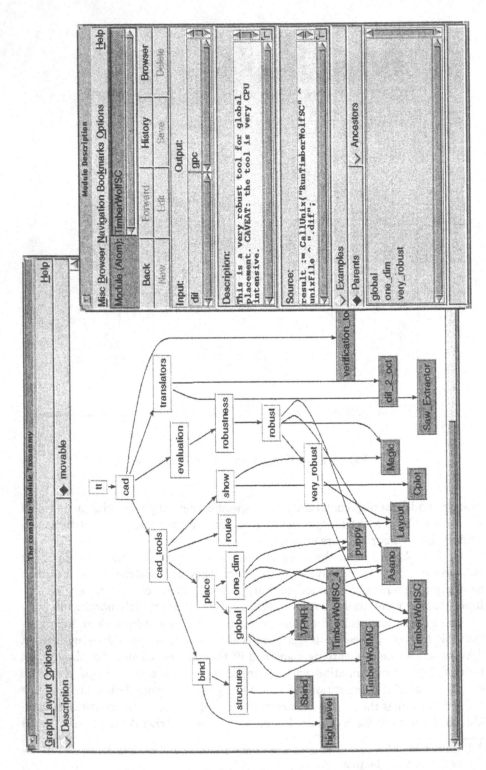

Fig. 3. Module Taxonomy and a Hypertext Card

of a taxonomic classification which establishes its application profile in terms of properties. Figure 3 shows the module taxonomy used in the following sections as presented by the hypertext system. It classifies the subset of tools available in the library that is relevant for the example. A *taxonomy* is a directed acyclic graph. Sinks represent concrete modules (labelled with the concrete tool names), which are atomic entities in the taxonomy, and intermediate nodes represent groups, i.e., sets of tools satisfying some basic property (expressed by predicates). Similarly, we have a taxonomy on the input/output types induced by the tools. This guarantees the flexible and efficient selectivity of the specifications and thus the good algorithmic performance of the synthesis component. Figure 2 shows the type taxonomy used in the example.

Our languages for expressing *local* constraints, capturing interfacing and single tool specifications, and *global* constraints, restricting the ordering between tools along a design plan, are presented in the next two paragraphs.

Local Constraints: The Static Aspect. Local constraints are the selection criteria for *single components*, i.e., single design steps allowed to appear in the final plan. They are based on the taxonomic classification of the repository components, whose design is the crucial part of the METAFrame instantiation for a specific application. We distinguish

- *Interface* or *Type constraints*, which describe the 'neighbourhood' of single elements of the repository in terms of type compatibility. They range over the type taxonomy, and
- *Module constraints*, which restrict the set of legal elementary tools which may appear in the design plan. They range over the module taxonomy.

Both forms of local constraints are formulated as simple propositional logic formulas over the respective taxonomies, which are regarded as definitions of sets of basic predicates (atoms). As an example, in the module taxonomy of Figure 3 the module constraint relative to placement tools

global and not robust

individuates the set { TimberWolfMC, TimberWolfSC_4, VPNR }, which are tools for global placement that are not considered robust.
Similarly, in the type taxonomy of Figure 2 the type constraint

cad_formats and hw_descr_lang

returns the empty set, since none of the types classified under cad_formats is also a hardware description language.

The *task schemata* approach in Hercules'workflow management [1] captures exactly local constraints. Information on functional and data dependencies between tools, there represented in a task schema, is found in CAP-METAFrame's module and type taxonomy. Hercules' task schemata are stepwise constructed by designers by means of successive *Expansion* and selection steps. (Type correct) expansion is equivalent to a type constraint for an atomic type, which retrieves all the neighbouring modules to a given one[3]. Selection corresponds to choosing one of them, which is then included in the task schema. Plans are therefore interactively constructed as type-correct successions of *single* modules.

The next paragraph describes the *innovative* features of our specification language, which allow automatic construction of plans from global constraints.

Global Constraints: The Temporal Aspect. Global constraints are the innovative feature of our planner. They allow users to specify a relative ordering between (some of) the components that form a solution. Using a temporal logic as a framework, we extend the two local kinds of specifications to an elegant and uniform specification language for global constraints, which is defined as follows:

Definition 1 (SLTL).

The syntax of Semantic Linear-Time Temporal Logic (SLTL) is given by:

$$\Phi ::= tt \mid \mathsf{type}(t_c) \mid \neg\Phi \mid \Phi \wedge \Phi \mid <m_c> \Phi \mid G\Phi \mid \Phi U\Psi$$

where t_c and m_c represent type and module constraints, respectively.

The logic can be regarded as a variant of PTL [9] or a linear-time variant of CTL [5]. The predicate 'semantic' accounts for the fact that atomic propositions and actions are interpreted over their own logics.

SLTL formulas are interpreted over the set of all *finite legal design plans*, i.e. all the sequences of design tasks where the output type (signature) of each task coincides with the input type (signature) of its successor. Intuitively,

- tt (meaning true) is satisfied by every plan.
- $\mathsf{type}(t_c)$ is satisfied by every design plan whose first tool satisfies the type constraint t_c.
- Negation $\neg$ and conjunction $\wedge$ are interpreted in the usual fashion.
- $<m_c> \Phi$ is satisfied by plans whose first module satisfies m_c and whose *continuation*[4] satisfies Φ. In particular, $<.> \Phi$ is satisfied by every plan whose continuation satisfies Φ.
- $G\Phi$ requires that Φ is satisfied for every suffix of the program composition. As we are dealing with finite paths only, certain properties of this kind will never hold. This operator is useful e.g. to express global type constraints: in our setting $G\neg\texttt{bitmap}$ excludes from the solution all the plans that feature modules reading/generating data of type { tiff, jpeg, gif }
- $\Phi U\Psi$ expresses that a property Φ holds for all components of the plan, until we reach a *border* position where the corresponding continuation satisfies a property Ψ. Note that $\Phi U\Psi$ guarantees that the property Ψ holds eventually (strong until). This is the most interesting construct of SLTL, since it allows to specify different properties to be met by different portions of a plan.

---

[3] An example for a user's local constraint query in CAP-meta is contained in Section 5.
[4] This continuation is simply the plan starting from the second module.

The last three operators are responsible for the global character of SLTL specifications. In particular, specifications can capture the *interdependencies* of neighbouring design tasks by means of the < > operator, and of distant design tasks by means of the **U** operator.

The on-line introduction of **derived operators** allows a modular and intuitive formulation of complex properties. In fact, as can be seen in Section 5, our built-in macro facility allows intuitive domain level specifications. As examples we introduce the dual operators

$$
\begin{aligned}
\textit{False}: &\quad \textit{ff} &=_{df}& \neg tt \\
\textit{Disjunction}: &\quad \Phi \vee \Psi &=_{df}& \neg(\neg\Phi \wedge \neg\Psi) \\
\textit{Box}: &\quad [m_c]\Phi &=_{df}& \neg <m_c> (\neg\Phi) \\
\textit{Eventually}: &\quad \mathbf{F}\,\Phi &=_{df}& \neg\mathbf{G}(\neg\Phi) \;=\; tt\,\mathbf{U}\,\Phi \\
\textit{Weak Until}: &\quad \Phi\,\mathbf{WU}\,\Psi &=_{df}& \neg(\neg\Psi\,\mathbf{U}\,\neg(\Phi \vee \Psi))
\end{aligned}
$$

and convenient synonyms and derived operators which occur in the examples:

$$
\begin{aligned}
\Phi \Rightarrow \Psi &=_{df} \neg\Phi \vee \Psi & \Phi,\Psi &=_{df} \Phi \wedge \Psi \\
\textbf{use } \Phi &=_{df} \mathbf{F}\Phi & \textbf{finally } \Phi &=_{df} \mathbf{F}\,(\Phi \wedge [.]\textit{ff})
\end{aligned}
$$

We give three further examples of constraints specified in SLTL:

1. <VPNR> *ff*
   imposes all legal design plans to use the VPNR tool as last module[5].
2. $\mathbf{F}(< \texttt{place} > tt)$
   This SLTL formula intuitively means: "place occurs eventually", i.e. a placement algorithm has to be used now or at a later design step.
3. Specification of a liveness property:
   $\mathbf{G}\,(\,(< \texttt{place} > tt\,) \;\Rightarrow\; \mathbf{F}(< \texttt{show} > tt)\,)$
   This SLTL formula intuitively means: "Whenever place occurs, then show occurs at the same time or later".

Note that users do not need to master the basic syntax of SLTL. They can define their constraints by means of the simpler derived operators, like in the examples of the next section.

Using a temporal logic like SLTL especially allows the formulation of *incomplete* (loose) specifications. In our setting this means in particular that SLTL enables the specification of a partial order on design tasks. This possibility is quite helpful, since there often exist situations where the order in which design tasks have to be executed is not known or irrelevant. This situation is precisely captured by the partial orders.

The next two sections illustrate the central features of our approach following a user session for the development of a new, complex special-purpose design tool, which we solve by synthesizing a corresponding design plan.

---

[5] The continuation *ff* is in fact not satisfiable by any module.

5 Working with the Synthesis Component

To illustrate the 'pure' synthesis process sketched in Figure 1, we revisit the *Lassie* task presented in [4] for the illustration of a user session with Cadweld.

The Lassie *Task.* In a context of 'physical level' design of VLSI chips, this task automatically creates a data path for a partially specified design. The design is partially specified since it is given as list of (functional) components, without any information neither on the physical realization of each of them (this is contained in a library within the framework) nor on the final spatial arrangement for the final chip. These mappings are computationally very intensive, have to be carried out in several steps with several tools, and their computational efficiency as well as the quality of the resulting layout (placement of each single transistor and of the necessary wirings) may vary greatly depending on the choice among the available tools and among the algorithms offered by the tools. The ideal goal is a fast computation of a compact layout with low power consumption from the given gate-level netlist. In [4] the design task was described as follows:

> *The Lassie task uses a design that consists only of logical components and their required connections and creates a VLSI chip with the appropriate inter-connections completed. To achieve this, the Lassie task needs a design specified in the* DIF *language[6] from which to* start. *It then determines the* structural binding *between logical components and actual physical realizations. Lassie then attempts a* global place *and* route *to determine where the parts of the design should be placed in the final chip. Once this is done, the actual wires are added to the design specification and the chip is transformed into its* final representation *(here,* CIF*).*

The remainder of this section presents the required ingredients and steps for the treatment of this task.

The Repository. The required fragment of our repository is shown in Figures 2 and 3. It has been reconstructed from the data in [4], e.g., the number and names of tools responding to a query, and has been added to our usual library of tools and algorithms for analysis and verification of distributed systems (as indicated e.g. by entries like verification_tools in the module taxonomy and by similar entries in the type taxonomy).

The taxonomic classification which defines groups over the atomic modules is shown in Figure 3 as it is displayed by our hypertext system, together with the card for the atom TimberWolfSC. Cards contain a concise textual description (expandable to full documentation via hypertext links), which may also include important warnings, links to examples of application and information about the collocation in the taxonomy (here, the parent groups are listed). For the atoms, the card also contains their input and output types, which serve as on-line links to the type taxonomy. In this card the types are dif and gpc, an abstract

---

[6] DIF and CIF are standard hardware Interchange Formats.

type indicating that the global placement has been completed. Taxonomies can reflect very different classification criteria: in the module taxonomy, not only the functionality of the tools has been captured (by means of predicates like route, place, cad_tools), but also the orthogonal robustness criterion, which plays an important role in the development of this example.

The Specification. Already the formulation of the Lassie task shown in Figure 4 (middle) is understood by the system. The formula largely consists of the highlighted keywords contained in the plain text description above. This formula is expanded in terms of primary SLTL operators to give

$$\text{type(dif)} \land$$
$$F(\text{bind} \land \text{structure}) \land F(\text{place} \land \text{global}) \land F \text{ route} \land$$
$$F(\text{type(cif)} \land [.]\mathit{ff})$$

which is passed to the synthesis algorithm. Note the looseness of the formula: no temporal constraints concern orderings between the modules. The only precise requirements are to start with type dif and to terminate with type cif.

The Solution Space. Given this formula, the system returns the set of shortest design plans in graph representation: every path from the start to the success node in the graph of Figure 4(left) is a possible shortest (i.e. minimal length, in terms of number of tools involved) solution to our synthesis problem. In the solution graph, nodes represent modules (atoms) labelled by their name, and edges are labelled by type information. The correct sequencing of the modules along each path is ensured by type correctness. Solutions can be investigated by means of the hypertext browser, which provides information about single modules and types as well as about the type and module taxonomies. The hypertext system offers via a mouse click a card for each node or edge of the graph.

The Execution. All the proposed solutions are directly executable. In fact, each path in the graph corresponds to a target program in our high-level programming language, which is implemented in C++. In order to invoke a solution, its corresponding path must be selected by means of the mouse. The system offers the option for execution, as soon as the selection is unambiguous. Input required during execution can either be typed in a pop-up window or loaded from a file.

In the original Cadweld session, only one of these plans could be constructed at a time. Moreover, this happened "on the fly", at design time. Unfortunately, the constructed plan did not meet the expectations of the designer, since additional properties (e.g. the 'robustness' of the placement tools) were interactively discovered to play a central role for a satisfactory completion of the task. That meant interrupting the design after having already run the 'wrong' placement tool, and trying to *backtrack stepwise* to an earlier (data safe and complete) stage, from which to resume the design under stricter plan requirements.

This time and resource consuming backtracking can be completely avoided *if a* global *solution space is available, which is not the case in the common CAD frameworks.*

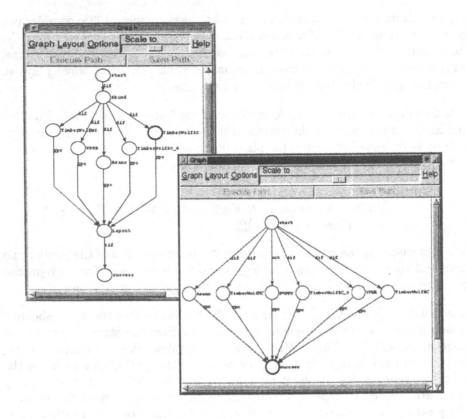

Fig. 4. Synthesis from the Original Specification

On the contrary, we have just shown that CAP-METAFrame offers the automatic generation and visualization of such a global solution space. Underspecifications are here easily detectable by inspection: domain experts may in fact notice that continuations of global plans after some operation do not meet their intuitive expectations. In this example a quick look at the proposed solutions lets a hardware designer immediately discover that some of the placement tools appearing there are not robust enough. Therefore the need for an additional requirement to the design plan is immediately detected, *prior to any execution*, and thus in particular without any run-time backtracking.

Exploring the Library. In our solution, looking at the graph of proposed design plans, experienced designers may know that there are still more global placement tools available in the library, and may ask METAFrame to show all of them via the local constraint

use global

This local constraint is similar to the placement of a request on the blackboard of a tool like Cadweld, or to asking for an expansion step in the course of constructing a task schema in Hercules. The tools corresponding to this description are the six shown in Figure 4(right). puppy did not appear in the previous solutions because it only accepts the .oct input format, which requires a format conversion via an additional translation step. Thus the design path through puppy would be one step longer than the ones in Figure 4(left), thus not shortest. In order to consider such plans we use the option for synthesis of *minimal*[7] rather than shortest solutions.

Modifying the Query. In the *prototyping* phase, the user approaches the desired plan by successively refining or relaxing an initial (usually loose) specification on the basis of some hypertext investigation, or experiments with automatically generated prototypes.

Most additional requirements do not really need running the tools in order to be discovered, but can be easily captured by a well-designed taxonomy and by inspection of the cards of the tools appearing in the proposed solutions. As an example, the warning in the description field relative to TimberWolfSC (see Figure 3(right)) suffices to rule out any path through this tool in case CPU-friendliness is important.

In the original Cadweld session it turned out that the previous specification was still insufficient. It was necessary to (1) start from a .ALL file, and (2) additional constraints (e.g. robustness, one-dimensional placement) on the placement tool emerged stepwise. The resulting layout (.CIF file) was also (3) wished to be successively inspected via MAGIC or plotted via CPLOT. The availability of global plans for inspection would have sufficed to spot the corresponding inadequacies, without requiring any run-time information.

In our setting, this domain-level knowledge immediately leads to the new specification of Figure 5. The result is shown in the same figure, this time after configuration of the synthesis algorithm in the *minimal* solutions mode. The two leftmost solutions would have been found in the shortest path mode too, however the solution through puppy is only minimal and not shortest. The three paths to the failure node, highlighted on the screen, indicate *failing* attempts. This indication has proved valuable for locating errors and to debug specifications without running the tools. E.g., although the module taxonomy shows that TimberWolfSC_4 is even more robust than required, it fails to satisfy the one-dimensional placement.

Note that solutions contain (necessary) modules which are not mentioned in the loose specification. They are automatically introduced by the synthesis algorithm as type correct (sequences of) modules which bridge gaps between different parts of the specification. Here the globality of the constraints comes into play. As an example, we are starting now with a .ALL file, but the binder Sbind needs a .DIF input. A call to the SAW_Extractor tool is therefore appropriately introduced in the design plan as a necessary type transformer. If we made extensive use of this completion feature, already the following, much more concise specification

---

[7] Minimal means that no sub-plan is a solution. It means in particular also cycle-free.

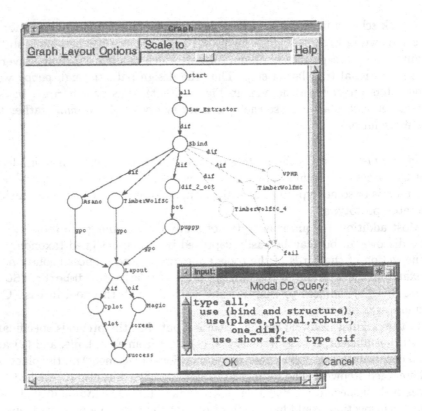

Fig. 5. Synthesis with the Additional Constraints

> **type all, use (global, robust, one_dim), finally show**

would deliver the same set of solutions in the given taxonomy.

The Compilation. Satisfactory plans can be made persistent through compilation into a new module that can be saved in the repository for later reuse. Repository updates are supported by the hypertext system by automatically associating with each new module a new card, which by default contains appropriately precomputed taxonomic criteria and a short textual description. These criteria are generated by the system from the corresponding criteria of its components. Thus the consistency of the taxonomies is automatically maintained. The user only needs to provide a new name for the new component, then the repository and taxonomies are updated automatically. Of course, the proposed content of the new hypertext card can be modified interactively too.

6   A Synthesis-Based Interactive Editor

The good performance of our global synthesis procedure is due to its restriction to linear compositions. More complex control structures glueing the linear portions together must be realized by hand, as it is the case in all the other design planning tools. Still, being able to synthesize linear plans improves drastically over previous methods, where only single components can be retrieved from the underlying repository along local criteria. The advantage of our method is already present if a designer is only interested in the functionality of single tools, because our synthesis algorithm will automatically determine (linear compositions of) required interfacing modules.

CAP-METAFrame can be regarded as a sophisticated editor for the interactive composition of reusable design plans on the large to huge grain level, which allows the automatic synthesis of the required linear portions. Altogether our synthesis-based editor works in a three-step rhythm:

1. decompose the problem into non-linear context components and their linear portions,
2. synthesize solutions to each linear subproblem along the lines of the previous section. In this step interaction allows to successively refine the specifications in order to obtain optimized solutions, and finally
3. construct the global implementation from the partial solutions synthesized in the previous steps.

7 Perspectives

The experience with CAP-METAFrame is very promising: not only is it unique in making available to the users an unprecedented wealth of possibilities, but it also efficiently helps them in mastering the corresponding diversity according to specific application profiles. This feature is essential in order to encourage experimentation with the new generation of tools, which often lack acceptance by practitioners because of their high complexities.

Our approach exactly meets the description expressed by Goguen and Luqi in [6] for the emerging paradigm of *Domain Specific Formal Methods*, which requires formal methods to be introduced also on a large or huge grain level, to support programming with whole subroutines, modules and tools as elementary building blocks. This is precisely what METAFrame is designed for. In our setting, this is reflected in the application of formal methods as a powerful aid in the coordination and combination of complex tasks, as in our synthesis of design plans which organize complex tools along formally described criteria.

Key factor to the acceptance of our methods in the industrial environment was, however, the *incremental formalization* approach [14] of METAFrame, ranging from 'no specification', which results in the old-fashioned development style, to 'detailed specification' with full tool support. This accounts for full compatibility with existing practice, and for offering (rather than demanding) a shift in the accustomed habits of individual developers.

The same principles and algorithms underlying the design planning facility of CAP-METAFrame are now being used as tool coordination engine in the Electronic Tool Integration platform (ETI) of the Springer Journal on *Software Tools for Technology Transfer* [12].

Acknowledgement We are grateful to Andreas Claßen for his constructive cooperation in the design and implementation of CAP-METAFrame.

References

1. J. Brockman, S. Director: *"The Schema-Based Approach to Workflow management"*, IEEE Trans. on Comp.-Aided Design Vol.14(10), Oct. 1995, pp. 1257-1267.
2. M. von der Beeck, T. Margaria, B. Steffen: *"A Formal Requirements Engineering Method Combining Specification, Synthesis, and Verification,"* Proc. IEEE SEE'97, Cottbus (D), April 1997, IEEE Comp. Soc. Press, pp.131-144.
3. M. Bushnell, S. Director: *"ULYSSES - A knowledge based VLSI design environment"*, Int. J. AI Eng., Vol.2, N.1, January 1987.
4. J. Daniell, S. Director: *"An Object Oriented Approach to CAD Tool Control,"* Trans. on Computer-Aided Design, Vol.10, N.6, June 1991, pp.698-713.
5. A. Emerson, E. Clarke: *"Using branching time temporal logic to synthesize synchonization skeletons,"* Sc. of Computer Progr., Vol.2, pp.241-266, 1982.
6. J.A. Goguen, Luqi: *"Formal Methods and Social Context in Software Development,"* Proc. TAPSOFT'95, Aarhus (DK), May 1995, LNCS N.915, pp.62-81.
7. E. Johnson, J. Brockman: *"Incorporating design schedule Management into a flow management system"*, Proc. 32nd ACM/IEEE DAC, June 1995.
8. D. Knapp, A. Parker: *"A design utility manager: the ADAM planning engine"*, Proc. DAC'86, IEEE, 1986, pp. 48-54.
9. Z. Manna, P. Wolper: *"Synthesis of Communicating Processes from Temporal Logic Specifications,"* ACM TOPLAS Vol.6, N.1, Jan. 1984, pp.68-93.
10. J. Miller, K. Groening, G. Schulz, C. White: *"The object-oriented integration methodology ogf the Cadlab workstation design environment"*, Proc. ACM/IEEE 26th Design Automation Conference, 1989.
11. *"Jessi Common Frame V2.0 - Desktop User's Guide,"* SNI AG, 1993.
12. B. Steffen, T. Margaria, V. Braun: *The Electronic Tool Integration Platform: Concepts and Design*, Int. Jour. on Softw. Tools for Techn. Transfer, Vol.1, Springer V., Dec. 1997. See http://eti.cs.uni-dortmund.de for informations on this service.
13. B. Steffen, T. Margaria, A. Claßen: *"Heterogeneous Analysis and Verification for Distributed Systems"*, Software: Concepts and Tools 17(1), pp.13-25, March 1996, Springer Verl.
14. B. Steffen, T. Margaria, A. Claßen, V. Braun: *"Incremental Formalization: a Key to Industrial Success"*, Software: Concepts and Tools 17(2), pp.78-91, Springer V., July 1996.
15. B. Steffen, T. Margaria, A. Claßen, V. Braun: *"The METAFrame '95 Environment"*, Proc. CAV'96, Aug. 1996, New Brunswick, NJ, USA, LNCS, Springer Verlag.
16. B. Steffen, T. Margaria, A. Claßen, V. Braun, M. Reitenspieß: *"An Environment for the Creation of Intelligent Network Services"*, in "The Advanced Intelligent Network: A Comprehensive Report", Int. Engin. Consort., Chicago, Dec. 1995.
17. P. van der Wolf, P. Bingley, P. Dewilde: *"On the Architecture of a CAD Framework: The NELSIS Approach,"* Proc. EDAC'90, IEEE Comp. Soc. Press, pp.29-33.
18. P. van der Wolf, O. ten Bosch, A. van der Hoeven: *"An enhanced flow model for constraint handling in hierarchical multi-view design environments"*, Proc. ICCAD'94, IEEE, Nov. 1994.

Model-Checking CSP-Z

Alexandre Mota   and   Augusto Sampaio
Federal University of Pernambuco
P. O. BOX 7851 Cidade Universitária
50740-540 Recife - PE Brazil
{acm,acas}@di.ufpe.br

Abstract. Model-checking is now widely recognised as an efficient method for analysing computer system properties, such as deadlock-freedom.
Its practical applicability is due to existing automatic tools which deal
with tedious proofs. Another increasingly research area is formal language integration where the capabilities of each language are used to
capture precisely some aspects of a system. In this paper we describe a
formal strategy for deadlock analysis of specifications in CSP-Z (a language which integrates CSP and Z). We also show how FDR (a model-
checker originally developed for CSP) can be adapted for CSP-Z. Finally,
we present a subset of a CSP-Z formal specification of a real Brazilian
artificial microsatellite, and use FDR to check that the specification is
deadlock-free.

1 Introduction

There is an increasing interest, among the Computer Science community, in
model-checkers. These are programs that work by checking every possible state
of a system to verify some specified property such as *deadlock-freedom*. Although
model-checking is limited to certain problems, those that have not the *exponential state explosion problem*, it has a great advantage over, for example, general
theorem proving because it is fully automatic whereas the latter is not.

Linking theories is also a recent trend in the area of formal methods. The
main advantage of these is to capture more than one aspect of a system using a
uniform notation. For example, concurrent specification languages, such as CSP
[12] or CCS [17], can characterise precisely the behaviour aspects of a system
meanwhile they are not suitable for stating concisely (and abstractly) the system
data structures. This is because the data structures in these languages are similar
to those of a programming language. On the other hand, languages such as Z
[20], VDM [14] and OBJ [11] have great expressive power to describe abstract
data structures but lack the notion of operation evaluation order. Currently,
there are a lot of language integration proposals. Some examples are LOTOS
[2], Temporal Logic and CSP [16], LOTOS and Z [6] and CSP-Z [7, 8].

In this paper we use CSP-Z, a language which integrates CSP and Z both
sintactically and semantically. CSP-Z was defined such that apart from enabling
one to deal with the behaviour and the data structure aspects of a system independently, the resulting specification can also be refined independently, i.e., the

approach to refinement is compositional in the sense that refining the CSP or the Z part (with some constraints) leads to the refinement of the entire CSP-Z specification. The main contribution of this paper is a strategy for deadlock analysis of CSP-Z based on [4] and its mechanisation by adapting the FDR model-checker [9], which was originally developed to deal exclusively with CSP specifications. Finally, we present a case study of a Brazilian artificial microsatellite (SACI-1) being developed by the Brazilian Space Research Institute (INPE), where we apply our strategy for deadlock analysis with the aid of FDR. This case study is a small subset of a detailed formalisation and analysis of the SACI-1, described in [1].

The rest of this paper is organised as follows. Section 2 introduces the CSP-Z language through an example, and briefly describes its syntax and semantics. In Section 3 we present a technique developed by Brookes and Roscoe [4] to analyse the deadlock-freedom property of a CSP specification, and explain how FDR implements this technique. Based on this technique we develop a deadlock analysis strategy for CSP-Z specifications and show how to adapt FDR to work for CSP-Z; this is presented in Section 4. Section 5 illustrates this approach through the specification and analysis of the On-Board Computer system (OBC) of the SACI-1 Brazilian microsatellite. Finally, we consider what are the benefits of using an integrated language and the practical advantages and limitations of using FDR in this setting. We assume some familiarity with the languages CSP and Z.

2   CSP-Z

The language CSP-Z [7, 8] is a conservative extension of both CSP and Z in the sense that the syntactical and semantical aspects of CSP is fully preserved while Z operations have a slightly different interpretation. In order to give an overview of CSP-Z we present part of the specification of our case study, fully described in Section 5. In [8] the integration of CSP with an object oriented extension of Z is presented. Here we consider the plain Z notation.

2.1   A simple Example

The Watch-Dog Timer or simply WDT is a process of the SACI-1 microsatellite responsible for waiting a reset signal that comes (periodically) from another SACI-1 process, the Fault-Tolerant Router (FTR). If this reset signal does not come, the WDT sends a recovery signal to the FTR in order to initiate a recovery process to normalise the situation. This procedure occurs three times and, if after that, the FTR does not respond, than the WDT considers the FTR faulty.

A CSP-Z specification is encapsulated into a spec and end_spec scope, where the name of the specification follows these keywords. The interface is the first part of a CSP-Z specification and is used to declare the external channels (keyword channel) and the local (or hidden) ones (keyword local_channel). Each list of channels has an associated Z schema type, where the empty schema type ([])

denotes a list of events, i.e., channels which do not communicate values. The concurrent behaviour of the system is introduced by the keyword main, where other equations can be added to obtain a more structured CSP specification.

spec *WDT*

    channel *clockWDT*:[clk : CLOCK]

    channel *reset, recover, failFTR*:[]

    local_channel *timeOut, noTimeOut*: []

The equation introduced below with the keyword main describes a totally independent behaviour between the processes *Signal* and *Verify* using the CSP interleaving operator (|||). *Signal* is simply characterised by waiting for consecutive reset signals, i.e., waiting for a *reset* and then (→) behaving like *Signal* again (i.e., waiting for another signal). *Verify* waits for a clock, then checks whether a reset signal arrived at the right period or not via the choice operator (□). If a *timeOut* occurs then the WDT tries to send a recovery signal to the FDR. If the FTR is not ready to synchronise in this event then the WDT assumes that the FTR is faulty and then finishes its execution (behaving like skip).

    main=*Signal* ||| *Verify*

    Signal=(*reset*→*Signal*)

    Verify=(*clockWDT*→(*noTimeOut*→*Verify*

                    □ *timeOut*→(*recover*→*Verify*

                         □ *failFTR*→skip))

After introducing the behaviour of the WDT, the data structures used are declared. In order to fix a timeout and to know if the clock achieved this maximum we introduce two constants, WDTtOut and WDTP. The system state (State) has simply a declarative part where is recorded the number of cycles that the WDT tries to recover the FTR and the value of the last clock received. The initialisation schema (Init) asserts that the number of cycles is initially zero.

| WDTtOut : CLOCK | State $\hat{=}$ [cycles : LENGTH; time : CLOCK] |
| WDTP : CLOCK $\leftrightarrow$ CLOCK | Init $\hat{=}$ [State' | cycles' = 0] |

The following schemas are standard Z schemas (with a declaration part and a predicate which constrains the values of the declared variables) except that their names are originated from the channel names, prefixing the keyword com_. Informally, the meaning of a CSP-Z specification is that, when a CSP event c occurs the respective Z operation com_c is executed, possibly changing the data structures. Further, when there is no schema name associated with a given channel, this means that no change of state occurs. An observation is that every external communication has a type, then when no type is explicit CSP-Z assumes the type signal, where the desired behaviour is merely that of a synchronisation and not a value passing. For events with an associated non-empty schema type, the Z schema must have input or output variables with corresponding names in order to exchange communicated values between the CSP and the Z parts. Hence, the input variable clk? receives values communicated through the *clockWDT* channel. For schemas where prime (') variables are omitted, we assume that no modifications occur, i.e., in the schema com_reset below it is implicit that the time component is not modified (time′ = time).

com_reset $\hat{=}$ [ΔState | cycles′ = 0]
com_clockWDT $\hat{=}$ [ΔState; clk? : CLOCK | time′ = clk?]

When a Z schema has a precondition differing from true then it imposes a restriction on the occurrence of a CSP event. It is like a CSP guard, i.e., if the precondition is true then the event is allowed to occur normally, otherwise it is refused and the process behaves like the canonical deadlock process (stop).

Note that the precondition of the schema com_noTimeOut is the predicate ¬ WDTP(time, WDTtOut) meaning that the timeout has not yet occurred, whereas the precondition of com_timeOut specifies the occurrence of timeout.

com_noTimeOut $\hat{=}$ [ΞState | ¬ WDTP(time, WDTtOut)]
com_timeOut $\hat{=}$ [ΔState | WDTP(time, WDTtOut) ∧ cycles′ = cycles + 1]

As already explained, the recovery process is attempted for 3 times, after which the WDT assumes that the FTR is faulty.

com_recover $\hat{=}$ [ΞState | cycles < 3]
com_failFTR $\hat{=}$ [ΞState | cycles = 3]

end_spec *WDT*

2.2 Brief Explanation of the Semantics of CSP-Z

The CSP semantical model assumed as standard is the Failures-Divergence model [3]. This means that a specification can be characterised by a set of pairs ($\mathcal{F}$, $\mathcal{D}$) where $\mathcal{F}$ is the failures set and $\mathcal{D}$ is the set of divergences. The failures of a process P is a set of pairs (s, X), of traces (observed events) and refusals, such that after P performs the trace s it cannot engage in any event of the refusal set X. The divergences of a process P are sets of traces such that after P performs any trace of this set it engages in an infinite loop of hidden events. The language CSP-Z is a semantical integration of CSP and Z in that it is given a Failures-Divergence meaning to Z [7, 8]. This interpretation is required in order to allow Z components to be combined using the CSP operators like interleaving (|||) and parallelism (||).

As explained above, a CSP-Z specification is a parallel combination of the CSP and the Z parts via the channel names, such that on the occurrence of a channel c the corresponding Z schema com_c is activated. As the semantics of CSP-Z is also based on the Failures-Divergence model, we should explain what happens when a given event c occurs successfully, when it is refused and when it leads to divergence. These situations are considered below.

Suppose that c is a CSP untyped channel with corresponding schema com_c. If the event c occurs, the guard of the event and the precondition of the schema com_c are satisfied, this characterises a successful execution step. In this case, the state space is subjected to the predicate part of com_c and the CSP part also evolves (where the event c is added to the trace of the process). Now, suppose that the channel c is a typed channel. If c?x is performed and the value v assigned to x cannot be treated by the input part of com_c, due to a type incompatibility, then c is refused. Similarly, if com_c exhibits a value v from one of its output variables which cannot be communicated through c!v then c is also refused. Finally, suppose that c is not refused by the Z part, according to the above explanation, then if the value communicated falsifies the precondition of com_c then the whole process diverges. A more formal presentation of the semantics is given in Appendix A.1.

Formalising the above explanation, we can state precisely a refusal or a divergence introduced by the Z part. Let c be a channel and tr be a trace then

- com_c is defined as a standard Z schema operation describing the state effect on the occurrence of c
- enable_c $\hat{=}$ ∃ State'; In?; Out! • com_c is a constraint between the values communicate from the CSP part to the Z part and vice-versa
- pre com_c $\hat{=}$ ∃ State'; Out! • com_c
- com_⟨⟩ $\hat{=}$ Init, for an empty trace
- com_(c ⌢ tr) $\hat{=}$ com_c ⨟ com_tr, where ⌢ is the concatenation operator and ⨟ is the Z schema composition operator

Thus, a refusal can occur if ¬enable_c and a divergence if enable_c∧¬ pre com_c.

3 Deadlock Analysis for CSP: Theory and Tools

Concurrent programming is more complex than sequential one mainly because the number of states grows exponentially with the number of processes that compose the system. Describing precisely a concurrent system and analysing its properties is essential to guarantee its expected behaviour. One of the most important properties of a concurrent system is deadlock-freedom, i.e., the system will work normally without an unforeseen and permanent interruption.

In this section we present the two main results of a deadlock analysis technique developed by Brookes and Roscoe[4]. We also show how the FDR model-checker analyses a specification for deadlock-freedom and how the work reported in [4] can guide one in an automatic deadlock analysis of a complex concurrent system using FDR. The theorems presented here are based on some concepts which are informally explained below and defined formally in Appendix A.2. Each of such concepts appears in this section in *slanted* font, to ease the references to the appendix.

The present approach to deadlock analysis considers only CSP processes that do not diverge. This requirement allows a simpler mathematical treatment while it is not too severe in practice, since almost all practical applications are expected to be divergence-free.

Theorem 1 deals with the case where an arbitrary *network* of CSP processes is analysed whereas Theorem 2 is used when one can partition the network into smaller ones. By network we mean a set of parallel processes; it is *busy* if all its processes are deadlock-free. Both theorems use the concept of *vocabulary* which is the set of events containing the synchronisation channels of each pair of processes of the network. A *request* between processes A and B is just a possibility of A synchronising with B. An *ungranted request* is a request (say, from A to B) that cannot be satisfied, i.e., B cannot offer any event needed by A. A *conflict* occurs when both processes involved in a request have ungranted requests to each other; and a *strong conflict* means that these two processes cannot communicate with a third one. A *cycle* of requests is a sequence of indices (identifying processes) in which each ordered pair of distinct indices form a request.

Theorem 1 *Let* V *be a busy network with vocabulary* Λ. *If* V *is free of strong* Λ*-conflict, any deadlock state of the network contains a proper cycle of ungranted requests with respect to* Λ. *If* V *is conflict-free then any deadlock state contains a proper cycle of ungranted requests* $(i_0, \ldots, i_{r-1})$ *with respect to* Λ $(r > 2)$, *such that the only requests being made in this state between processes involved in the cycle are the requets recorded in the cycle.*

We can visualise a network using a graph where the processes are the nodes of the graph and the edges are events that synchronise two processes, i.e., events common to two processes. Thus, by *disconnecting edges* we mean those whose removal increase the number of partitions of the graph, and by *essential components* those that stay after removing all disconnecting edges. A pair of processes is *conflict-free* if one cannot find a trace which introduces a reciprocal ungranted request or a strong one between these processes.

Theorem 2 *Suppose* V *is a network with essential components* $V_1, \ldots, V_k$ *where the pair of processes joined by each disconnecting edge are conflict-free with respect to the vocabulary* Λ. *Then if each of the* V_i *is deadlock-free, so is* V.

The above theorem establishes a connection between deadlock freedom and pairwise conflict freedom of the essential components of a network. The conflict-freedom constraint is necessary because if one essential component blocks then it can infect others if the edge linking two essential components has conflict. This is a very important result because for large networks one can arrange them such that they can be partitioned into simpler ones. Then Theorem 2 tells us that it suffices to check for deadlock-freedom of the essential components.

3.1 FDR

FDR [9] stands for **F**ailures-**D**ivergence **R**efinement and is a model-checker for CSP specifications. Since the specifier uses his knowledge about the theory of communicating processes to overcome the problem of the exponential state explosion, this tool is very efficient to analyse properties such as determinism, deadlock and livelock and to verify some refinement relations among processes.

Differences between CSP and FDR-CSP. FDR adopts a rather different interpretation (defined in [18]) of two elements of the earlier definition of CSP [12]. The first one is the treatment of alphabets that is considered by FDR as a global parameter of the specification. Hence, let $P_1, \ldots, P_n$ be the processes of the specification then the global alphabet Σ is now denoted as $\alpha P_1 \cup \alpha P_2 \cup \cdots \cup \alpha P_n$. Because of this new view of the alphabet, the parallel operator must have an explicit characterisation of the synchronisation events. In [12], the parallel operator is denoted simply as $\|$ because the synchronisation events are precisely determined by the alphabet of the two processes involved, while FDR uses two new (alphabetised) parallel operators: let P and Q be two processes then $P[A \| C]Q$ (with $A \subseteq \alpha P$ and $C \subseteq \alpha Q$) is the process that acts as P for events in A, as Q for events in C and as P and Q (synchronisation) for events in $A \cap C$; $P[\| B \|]Q$ (with $B = A \cap C \subseteq \alpha P \cap \alpha Q$) acts as P for events in $\alpha P - B$, as Q for events in $\alpha Q - B$ and as P and Q for events in B. Regarding notation, FDR-CSP uses a machine-readable version of CSP.

Deadlock analysis using FDR. FDR can analyse a CSP specification using one of the three semantical models defined for CSP, namely the Traces model (T), the Failures model (F) and the Failures-Divergence model (FD). With the first model one can prove safety properties of a system, the second can be used to prove safety, liveness and a combination of these properties and, in addition to the previous properties, the last one can be used to check divergence-freedom. Thus, to check deadlock for a divergent-free specification it is sufficient and more efficient to use the Failures model.

We consider how FDR prove deadlock-freedom and how to use the previous results to ease the analysis for complex networks. Initially let DF (Deadlock-Free) be a process such that

$$DF = \sqcap_{a \in \Sigma} a \to DF$$

Informally, DF can perform any trace, selecting any event a of the alphabet Σ, but may not refuse all events. In FDR, proving that a process P is deadlock-free is simply verifying if P refines DF, i.e., $DF \sqsubseteq_F P$, where F denotes the Failures model. Hence, FDR checks for deadlock based on the Definition 2 (see Appendix A.2), that is, if FDR finds a trace s of P such that after P performs s its refusal set X equals its alphabet αP, then P deadlocks. Further, FDR checks deadlock-freedom through a refinement relation. The relation $DF \sqsubseteq_F P$ is satisfied iff $\mathcal{F}[P] \subseteq \mathcal{F}[DF]$, that is, $s_P \subseteq s_{DF}$ and $X_P \subseteq X_{DF}$. The first relation is always satisfied because DF can perform any trace (interleaving events) formed by the events of the alphabet of P, but the second will not hold when if P refuses all its events because DF cannot.

The verification of $DF \sqsubseteq_F P$ is done by FDR through a normalisation of the transition system of DF where a transition system equivalent to the original one is built such that there is a one-to-one relation between states and traces. Although the normalisation transition system of any process is smaller than its original one and FDR can also apply compression techniques, one can always get a process that exhibits the exponential state explosion problem. Therefore, it is convenient to apply the decomposition techniques captured by Theorem 2 whenever possible. The deadlock analysis strategy is compositional in the sense that we verify smaller processes and use the theorems to conclude the deadlock-freedom of their parallel compositions. With FDR we can easily check if a network is busy, verifying its individual components for deadlock. Also we can prove whether two processes are conflict-free, using Theorem 2, simply checking if its parallel composition is deadlock-free.

4 Deadlock Analysis for CSP-Z: Theory and Tools

According to the requirements of the formal strategy for deadlock analysis presented in the previous section, a network can only be investigated if it is divergence-free, triple-disjoint, uses an associative parallel operator such as ‖ (defined in [12]) and has a static topology.

If one can prove that a network has all these properties than all the results of the preceding section can be used. In this section we show what are the conformity obligations for such results to generalise for CSP-Z specifications. We also suggest an approach to adapt the FDR system to work for CSP-Z.

The conformity obligations that must be verified are:

1. When is the parallel operator [‖] used by CSP-Z equivalent to ‖?
2. How to guarantee that the Z part does not introduce divergence?
3. How to manage the dynamic aspects introduced by the Z part?

Theorem 3 *(Associativity of* [‖]*)*
   Let V *be a triple-disjoint network. Then* [‖] *is associative. Thus, for all processes* P, Q *and* R *of* V *we have* P [‖ X ‖] (Q [‖ Y ‖] R) = (P [‖ X' ‖] Q) [‖ Y' ‖] R *such that* $X \cup Y = X' \cup Y'$.

Informally, if one finds an event of X which is not in Y (the set $(\alpha Q \cup \alpha R) \setminus Y$) and this event cannot be performed by Q and R (the set $\alpha Q \cap \alpha R$) then [‖] is associative. Hence, the set X' equals $X \cap \alpha Q$ and Y' equals $Y \cup (X \cap \alpha R)$.

Theorem 4 *(Divergence-freedom of Z)*
   Let T_c *be the type of a channel* c *and* T_v *be the type of a variable* v *of the state space such that values carried out by* c *are assigned to* v *. If* $T_c \subseteq T_v$ *then the Z part of a CSP-Z specification does not introduce divergence, i.e.,* (enable_c $\wedge \neg$ pre com_c) $\equiv$ false. *Actually, under the above assumptions it is possible to prove a stronger result:* enable_c $\equiv$ pre com_c.

See [1] for a more detailed consideration about Theorems 3 and 4.

   Because of the above theorem we can encapsulate the enable_c schema into the precondition of the com_c one, changing the refusals of the channel c from ¬enable_c to ¬ pre com_c. This simplifies the mathematical treatment of CSP-Z specifications because one does not need to refer to enable_c, only to pre com_c. This is extensively used in what follows.

   Finally, we arrive at the point to consider how to manage the dynamic aspects introduced by the Z part. This characteristic makes the topology of any network built using CSP-Z dynamic; hence, we cannot carry out only a static analysis such as described in Section 3. According to the CSP-Z semantics, if c is a channel and pre com_c ≡ false then c is refused even if its environment enables it. Therefore, it is not sufficient to consider only the CSP equations, but one must also consider the state space on every occurrence of a CSP event.

The impact of the refusal sets of the Z part on the theoretical analysis is that CSP maximal refusal sets are not CSP-Z maximal refusal sets. In order to use that strategy for CSP-Z, apart from the CSP maximal refusal sets, one must also consider the pre com_c schema for every event c of every trace tr.

In [4], dynamic networks are not considered. The dynamic aspects, introduced by the Z part, can only be managed keeping track of the network's structure during execution; so, it seems very convenient to use FDR for CSP-Z. Therefore, for analysing a CSP-Z specification it is necessary to consider what happens to the network after its data structures initialisation. Let S be a CSP-Z specification such that the CSP part has a cyclic behaviour as $\langle a, b, c, a, b, c, a, b, c, \ldots \rangle$ then if one can prove that $\forall e : \{a, b, c\} \bullet$ pre com_e ≡ true then the CSP-Z behaviour is equal to the CSP one, otherwise this cyclic trace is broken. The analysis is no more static because for the trace $\langle a, b, c \rangle$, the data structures are affected by the following Z composition com_a ⨟ com_b ⨟ com_c, according to the CSP-Z semantics. Therefore, the next occurrence of a might happen in the context of a state which falsifies pre com_a.

4.1 FDR for CSP-Z

Deadlock analysis is not trivial even if one considers only CSP processes. Hence, it is essential to find out a strategy to mechanise deadlock analysis for CSP-Z. In this section we present how to adapt FDR for analysing CSP-Z specifications.

In order to use FDR to analyse CSP-Z we have to define the following elements in FDR: State (the system state space), Init (the initialisation schema), com_c (schema associated to the channel c), pre com_c (precondition of the schema com_c) and the communication of values between the CSP and the Z parts of the specification. The translation strategy is defined as follows. In general, Z operations are relations between initial and final states, as well as input and output values. However, for simplicity we assume in the following that these relations are functional.

• State: FDR has no means to represent a global state space due to its foundations on CSP. However, FDR processes can have parameters which are commonly used for indexing. Therefore, the system state space can be represented as a parameter of all processes of the specification. When a schema com_c updates the state space the final state produced must be taken as the initial state for the next execution step.

• Init: As FDR cannot represent a state space globally then the Init schema is translated into FDR as a process such that it initialises the data structures used by the main equation. Thus, Init = main(InitialState), where InitialState is a tuple which defines an initial value for each state component.

• com_c: A Z schema can be translated into FDR as a function. The arguments to this function are the (current) state and the values of the input variables; the function result is formed by the final state defined by the schema and the values of the output variables. This function does not embody the precondition part of the schema, only the effect.

• pre com_c: A precondition is also encoded as an FDR function of type State × Input ⇸ $\mathbb{B}$; it evaluates to true in the states and input values which satisfy the precondition of the com_c schema, and to false otherwise.

• **Communications**: Values communicated in the CSP part of the FDR script must be passed to the Z part, and vice-versa. All conversion patterns below have the form of a CSP guarded command. For an input, the condition of the guard is a prefix choice of a suitable value for the input parameter. The expression a?x : {a.x • x : T, pre_com_a(S, x)} is a set comprehension which generates the set of elements a.x where x ranges over T and satifies the predicate pre_com_a(S, x). For an output we simply pass the result of the Z part to the CSP part.

The following conversion patterns implement the above strategy and ease the encoding of a CSP-Z specification into FDR:

CSP-Z	FDR CSP-Z
$P=a \rightarrow P$	P(S)=pre_com_a(S) & (let S'=com_a(S) within a -> P(S'))
$P=a?x \rightarrow P$	P(S)=a?x:{a.x @ x:T,pre_com_a(S,x)} & (let S'=com_a(S,x) within P(S'))
$P=a!e \rightarrow P$	P(S)=pre_com_a(S) & (let (S',e)=com_a(S) within a!e -> P(S'))

The translation of channel declarations, constants and free types is a straight-forward syntactical conversion, as presented in [1].

5 Case Study

In this section we present the CSP-Z specification of two processes which combined in parallel with that introduced in Section 2 results in a final specification that represents the simplified behaviour of the SACI-1 OBC. We also show how to translate the specification into our FDR representation and then we carry out a deadlock analysis using FDR.

The SACI-1 OBC is a fault-tolerant distributed processing system which combines software and hardware components [5]. Its main parts are: its Watch-Dog Timer (WDT) and its Fault-Tolerant Router (FTR). Due to its fault-tolerant aspects, the SACI-1 was designed with redundant components. It has three WDT's, three FTR's, etc. However, for illustrative purposes we consider here a simplification of the real configuration, removing indices and presenting its behaviour.

5.1 The SACI-1 Main Components

Fault-Tolerant Router. The FTR is responsible for some tasks and for periodically sending a reset signal to the WDT. In order to model the FTR as close as possible to its original conception we consider that it can stop temporarily or permanently. In a temporary stop, the FTR can be reanimated through a recover signal. However, in a permanent one the WDT cannot be restarted.

spec *FTR*

    channel *clockFTR*:[clk : CLOCK]

    channel *reset, recover*:[]

    local_channel *resetWDT, task, taskDone, problem*:[]

    main=*clockFTR*→*Work*

     Work=(*Normal* ||| *Problem*)

    Normal=(*resetWDT*→ *reset*→main

            □ *task*→((*taskDone*→main) ^ (*problem*→stop)))

    Problem=(*recover*→ main)

$$\boxed{\begin{array}{l}\text{State} \\ \hline \text{time : CLOCK} \end{array}}$$

| WDTRstP : CLOCK

com_task $\widehat{=}$ ¬ com_resetWDT

$$\boxed{\begin{array}{l}\text{com\_resetWDT} \\ \hline \Xi\text{State} \\ \hline \text{WDTP(time, WDTRstP)} \end{array}}$$

$$\boxed{\begin{array}{l}\text{clockFTR} \\ \hline \Delta\text{State} \\ \text{clk? : CLOCK} \\ \hline \text{time}' = \text{clk?} \end{array}}$$

end_spec *FTR*

OBC Clock. As CSP-Z cannot capture precisely temporal aspects of a system, we need some way to characterise the SACI-1 as a system dependent of time. We model a process which exhibits events, carrying clock values, that control the behaviour of the WDT and the FTR.

spec *SCLOCK*

    channel *clockWDT, clockFTR* : [clk : CLOCK]

    local_channel *tic*: []

    main=(*clockWDT*→skip ||| *clockFTR* →skip)⨾(*tic*→main)

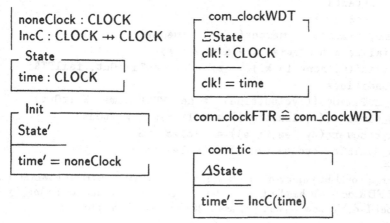

$$\boxed{\begin{array}{l}\text{noneClock : CLOCK} \\ \text{IncC : CLOCK} \rightarrowtail \text{CLOCK} \\ \boxed{\begin{array}{l}\text{State} \\ \hline \text{time : CLOCK}\end{array}}\end{array}}$$

$$\boxed{\begin{array}{l}\text{com\_clockWDT} \\ \hline \Xi\text{State} \\ \text{clk! : CLOCK} \\ \hline \text{clk!} = \text{time} \end{array}}$$

$$\boxed{\begin{array}{l}\text{Init} \\ \hline \text{State}' \\ \hline \text{time}' = \text{noneClock} \end{array}}$$

com_clockFTR $\widehat{=}$ com_clockWDT

$$\boxed{\begin{array}{l}\text{com\_tic} \\ \hline \Delta\text{State} \\ \hline \text{time}' = \text{IncC(time)} \end{array}}$$

end_spec *SCLOCK*

SACI-1. The simplified behaviour of the SACI-1 microsatellite is given by an alphabetised parallel composition ([|||]) of the previous three CSP-Z components. In this specification, the elements inside the brackets of the parallel operator are the synchronisation points.

spec *SACI-1*

    main=*(WDT [| {reset, recover} |] FTR)*
                     [| {clockWDT, clockFTR} |] *SCLOCK*

end_spec *SACI-1*

5.2 *WDT* in FDR

In this section we present the translation of the *WDT* into FDR. Comments (--) are added to ease the FDR script[1].

```
-- The CLOCK data type (Free type)
datatype CLOCK = noneClock | c1 | c2 | c3 | c4 | c5 | c6
-- spec WDT
channel clockWDT : CLOCK
channel reset, recover, failFTR, timeOut, noTimeOut
-- The main equation and its descendents
main(S)   = Signal(S) ||| Verify(S)
Signal(S) = reset -> Signal(com_reset(S))
Verify(S) = (clockWDT?c ->
             (pre_com_noTimeOut(com_clockWDT(S,c)) &
               noTimeOut -> Verify(com_clockWDT(S,c))
          [] pre_com_timeOut(com_clockWDT(S,c)) &
               timeOut ->
               (pre_com_recover(com_timeOut(com_clockWDT(S,c))) &
                 recover -> Verify(com_timeOut(com_clockWDT(S,c)))
               [] pre_com_failFTR(com_timeOut(com_clockWDT(S,c))) &
                 failFTR -> SKIP)))
-- The constants
WDTtOut = {c3, c6}
WDTP(time, timeout) = member(time, timeout)
-- Initialisation schema (now a process)
Init = main((0, noneClock)) \ {timeOut, noTimeOut, failFTR}
-- Preconditions
pre_com_noTimeOut((cycles,time)) = not WDTP(time, WDTtOut)
pre_com_timeOut((cycles,time)) = WDTP(time, WDTtOut)
pre_com_recover((cycles,time)) = cycles < 3
pre_com_failFTR((cycles,time)) = cycles == 3
```

---

[1] This script could be improved using the let ... within construct; however, release 2.11 of FDR does not handle this construct correctly. According to Formal Systems (Europe) Ltd, the new version (release 2.20) has solved the problem.

```
-- Schemas
com_reset((cycles,time)) = (0, time)
com_clockWDT((cycles,time),clk) = (cycles, clk)
com_timeOut((cycles,time)) = (cycles + 1, time)
-- end_spec WDT
```

The other two processes are translated into the FDR notation in a similar way. We have done that, loaded into FDR and checked that the *SACI-1* specification is deadlock-free.

6 Conclusion

In this paper we proposed a strategy for model-checking CSP-Z specifications based on previous work for model-checking CSP and on the semantics of the CSP-Z language, verifying its conformity, and adapting the FDR model-checker to work with the state part of CSP-Z specifications. We presented a formal specification in CSP-Z of a subset of the SACI-1 microsatellite OBC as well as a deadlock analysis of this specification using the FDR tool.

The SACI-1 project as developed by the Brazilian Space Research Institute lacked formal documentation, hence our first contribution was to formally define a subset of the SACI-1 [1]: its OBC system. From the very beginning, the goal of the formalisation task was to develop a formal specification free from problems and hence we did not find any deadlocks in our specification, as required. However, some problems in the informal documentation were detected: the informal documentation was found to be ambiguous (difficulting the understanding of the system), and the description of many processes which were supposed to cooperate did not specify synchronisation points. These problems were reported to the members of the SACI-1 project and the specification reported in [1] serves today as a formal reference for the implementation of this project.

One research direction we intend to pursue is the derivation of an implementation in a language like OCCAM [15] from CSP-Z specifications. To this end, we count with an important theoretical result [7, 8]: refinement of the CSP and of the Z part (subject to some constraints) of a CSP-Z specification leads to refinement of the entire CSP-Z specification.

Another topic for further research is the integration of tools to deal with CSP-Z specifications. In [1], we have shown how to use Z-EVES [19] to type-check the Z part of the SACI-1 specification and to refine some of its data structures. Furthermore, the ZANS animator [13] was also used in [1] to analyse the behaviour of the data structures in the Z part of the SACI-1 specification. Ideally, these tools should also be adapted to work for CSP-Z, as we did with FDR. The ultimate goal would be linking all these tools into a uniform development environment for CSP-Z.

A final remark is that although we have based our work on CSP-Z, the results could, in principle, be easily adapted to other approaches to integrate CSP and Z, such as, for example [10].

7 Acknowledgements

We thank people from the Brazilian Space Research Institute (INPE), and in particular Alderico R. Paula Jr. for help in the understanding of the SACI-1. We also thank Clemens Fischer and Paulo Borba for discussions about CSP-Z and FDR, and for suggestions and criticisms which helped us to improve our approach to model-checking CSP-Z.

A Formal Definitions

The whole paper was intended to describe the development of our strategy to model-checking CSP-Z specifications without too much technical details. In this section we present the Failures-Divergence model for Z and the some definitions which were only informally presented in Section 3.

A.1 Failures-Divergence Semantics of Z

Let c be a channel, tr be a trace, $\mathsf{Chans}(\mathsf{I})$ be the set of channels of an interface I and $Comm$ be the set of communications (pairs (c, v), where c is a channel and v is a communication value), thus:

The Failures-Divergence interpretation for the Z part is given by the following definition:

Definition 1. Let I be an interface and O_Z a list of Z-schemas with exactly one schema enable_c and effect_c for every channel c from $\mathsf{Chans}(\mathsf{I})$. Then the semantics of the corresponding CSP-Z specification is defined as follows:

$$[\text{spec } I; State; Init; O_Z \text{ end\_spec}] = (\mathcal{F}, \mathcal{D})$$

$$where$$

$$\mathcal{D} = \{s^\frown t : \text{seq } Comm \mid \exists State' \bullet effect\_s \wedge (enable\_head(t))' \wedge \neg(\text{pre } effect\_head(t))'\}$$

$$\mathcal{F} = \{(tr, \mathcal{R}) : \text{seq } Comm \times \mathbf{P} \, Comm \mid \exists State' \bullet (effect\_tr \wedge \mathcal{R} \subseteq REF)\}$$
$$\cup \{(tr, \mathcal{R}) : \mathcal{D} \times \mathbf{P} \, Comm\} \cup \{(\langle\rangle, \varnothing)\}$$
$$REF == \{(c, v) \mid \neg(enable\_(c, v))'\}$$

In the above definition, $\mathcal{D}$ is the refusal set introduced by the Z part where the predicate enable_c$\wedge\neg$ pre effect_c is verified and $\mathcal{F}$ is the failures set of the Z part, where REF is the set of communications that can be refused, i.e., the predicate $\neg$enable_c is satisfied.

A.2 Definitions for Deadlock Analysis

Definition 2. The process P is *deadlock-free* if $\forall s \in (\alpha P)^* \bullet (s, \alpha P) \notin \mathcal{F}[P]$.

CSP operators are compositional in the sense that given two processes P and Q, P $\square$ Q or P $\parallel$ Q are also processes. Thus, we can see a concurrent system as a composition of parallel processes.

Definition 3. A *network* is a parallel combination of processes. Let V be a network composed of the processes $P_1, \ldots, P_n$ then $V = \langle P_1, \ldots, P_n \rangle$.

In the following definitions, let V be a network such that $V = \langle P_1, \ldots, P_n \rangle$.

Definition 4. A network is *triple-disjoint* iff $\alpha P_i \cap \alpha P_j \cap \alpha P_k = \emptyset$, $i \neq j \neq k$.

Definition 5. A graphical view of a network is a *communication graph* where the processes are the nodes and an arc exists between two nodes iff $\alpha P_i \cap \alpha P_j \neq \emptyset$, $i \neq j$.

Definition 6. The *vocabulary* Λ of a network V is the set $\bigcup \{\alpha P_i \cap \alpha P_j \mid 1 \leq i < j \leq n\}$.

Definition 7. A *state* σ of a network V is a trace s of V and an indexed tuple $\langle X_1, \ldots, X_n \rangle$ of refusal sets X_i such that for each i, $(s \restriction \alpha P_i, X_i) \in \mathcal{F}[P_i]$.

Definition 8. Let $\sigma = (s, X)$ be a state and Λ be the vocabulary of the network V. A pair of indices $\langle i, j \rangle$ (with $i \neq j$) is:

* a *request* if $(\alpha P_i - X_i) \cap \alpha P_j \neq \emptyset$ $(P_i \overset{\sigma}{\to} P_j$ or $P_i \overset{\sigma, \Lambda}{\to} P_j)$;

* a *strong request* if $\emptyset \neq (\alpha P_i - X_i) \subseteq \alpha P_j$ $(P_i \overset{\sigma}{\Rightarrow} P_j$ or $P_i \overset{\sigma, \Lambda}{\Rightarrow} P_j)$;

* *ungranted* if in addition $\alpha P_i \cap \alpha P_j \subseteq X_i \cup X_j$ $(P_i \overset{\sigma}{\to}_\bullet P_j$ or $P_i \overset{\sigma, \Lambda}{\to}_\bullet P_j)$.

Definition 9. A state σ of the pair $\langle P, Q \rangle$ is a Γ-*conflict* if $P \overset{\sigma, \Gamma}{\to}_\bullet Q$ and $Q \overset{\sigma, \Gamma}{\to}_\bullet P$ and *strong* Γ-*conflict* if $P \overset{\sigma, \Gamma}{\Rightarrow}_\bullet Q$ or $Q \overset{\sigma, \Gamma}{\Rightarrow}_\bullet P$ (with respect to Γ).

Definition 10. A pair $\langle P, Q \rangle$ is *free of* Γ-*conflict* if none of its states is a Γ-conflict.

Definition 11. A network V is *(strong) conflict-free* iff for all $i \neq j$ the pair $\langle P_i, P_j \rangle$ is free of strong Λ-conflict.

Definition 12. The edges (nodes) $V_1, \ldots, V_k$ are the *disconnecting edges* of the network V iff they are nodes of the communication graph of V whose removal would increase the number of connected components (partitions).

Definition 13. The *essential components* of V are the connected components of the graph that remains after all disconnecting edges were removed.

References

1. A. C. Mota. Formalisation and Analysis of the SACI-1 Microsatellite in CSP-Z. Master's thesis, Federal University of Pernambuco, 1997.
2. T. Bolognesi and Ed Brinksma. Introduction to the ISO specification language LOTOS. *Computer Networks and ISDN Systems*, 14(1):25–59, January 1987.
3. S. D. Brookes and A. W. Roscoe. An improved failures model for communication processes. In *Lecture Notes on Computer Science*, volume 197, pages 281–305, 1985.
4. S. D. Brookes and A. W. Roscoe. Deadlock analysis in networks of communicating processes. *Distributed Computing*, pages 209–230, 1991.
5. A. R. de Paula Jr. Fault-Tolerance Aspects of the On-Board Computer of the First INPE Microsatellite for Scientific Applications. *VI Brazilian Symposium on Fault-Tolerant Computers*, August 1995.

6. E. Boiten, H. Bowman, J. Derrick and M. Steen. Viewpoint Consistency in Z and LOTOS: A Case Study. In *FME'97: Industrial Applications and Strengthened Foundations of Formal Methods*, pages 644–664. Springer Verlag, 1997.

7. C. Fischer. Combining CSP and Z. Technical report, University of Oldenburg, 1996.

8. C. Fischer. CSP-OZ: A Combination of Object-Z and CSP. In *2nd IFIP International Conference on Formal Methods for Open Object-based Distributed Systems (FMODDS'97)*. Chapman Hall, 1997.

9. Formal Systems (Europe) Ltd. *FDR: User Manual and Tutorial, version 2.01*, August 1996.

10. G. Smith. A Semantic Integration of Object-Z and CSP for the Specification of Concurrent Systems. In *FME'97: Industrial Applications and Strengthened Foundations of Formal Methods*, number 1313 in Lecture Notes in Computer Science, pages 62–81. Springer Verlag, 1997.

11. J. A. Goguen and T. Winkler. Introducing OBJ3. Technical report, SRI International, SRI-CSL-88-9, August 1988. Revised version to appear with additional authors José Meseguer, Kokichi Futatsugi and Jean-Pierre Jouannaud, in *Applications of Algebraic Specification using OBJ,*.

12. C. A. R. Hoare. *Communicating Sequential Processes*. Prentice-Hall, 1985.

13. X. Jia. *A Tutorial of ZANS - A Z Animation System*, 1995.

14. C. B. Jones. *Systematic Software Development Using VDM*. Prentice-Hall International, 1986.

15. G. Jones and M. Goldsmith. *Programming in OCCAM 2*. Prentice-Hall International, 1988.

16. Z. Manna and A. Pnueli. *The Temporal Logic of Reactive and Concurrent Systems*. Springer-Verlag, 1991.

17. R. Milner. A Calculus of Communicating Systems. In *Lecture Notes in Computer Science 92*. Springer-Verlag, 1980.

18. A. W. Roscoe. *The Theory and Practice of Concurrency*. Prentice-Hall International, 1997.

19. M. Saaltink. The Z/EVES System. In *ZUM'97: The Z Formal Specification Notation*, pages 72–85. Lecture Notes in Computer Science, 1212, Springer, 1997.

20. M. Spivey. *The Z Notation: A Reference Manual*. Prentice-Hall International, 2nd edition, 1992.

Rule-Based Refinement of High-Level Nets Preserving Safety Properties

J. Padberg, M. Gajewsky, C. Ermel

e-mail: {padberg, gajewsky, lieske}@cs.tu-berlin.de

Technical University of Berlin**

Abstract. The concept of rule-based modification developed in the area of algebraic graph transformations and high-level replacement systems has recently shown to be a powerful concept for vertical stucturing of Petri nets. This includes low-level and high-level Petri nets, especially algebraic high-level nets which can be considered as an integration of algebraic specifications and Petri nets. In a large case study rule-based modification of algebraic high-level nets has been applied successfully for the requirements analysis of a medical information system. The main new result in this paper extends rule-based modification of algebraic high-level nets such that it preserves safety properties formulated in terms of temporal logic. For software development based on rule-based modification of algebraic high-level nets as a vertical development strategy this extension is an important new technique. It is called rule-based refinement. As a running example an important safety property of a medical information system is considered and is shown to be preserved under rule-based refinement.

Keywords: Petri nets, high-level nets, algebraic specification, safety property, rule-based refinement

1 Introduction

Petri nets are well-known as a basic model for the general theory of concurrency and as a formal specification technique for distributed and concurrent systems. High-level nets can be considered as the integration of process and data type description, most prominent classes are Coloured Petri nets [Jen92, Jen95], Predicate/Transition nets [GL81, Gen91] and algebraic high-level nets [Vau87, Rei91, PER95]. The practical relevance of high-level Petri nets is considered to be very high, as there are many high-level Petri net tools used in real software production (e.g. LEU [SM97] , Design/CPN [JCHH91], INCOME [OSS94]). Since algebraic specifications are well developed for abstract data types (see e.g. [EM85]) we use algebraic high-level nets, but there is no problem of transfering results to other

** This work is part of the joint research project "DFG-Forschergruppe PETRINETZ-TECHNOLOGIE" between H. Weber (Coordinator), H. Ehrig (both from the Technical University Berlin) and W. Reisig (Humboldt-Universität zu Berlin), supported by the German Research Council (DFG).

high-level net classes as these classes can be conceived as different instances of a general theory of abstract Petri nets (see [Pad96]).

One main problem of verification in formal software engineering can be described by the following demand: Rigorous software development requires continuous verification during all phases of the software development process. Nevertheless, resources are restricted and an entirely new verification at each step is usually considered to be too expensive and time consuming. Thus, vertical structuring techniques should preserve verified properties.

In the area of Petri nets there are many contributions concerning verification with temporal logic [DDGJ90, BS90, HRH91] and refinement [BGV90, DM90, GG90, BDH92, Peu97]. They are mainly in the area of low-level nets. In the area of high-level nets, verification [Jen95, Sch96] is much more difficult and even more the compatibility of system properties with refinement.

In this paper we consider our notion of rule-based modification of algebraic high-level nets (developed in [PER95]) and extend it to rule-based refinement preserving safety properties. The theory of rule-based modification is an instance of the theory of high-level replacement systems [EHKP91], a generalization of graph transformation [Ehr79] in a categorical way. Rules describe which parts of a net are to be deleted (left side of the rule) and which new parts are to be added (right side of the rule). This transformation of nets yields a resulting net which is well-defined and no unspecified changes have been made. The advantage of this approach is the local description of change.

In order to extend rule-based modification of algebraic high-level nets we introduce morphisms for algebraic high-level nets, that – in contrast to transition preserving morphisms in [PER95] – preserve safety properties, in the sense of [MP92]. These morphisms, called place preserving morphisms, allow transfering specific temporal logic formulas expressing net properties from the source to the target net. This fact is captured by our first main theorem 3.5 that states the fact that place preserving morphisms preserve invariant formulas. As invariant formulas describe safety properties we hereby obtain safety property preserving algebraic high-level net morphisms.

Moreover, we combine these place preserving morphisms with rule-based modification. The second main result of this paper is formulated in theorem 4.2. It states the preservation of safety properties under transformation of nets via some rule that is provided with such a safety property preserving morphism. This allows the formulation of the new concept 4.1 that is the extension of rule-based modification to rule-based refinement, a formal technique for vertical structuring in software development.

Throughout the whole paper we give an ongoing example which illustrates the results of this paper in the context of a case study [Erm96, EPE96] concerning the development of a medical information system. A sketch of this case study as well as a review of the basic notions of algebraic high-level nets and rule-based modification is given in the next section. In section 3 we introduce the notion of place preserving morphisms. Our first main result states that these morphisms preserve safety properties. In section 4, rule-based modification is integrated with these morphisms. We present our second main theorem, showing that rule-based refinement preserves safety properties. Moreover, we discuss the relevance of our results for software engineering, especially the combination of horizontal structuring and refinement.

In this paper we merely give the proof ideas due to space limitations, in full detail the proofs are given in [PGE97].

2 Rule Based Modification and Safety Properties in a Medical Information System

In this section we sketch our case study and motivate the notions and results of the subsequent sections in terms of this case study. The motivation addresses general problems in software engineering. Any large and complex system can only be developed using horizontal and vertical structuring that is, stepwise development of subsystems. This implies that the entire system is given only implicitly. Thus, verification has to be achieved according to horizontal and vertical structuring. We now show an example of verifying a safety property, first in a net and then for one development step. Note, this is merely a small example from the larger context of the medical information system.

The medical information system HDMS

A medical information system, called Heterogeneous Distributed Information Management System (HDMS), has been developed in a large project, that included the whole reorganisation of the medical and management data of the German Cardiac Center Berlin, Deutsches Herz-Zentrum Berlin (DHZB). This project has been developed by the Projektgruppe Medizin/Informatik at the DHZB and the Technische Universität Berlin[1]. The DHZB is a clinical center dedicated to the treatment of all kinds of cardiac diseases. In our case study [Erm96, EPE96] we provide a formal requirement analysis for an important part of the medical information system HDMS at the DHZB using algebraic high-level nets. The transformation sequence from the actual state to the functional essence comprises about 100 rules and uses in a significant way compatibility results from [PER95] between horizontal structuring and rule-based modification. Here we present one transformation step of the whole rule-based modification. We demonstrate how safety properties are preserved using a special kind of algebraic high-level net morphisms and the new concept of rule-based refinement.

Example 2.1 (Safety Properties for Vital Values Measurement)
An algebraic high-level (AHL) net can be considered as a Petri net inscribed with terms over a specification, in this case the specification VVM-Spec which is merely sketched below due to space limitations. Tokens are elements of a VVM-Spec-algebra.

---

[1] The case study HDMS, the basis for our work, has been a part of the German BMFT-project KORSO, (KORrekte SOftware), funded by the Minister of Research and Technology (BMFT) between 1991 and 1994 [CHL95].

Let us shortly explain the idea of the net VVM in figure 1. In the DHZB we have the following situation: The patient is located at the ward. His blood pressure is taken, for example, if this has been demanded in the prescription sheet. The measured value is written down into the temperature chart. Other vital values, as medium arterial blood pressure, temperature, pulse, central venous pressure and import/export are also measured, if demanded in the prescription sheet. The temperature chart belongs to the patient record that is kept at the ward. All these activities are represented as transitions in the net VVM in figure 1. Note, that we restrict our example to this small subsystem concerning the measurement of vital values.

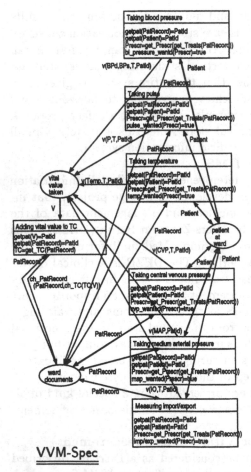

VVM-Spec

Fig. 1: The Algebraic High-Level Net Vital Values Measurement (VVM)

We merely state the sorts and operations of **VVM-Spec** used explicitly in the subsequent argument.

sorts: Name, Patient, PatId, PatRecord, ...

opns: patient: Name, Sex, Adress, PatId $\rightarrow$ Patient
getpat: Patient $\rightarrow$ PatId
getpatient: PatId $\rightarrow$ Patient
getpat: PatRecord $\rightarrow$ PatId

In the following, we give the marking and one safety property of the net VVM explicitly. We consider the A-quotient algebra (see [EM85]), that is the algebra generated according to the specification over carrier sets for names, doctors, resources etc. Assuming a carrier set $A_{Name} = \{Smith, Miller, ...\}$ we can suppose the following marking: $(patient(Smith, ...), \textbf{patient at ward}) \oplus (d, \textbf{ward documents})$ where $d \in A_{PatRecord}$ with $getpat(d) = getpat(patient(Smith, ...))$.

This marking means that there is a patient *Smith* and his patient record at the ward, represented by tokens $(patient(Smith, ...)$ and d on the places **patient at ward** and **ward documents** respectively.

We consider the safety property $\square[(patient(Smith, ...), \textbf{patient at ward}) \iff (d, \textbf{ward documents})]$ with $getpat(d) = getpat(patient(Smith, ...))$ for some $d \in A_{PatRecord}$ where $\lambda(a, p)$ for $(a, p) \in A \times P$ is an atomic formula (see def. 3.3) and $\square$ the always operator from temporal logic [MP92].

We informally argue that this safety property holds. For each transition except *Adding vital value to TC* the patient record is only read, denoted by double arrows with the inscription of a variable of sort *PatRecord*. The transition *Adding vital value to TC* changes the record, but by structural induction we can prove that no operation changes the initial patient identity. Thus, after firing of any transition the safety property still holds.

In general we assume a marking of the net VVM

$$M^{\text{VVM}} := \sum_{i=1}^{n} (a_i, \textbf{patient at ward}) \oplus (d_i, \textbf{ward documents})$$

s.t. $getpat(a_i) = getpat(d_i)$ for $a_i \in A_{Patient}$ and $d_i \in A_{PatRecord}$.

The more general formulation of our safety property φ^{VVM} is

$$\Box[(a, \textbf{patient at ward}) \Longleftrightarrow (d, \textbf{ward documents})]$$

s.t. $getpat(a) = getpat(d)$ for $a \in A_{Patient}$ and $d \in A_{PatRecord}$.

This safety property means *"At any time we have: there is some patient at the ward if and only if the corresponding patient record is at the ward."* and holds due to the same argument as above. ◇

Algebraic High-Level Nets and Refinement Techniques

An algebraic high-level net consists – roughly speaking – of a Petri net with inscriptions of an algebraic specification $SPEC$ defining the data type part of the net. The data type in our case study is given by a suitable $SPEC$ algebra. In contrast to other variants of algebraic high-level nets ([DHP91, Hum89, Lil94]) we do not label places with sorts. Note, that the pre and post domain of a transition is given by a multiset of pairs of terms and places. Multisets can be considered as elements of a commutative monoid. Here, we use free commutative monoids for the description of the pre and post domain of a transition as this representation allows a more categorical treatment.

Morphisms between different AHL nets are given componentwise and have to preserve the firing conditions and each transition's pre and post domain. This is characterized by the commutativity of diagrams (1) and (2) in def. 2.2.

Definition 2.2 (Algebraic High-Level Nets)

– An **algebraic high-level net** $N = (SPEC, P, T, pre, post, cond, A)$ consists of an algebraic specification $SPEC = (S, OP, E)$, a set of places P, a set of transitions T, two functions $pre, post : T \longrightarrow (T_{OP}(X) \times P)^{\oplus}$, assigning to each $t \in T$ an element of the free commutative monoid[2] over the cartesian product of terms $T_{OP}(X)$ with variables in X and the set P of places, a function $cond : T \longrightarrow \mathcal{P}_{fin}(EQNS(SIG))$ assigning to each $t \in T$ a finite set $cond(t)$ of equations over $SIG = (S, OP)$, the signature of $SPEC$ and a $SPEC$ algebra A.

– A **(transition preserving) AHL net morphism** $f = (f_{SPEC}, f_P, f_T, f_A) : N_1 \to N_2$ is given componentwise by the specification morphism $f_{SPEC} : SPEC_1 \to SPEC_2$, the functions $f_P : P_1 \to P_2$ and $f_T : T_1 \to T_2$ and the isomorphism $f_A : A_1 \xrightarrow{\sim} V_{f_{SPEC}}(A_2)$ on the algebras such that the following diagrams (1) and (2) commute:

---

[2] The free commutative monoid implies the following operations on linear sums: $\oplus, \ominus, \leq$.

$$\mathcal{P}_{fin}(EQNS(SIG_1)) \xleftarrow{cond_1} T_1 \underset{post_1}{\overset{pre_1}{\Longrightarrow}} (T_{OP_1}(X_1) \times P_1)^\oplus$$

$$f_E := \mathcal{P}_{fin}(f^\sharp_{SPEC})\ (1) \qquad f_T \qquad (2)\ (f^\sharp_{SPEC} \times f_P)^\oplus := f_S$$

$$\mathcal{P}_{fin}(EQNS(SIG_2)) \xleftarrow{cond_2} T_2 \underset{post_2}{\overset{pre_2}{\Longrightarrow}} (T_{OP_2}(X_2) \times P_2)^\oplus$$

The sets of variables are defined by indexing a fixed set $X_i := (X_{fix_s})_{s \in S_i}$ for $i = 1, 2$. In the following, we will use abbreviations for the mappings of markings (f_M), symbolic markings, that is terms with variables (f_S) and sets of equations (f_E):

$$f_M := ((f_{SPEC}, f_A) \times f_P)^\oplus, f_S := (f^\#_{SPEC} \times f_P)^\oplus \text{ and } f_E := \mathcal{P}_{fin}(f^\sharp_{SPEC}).$$

- AHL nets and AHL net morphisms are defining the category **AHL** of algebraic high-level nets.

- The **behaviour** of an AHL net N is given by firing of transitions. Transitions are enabled under a marking $M \in (A \times P)^\oplus$ for an assignment $asg : X \to A$ inducing $ASG : (T_{OP}(Var(t)) \times P)^\oplus \to (A \times P)^\oplus$ with $ASG(term, p) = (\overline{asg}(term), p)$ if $ASG(pre(t)) \leq M$. $Var(t)$ is the set of variables that occur in the firing condition $cond(t)$ and in the pre and post domains $pre(t)$ and $post(t)$ for each $t \in T$. The follower marking M' then is constructed by $M' = M \ominus ASG(pre(t)) \oplus ASG(post(t))$, denoted by: $M[t, asg > M'$. The set of all follower markings is denoted by $[M >$.

$$\triangle$$

We review rule-based modification as a vertical structuring technique of Petri nets [PER95]. The idea is to present rules denoting the replacement of one subnet by another without changing the remaining part of the whole net. This has the advantage of a local description of changes inducing global changes without side effects. We consider to have a rule r with a left-hand side net L that is replaced by a right-hand side net R. This rule can be applied to some net N, yielding the new net M. This application of a rule, called transformation, is denoted by $N \overset{r}{\Longrightarrow} M$. The rule is given by $r = (L \leftarrow K \to R)$ where K is a net and $K \to L$ and $K \to R$ are injective AHL net morphisms. Deleted are those parts of the net L that are not in the image of the morphism $K \to L$. Adding works symmetrically, all those parts of R are added, that are not in the image of the morphism $K \to R$. Thus, K denotes the common interface between deleting and adding, that is the part of the rule that has to be present but is not changed by the rule. The transformation $N \overset{r}{\Longrightarrow} M$ is defined using two pushout squares (1) and (2) in def. 2.3 in the category **AHL**. C is the context net (N after the deletion of items by the rule and before the addition of the new items from R).

Definition 2.3 (Rule and Transformation)
A rule $r = (L \leftarrow K \to R)$ consists of two AHL nets L and R (called left and right hand sides of the rule), an AHL net K (called interface) and two injective AHL net morphisms $L \leftarrow K$ and $K \to R$.

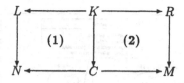

A **(direct) transformation** $N \overset{r}{\Longrightarrow} M$ of a net N to M via rule $r = (L \leftarrow K \rightarrow R)$ at the match $L \rightarrow N$ is defined using two pushout squares **(1)** and **(2)** shown in the diagram in the category **AHL**.

$\triangle$

This definition is the technical basis for the vertical structuring technique of rule-based modification. Results concerning parallel and concurrent application of rules and compatibility with horizontal structuring can be found in [PER95].

Example 2.4 (Blood Hypertension Test)

We now want to describe the refinement step that adds an exception in case of blood hypertension. In this case the doctor shall be notified immediately.

The transformation rule $r^{\text{vvm}} : L \leftarrow K \rightarrow R$ in figure 2 describes the refinement of the net VVM depicted in figure 1 by an exception for blood hypertension. For each blood pressure value taken an additional test for hypertension is performed. In case of hypertension the doctor is notified. The transition *Adding vital value to TC* is part of the interface K in order to ensure the application of r^{vvm} only in the context of vital value measurement.

The inclusion morphism $K \rightarrow L$ means that the transition *taking blood pressure* is deleted. Additionally, the right hand side net R contains the places **values for hypertension test** and **doctor**, and the transitions *notifying doctor* and *taking blood pressure*. The corresponding algebraic specification also has to be adapted coherently and persistently by adding the equations used for the entry of blood hypertension (for details see [PGE97]).

The application of rule r^{vvm} to the net VVM yields the following transformation shown in figure 2: The deletion of the transition *taking blood pressure* yields the context net C and the addition of the places **values for hypertension test**, **doctor**, and the transitions *notifying doctor* and *taking blood pressure* yields the net BEX (short for Blood hypertension EXception).

Now the main problem is the transfer of the safety property φ^{vvm} "*At any time we have: there is some patient at the ward if and only if the corresponding patient record is at the ward.*" This transfer should be induced by the rule $r^{\text{vvm}} = (L \leftarrow K \rightarrow R)$. To achieve the rule-based refinement we have to find a property of the rule such that the transformation preserves the safety property. We are looking for proof rules of the following form:

$$\text{some property for } r^{\text{vvm}}, \text{VVM satifies } \varphi^{\text{vvm}}$$
$$\overline{}$$
$$\text{BEX satisfies } \varphi^{\text{vvm}}$$

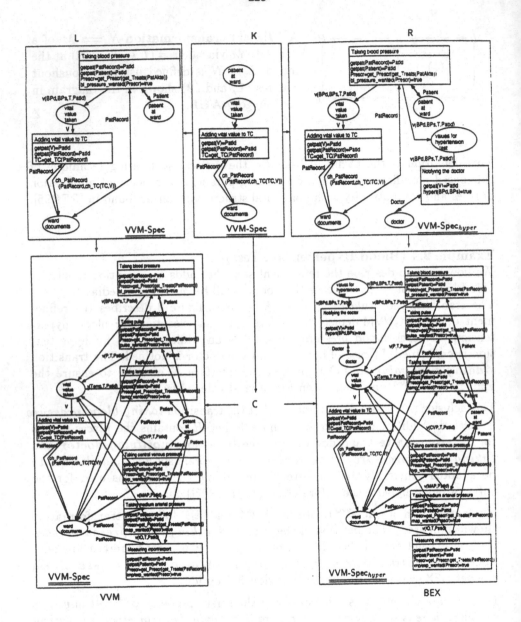

Fig. 2. Vital Value Measurement with Hypertension Exception

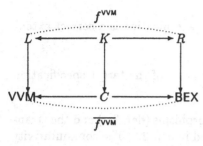

The main idea of our approach is to use a class of morphisms, called *place preserving*, that on the one hand preserve safety properties (section 3) and on the other hand are stable under transformations (section 4). As a result of a cooperation within the "DFG-Forschergruppe Petrinetztechnologie" (see first page), it has recently been shown in [Peu97] that safety properties are preserved by *place preserving* morphisms for low level nets. In this paper in section 3 we show that the idea can be transferred to high-level nets. Thus, we can transfer safety properties via transformations. The fact that $f^{VVM} : L \to R$ preserves safety properties (theorem 3.5) *always* implies that $\overline{f^{VVM}} : VVM \to BEX$ preserves safety properties (theorem 4.2). Thus we have the desired property so that the following proof rule holds:

$$\frac{(r^{VVM}, f^{VVM} : L \to R) \text{ preserves safety properties, } VVM \text{ satisfies } \varphi^{VVM}}{BEX \text{ satisfies } \varphi^{VVM}} \qquad \Diamond$$

3   Morphisms Preserving Safety Properties

In this section we define morphisms preserving safety properties of algebraic high-level nets. To be able to preserve safety properties (expressed via formulas on markings), we must take care that no new arcs are added to the context of mapped places by the morphism and no old (mapped) arcs are deleted from their context. Otherwise new transitions could add or delete tokens on "old" (mapped) places in an unpredictable way. We therefore call morphisms with these features *place preserving*.

Definition 3.1 (Place Preserving AHL Net Morphism)
Let $N_i = (SPEC_i, P_i, T_i, pre_i, post_i, cond_i, A_i), i \in \{1, 2\}$ be two AHL nets, then $f = (f_{SPEC}, f_P, f_T, f_A) : N_1 \to N_2$ is called a **place preserving AHL net morphism** if the following holds:
1. Preservation of firing conditions: $f_E \circ cond_1 = cond_2 \circ f_T$
2. Place preserving condition: $\bullet(f_S(term, p)) = f_T(\bullet(term, p))$ and
   $(f_S(term, p))\bullet = f_T((term, p)\bullet)$ for all $p \in P_1$ and $term \in T_{OP_1}(X_1)$
   where $\bullet(term, p) = \{t | (term, p) \leq post(t)\}$ and
   $(term, p)\bullet = \{t | (term, p) \leq pre(t)\}$ define the pre and post sets of p.
3. f_T, f_P and f_{SPEC} are injective and f_{SPEC} is persistent (compare [EM85]).
4. Embedding condition: $f_S(pre_1(t)) \leq pre_2(f_T(t))$ and
   $f_S(post_1(t)) \leq post_2(f_T(t))$ for all $t \in T_1$
5. $f_A : A_1 \xrightarrow{\sim} V_{f_{SPEC}}(A_2)$ is an isomorphism in $\mathbf{Alg}(SPEC_1)$ $\qquad \triangle$

Remark: Intuitively, the conditions ensure that

1. the firing conditions are preserved by the morphism,
2. arcs adjacent to places are not changed,
3. the morphism is an injection and the target specification is a correct extension of the source specification,
4. the morphism has to map all arcs,
5. the algebra is merely extended for the new parts of the target specification or it is merely renamed.

Note the difference between place preserving morphisms (def. 3.1) and the (transition preserving) AHL net morphisms as defined in def. 2.2. The commutativity of diagram (2) in def. 2.2 yields a preservation of transitions in the sense that no new arcs are added to mapped transitions and no old (mapped) arcs are deleted from their pre and post domains. Place preserving morphisms are in general not transition preserving because condition 4 in def. 3.1 expresses that the pre and post domain of a transition in N_2 may contain more places than the original transition in N_1. A morphism $f : N_1 \to N_2$ that is place preserving and transition preserving at the same time merely yields a disjoint embedding of N_1 into N_2.

Example 3.2 (Place Preserving Morphism in Hypertension Test)
We sketch that the morphism $f^{\text{VVM}} : L \to R$ determined by figure 2 is place preserving. The inclusions $f^{\text{VVM}}{}_P$ and $f^{\text{VVM}}{}_T$ are given implicitly using name identity. The specification morphism $f^{\text{VVM}}{}_{SPEC}$ is an inclusion as sorts, operations and equations concerning the hypertension test are added in VVM-Spec$_{hyper}$ such that $f^{\text{VVM}}{}_{SPEC}$ is persistent (see [PGE97]). The conditions of def. 3.1 hold such that the morphism $f^{\text{VVM}} : L \to R$ is place preserving:
Condition 1 is satisfied because transitions in net R that lie in the image of f^{VVM} have the same firing conditions as their originals in net L. Condition 2 is satisfied as no new arcs are adjacent to mapped places. For the place **vital value taken** this is formally shown, for the other places it is analogous:
$\bullet(f^{\text{VVM}}{}_S(v(BPd, BPs, T, PatId), \text{vital value taken}))$
$= \quad \{Taking\ blood\ pressure\}$
$= \quad f^{\text{VVM}}{}_T(\{Taking\ blood\ pressure\})$
$= \quad f^{\text{VVM}}{}_T(\bullet(v(BPd, BPs, T, PatId), \text{vital value taken}))$
analogously $\quad (f^{\text{VVM}}{}_S(V, \text{vital value taken}))\bullet = f^{\text{VVM}}{}_T((V, \text{vital value taken})\bullet)$
Moreover, $f^{\text{VVM}} : L \to R$ is an embedding (condition 4) as no arcs are deleted. The morphism f^{VVM} is not transition preserving in the sense of def. 2.2 because the transition *Taking blood pressure* in R has more places in its post set than the original *Taking blood pressure* in L. $\diamond$

We will now define formulas over AHL net markings and their translations via morphisms to be able to express safety properties and prove their preservation via morphisms in a formal way.
The invariant formula $\Box\varphi$ expresses safety properties in the sense of [MP92]. Note that we use a restricted notion as φ is merely a static formula whereas in [MP92] backward operators are allowed.

Definition 3.3 (Formulas and Translations)
Let N be an AHL net according to definition 2.2. We define

- **Formulas**: For $\lambda \in \mathbb{N}$ and $(a, p) \in (A \times P)$: $\lambda(a, p)$ is a **static formula**.
  For φ_1, φ_2 static formulas: $\neg\varphi_1, \varphi_1 \wedge \varphi_2$ are static formulas.
  Let φ be a static formula over N. Then $\Box\varphi$ is an **invariant formula**.
- **Validity of formulas**: Let $M \in (A \times P)^\oplus$ be a marking and let φ_1 and φ_2
  be static formulas. A static formula under the marking M is valid if:

$$M \models_N \varphi_1 \Longleftrightarrow \varphi_1 \leq M \qquad for\ \varphi_1 = \lambda(a, p)$$
$$M \models_N \neg\varphi_1 \Longleftrightarrow \neg(M \models_N \varphi_1)$$
$$M \models_N \varphi_1 \wedge \varphi_2 \Longleftrightarrow (M \models_N \varphi_1) \wedge (M \models_N \varphi_2)$$

The invariant formula $\Box\varphi$ holds in N under M iff φ holds in all states
reachable from M: $M \models_N \Box\varphi \Longleftrightarrow \forall M' \in [M >: M' \models_N \varphi$

- **Translation of formulas**: Let $f = (f_{SPEC}, f_P, f_T, f_A) : N_1 \to N_2$ be a
  place preserving AHL net morphism. Then the translation $\mathcal{T}_f$ of formulas
  over N_1 under the marking $M_1 \in (A_1 \times P_1)^\oplus$ to formulas over N_2 is given
  as follows, where f_M is defined as in def. 2.2:

$$\mathcal{T}_f(\varphi) = f_M(\varphi) \qquad for\ \varphi = \lambda(a, p) \in (A_1 \times P_1)^\oplus$$
$$\mathcal{T}_f(\neg\varphi) = \neg\mathcal{T}_f(\varphi)$$
$$\mathcal{T}_f(\varphi_1 \wedge \varphi_2) = \mathcal{T}_f(\varphi_1) \wedge \mathcal{T}_f(\varphi_2)$$
$$\mathcal{T}_f(\Box\varphi) = \Box\mathcal{T}_f(\varphi) \qquad\qquad\qquad \triangle$$

Next, we explain how a translated formula $\mathcal{T}_f(\varphi)$ is evaluated under a translated
marking $M_2 \in (A_2 \times P_2)^\oplus$. Let us define the notion of a translated marking M_2
via the notion of a restriction of the marking M_2 with respect to f as we are
only interested in the marked places of M_2 that are images of places of N_1.

Definition 3.4 (Restriction of Marking)
Let $f : N_1 \to N_2$ be a place preserving AHL net morphism, $M_1 \in (A_1 \times P_1)^\oplus$ a
marking of N_1 and $M_2 \in (A_2 \times P_2)^\oplus$ a marking of N_2
s.t. $\quad M_2 = f_M(M_1) \quad \oplus \quad \sum_{j=1}^{m} \mu_j(a_j, p_j) \quad$ with $\mu_j(a_j, p_j) \notin f_M(A_1 \times P_1)^\oplus$
Then the **restriction** $M_{2|f}$ of the marking M_2 to the net N_1 with respect to f
is given as follows: $\quad M_{2|f} := M_1 \qquad\qquad\qquad\qquad\qquad\qquad \triangle$

$M_{2|f}$ is well-defined due to the injectivity of the underlying morphisms.

Now we come to the main theorem concerning the preservation of formulas by
morphisms.

Theorem 3.5 (Place Preserving Morphisms Preserve Safety Properties)
Let $f : N_1 \to N_2$ be a place preserving AHL net morphism and $M_1 \in (A_1 \times P_1)^\oplus$
and $M_2 \in (A_2 \times P_2)^\oplus$ be markings of N_1 and N_2 with $M_{2|f} = M_1$. Let $\Box\varphi$ be
an invariant formula. Then the following holds:

$$M_1 \models_{N_1} \Box\varphi \Longrightarrow M_2 \models_{N_2} \mathcal{T}_f(\Box\varphi) \qquad\qquad \triangle$$

Example 3.6 (Preserving a Safety Property in Hypertension Test)

As example we consider the place preserving morphism $f^{\text{VVM}} : L \to R$ as given in ex. 3.2. Assume we have a marking M_1 in L analogously to ex. 2.1 and 2.4. Then we have $M_1 \models_L \varphi^{\text{VVM}}$ due to the same argument as in ex. 2.1. As we have a place preserving morphism (see ex. 3.2), we can apply theorem 3.5. Note that marking and safety property do not change, as f^{VVM} is an inclusion. Thus, we have $M_1 \models_L \varphi^{\text{VVM}}$ implies $M_2 \models_R \varphi^{\text{VVM}}$, where M_2 contains M_1. $\diamond$

Proof Idea of Theorem 3.5

For a complete proof we refer to the detailed technical report [PGE97].

The proof takes four steps: First the effect of restriction to the pre and post domains of transitions is investigated. Then we can show that the follower marking is preserved. Thirdly we show the preservation of static formulas. At last we prove the preservation of invariant formulas.

Let N_1, N_2 be AHL nets and $f : N_1 \to N_2$ a place preserving AHL net morphism. Let $M_1 \in (A_1 \times P_1)^{\oplus}$ be a marking of N_1 and $M_2 \in (A_2 \times P_2)^{\oplus}$ be a marking of N_2 with $M_{2|f} = M_1$.

Restriction and Place Preserving Morphisms $\hfill (*)$

(1) For all $t_2 \in T_2$ with $f_T(t_1) = t_2$:
    (i) $pre_2(t_2)_{|f} = pre_1(t_1)$ and (ii) $post_2(t_2)_{|f} = post_1(t_1)$
(2) For all $t_2 \in T_2 \backslash f_T(T_1)$:
    (i) $pre_2(t_2)_{|f} = \epsilon$ and (ii) $post_2(t_2)_{|f} = \epsilon$

For the proof of (1)(i) we show $pre_2(f_T(t_1))_{|f} \geq pre_1(t_1)$ directly, due to the embedding condition and $pre_2(f_T(t_1))_{|f} \leq pre_1(t_1)$ by contradiction, using the place preserving condition. The proof of (1)(ii) is analogous.

For the proof of (2)(i) assume $pre_2(t_2)_{|f} \neq \epsilon$. Let $(term_2, p_2) \leq pre_2(t_2)$ with $f_S(term_1, p_1) = (term_2, p2)$. Then $t_2 \in (term_2, p2)\bullet$ implies $t_2 \in (f_S(term_1, p_1))\bullet$. Thus f place preserving (see def. 3.1) implies $t_2 \in f_T((term_1, p_1)\bullet)$. This contradicts to our assumption $t_2 \in T_2 \backslash f_T(T_1)$. Hence $pre_2(t_2)_{|f} = \epsilon$. The proof of (2)(ii) is analogous.

Preservation of Follower Marking $\hfill (**)$

We prove $\forall M_2' \in [M_2 >: M_{2|f}' \in [M_1 >$ by induction over the firing of every transition in N_2 beginning with the induction base that no transition has been fired. As induction step we show that $M_2'[t_2, \overline{asg_2} > M_2''$ implies $M_{2|f}'' \in [M_1 >$.

For $t_2 \in T_2 \backslash f_T(T_1)$ we show with the help of $(*)(2)$ that $M_{2|f}'' = M_{2|f}' \in [M_1 >$.

For $t_2 = f_T(t_1)$ we first show that t_1 is enabled under $\overline{asg_1}$ and $M_{2|f}'$ with $\overline{asg_1} = X_1 \longrightarrow X_2 \overset{asg_2}{\longrightarrow} A_2 \overset{iso}{\longrightarrow} A_1$. With t_1 enabled we can show that $M_{2|f}'[t_1, \overline{asg_1} > M_{2|f}''$. Together with $M_{2|f}' \in [M_1 >$ we have: $M_{2|f}'' \in [M_1 >$.

Preservation of Static Formulas $\hfill (***)$

We show that $M_1 \models_{N_1} \varphi \Longleftrightarrow M_2 \models_{N_2} T_f(\varphi)$ by induction over the structure of static formulas as given in def. 3.3.

Preservation of Invariant Formulas

We show $M_1 \models_{N_1} \Box\varphi$ implies $M_2 \models_{N_2} \mathcal{T}_f(\Box\varphi)$ by

$$
\begin{aligned}
M_1 \models_{N_1} \Box\varphi &\Longleftrightarrow \forall M_1' \in [M_1 >: M_1' \models_{N_1} \varphi &&\text{due to def. 3.3} \\
&\Longrightarrow \forall M_2' \in [M_2 >: M_{2|f}' \models_{N_1} \varphi &&\text{due to } (**) \\
&\Longleftrightarrow \forall M_2' \in [M_2 >: M_2' \models_{N_2} \mathcal{T}_f(\varphi) &&\text{due to } (***) \\
&\Longleftrightarrow M_2 \models_{N_2} \Box\mathcal{T}_f(\varphi) &&\text{due to def. 3.3} \\
&\Longleftrightarrow M_2 \models_{N_2} \mathcal{T}_f(\Box\varphi) && \surd
\end{aligned}
$$

4 Rule-Based Refinement Preserving Safety Properties

In software engineering it is most desirable to "automatically" derive properties of a refined net from its abstraction. The main advantage of such refinements is that those properties do not have to be proven again. For our example in section 2 it is obvious that the safety property φ^{VVM} "*At any time we have: there is some patient at the ward if and only if the corresponding patient record is at the ward.*" should hold again in the resulting net after the application of a rule r^{VVM} to a net with that property. This is captured by the notion of 'rule-based refinement', which is rule-based modification plus the preservation of (safety) properties. A main advantage of rules is that modifications are described locally, i.e. in a small context. Moreover — as we will show in this section — the preservation of safety properties can already be checked on the level of rules. Applying these rules means an intrinsic propagation of safety properties to the resulting net. This, of course, is of high importance from a software engineering point of view, especially for our case study in section 2 because there is no need of verifying these properties in the resulting net.

Concept 4.1 (Vertical Structuring Technique: Rule-Based Refinement)

Rule-based refinement is the extension of rule-based modification with morphisms that preserve system properties. In this case we have place preserving morphisms that preserve safety properties. A safety property preserving rule in rule-based refinement is given by (r, f) with a rule $r : L \leftarrow K \rightarrow R$ (see def. 2.3) and $f : L \rightarrow R$ a place preserving morphism (see def. 3.1) which are compatible in the sense that the composition of $K \rightarrow L$ and $L \rightarrow R$ equals $K \rightarrow R$, i.e. $K \rightarrow L \rightarrow R = K \rightarrow R$. $\diamond$

The following theorem provides sufficient conditions for propagating safety properties from one net to its modification. The general idea is that the application of a rule that preserves safety properties leads to a net transformation that preserves the same safety properties. In fact, these rules that have place preserving morphisms from the left to the right hand side, preserve safety properties.

Theorem 4.2 (Rule-Based Refinement Preserves Safety Properties)

Let (r, f) be a safety property preserving rule (see con. 4.1), $N_1 \overset{r}{\Longrightarrow} N_2$ the application of r to the net N_1. Furthermore let M_1 be a marking of N_1 and M_2

a marking of N_2 with $M_2|_f = M_1$ (see def. 3.4).

Then there is a well-defined morphism $\overline{f} : N_1 \to N_2$ induced by $f : L \to R$ with:

$$M_1 \models_{N_1} \Box\varphi \quad \Longrightarrow \quad M_2 \models_{N_2} T_{\overline{f}}(\Box\varphi) \qquad\qquad \triangle$$

Example 4.3 (Refinement in Hypertension Test)

Again we consider the example given in figure 2 with respect to the safety property φ^{VVM} "At any time we have: there is some patient at the ward if and only if the corresponding patient record is at the ward." It has already been shown that $f^{\text{VVM}} : L \to R$ is place preserving (see ex. 3.2) and the above safety property holds in VVM with marking M^{VVM} (see ex. 2.1). Furthermore we have $K \to L \to R = K \to R$ as all morphisms are inclusions. Thus, due to theorem 4.2 for any M_2 with $M_2|_{\overline{f^{\text{VVM}}}} = M^{\text{VVM}}$ we have: $\quad M_2 \models_{\text{BEX}} \varphi^{\text{VVM}}$

Note, $\varphi^{\text{VVM}} = T_{\overline{f^{\text{VVM}}}}(\varphi^{\text{VVM}})$ as $\overline{f^{\text{VVM}}} :$ VVM $\to$ BEX is also an inclusion. $\qquad \diamond$

In order to prove theorem 4.2 we apply results of [Pad96] that are formulated for an arbitrary category and a distinguished class Q of morphisms used to classify different types of rules. In this case the class Q is given by the place preserving morphisms, those preserving safety properties as shown in theorem 3.5.

Technically, we must prove the assumptions given in [Pad96], def. 4.3.1. We therefore define a category (**QAHL**) that contains both the category **AHL** (see def. 2.2) and place preserving morphisms. In this category pushouts of the subcategory **AHL** must be preserved, and the class of place preserving morphisms must be closed under pushouts and coproducts. Note, that we only sketch the proof for restrictions of space. They can all be found in detail in [PGE97].

Proof Idea of Theorem 4.2:

We first present the general definition of Q-morphisms according to [Pad96], (def. 4.3.1).

> Let **QCAT** be a category so that **CAT** is a subcategory **CAT** $\subseteq$ **QCAT** and the inclusion functor $I :$ **CAT** $\to$ **QCAT** preserves pushouts.
>
> Let Q be a class of morphisms in **QCAT**, closed under the construction
>
> - of pushouts in **QCAT**: Given $C \xrightarrow{f'} D \xleftarrow{g'}$ a pushout of $B \xleftarrow{f} A \xrightarrow{g} C$, then $f \in Q \implies f' \in Q$.
> - of coproducts in **QCAT**: For $A \xrightarrow{f} B$ and $A' \xrightarrow{f'} B'$, we have $f, f' \in Q \implies f + f' \in Q$ provided the coproduct $A + A' \xrightarrow{f+f'} B + B'$ of f and f' exists in **QCAT**.

We instantiate this definition with algebraic high-level nets, that is **AHL** and **QAHL** correspond to **CAT**, resp. **QCAT**.

Category QAHL: Objects in **QAHL** are AHL nets as defined in def. 2.2. Given two AHL nets $N_i = (SPEC_i, P_i, T_i, pre_i, post_i, cond_i, A_i)$ for $i = 1, 2$, a morphism $f : N_1 \to N_2$ is a quadrupel $f = (f_{SPEC}, f_P, f_T, f_A)$, where the components are morphisms in the underlying categories **SPEC** and **SETS** and f_E, f_S are defined as in def. 2.2 , satisfying the following conditions:

   (i) $f_E \circ cond_1 = cond_2 \circ f_T$

  (ii) arcs are preserved, i.e. $\forall t_1 \in T_1$:

     (a) $f_S(pre_1(t_1)) \leq pre_2(f_T(t_1))$

     (b) $f_S(post_1(t_1)) \leq post_2(f_T(t_1))$

 (iii) $f_A : A_1 \xrightarrow{\sim} V_{f_{SPEC}}(A_2)$ is an isomorphism in the category $\mathbf{Alg(SPEC_1)}$ of $SPEC_1$-algebras.

Preservation of Pushouts: The proof uses the fact that pushouts in **AHL** are constructed componentwise in **SPEC**, **SETS** and **Alg(SPEC)** (see e.g. fact 5.2 in [PER95]). Thus, there are unique induced morphisms in these categories, whose combination is a unique **QAHL**-morphism.

Class Q: The class Q of morphisms is given by the place preserving morphisms (see def. 3.1).

Preservation of Q under Pushouts: We have to show that the induced pushout morphisms satisfy the conditions of definition 3.1. The preservation of firing conditions (condition 1), the embedding condition (condition 4) and condition 5 are due to the notion of **QAHL**-morphisms. Condition 3 immediately follows by preservation of monomorphisms and the extension lemma 8.15 in [EM85]. Condition 2 (place preserving condition) can be shown by the mutual inclusion of sets. In one direction we use the linearity of free commutative monoids. For the other inclusion it is shown that an arc, decorated by an image term, between a transition and an image place in the pushout object must already exist in the source net.

Preservation of Q in Coproducts: We show, that coproducts in **QAHL** are constructed componentwise and the inclusions are place preserving. The actual proof is straightforward and uses mainly inclusions.

These conditions and fact 4.3.3 in [Pad96] yield: $N_1 \overset{r}{\Longrightarrow} N_2$ and $f : L \to R$ in Q implies a well-defined induced morphism $\overline{f} : N1 \to N2$ in Q. This and theorem 3.5 proves the stated fact. $\checkmark$

Implication for Formal Software Development and Open Problems

As illustrated above rule-based refinement allows deducing safety properties of the refined net under very weak assumptions. We have shown that the preservation of safety properties can be expressed in terms of the transforming rule and the source net. Only the source net has to satisfy this property (under a marking) and the rule has to be place preserving. In so far verification of these properties in a target net can exploit the properties of the source net, which seems to be very natural in the context of system development. Thus, iterative verification becomes possible: the safety property has to be verified once for a starting net and from there on the safety property is propagated by place preserving rules.

A further important aspect is the relation between vertical, i.e. rule-based refinement, and horizontal structuring realized by the notion of union and fusion. Intuitively, union is the gluing of two nets sharing a common subnet. It serves the purpose of joining two parts over a common interface. Fusion is the identification of distinct items in one net, which means unification or abstraction. In fact, the general theory of Q-morphisms developed in [Pad96] states the compatibility of rule-based refinement with horizontal structuring (see [Pad96], theorem

4.5.5 and 4.5.9). This is a fundamental issue from the software engineering point of view as it allows concurrent refinement and composition of the system. The following diagram illustrates this fact:

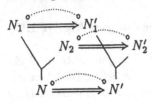

The preservation of safety properties, which is supplied on the level of rules, cannot only be transferred to transformations but also to the horizontal composition of transformations. This means, that we can do horizontal structuring (denoted by the forking lines) and rule-based refinement (denoted by the double arrows) in any ordering.

From a software engineering point of view an additional compatibility is essential, namely the propagation of safety properties from a component net (N_1) to the composed net (N). By transitivity this would ensure, that a safety property of a component net would be preserved in the refined and composed net (N'). This has been subject to our paper [EG97], where we show that propagation of safety properties is possible in special cases. However, a corresponding general theory still has to be developed.

5 Conclusion and Future Research

We have presented a new, formal vertical structuring technique, the rule-based refinement of algebraic high-level nets. This technique combines the advantages of a rule-based approach to stepwise development with a refinement that preserves safety properties. We have shown that a specific kind of AHL morphisms, called place preserving, allows transfering safety properties from the source to the target net. In combination with rule-based modification we obtain rule-based refinement – based on the theory of Q-transformations in [Pad96] – that preserves safety properties. We have illustated this rule-based refinement for one refinement step using our main theorem 4.2 to transfer an important safety property in the context of our case study HDMS. This transfer is guaranteed in terms of the corresponding rule, and has not to be done for the whole subsystem. Moreover, this new technique of rule-based refinement can be adapted easily to other high-level Petri net formalisms, because in [Pad96, EP97] a uniform approach to Petri nets is developed where the abstract frame for rule-based refinement is already formulated.

Further research, aside from the compatibility of safety properties with horizontal structuring as discussed in section 4, concerns the transfer of other system properties as liveness, obligations, persistency and others as in [MP92] along the rules within the frame of rule-based refinement.

Moreover, as one of our referees suggested, the extension of our approach to different notions of time is also an exciting idea. This would lead to the notion of time preserving morphisms and rules which could be very helpful for the specification of real time systems.

References

[BDH92] E. Best, R. Devillers, and J. Hall. The Box Calculus: a new causal algebra with multi-label communication. In *Advances in Petri Nets*, pages 21–69. Lecture Notes in Computer Science, 1992. 609.

[BGV90] W. Brauer, R. Gold, and W. Vogler. A Survey of Behaviour and Equivalence Preserving Refinements of Petri Nets. *Advances in Petri Nets, LNCS 483*, 1990.

[BS90] J. Bradfield and C. Stirling. Verifying temporal properties of processes. In J. C. M. Baeten et al., editors, *LNCS; CONCUR'90, Theories of Concurrency: Unification and Extension. (Conference, 1990, Amsterdam, The Netherlands)*, pages 115–125, Springer, Berlin, 1990.

[CHL95] F. Cornelius, H. Hußmann, and M. Löwe. The KORSO Case Study for Software Engineering with Formal Methods: A Medical Information System. In M. Broy and S. Jähnichen, editors, *KORSO: Methods, Languages, and Tools for the Construction of Correct Software*, pages 417–445. Springer LNCS 1009, 1995. Also appeared as technical report 94-5, TU Berlin.

[DDGJ90] W. Damm, G. Döhmen, V. Gerstner, and B. Josko. Modular verification of petri nets: The temporal logic approach. In J. W. de Bakker et al., editors, *LNCS; Proceedings of the REX Workshop on Stepwise Refinement, 1989, Mook, The Netherlands*, pages 180–207, Springer, Berlin, 1990.

[DHP91] C. Dimitrovici, U. Hummert, and L. Petrucci. Composition and net properties of algebraic high-level nets. In *Advances of Petri Nets*. Springer Verlag Berlin LNCS 524, 1991.

[DM90] J. Desel and A. Meceron. Vincinity Respecting Net Morphisms. In *Advances in Petri Nets*, pages 165–185. Springer Verlag LNCS 483, 1990.

[EG97] C. Ermel and M. Gajewsky. Expanding the Use Of Structuring: Formal Justification for Working on Subnets. In Proceedings of *Workshop Petri Nets in System Engineering '97*, pages 44 – 54, University Hamburg, 1997. FBI –HH–B–205/97.

[EHKP91] H. Ehrig, A. Habel, H.-J. Kreowski, and F. Parisi-Presicce. Parallelism and concurrency in high-level replacement systems. *Math. Struct. in Comp. Science*, 1:361–404, 1991.

[Ehr79] H. Ehrig. Introduction to the algebraic theory of graph grammars. In V. Claus, H. Ehrig, and G. Rozenberg, editors, *1st Graph Grammar Workshop, LNCS 73*, pages 1–69. Springer Verlag, 1979.

[EM85] H. Ehrig and B. Mahr. *Fundamentals of Algebraic Specification 1: Equations and Initial Semantics*, volume 6 of *EATCS Monographs on Theoretical Computer Science*. Springer Verlag, Berlin, 1985.

[EP97] H. Ehrig and J. Padberg. Introduction to Universal Parametrized Net Classes. In H. Weber, H. Ehrig, and W. Reisig, editors, *MoveOn-Proc. der DFG-Forschergruppe "Petrinetz-Technologie"*, Technical Report 97-21, TU Berlin, 1997.

[EPE96] C. Ermel, J. Padberg, and H. Ehrig. Requirements Engineering of a Medical Information System Using Rule-Based Refinement of Petri Nets. In D. Cooke, B.J. Krämer, P. C-Y. Sheu, J.P. Tsai, and R. Mittermeir, editors, *Proc. Integrated Design and Process Technology*, pages 186 – 193. Society for Design and Process Science, 1996. Vol.1.

[Erm96]   C. Ermel. Anforderungsanalyse eines medizinischen Informationssystems mit Algebraischen High-Level-Netzen. Techn. Report 96-15, TU Berlin, 1996.

[Gen91]   H.J. Genrich. Predicate/Transition Nets. In *High-Level Petri Nets: Theory and Application*, pages 3–43. Springer, 1991.

[GG90]   R.J. van Glabbeck and U. Golz. Equivalences and Refinement. In *Semantics of Systems of Concurrent Processes*, pages 309–333. Springer, 1990. Lecture Notes in Computer Science 469.

[GL81]   H.J. Genrich and K. Lautenbach. System modelling with high-level Petri nets. *Theorétical Computer Science*, 13:109–136, 1981.

[HRH91]   R. R. Howell, L. E. Rosier, and Chun Yen Hsu. A taxonomy of fairness and temporal logic problems for petri nets. *Theoretical Computer Science*, 82(2):341–372, 1991.

[Hum89]   U. Hummert. *Algebraische High-Level Netze*. PhD thesis, Technische Universität Berlin, 1989.

[JCHH91]   K. Jensen, S. Christensen, P. Huber, and M. Holla. *Design/CPN. A Reference Manual*. Meta Software Cooperation, 125 Cambridge Park Drive, Cambridge Ma 02140, USA, 1991.

[Jen92]   K. Jensen. *Coloured Petri Nets. Basic Concepts, Analysis Methods and Practical Use*, volume 1. Springer, 1992.

[Jen95]   K. Jensen. *Coloured Petri Nets. Basic Concepts, Analysis Methods and Practical Use*, volume 2. Springer, 1995.

[Lil94]   J. Lilius. *On the Structure of High-Level Nets*. PhD thesis, Helsinki University of Technology, 1994.

[MP92]   Zohar Manna and Amir Pnueli. *The Temporal Logic of Reactive and Concurrent Systems, Specification*. Springer-Verlag, 1992.

[OSS94]   A. Oberweis, G. Scherrer, and W. Stucky. INCOME/STAR: Methodology and Tools for the Development of Distributed Information Systems. *Information Systems*, 19(8):643–660, 1994.

[Pad96]   J. Padberg. *Abstract Petri Nets: A Uniform Approach and Rule-Based Refinement*. PhD thesis, Technical University Berlin, 1996. Shaker Verlag.

[PER95]   J. Padberg, H. Ehrig, and L. Ribeiro. Algebraic high-level net transformation systems. *Math. Struct. in Computer Science*, 5:217–256, 1995.

[Peu97]   S. Peuker. Invariant property preserving extensions of elementary petri nets. *Technical Report No.97-21, TU Berlin*, 1997.

[PGE97]   J. Padberg, M. Gajewsky, and C. Ermel. Refinement versus Verification: Compatibility of Net-Invariants and Stepwise Development of High-Level Petri Nets. Technical Report 97–22, TU Berlin, 1997. to appear.

[Rei91]   W. Reisig. Petri Nets and Algebraic Specifications. *Theoretical Computer Science*, 80:1–34, 1991.

[Sch96]   K. Schmidt. *Symbolische Analysemethoden für algebraische Petri-Netze*, volume 4. Bertz Verlag, versal edition, 1996.

[SM97]   J. Svensson and M. Meier. *Handbuch LEU Support-Guide*. Vebacom Service GmbH. Also, http://www.lion.de/PRODUKT/produkt.html.

[Vau87]   Vautherin, J. Parallel System Specification with Coloured Petri Nets. In Rozenberg, G., editor, *Advances in Petri Nets 87*, pages 293–308. LNCS 266, Springer, 1987.

Automated Formal Analysis of Networks: FDR Models of Arbitrary Topologies and Flow-Control Mechanisms *

JN Reed[1], DM Jackson[2], B Deianov[3], and GM Reed[4]

[1] Oxford Brooks University, Oxford, UK
[2] Praxis Critical Systems, Ltd, Bath, UK
[3] Cornell University, Ithaca, NY, USA
[4] Oxford University, Oxford, UK

Abstract. We present new techniques for formally modeling arbitrary network topologies and control-flow schemes, applicable to high-speed networks. A novel induction technique suitable for process algebraic, finite-state machine techniques is described which can be used to verify end-to-end properties of certain arbitrarily configured networks. We also present a formal model of an algorithm for regulating burstiness of network traffic, which incorporates discrete timing constraints. Our models are presented in CSP with automatic verification by FDR.

1 Introduction

The dynamic nature and arbitrary configuration of advanced network environments and network protocols make the problems of their design, control and analysis inherently complex. This is particularly the case where timeliness as well as correctness of service delivery is a priority.

This paper presents elements of formal models of networks which capture various properties of resource-management and control-flow schemes, of special relevance for high-speed, multiservice networks. These models are analysed with FDR [FDR94,RGG95], a software package offered by Formal Systems (Europe) Ltd, which allows automatic checking of many properties of finite state systems and the interactive investigation of processes which fail these checks. It is based on the mathematical theory of Communicating Sequential Processes, developed at Oxford University and subsequently applied successfully in a number of industrial applications.

Previous CSP/FDR network applications primarily centre on protocols. These applications do not specifically address arbitrary network topologies nor rate-based, flow-control mechanisms for network traffic. In this paper we describe a novel induction technique which used in conjunction with hiding and renaming

---

* This work was supported by the US Office of Naval Research and a research grant from Oxford Brookes University. Technical staff at Formal Systems (Europe) Ltd provided valuable advice on the use of FDR.

can be used to establish properties of arbitrary network configurations. This technique would prove extremely valuable for verifying livelock and deadlock freedom for complex protocols exercised by arbitrary numbers of network nodes. We illustrate its applicability with an example patterned after the Resource reSerVation Protocol (RSVP) [ZDE93,BZB96], a protocol designed to support resource reservation for high-bandwidth multicast transmissions over IP networks.

We also formalise the *leaky bucket* algorithm, a scheme for regulating *burstiness* (variance of delay) of transmitted traffic at a network node. A key component in this model is a ticking clock capturing aspects of a discrete time model.

2 Formal Models of Network Protocols

CSP/FDR belong to the class of formalisms which combine programming languages, and finite state machines. Two similar approaches standardised by ISO for specification and verification/validation of distributed services and protocols are LOTOS [ISOL] [wwwl] and Estelle [ISOE] [ftpe] These techniques are particularly suited for modeling layered protocols, which has come to be a conventional approach for formalising computer networks.

These layered protocols are structured as a fixed number of layers, each with fixed service interfaces. Correctness properties for a given layer typically take the form of an assumption of correct service from the immediate lower level in order to guarantee correct service to the immediate higher level. Properties of the entire "protocol stack" are established by chaining together the service specifications for the fixed number of intermediate layers, ultimately arriving at the service guaranteed by the highest level. The formal layered model naturally reflects the specification and implementation structure of these protocols as adopted by the network and communications community, such as the seven-layer OSI Reference Model developed by the International Standards Organisation. There are numerous examples of formalisations of layered protocols, including Ethernet: CSMA/CD (in non-automated TCSP [Dav91]) (in non-automated algebraic-temporal logic [Jma95]), TCP (in non-automated CSP [GJ94]), DSS1 / ISDN SS7 gateway (in LOTOS [LY93]), ISDN Layer 3 (in LOTOS [NM90]), ISDN Link Access Protocol (in Estelle [GPB91]), ATM signalling (in TLT, a temporal logic/UNITY formalism [BC95]).

An essential feature of these approaches is that system correctness properties are specified in terms of a high-level black box, with a predetermined set of intermediate subcomponents. None of these examples incorporate an unspecified (nor even arbitrary but fixed) set of intermediate nodes. For example, a useful approach for verifying correctness of communication protocols suitable for mechanical support is to prove that an implementation satisfies a variation of what is sometimes known as the $COPY$ property, whereby a message is passed by a "black box" process from a specific *sender* to a specific *receiver*. Examples include the alternating bit, sliding window, and multiplexed switches [PS91,FDR94]. In all of these examples the black box connecting the sender to the receiver is refined by an implementation with a fixed number of subcomponents, each with a fixed interface (set of communication channels).

An *arbitrary* network topology is modelled with action systems [But92] and extended in [Sin97]. The system consists of an (arbitrary but) fixed set of node pairs denoting pairwise channels, together with a complete, noncyclic set of routes. A correctness property analogous to *Copy* is straightforwardly established for the store and forward network. Such deductive-reasoning techniques are not possible for model-checkers such as FDR.

3 CSP and FDR

CSP [Hoa85] models a system as a *process* which interacts with its environment by means of atomic *events*. Communication is synchronous; that is, an event takes place precisely when both the process and environment agree on its occurrence. CSP comprises a process-algebraic programming language (see appendix), together with a related series of semantic models capturing different aspects of behaviour. A powerful notion of refinement intuitively captures the idea that one system implements another. Mechanical support for refinement checking is provided by Formal Systems' FDR refinement checker, which also checks for system properties such as deadlock or livelock.

The simplest semantic model identifies a process as the sequences of events, or *traces* it can perform. We refer to such sequences as *behaviours*. More sophisticated models introduce additional information to behaviours which can be used to determine liveness properties of processes.

We say that a process P is a refinement of process Q, written $Q \sqsubseteq P$, if any possible behaviour of P is also a possible behaviour of Q. Intuitively, suppose S (for "specification") is a process for which all behaviours are in some sense acceptable. If P refines S, then the same acceptability must apply to all behaviours of P. S can represent an idealised model of a system's behaviour, or an abstract property corresponding to a correctness constraint, such as deadlock freedom.

The theory of refinement in CSP allows a wide range of correctness conditions to be encoded as refinement checks between processes. FDR performs a check by invoking a normalisation procedure for the specification process, which represents the specification in a form where the implementation can be checked against it by simple model-checking techniques. When a refinement check fails, FDR provides the means to explore the way the error arose. The system provides the user with a description of the state of the implementation (and its subprocesses) at the point where the error was detected, as well as the sequence of events that lead to the error. The definitive sourcebook for CSP/FDR can now be found in [Ros97].

Unlike most packages of this type, FDR was specifically developed by Formal Systems for industrial applications, in the first instance at Inmos where it is used to develop and verify communications hardware (in the T9000 Transputer and the C104 routing chip). Existing applications include VLSI design, protocol development and implementation, control, signalling, fault-tolerant systems and security. Although the underlying semantic models for FDR do not specifically address time (in contrast to Timed CSP formalism [RR86,TCSP92,KR93]), work has been carried out modeling discrete time with FDR [Sid93,Ros97]. A class of embedded real-time scheduler implementations [Jac96] is analysed with FDR by extracting numerical information from refinement checks to show not only that a timing requirement is satisfied, but also to determine the margin by which it is met.

4 Properties of Arbitrarily Configured Networks

Certain desirable network properties may not be expressible in terms of pre-determined numbers of nodes and interfaces. For example, we might wish to establish deadlock-livelock freedom for an end-to-end protocol which operates with an arbitrary number of intermediate nodes. We would therefore want to express models and properties in a topology dependent manner. To achieve this, we base our specification on single network nodes plus immediate neighbours, and inductively establish the property for arbitrary chains of such nodes. Further discussion of our inductive technique is given in [CR,Cre].

Suppose for a single node we can characterise the interface which a sender or routing node presents to the next node downstream by a property P. If we can demonstrate that under the assumption that all incoming interfaces satisfy P then so do all outgoing onees, we have established an inductive step which allows arbitrary acyclic graphs to be built up, always presenting an interface satisfying P to the nodes downstream. The essential base condition, of course, is that an individual data source meets P. The symmetric case starting with a property of a receiving node and building back towards a source is equally sound. The power of this proof strategy depends on the properties which can be proven of particular nodes, and the ability to structure a collection of nodes inductively with these nodes. Shankar [Shan] uses an induction scheme for PVS model checking for a shared memory algorithm for mutual exclusion, but to our knowledge there has been no published work addressing network protocols.

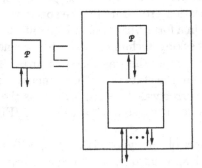

Fig. 1. Simple Induction Scheme

5 RSVP and CSP Models of Reservation Protocols

RSVP is a protocol for multicast resource reservation intended for IP based networks. The protocol addresses those requirements associated with a new generation of applications such as remote video, multimedia conferencing, and virtual reality, which are sensitive to the quality of service provided by the network. These applications depend on certain levels of resource (bandwidth, buffer space, etc.) allocation in order to operate acceptably. The RSVP approach is to create and maintain resource reservations along each link of a previously determined multicast route, with receivers initiating resource requests. This is analogous to a signalling phase prior to packet/cell transmission (such as found in ATM networks).

The technical specification for RSVP as given by its developers appears as a working document of the Internet Engineering Task Force [BZB96]. The protocol assumes a multicast route, which may consist of multiple senders and receivers. RSVP messages carrying reservation requests originate at receivers and are passed upstream towards the senders. Along the way if any node rejects the reservation, a RSVP reject message is sent back to the receiver and the reservation message discarded; otherwise the reservation message is propagated as far as the closest point along the way to the sender where a reservation level greater than or equal to it has been made. Thus reservations become "merged" as they travel upstream; a node forwards upstream only the "maximum" request.

Receivers can request confirmation messages to indicate that the request was (probably) successful. A successful reservation propagates upstream until it reaches a node where there is a (pending) smaller or equal request; the arriving request is then merged with the request in place and a confirmation sent back to the receiver. The receipt of this confirmation is thus a high-probability indication rather than a guarantee of a successful reservation. There is no easy way for a receiver to determine if the reservation is ultimately successful although enhancements involving control packets travelling downstream contain pertinent information to predict the result.

Several interesting aspects emerge from the intuitive description of the RSVP protocol. The protocol is defined for arbitrary routing graphs consisting of several senders and receivers. Confirmations sent by intermediate nodes to receivers are ultimately valid only for the receiver making the largest request; i.e., a requester may receive a confirmation although subsequently the end-to-end reservations fails because of further upstream denial. Global views involving intermediate nodes, (e.g., successful reservations propagate upstream until there are pending smaller or equal requests) present problems for building models consisting of predetermined sets of components. Clearly we are dealing with end-to-end properties inherently defined for arbitrary configurations of intermediate nodes.

We note some interesting design decisions distinctive to RSVP but which are not explicit in [BZB96]. Acknowledgements returned to receivers are only a reflection of a full path back to the specified source for the receiver which has made the (globally) largest request – other receivers may receive acknowledgements when reservations are in place along part of the path. Acknowledgements from different sources are considered independently: a receiver requesting an acknowledgement which is greater than any existing one will receive an acknowledgement from each data source. Receivers making smaller reservations may receive acknowledgements from intermediate nodes or from sources, depending on the partial ordering among requests.

Extending RSVP to provide more exact information for sender/receiver pairs would involve algorithmic changes, including maintaining more state at intermediate nodes. An interesting technical consideration arises in the context of mechanical verification, where we might identify a hierarchy of approaches: if we maintain state for each reservation, then the system will be potentially infinite, as duplicate reservations must be counted; if we maintain confirmation state for only a single request for each interface, we lose the ability to provide exact acknowledgements. As a compromise, we maintain a record of the confirmed status of each *unique* request, and ignore duplicates.

5.1 CSP Models for Reservation Protocols

We build a general model of a network node, and inductively establish appropriate properties desirable from a receiver's perspective. We illustrate here a very simple model (immediate acknowledgements for previously accepted requests). Similar properties amenable to inductive argument but requiring more complex models include automatic rejection of requests exceeding those previously rejected upstream and filtering requests according to selected sources.

The general communications convention used is that a node has access to two channels, one upstream to toward the source, and another downstream towards the sender. We model resources as small integers and define a single type to distinguish acknowledgements from errors, and define internal channels to relay messages and implement a voting protocol.

```
MAX_RESOUCE = 3
RESOURCE = {0 . . MAX_RESOURCE}
datatype RESULT = accept | reject
datatype MESSAGE = request . RESOURCE
                 | reply . RESOURCE . RESULT

channel upstream, downstream: MESSAGE

datatype INTERNAL = msg . MESSAGE |
    sync . RESOURCE | vote . RESOURCE . RESULT
channel internal : INTERNAL
```

– PROTOCOL NODE: To avoid state explosion, a node is structured as a series of "slices" each maintaining one value of the resource. In practice this would be implemented by fewer processes sharing state. The "down" section of a node manages downstream communications with receivers. Each slice has a parameter v indicating which resource value it is concerned with, and maintains a current reservation state, and an idle flag which indicates if a request is pending.

```
DownSlice(curr, v, idle) =
  idle & downstream . request . v ->
    (if curr >= v
      then DownSlice(curr, v, false)
      else (internal . msg . request ! v -> DownSlice(curr, v, false)
            |~|
            downstream . reply ! v ! reject -> DownSlice(curr, v, true)))
  []
  not idle and curr >= v & downstream . reply ! v ! accept ->
    DownSlice(curr, v, true)
  []
  internal . msg . reply ? vv ! reject ->
    (if vv == v and not idle
      then downstream . reply ! v ! reject -> DownSlice(curr, v, true)
      else DownSlice(curr, v, idle))
  []
  internal . msg . reply ? vv ! accept -> DownSlice(max(curr,vv), v, idle)
```

– Requests which cannot be trivially satisfied are forwarded on the internal message channel. The whole receiver interface is a combination of such slices:

```
Down = || v: RESOURCE @ [{|internal . msg . reply ,
                          internal. msg.request.v,
                          downstream.request.v,
                          downstream.reply.v|}] DownSlice(0, v, true)
```

– The interface to a sender is similarly structured: In the RSVP wild-card model, it simply relays requests upstream and then votes on the returned status value. If a reservation succeeds, it will allow both synchronisation's to happen without intervening events. Otherwise, it will insist that the rejection is recorded. Different upstream interfaces all synchronise on sync but interleave on vote.

```
UpSlice(v) =
  internal . msg . request . v -> upstream . request ! v ->
    upstream . reply . v ? result -> internal . sync ! v ->
    if result == accept
      then internal . sync ! v  -> UpSlice(v)
      else internal . vote ! v ! reject ->
              internal . sync ! v  -> UpSlice(v)
```

– Instantiation:

```
Up = || v: RESOURCE @ [{|internal . msg . request.v,
                        internal.vote.v,
                        internal. sync.v,
                        upstream.request.v,
                        upstream.reply.v|}] UpSlice(v)
```

– The final part of the node is a central co-ordinator which is responsible for monitoring the results of propagated requests and passing the resulting vote down to the receiver components. All upstream interfaces should register their vote on sync, with only rejecting also choosing to vote reject.

– This rather complex voting structure accommodates multiple upstream interfaces; a downstream request is ultimately accepted only if all upstream interfaces accept.

```
CoordinatorSlice(v) =
let
  Accept = internal . sync . v ->
                internal . msg . reply ! v ! accept ->
                CoordinatorSlice(v)
             []
             internal . vote . v . reject -> Reject
  Reject = internal . sync . v ->
                internal . msg . reply ! v ! reject ->
                CoordinatorSlice(v)
             []
             internal . vote . v . reject -> Reject
  within internal . sync . v -> Accept
```

– In this case there is no communication between co-ordinator slices.

```
Coordinator = ||| v : RESOURCE @ CoordinatorSlice(v)
```

– The simplest possible node has a single upstream and single downstream interface, and a coordinator (see Fig. 2):

```
SimpleNode =  ((Up
              [|{|internal.vote,internal.sync|}|]
              Coordinator \ {|internal.vote,internal.sync|})
              [|{|internal|}|]
              Down \ {|internal|})
```

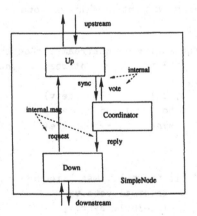

Fig. 2. Simple Node

– The following specification for a receiver access point has two principle properties: acknowledgements are issued only for previously observed request values, and requests for values which have not yet been seen are always accepted.

```
RAO =
let
SPEC({}) = downstream.request?v -> SPEC({v})
SPEC(seen) =
            (downstream.request?v -> SPEC(union(seen,{v})))
        |~|
    downstream.request?v:diff(RESOURCE,seen) ->
SPEC(union(seen,{v}))
    |~|
(|~| h : seen,  v: RESULT @
                        downstream . reply ! h ! v -> SPEC(seen))
within SPEC({})
```

– The simplest specification that a sender must satisfy is that it must present an interface satisfies this condition; we achieve this by using RAO. We can then connect such an abstract source to a simple protocol node as follows:

```
SimpleSystem = (RAO[[ downstream <- upstream ]]
[| {|upstream|} |]
SimpleNode) \ {| upstream |}
```

– This should preserve the RAO property (see Figure 3):

```
assert RAO [FD= SimpleSystem
```

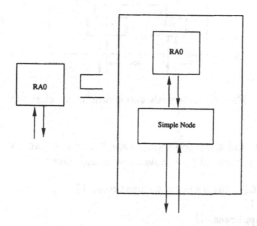

Fig. 3. Receiver's perspective

– To add a second receiver interface, we introduce a second downstream channel, and add an appropriately renamed interface process.

```
channel down' : MESSAGE
channel localreq : RESOURCE
```

– A new local request channel is introduced to allow requests from the two downstream channels to be interleaved. The `intrnal.msg.request` channel seen by the first down node (`down'`) is renamed to `localreq` before it becomes hidden (and thus unavailable to the second down node). Then this `localreq` is renamed back to `internal.msg.request` in order to open it up to the second down node. This clever technique enables the synchronised parallel operator (`[| |]`) with both synchronous (`internal.msg.reply`) and asynchronous channels (`internal.msg.request`).

```
DualNode = ((( (normal(((Up
          [|{|internal.vote,internal.sync|}|]
          Coordinator \ {|internal.vote,internal.sync|})
                     [[ internal.msg.request  <- localreq,
 internal.msg.request <- internal.msg.request ]]
          [|{|internal|}|]
          Down[[downstream <- down']]) \ {|internal.msg.request|})
      [[ localreq <- internal.msg.request ]])
   [|{|internal.msg.reply|}|]
          Down)) \ {|internal|})
```

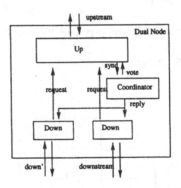

Fig. 4. Node with two downstream channels

– Again we can add a pseudo-sender (see Figures 4 and 5). The system should present the same interface on both **downstream** and **down'**: :

```
DualSystem = (RAO[[ downstream <- upstream ]]
[| {|upstream|} |]
DualNode) \ {| upstream |}

assert RAO  [F= DualSystem \ {|down'|}
assert RAO[[downstream <- down']] [F= DualSystem \ {|downstream|}
```

In the refinement above we employ the CSP hiding operator \, but a stronger criteria is obtained if we use lazy evaluation [Ros97]. The assertions illustrated in Fig 5 inductively establishing properties for, in this instance, any network made up of nodes with downstream branching degree of two. Thus we can prove correctness for finite but unbounded topologies.

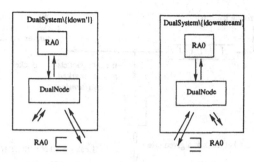

Fig. 5. Each downstream channel satisfies RA0

6 Leaky Bucket

Traffic congestion caused by burstiness of data transmission presents problems for today's multimedia networks, particularly for video and audio which do not tolerate variable rates of flow well. One approach to congestion management in ATM networks is called traffic shaping, which attempts to regulate the average rate and burstiness of network traffic. If senders agree to certain transmission patterns, then the network can agree to provide a certain quality of service. Monitoring a traffic flow for conformance of transmission pattern is called traffic policing.

The leaky bucket algorithm [Tur86] attempts to regulate traffic burstiness at a network node. It does not preclude buffer overflow nor guarantee an upper bound on packet delay; but with proper choice of bucket parameters, overflow and delay can be reduced.

Our model utilises an idiom introduced in [Ros97] which was applied very effectively to the verification of timing requirements of a real-time embedded scheduler [Jac96]. Passing of time is marked by a clock process synchronising with other system components. However because of CSP's particular treatment of internal events, care must be taken to prevent the system from diverging (livelocking).

Overview of Algorithm

This description is adapted from Tanenbaum [Tan96]. Imagine a bucket with capacity L which holds packets and leaks them at a given rate I when not empty and rate 0 when empty. Arriving packets join the bucket if the bucket is not full and are marked *conforming*. If the bucket is full, arriving packets do not join and are marked as *nonconforming*. This mechanism can be used to smooth out burstiness to a more even flow.

For example, assume that we want to achieve a transmission rate of 2MB/sec, and assume that data is coming in at a rate of 25MB/sec for the first 40 msec of a 1 second period. If the bucket has capacity 1MB, and leaks packets at a rate of 2 MB/sec, then the described burst of 1MB/sec is conforming. However an additional 25MB/sec over the next 10 msec would be marked as nonconforming.

The first example below models a policing function using a leaky buffer. The second example contains an additional space controller which attempts to smooth burstiness by buffering incoming cells.

We outline a model indicated in Fig 7 of the Leaky-Bucket algorithm, with and without a Space Controller. We omit the code for most of the components, but explicitly give that for the crucial modules Space Controller and the Timer.

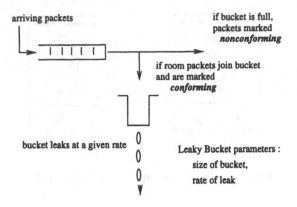

Fig. 6. Leaky Bucket

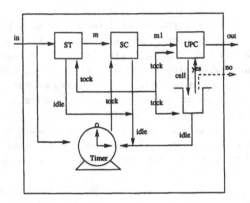

Fig. 7. Leaky Bucket with Space Controller

```
DATA = {0,1}
channel in,out,m,m1 : DATA
channel cell,yes,no,error,tock,idle
```

A tock event indicates that one unit of time has passed. A process performing the idle event will not change state until some non-tock event takes place. BUFF(B) is a B place buffer.

LB(I,L) models a leaky bucket with parameters I (agreed rate) and L (tolerance/bucket size); it remembers the current value of the bucket. With each tock, when the bucket is not empty, leak one otherwise indicate that the bucket is idle. A cell event is non-conforming (output no) if the bucket is too full and conforming (yes) otherwise; put I more in the bucket. The significance of a no event is that a non-conforming cell will cause the system to fail the specification. The bucket is initially empty.

The UPC process simply relays out those cells which are nonconforming. It must always listen to tock events.

A space controller with parameters I (release rate) and B (buffer size); s is the current contents of the buffer; t is the time since the last cell was released. If enough time has passed release the next cell – otherwise record the passage of time. The space controller is idle only if its buffer has been empty for I units of time. If there is space in the buffer, store cells when they arrive –if not, release a cell even if it is too early, to prevent the buffer from overflowing.

```
SC(I,B) = let
  SC1(s,t) = if t == 0 and not null(s)
              then m1!head(s) -> SC1(tail(s),I)
              else (tock -> if t > 0
                              then SC1(s,t-1)
                              else if null(s)
                                      then idle -> SC1(<>,0)
                                      else SC1(s,0))
                  []
                  (m?c -> if #s < B
                            then SC1(s^<c>,t)
                            else m1!head(s) -> SC1(tail(s)^<c>,I))
within SC1(<>,0)
```

A transmitter process ST(I,B) inputs cells from the environment and puts them into the system, but no more than B every I*B units of time (overall rate 1 every I tocks); it maintains a value bits as a binary record of the last I*B+B events: a bit is 1 if the event was a cell put into the system, 0 if it was a tock; count is the number of 1s in bits. If no cells have been transmitted recently, the transmitter is idle – otherwise change the state with the passage of time. If no more than B cells have been transmitted in the last B*I tocks transmit the next cell and record that.

The purpose of TIMER is to stop time when the system is idle - this stops the system from diverging as it can't perform the tock event an infinite number of times without engaging in external communication. N is the number of components in the system; M is the number of components that are still not idle, when 0 time stops. An input from the timer wakes up the clock. Only allow the tock event if the system is not idle.

```
TIMER(N) = let
TIMER1(M) = M != 0 & (tock -> TIMER1(N)
                      []
                      idle -> TIMER1(M-1))
            []
            in?c -> TIMER1(N)
within TIMER1(N)
```

A complete system (without space controller) with parameters I1 (transmission rate), B1 (burstiness), I2 (agreed rate), L2 (bucket size/tolerance).

```
SYS(I1,B1,I2,L2) = (ST(I1,B1) [|{|m,tock|}|] LB(I2,L2) \ {|m|})
                    [|{|in,tock,idle|}|]
                    TIMER(2) \ {|tock,idle|}
```

A complete system (with space controller). Additional parameter: B2 (space controller buffer size).

```
SYSC(I1,B1,I2,L2,B2) = ((ST(I1,B1) [|{|m,tock|}|]
                         SC(I2,B2) \ {|m|}) [|{|m1,tock|}|]
                         LB(I2,L2) [[m <- m1]] \ {|m1|})
                         [|{|in,tock,idle|}|]
                         TIMER(3) \ {|tock,idle|}
```

`assert BUFF(1) [FD= SYS(5,1,5,3)`   `-- Checks !`

– Transmission is at agreed rate with equal delay between cells; all cells are conforming.

`assert BUFF(2) [FD= SYS(5,3,5,8) -- Fails !`

– Transmission at the agreed rate, but the traffic is bursty; the bucket is too small and the third cell is non-conforming.

`assert BUFF(3) [FD= SYSC(5,3,5,8,2) -- Checks !`

– Same as above, but with a space controller; all cells are now conforming.

`assert BUFF(6) [FD= SYSC(4,1,5,8,5) -- Fails !`

– Transmission is too fast and eventually both the buffer of the space controller and the leaky bucket overflow.

7   Conclusions

We described an induction technique for proving properties of arbitrary configurations of nodes. This technique was illustrated with RSVP, a resource reservation protocol which is intended for and most naturally described using arbitrary network topologies. Whilst unspecified topologies are straightforwardly handled by state-based formal methods such as action systems or Z, corresponding methods for automated model-checking approaches such as FDR have not been identified. Our contribution is to identify induction schemes which require no extension to the underlying theory, but which have not been used in previous applications and rely on various "coding tricks" which have not been illustrated in previously published works. Such techniques would prove especially valuable for proving deadlock/livelock freedom for complex protocols among arbitrary numbers of nodes, provided that we can model the protocol using an inductive structure.

We have also presented an FDR model incorporating discrete time which is applied to the leaky bucket algorithm for traffic policing. FDR is not immediately associated with applications dealing with time, but the treatment of discrete time proves very effective in this case.

References

[BC95] D Barnard and Simon Crosby, The Specification and Verification of an Experimental ATM Signalling Protocol, *Proc. IFIP WG6.1 International Symposium on Protocol Specification, Testing and Verification XV*, Dembrinski and Sredniawa, eds,Warsaw, Poland, June 1995, Chapman Hall.

[But92] R Butler. A CSP Approach to Action Sysems, DPhil Thesis, University of Oxford, 1992.

[BZB96] R Braden, L Zhang, S. Berson, S. Herzog and S. Jamin. Resource reSerVation Protocol (RSVP) – Version 1, Functional Specification. Internet Draft, Internet Engineering Task Force. 1996.

[Cre] S Creese, An inductive technique for modelling arbitrarily configured networks, MSc Thesis, University of Oxford, 1997.

[CR] S Creese and J Reed, Inductive Properties and Automatic Proof for Computer Networks, (to appear).

[Dav91] J Davies, Specification and Proof in Real-time Systems, D.Phil Thesis, Univ. of Oxford, 1991.

[FDR94] Formal Systems (Europe) Ltd. Failures Divergence Refinement. *User Manual and Tutorial*, version 1.4 1994.

[ftpe] Estelle Specifications, ftp://louie.udel.edu/pub/grope/estelle-specs

[GJ94] JD Guttman and DM Johnson, Three Applications of Formal Methods at MITRE, *Formal Methods Europe*, LNCS 873, M Naftolin, T Denfir, eds, Barcelona 1994.

[GPB91] R Groz, M Phalippou, M Brossard, Specification of the ISDN Linc Access Protocol for D-channel (LAPD), CCITT Recommendation Q.921, ftp://louie.udel.edu/pub/grope/estelle-specs/lapd.e

[Hoa85] CAR Hoare. *Communicating Sequential Processes*. Prentice-Hall 1985.

[ISOE] ISO Recommendation 9074, The Extended State Transition Language (Estelle), 1989.

[ISOL] ISO: Information Processing System - Open System Interconnection - LOTOS - A Formal Description Technique based on Temporal Ordering of Observational Behavior, IS8807, 1988.

[Jac96] DM Jackson. Experiences in Embedded Scheduling. *Formal Methods Europe*, Oxford, 1996.

[Jma95] M Jmail, An Algebraic-temporal Specification of a CSMA/CD Protocol, *Proc. IFIP WG6.1 International Symposium on Protocol Specification, Testing and Verification XV*, Dembrinski and Sredniawa, eds,Warsaw, Poland, June 1995, Chapman Hall.

[KR93] A Kay and JN Reed. A Rely and Guarantee Method for TCSP, A Specification and Design of a Telephone Exchange. *IEEE Trans. Soft. Eng.*. 19,6 June 1993, pp 625-629.

[LY93] G Leon, JC Yelmo, C Sanchez, FJ Carrasco and JJ Gil, An Industrial Experience on LOTOS-based Prototyping for Switching Systems Design, *Formal Methods Europe*, LNCS 670, JCP Woodcock and DG Larsen, eds., Odense Denmark, 1993.

[NM90] J Navarro and P s Martin, Experience in the Development of an ISDN Layer 3 Service in LOTOS, *Proc. Formal Description Techniques III*, J Quemada, JA Manas, E Vazquez, eds, North-Holland, 1990.

[PS91] K Paliwoda and JW Sanders. An Incremental Specification of the Sliding-window Protocol. *Distributed Computing*. May 1991, pp 83-94.

[RGG95] AW Roscoe, PHB Gardiner, MH Goldsmith, JR Hulance, DM Jackson, JB Scattergood. H ierarchical compression for model-checking CSP or How to check 10^{20} dining philosphers for deadlock, Springer LNCS 1019.

[Ros97] AW Roscoe. *The CSP Handbook*, Prentice-Hall International, 1997.

[RR86] GM Reed and AW Roscoe, A timed model for communicating sequential processes, Proceedings of ICALP'86, Springer LNCS 226 (1986), 314-323; *Theoretical Computer Science* 58, 249-261.

[Shan] N Shankar, Machine-Assisted Verification Using Automated Theorm Proving and Model Checking, *Math. Prog. Meothodology*, ed. M Broy.

[Sid93] K Sidle, Pi Bus, *Formal Methods Europe*, Barcelona, 1993.

[Sin97] J Sinclair, Action Systems, Determinism, and the Development of Secure Systems, PHd Thesis, Open University, 1997.

[Tan96] AS Tanenbaum. *Computer Networks*. 3rd edition. Prentice-Hall 1996.

[TCSP92] J Davies, DM Jackson, GM Reed, JN Reed, AW Roscoe, and SA Schneider, Timed CSP: Theory and practice. *Proceedings of REX Workshop, Nijmegen*, LNCS 600, Springer-Verlag, 1992.

[Tur86] JS Turner. New Directions in Communications (or Which Way to the Information Age). *IEEE Commun. Magazine*. vol 24, pp 8 -15, Oct 1986.

[wwwl] LOTOS Bibliography, http://www.cs.stir.ac.uk/ kjt/research/well/bib.html

[ZDE93] L Zhang, S Deering, D Estrin, S Shenker and D. Zappala. RSVP: A New Resource ReSerVation Protocol. *IEEE Network*, September 1993.

Appendix A. The CSP Language

The CSP language is a means of describing components of systems, *processes* whose external actions are the communication or refusal of instantaneous atomic *events*. All the participants in an event must agree on its performance. The CSP processes that we use are constructed from the following (overview from [Jac96]):

STOP is the simplest CSP process; it never engages in any action, and never terminates.

SKIP similarly never performs any action, but instead terminates successfully, passing control to the next process in sequence (see ; below).

a -> P is the most basic program constructor. It waits to perform the event a and after this has occurred subsequently behaves as process P. The same notation is used for outputs (c!v -> P) and inputs (c?x -> P(x)) of values along named channels.

P |~| Q represents *nondeterministic* or internal choice. It may behave as P or Q arbitrarily.

P [] Q represents external or *deterministic* choice. It will offer the initial actions of both P and Q to its encironment at first; its subsequent behaviousr is like *P* if the initial action chosen was possible only for P, and like Q if the action selected Q. If both P and Q have common initial actions, its subsequent behaviour is nondeterministic (like |~|). A deterministic choice between STOP and another process, STOP [] P is identical to P.

P |[A]| Q represents parallel (concurrent) composition. P and Q evolve separately, except that events in A occur only when P and Q agree (i.e. *synchronise*) to perform them.

P ||| Q represents the interleaved parallel composition. P and Q evolve separately, and do not synchronize on their events.

P ; Q is a sequential, rather than parallel, composition. It behaves as P until and unless P terminates successfully: its subsequent behaviour is that of Q.

P \ A is the CSP abstraction or hiding operator. This process behaves as P except that events in set A are hidden from the environment and are solely determined by P; the environment can neither observe nor influence them.

P [[a <- b]] represents the process P with a renamed to b.

There are also straighforward generalisations of the choice operators over non-empty sets, written |~| x:X @ P(x) and [] x:X @ P(x).

Behaviour Analysis and Safety Conditions:
A Case Study in CML

Hanne Riis Nielson   Torben Amtoft   Flemming Nielson

Computer Science Department, Aarhus University, Denmark
e-mail: {hrn,tamtoft,fn}@daimi.aau.dk

Abstract. We describe a case study where novel program analysis technology has been used to pinpoint a subtle bug in a formally developed control program for an embedded system. The main technology amounts to first defining a process algebra (called behaviours) suited to the programming language used (in our case CML) and secondly to devise an annotated type and effect system for extracting behaviours from programs in a such a manner that an automatic inference algorithm can be developed. The case study is a control program developed for the "Karlsruhe Production Cell" and our analysis of the behaviours shows that one of the safety conditions fails to hold.

Keywords. Embedded systems, formal program development, program analysis.

1   Introduction

There are several approaches for how to close the gap between the specification of a system and its actual realisation as a program in some programming language. Different procedures for systematic design have been developed with the goal of reducing the likelihood of introducing errors, and concise notations have been introduced for documenting and reasoning about systems.

Unfortunately, a system may have been developed using formal methods but still have bugs. Advanced proof techniques may have been used to show that the specification fulfils certain safety and liveness properties, but there is always the risk that the formalisation does not fully correspond to the informal description (or even a formal description in another framework) and that the code written does not fully correspond to the specification. Clearly the risk of such unfortunate scenarios gets smaller the more care is taken in the development of the system but we believe that it is not feasible to completely eliminate the risk. Indeed there always is the risk of human mistake (like using a previous incorrect version of the system instead of the current correct version) and of malicious behaviour (a subcontractor cutting corners to increase profit).

While formal methods clearly are very useful for increasing our confidence in the system, it would seem that more is needed. In this paper we demonstrate that technology from program analysis can be invaluable in spotting some of the subtle bugs that may have survived the careful use of formal methods. Traditionally, program analysis has been used in optimising compilers but due to their ability to analyse programs automatically and systematically we claim that they also have an important role to play in program validation. Although the kind of properties of interest in program validation may differ from those of interest in optimising compilers, we demonstrate in this paper that recent developments have paved the way for adapting program analysis to the new application domain.

Background. In [7,8] we present an annotated type system for extracting the communication topology of programs written in a subset of CML [9]. We introduce a formalism of behaviours, a process algebra like CCS or CSP but tailored to the characteristics of CML. The traditional type system for CML is then extended such that it determines behaviours of expressions as well as their types. Both CML and the behaviours are equipped with a small-step operational semantics and a key theoretical result is a subject reduction result ensuring that whenever the CML program engages in a communication, then also the behaviour will be able to do so. This means that safety results obtained by analysing the behaviour also apply to the original CML program.

In [1] we develop an algorithm for type and behaviour reconstruction. The development is sufficiently general that (1) the behaviours contain causality information, (2) ML-like polymorphism is supported, and (3) the algorithm is sound as well as complete with respect to the annotated type system. These properties are crucial for the application described in the present paper. The causality of the various operations is often an integral part of safety conditions for systems; without causal behaviours one can only validate rather few properties of interest. Polymorphism is important when analysing generic programs; without polymorphism (or perhaps polyvariance) one will need to merge information from different function calls and this may make it impossible to validate many interesting properties. The soundness result ensures that the behaviours obtained by the algorithm are correct with respect to the semantics of the program and the completeness result ensures that the behaviours are as precise as is possible according to the annotated type system; it should be obvious that these are crucial properties as well.

Having established the theoretical foundations [1] we have implemented a prototype for extracting behaviours from programs [2]. The present version is able to deal with a fairly large subset of CML and provides the basis for the experiments reported here.

Accomplishments. We study a CML program for the well-known "Production Cell" [4] developed by FZI in Karlsruhe as a benchmark for the development of verified software for embedded systems. The CML program used has been developed using systematic design methods: its functionality has been specified in CSP and many of its safety conditions have been formally verified [10]. Furthermore, it has been combined with the FZI simulator to a working prototype that has subsequently been tested.

None the less, our program analysis reveals that the program does *not* fulfil all of its safety conditions. Our experiments show that the program makes certain assumptions about the initial configuration of the system – a bug that has escaped the formal verification. Furthermore, it turns out that the simulator makes similar assumptions about the initial configuration so that this particular bug will never turn up during testing. We should stress that we do not mean to criticise neither the formal development nor the verification methods nor the programmers. We merely see it as an illustration of a typical problem in the development of complex software systems as was alluded to above.

We believe that the results of our case study presents convincing arguments for also using novel program analysis techniques when validating safety conditions of embedded systems. Although we have been able to validate many of the safety conditions of interest, and to find one that does not hold, there is room for extending our techniques because some of the safety conditions require information not presently included in the behaviours.

Overview. In Section 2 we give a brief introduction to the basic primitives of CML and we present a fragment of the program used in the case study. Then in Section 3 we introduce the behaviours and sketch some of the central rules for how to obtain behaviours from a CML program. In Section 4 we examine three of the safety conditions of the Production Cell and in Section 5 we discuss some further enhancements of our techniques. Finally, Section 6 contains the concluding remarks.

2 The case study

The Production Cell is designed to process metal blanks in a press [4]; its various components are shown from above on Figure 1 which is a picture from the FZI simulator. The work pieces (metal blanks) enter the system on the feed belt (the bottom one on Figure 1) and are then transfered one at a time to a rotating table; the table is then lifted and rotated such that one of the two robot arms can take the work piece and place it in the press. After processing the work piece, the other robot arm will take it out of the press and deliver it to a deposit belt (the top one on Figure 1). For testing purposes a crane has been added to move the work pieces from the deposit belt back to the feed belt.

We shall concentrate on just one of these entities, namely the rotating table. The table can be in one of two vertical positions and it can be rotated clockwise as well as counterclockwise. The following safety conditions have been supplied for the table:

1: The table must not be moved downward if it is in its lower position, and it must not be moved upward if it is in its upper position.

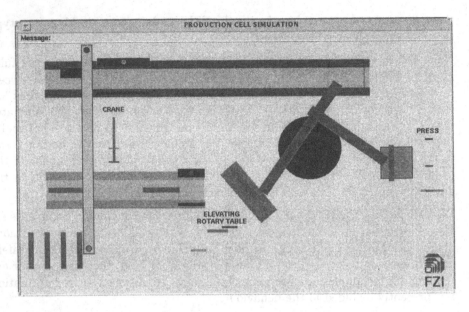

Fig. 1. The Karlsruhe Production Cell.

2: The table must not be rotated clockwise if it is in the position required for transferring work pieces to the robot, and it must not be rotated counterclockwise if it is in the position to receive work pieces from the feed belt.

3: There can only be one work piece at the table at any time.

The program. CML [9] is an extension of the higher-order functional language SML [5] with constructs for communication. Processes and channels can be created dynamically using the constructs **spawn** and **channel**; the constructs **send** and **accept** are available for synchronous communication. Functions as well as channels are first class values and so are events: an event is a potential communication created by one of the constructs **transmit** and **receive**. There is also an explicit synchronisation operation **sync** so the construct **send(ch,v)** is equivalent to **sync(transmit(ch,v))** and similarly **accept(ch)** is equivalent to **sync(receive(ch))**. Events can be manipulated using the construct **wrap**; this corresponds to a kind of speculative post-processing of an event in that it will only take effect if and when the event is synchronised. Finally, we shall mention the construct **choose** which can be used to choose one of several events.

The CML program for the Production Cell consists of 7 processes. They communicate with the simulator using 63 channels and they communicate internally using 16 channels. The part of the program controlling the movements of the table is shown in Figure 2. It uses the following channels for communicating with the simulator:

```
(* actuator channels *)
val table_left     = channel(): unit chan;
val table_stop_h   = channel(): unit chan;
val table_right    = channel(): unit chan;
val table_upward   = channel(): unit chan;
val table_stop_v   = channel(): unit chan;
val table_downward = channel(): unit chan;

(* sensor channels *)
val table_is_bottom     = channel(): unit chan;
val table_is_not_bottom = channel(): unit chan;
val table_is_top        = channel(): unit chan;
val table_is_not_top    = channel(): unit chan;
val table_angle         = channel(): int  chan;
val new_table_angle     = channel(): unit chan;
```

Internally, the table synchronises its movements with the feed belt and the robot and for this it uses the following channels:

```
val belt1_transmit_ready = channel(): unit chan;
val belt1_transmit_done  = channel(): unit chan;

val table_transmit_ready = channel(): unit chan;
val table_transmit_done  = channel(): unit chan;
```

We shall not explain the program in detail here; some of the points will naturally be dealt with when we come to discussing aspects of its behaviour.

3 Behaviours

The safety requirements imposed on the Production Cell are to a large extent concerned with the order in which the communications are performed. This is exactly the kind of information that is available in the behaviours. The behaviours are terms of a process calculus designed to match the structure of CML. The basic behaviours are:

- ϵ is the behaviour of a program that does not create any channels or processes and that is not involved in any communication;
- t CHAN r is the behaviour of a program that creates a channel that can be used to communicate values of type t and where the channel belongs to the region r (a region is an indication of where in the program the channel has been created);
- FORK b is the behaviour for a program that spawns a new process that will behave as described by the behaviour b;
- $r!t$ is the behaviour of a program that sends a value of type t on one of the channels created in the region r; and

```
fun table () =
let
    fun clockwise (a) =                        (*rotate clockwise until degree a*)
        let val x = accept(table_angle)
        in (send(table_right,());
            while (accept(new_table_angle); accept(table_angle)) < a
            do ();
            send(table_stop_h,()) )
        end;

    fun counterclockwise (a) =   (*rotate counterclockwise until degree a*)
        let val x = accept(table_angle)
        in (send(table_left,());
            while (accept(new_table_angle); accept(table_angle)) > a
            do ();
            send(table_stop_h,()) )
        end;

    fun main () =
        (accept(belt1_transmit_ready); accept(belt1_transmit_done);
         clockwise(50);
         send(table_upward,());
         accept(table_is_top);
         send(table_stop_v,());
         send(table_transmit_ready,()); send(table_transmit_done,());
         send(table_downward,());
         accept(table_is_bottom);
         send(table_stop_v,());
         counterclockwise(0);
         main())
in
    spawn(fn () => main())
end;
```

Fig. 2. CML program for the table.

- $r?t$ is the behaviour of a program that receives a value of type t on one of the channels created in the region r.

The basic behaviours can then be combined using sequencing (expressed by ';') and choice (expressed by '+') and they can be recursively defined.

As an example consider the following behaviours:

$$B_c = \{\text{table\_angle}\}?\text{int};\{\text{table\_right}\}!\text{unit};B_1;\{\text{table\_stop\_h}\}!\text{unit}$$

$$B_1 = \{\text{new\_table\_angle}\}?\text{unit};\{\text{table\_angle}\}?\text{int};(\epsilon + B_1)$$

The behaviour B_c expresses that first there will be a communication on the channel table_angle (obtaining the current angle of the table) and next there will be a communication on the channel `table_right` (starting a clockwise rotation of the table). Then the behaviour of B_1 will be executed and finally there will be a communication on the channel `table_stop_h` (stopping the rotation). The behaviour B_1 is recursive: first there will be a communication over the channel `new_table_angle` (indicating that the angle has changed) and subsequently there is a communication on the channel `table_angle` (to obtain the new angle). After that the program may exit (the angle has the required value) or it may repeat the behaviour of B_1 (still waiting for the angle to get the required value).

It turns out that B_c is the behaviour corresponding to the body of the function `clockwise` of Figure 2. Comparing the code for the function with the behaviour above shows that we have recorded which communications take place and in which order, but we have ignored all values and tests. So while the behaviour retains the overall control structure of the code, it loses those details of tests that determine which branch is taken in conditionals (as e.g. that the clockwise rotation of the table is stopped at the angle given as argument to the function).

Construction of behaviours. The behaviours are extracted from the CML program by an extension of the standard polymorphic type system. The idea is that each of the concurrency primitives when supplied with the appropriate parameters gives rise to one of the basic behaviours, and the composite expressions will tell how these behaviours are combined into larger behaviours. A function may require some arguments in order to exhibit its behaviour and an event may need to be synchronised in order to exhibit its behaviour, and to capture this we shall annotate the types with behaviour information. So a function may have the type $t_1 \rightarrow^b t_2$ meaning that it takes an argument of type t_1, gives a result of type t_2 and in doing so it will perform communications as described by the behaviour b. Similarly, an event may have the type t event b meaning that when synchronised it will give rise to a value of type t and in doing so it will perform communications as described by b. The following specifies the annotated types of some of the primitive operations:

send:	$(t \text{ chan } r) \times t \rightarrow^{r!t} \text{unit}$
accept:	$(t \text{ chan } r) \rightarrow^{r?t} t$
transmit:	$(t \text{ chan } r) \times t \rightarrow^{\epsilon} \text{unit event } (r!t)$
receive:	$(t \text{ chan } r) \rightarrow^{\epsilon} t \text{ event } (r?t)$
sync:	$(t \text{ event } b) \rightarrow^b t$
wrap:	$(t_1 \text{ event } b_1) \times (t_1 \rightarrow^b t_2) \rightarrow^{\epsilon} t_2 \text{ event } (b_1; b)$
choose:	$(t \text{ event } b) \text{ list } \rightarrow^{\epsilon} t \text{ event } b$

The construction of the behaviours can be formulated as an annotated type system and below we illustrate the basic idea; for the details we refer to [7, 1].

A type environment *tenv* gives the annotated type of a variable and just mentioning a variable x (in a call-by-value language like CML) does not give rise to any interesting behaviour so we write this as

$$tenv \vdash x : t \ \& \ \epsilon \quad \text{if } tenv(x) = t$$

We have a similar axiom for constants: mentioning a constant (like a numeral or one of the primitive operators above) does not involve any computation so we have

$$tenv \vdash c : t_c \ \& \ \epsilon$$

where t_c is (an instance of) the type of c.

For ordinary function abstraction we take

$$\frac{tenv[x \mapsto t_1] \vdash e : t_2 \ \& \ b}{tenv \vdash \text{fn } x \Rightarrow e : t_1 \rightarrow^b t_2 \ \& \ \epsilon}$$

So we guess a type t_1 for the formal parameter x and analyse the body of the abstraction to determine its type t_2 and its behaviour b. We record the behaviour as part of the overall type of the abstraction and note that as far as communication goes nothing interesting has happened so the overall behaviour will again be ϵ. The case of recursive function definition is fairly similar

$$\frac{tenv[f \mapsto t_1 \rightarrow^b t_2; x \mapsto t_1] \vdash e : t_2 \ \& \ b}{tenv \vdash \text{fun } f \ x \Rightarrow e : t_1 \rightarrow^b t_2 \ \& \ \epsilon}$$

and here we will typically rely on b being a recursive behaviour that can be unfolded as demanded by the unfolding of the recursive function call.

Turning to the rule for function application we have

$$\frac{tenv \vdash e_1 : t_1 \rightarrow^b t_2 \ \& \ b_1, \quad tenv \vdash e_2 : t_1 \ \& \ b_2}{tenv \vdash e_1 \ e_2 : t_2 \ \& \ (b_1; b_2; b)}$$

The idea is that we first determine the annotated type and the behaviour of the operator and the operand. CML has a call-by-value parameter mechanism so operationally we will first observe the communications originating from the operator, then those from the operand and finally those from the called function. Hence the application will have the behaviour $b_1; b_2; b$ – note that the causality of the communications are recorded.

In order for this approach to work we have to be able to enlarge the behaviours. As an example, all the elements in the argument list to the choose primitive must have the same behaviour and to achieve this we shall need a subsumption rule like

$$\frac{tenv \vdash e : t \ \& \ b}{tenv \vdash e : t \ \& \ b'} \quad \text{if } b \sqsubseteq b'$$

Here $b \sqsubseteq b'$ is some ordering on behaviours that for example will express that $+$ is an upper bound operator so b_1 can be enlarged to $b_1 + b_2$. The ordering will also express that ϵ is a left and right identity for sequencing ($\epsilon; b = b = b; \epsilon$) and this allows us to get rid of a lot of uninteresting occurrences of ϵ.

The full type system employs a general subtyping rule and also has rules for dealing with ML-like polymorphism; we shall spare the reader for these details as they do not seem so important for the current discussion. Instead we refer

$B = \text{FORK}(B_0)$

$B_0 = \{\texttt{belt1\_transmit\_ready}\}?\texttt{unit}; \{\texttt{belt1\_transmit\_done}\}?\texttt{unit};$
$\quad \{\texttt{table\_angle}\}?\texttt{int}; \{\texttt{table\_right}\}!\texttt{unit}; B_1; \{\texttt{table\_stop\_h}\}!\texttt{unit};$
$\quad \{\texttt{table\_upward}\}!\texttt{unit}; \{\texttt{table\_is\_top}\}?\texttt{unit}; \{\texttt{table\_stop\_v}\}!\texttt{unit};$
$\quad \{\texttt{table\_transmit\_ready}\}!\texttt{unit}; \{\texttt{table\_transmit\_done}\}!\texttt{unit};$
$\quad \{\texttt{table\_downward}\}!\texttt{unit}; \{\texttt{table\_is\_bottom}\}?\texttt{unit}; \{\texttt{table\_stop\_v}\}!\texttt{unit};$
$\quad \{\texttt{table\_angle}\}?\texttt{int}; \{\texttt{table\_left}\}!\texttt{unit}; B_1; \{\texttt{table\_stop\_h}\}!\texttt{unit};$
$\quad B_0$

$B_1 = \{\texttt{new\_table\_angle}\}?\texttt{unit}; \{\texttt{table\_angle}\}?\texttt{int}; (\epsilon + B_1)$

Fig. 3. Behaviour for the table.

to the development in [1] for the many fine details concerning the ordering $\sqsubseteq$, subtyping, polymorphism, constraint simplification, semantic soundness of the inference system, and syntactic soundness and completeness of the inference algorithm.

The type and behaviour reconstruction algorithm has been implemented in Moscow ML and is available on the web[1]. It has been used to analyse the CML program implementing the Production Cell. For the part of the program corresponding to Figure 2 the algorithm will determine the type unit $\rightarrow^B$ thread_id where B is the behaviour of Figure 3.

Correctness issues. The language CML as well as the language of behaviours are equipped with a small-step operational semantics. This forms the basis for a correctness proof that essentially says that whenever the CML program performs a sequence of steps then also the associated behaviour can perform similar steps. To be more specific: when the semantics of the CML program performs a step corresponding to sending a value v of type t on some channel ch in some region r then the semantics of the behaviour can take a step that will execute the basic behaviour $r!t$, and similarly for the other primitive actions. Thus the behaviours give a *safe* approximation of the communications performed by the CML program.

The behaviour may be able to perform more actions than are possible by the CML program, for example because it will always be able to take both branches of a conditional. However, in the case where the behaviour only can perform one action then the CML will eventually have to perform a matching action – unless it is deadlocked or is looping. To illustrate this, consider a behaviour that contains the sequence

$$\{\texttt{table\_is\_not\_top}\}?\texttt{unit}; \{\texttt{table\_upward}\}?\texttt{unit}$$

---
[1] http://www.daimi.aau.dk/~bra8130/TBAcml/TBA_CML.html

and assume the behaviour of the process of interest only has those two occurrences of communications on the channels `table_is_not_top` and `table_upward`. Then the correctness result will tell us two things. First, if the CML program engages in a communication on `table_upward` then it will already have communicated on `table_is_not_top`. Second, after having engaged in a communication on `table_is_not_top` then it will eventually perform a communication on `table_upward` – unless it enters a looping computation or a deadlock between the two communications.

4 Safety conditions

Most safety conditions of the Production Cell [4] are concerned about the interplay between communications of only a few channels. Much of this information is directly available in the behaviours and we can easily attempt validating the three conditions mentioned in Section 2 based on the behaviours given in Figure 3. However, it is convenient to be able to ignore those channels that are not relevant for validating the condition at hand, i.e. to abstract away from communications on those channels.

As an example, suppose that we want to validate the following safety condition:

> *The engine starting the vertical movement of the table is always turned off before it is turned on (assuming that it is initially turned off).*

We shall rely on some assumptions about the environment: The engine can only be turned on using one of the two channels `table_upward` and `table_downward` and it can only be turned off using the channel `table_stop_v`. We shall therefore replace all communications mentioned in Figure 3 that do *not* involve any of these three channels with ellipses and then we shall apply some straightforward simplifications in order to obtain:

$$B_0 = \cdots ; \{\texttt{table\_upward}\}!\texttt{unit}; \cdots ; \{\texttt{table\_stop\_v}\}!\texttt{unit};$$
$$\cdots ; \{\texttt{table\_downward}\}!\texttt{unit}; \cdots ; \{\texttt{table\_stop\_v}\}!\texttt{unit};$$
$$\cdots ; B_0$$

This simplified behaviour clearly shows that the engine is turned on and off in the manner described by the safety condition.

Just as our prototype is responsible for producing the behaviour of Figure 3 it can also be used to produce the above simplified behaviours. The theoretical foundations for the simplified behaviours are established in [1].

We shall now go through the three safety conditions of the rotating table mentioned in Section 2 and discuss to what extent they can be validated using the behaviours. Based on the informal description of the condition and some overall assumptions about the environment we shall decide which channels are of relevance for the condition and extract that part of the behaviour. It turns out that this will be a fairly simple behaviour so we can immediately judge whether or not the safety condition is fulfilled; clearly a more formal approach is possible as well.

Condition 1.

The table must not be moved downward if it is in its lower position, and it must not be moved upward if it is in its upper position.

Validation of this condition relies on some assumptions about the environment: The vertical movement of the table can only be initiated by communicating on the two channels `table_upward` and `table_downward`. Information about the vertical position of the table can only be obtained from the four channels `table_is_bottom`, `table_is_not_bottom`, `table_is_top` and `table_is_not_top`.

We therefore select these six channels and obtain the following simplified behaviour from Figure 3:

$$B_0 = \cdots; \{\texttt{table\_upward}\}!\texttt{unit};\{\texttt{table\_is\_top}\}?\texttt{unit};$$
$$\cdots;\{\texttt{table\_downward}\}!\texttt{unit};\{\texttt{table\_is\_bottom}\}?\texttt{unit};$$
$$\cdots;B_0$$

Thus we see that all communications on `table_downward` are preceeded by a communication on `table_is_top`. By unfolding the behaviour is is also easy to see that, except for the initial case, all communications on `table_upward` are preceeded by a communication on `table_is_bottom`.

However, this is not the case for the initial communication on `table_upward`. The behaviour will *never* allow a communication on any of the four channels giving information about the vertical position of the table before the initial communication on the channel `table_upward`. It follows that the CML program will never be able to do that either. Hence the analysis has shown that the CML program does *not* fulfil Condition 1!

Condition 2.

The table must not be rotated clockwise if it is in the position required for transferring work pieces to the robot, and it must not be rotated counterclockwise if it is in the position to receive work pieces from the feed belt.

Again we have to rely on some assumptions about the environment. The rotation of the table can only be initiated by communication on one of the two channels `table_right` and `table_left` and it is stopped by communication on the channel `table_stop_h`. The horizontal position of the table can be obtained from the channel `table_angle`.

We therefore extract the behaviour involving the four channels mentioned above and get:

$B_0 = \cdots ; \{\texttt{table\_angle}\}?\texttt{int}; \{\texttt{table\_right}\}!\texttt{unit}; B_1; \{\texttt{table\_stop\_h}\}!\texttt{unit};$
$\qquad \cdots ; \{\texttt{table\_angle}\}?\texttt{int}; \{\texttt{table\_left}\}!\texttt{unit}; B_1; \{\texttt{table\_stop\_h}\}!\texttt{unit};$
$\qquad B_0$
$B_1 = \cdots ; \{\texttt{table\_angle}\}?\texttt{int}; (\epsilon + B_1)$

From this it is easy to see that we have validated the following version of the safety condition:

> *The table is alternating between being rotated clockwise and counterclockwise.*

However there is no information in the behaviours ensuring that the clockwise rotation stops when the angle is 50 (as required for the robot) or that the counterclockwise rotation stops when the angle is 0 (as required for the feed belt). More powerful analysis techniques will be needed to capture this kind of information; we shall return to this in Section 5.

Condition 3.

> *There can only be one work piece at the table at any time.*

This condition is concerned about the synchronisation between the individual processes of the system and hence its validation will depend on properties of the other processes, in particular those for the feed belt and the robot. The table is the passive part in both of these synchronisations. The channels `belt1_transmit_ready` and `belt1_transmit_done` are used to synchronise with the feed belt; between these two communications it is the responsibility of the feed belt to place a work piece on the table. The channels `table_transmit_ready` and `table_transmit_done` are used to synchronise with the robot; between these two communications it is the responsibility of the robot to remove a work piece from the table.

The analysis of the table will therefore need to make some assumptions about the feed belt and the robot. These assumptions will later have to be validated by analysing the behaviour of the program fragments for the respective processes. The assumptions are:

(a) Whenever the feed belt leaves the critical region specified by the two channels `belt1_transmit_ready` and `belt1_transmit_done` it will have moved one (and only one) work piece to the table.
(b) Whenever the robot leaves the critical region specified by the two channels `table_transmit_ready` and `table_transmit_done` it will have emptied the table.

Under these assumptions we can now validate Condition 3.

We shall concentrate on the four channels specifying the critical regions and we obtain the following simplified behaviour for the table:

$$B_0 = \{\texttt{belt1\_transmit\_ready}\}?\texttt{unit};\{\texttt{belt1\_transmit\_done}\}?\texttt{unit};\cdots;$$

$$\{\texttt{table\_transmit\_ready}\}!\texttt{unit};\{\texttt{table\_transmit\_done}\}!\texttt{unit};\cdots;$$

$$B_0$$

Clearly this shows that the two pairs of communications alternate. Also it shows that the synchronisation with the feed belt happens first and by assumption (a) a work piece is placed on the table. The simplified behaviour shows that subsequently there will be a synchronisation with the robot and by assumption (b) the work piece will be removed from the table. Hence Condition 3 has been validated with respect to the assumptions.

5 Discussion and further work

The results obtained from the analysis depend to a large extent on the programming style. As an example, an alternative program for the Production Cell uses the following function instead of the two functions clockwise and counterclockwise:

```
fun turn_to(a) =
    let val x = accept(table_angle) in
    if x < a then
        (send(table_right,());
        while (accept(new_table_angle); accept(table_angle)) < a
        do ();
        send(table_stop_h,()) )
    else if x > a then
        (send(table_left,());
        while (accept(new_table_angle); accept(table_angle)) > a
        do ();
        send(table_stop_h,()) )
    else ()
    end;
```

In the setting provided by Condition 2 we now get the following simplified behaviour for the program:

$$B_0 = \cdots;B_1;\cdots;B_1;B_0$$

$$B_1 = \{\texttt{table\_angle}\}?\texttt{int};$$

$$(\epsilon + \{\texttt{table\_left}\}!\texttt{unit};B_2;\{\texttt{table\_stop\_h}\}!\texttt{unit}$$

$$+ \{\texttt{table\_right}\}!\texttt{unit};B_2;\{\texttt{table\_stop\_h}\}!\texttt{unit})$$

$$B_2 = \cdots;\{\texttt{table\_angle}\}?\texttt{int};(\epsilon + B_2)$$

As expected we cannot validate Condition 2 from this. But even worse, we cannot even validate that the table is alternating between being rotated clockwise and counterclockwise; only that it is rotated an even number of times. The reason for the latter is that the current version of our technology does not incorporate any information about values of variables and the entities communicated and therefore we cannot prune the behaviour for turn_to to take the branch of interest for a given value of the parameter. We expect that techniques from Control Flow Analysis [3, 6] will prove useful when further developing the technology.

The CML program for the Production Cell is basically a first-order program and hence it does not exploit the higher-order constructs of CML. Our technique has no problems handing higher-order functions nor communication of channels. To illustrate a simple version of this, consider the following generic function

```
fun move start doit stop = (send(start,()); doit(); send(stop,()))
```

that takes a channel, a function and yet another channel as arguments. Let us rewrite the program to use this function:

```
fun table () =
let
    fun clockwise (a) =
        let val x = accept(table_angle);
        in move table_right
                (fn () => while (accept(new_table_angle);
                                 accept(table_angle)) < a do ())
                table_stop_h
        end;

    fun counterclockwise (a) =
        let val x = accept(table_angle)
        in move table_left
                (fn () => while (accept(new_table_angle);
                                 accept(table_angle)) > a do ())
                table_stop_h
        end;

    fun main () =
        (accept(belt1_transmit_ready); accept(belt1_transmit_done);
         clockwise(50);
         move table_upward (fn () => accept(table_is_top)) table_stop_v;
         send(table_transmit_ready,()); send(table_transmit_done,());
         move table_downward (fn () => accept(table_is_bottom)) table_stop_v;
         counterclockwise(0);
         main())
    in
        spawn(fn () => main())
    end;
```

The behaviour of this version of the program is exactly as in Table 3; in particular the techniques easily distinguish between the different sets of parameters supplied to the four calls of the move function.

6 Conclusion

We have argued that even the careful use of formal program development techniques may in practice produce bugs that go undetected. To increase the available techniques for validating embedded systems we have argued that the use of novel program analysis technology is likely to be indispensable and we have substantiated this claim by the development of a prototype.

Acknowledgements. We should like to thank H. Rischel for providing us with the simulator for Production Cell as well as the CML program for controlling the Production Cell, and also A. P. Ravn for general discussions about the analysis of embedded systems. This work has been supported in part by the DART project funded by the Danish Science Research Council and also builds on theories and tools developed during the LOMAPS project funded by ESPRIT BRA.

References

1. T. Amtoft, F. Nielson, and H. R. Nielson. Polymorphic subtyping for side effects. Book manuscript, DAIMI PB-529, Aarhus Univesity, 1997.
2. T. Amtoft, H. R. Nielson, and F. Nielson. Behaviour analysis for validating communication patterns. DAIMI PB-527, Aarhus University, 1997.
3. K. L. S. Gasser, F. Nielson, and H. R. Nielson. Systematic realisation of control flow analyses for CML. In *Proceedings of ICFP'97*, pages 38–51. ACM Press, 1997.
4. C. Lewerentz and T. Lindner. *Formal Development of Reactive Systems, Case Study "Production Cell"*. SLNCS vol 891, Springer Verlag, 1995.
5. R. Milner, M. Tofte, and R. Harper. *The definition of Standard ML*. MIT Press, 1990.
6. F. Nielson, H. R. Nielson, and C. L. Hankin. *Principles of Program Analysis: Flows and Effects*. To appear, 1999.
7. H. R. Nielson and F. Nielson. Higher-Order Concurrent Programs with Finite Communication Topology. In *Proc. POPL '94*, 1994.
8. H. R. Nielson and F. Nielson. Communication analysis for Concurrent ML. In *ML with Concurrency*, Monographs in Computer Science. Springer-Verlag, 1997.
9. J.H. Reppy. Concurrent ML: Design, application and semantics. In *Proc. Functional programming, Concurrency, Simulation and Automated Reasoning, SLNCS 693*, pages 165–19, 1993.
10. H. Rischel and H. Sun. Design and prototyping of real-time systems using CSP and CML. In *Proc. 9th Euromicro Workshop on Real-Time Systems*, pages 121–127. IEEE Computer Society Press, 1997.

Distributed Safety Controllers for Web Services

Anders Sandholm and Michael I. Schwartzbach

BRICS*, Department of Computer Science
University of Aarhus, Ny Munkegade
DK-8000 Aarhus C, Denmark
{sandholm,mis}@brics.dk

Abstract. We show how to use high-level synchronization constraints, written in a version of monadic second-order logic on finite strings, to synthesize safety controllers for interactive web services. We improve on the naïve runtime model to avoid state-space explosions and to increase the flow capacities of services.

1 Introduction

An Interactive Web Service consists of a global state (typically a database) and a number of distinct sessions that each contain some local state and a sequential, imperative action. A web client may invoke an individual thread of one of the given session kinds. The execution of this thread may interact with the client and inspect or modify the global state.

To alleviate laborious low-level encodings of such services, the Mawl language [6, 2] has been suggested as a high-level notation that is compiled into low-level CGI-scripts. It directly provides programming constructs corresponding to global state, dynamic document, sessions, local state, imperative actions, and client interactions. This system shows great promise to facilitate the efficient production of reliable web services.

While Mawl thus offers automatic synthesis of many advanced concepts, it still relies on standard low-level semaphore programming for concurrency control. We have designed a variation of Mawl, called Wig, on which we are currently performing a number of experiments. One of these is to synthesize the concurrency control from a high-level notation that is designed to be simple and intuitive. Our notation is based on second-order monadic logic on finite strings, M2L-Str.

As an example of a Wig service, consider the example in Fig. 1, which provides a counter for a page. The intended behavior should be clear. By default Wig provides exclusive write-access to components of the global state, but this is clearly not enough even for this simple example, where the updates of the counter variable must be atomic, which requires some sort of critical region.

Larger web services often require quite complicated concurrency control, which is hard to implement and maintain (and not the kind of issue on which most web programmers want to spend their time).

---

* Basic Research in Computer Science,
  Centre of the Danish National Research Foundation.

```
service {
    global counter: int = 0;
    document ThePage { You are visitor number <var name="num">. };
    session ReadMe {
        counter:=counter+1;
        show ThePage[num ← counter]
    }
}
```

Fig. 1. A simple Wig service.

The web programming environment, with rapidly changing code, fast machines, and slow networks seems an ideal niche for a radical approach of synthesizing finite-state controllers from high-level specifications without suffering an unacceptable performance loss compared to hand-written code. This paper provides the foundations for these ideas.

2 Labeled Services

Before presenting the actual high-level notation for concurrency control we need to make one important extension to the basic language for writing service code. The high-level notation for concurrency control needs a way of referring to points in the service code. For this purpose we add the possibility of having labels in the code. As an example it might very well later turn out to be advantageous to be able to refer to, say, the beginning and the end of a critical region.

With labels in the service code, a run of a service gives rise to the sequence of labels that are passed in turn during the run. We have the basic assumption that no two labels are passed at exactly the same time. In the absence of this assumption, we should replace the word sequence by pomset, partially ordered multi-set. Later, though, we do consider independence models in order to avoid the state explosion problem and to increase parallelism.

In addition to the labels added by the programmer, the following labels are generated automatically because standard safety requirements almost always involve these labels.

- For each global variable X we generate the labels take-X and give-X. These labels are put in just before and just after each assignment to the global variable X. They will make us able to ensure that global variables can only be updated by one session thread at a time.
- For each session definition A we generate labels start-A and end-A. They are put at the beginning and at the end of session A, respectively.

The kind of sequences that a run of a service S gives rise to will thus be strings over the alphabet Σ_S given by

$$\Sigma_S = \mathit{labels}(S) \cup \{\text{take-X} \mid X \in \mathit{globals}(S)\} \cup \{\text{give-X} \mid X \in \mathit{globals}(S)\}$$
$$\cup \{\text{start-A} \mid A \in \mathit{sessions}(S)\} \cup \{\text{end-A} \mid A \in \mathit{sessions}(S)\},$$

where *labels*, *globals*, and *sessions* are the functions that given a service S evaluates to the names of the labels, global variables, and sessions of S, respectively. Where obvious from the context we will drop the subscript S.

An *automaton* is a structure $A = (Q, \hat{q}, \Sigma, \rightarrow, F)$, where Q is a set of states with initial state $\hat{q} \in Q$, Σ is a set of labels, $\rightarrow \subseteq Q \times \Sigma \times Q$ is the transition relation, and $F \subseteq Q$ the set of acceptance states. We shall use $q_1 \xrightarrow{\sigma} q_2$ as notation for $(q_1, \sigma, q_2) \in \rightarrow$.

A string $w = \sigma_0 \sigma_1 \ldots \sigma_{n-1} \in \Sigma^*$ is said to be *accepted* by the automaton A if there exists a run of A that reads the string w and ends up in an accepting state q, i.e., if there exist $q_1, \ldots, q_{n-1} \in Q$ and $q \in F$, such that

$$\hat{q} \xrightarrow{\sigma_0} q_1 \xrightarrow{\sigma_1} \ldots \xrightarrow{\sigma_{n-2}} q_{n-1} \xrightarrow{\sigma_{n-1}} q.$$

We shall denote by $L(A)$ the *language* recognized by an automaton, i.e.,

$$L(A) = \{w \in \Sigma^* \mid A \text{ accepts } w\}.$$

One can observe that a service S induces—in a natural way—an infinite state automaton with alphabet Σ_S, transitions corresponding to passing a label during execution, and $F = Q$, where the language accepted by the induced automaton will then be the set of (finite prefixes of) possible runs of that service. We shall denote by $A_S = (Q_S, \hat{q}_S, \Sigma_S, \rightarrow_S, F_S)$ the automaton induced by S. Again we may omit the subscript S.

3 Safety Requirements

While programming a service, one often needs to make sure certain properties hold. We offer a way of synthesizing runtime controllers from static *safety requirements*. These requirements—written in a dialect of M2L-Str—can together with the service code be compiled into executable code containing a runtime system that automatically ensures that the safety requirements are met, namely by compiling the safety requirements into a runtime safety controller. For a diagram of the overall compilation process see Fig. 2.

M2L-Str is a very expressive logic in which several other logics can be encoded, e.g., interval logic and all sorts of linear time temporal logics. For an introduction to and a discussion of M2L-Str see [4]. The specific high-level notation built on top of M2L-Str for writing Wig safety requirements is called the Wig *service logic* (WSL). The specifics of WSL are dealt with later in this paper. One might argue in favor of other specification formalisms, e.g., Colored Petri Nets or Message Sequence Chart Diagrams. One of the reasons why we have chosen M2L-Str is

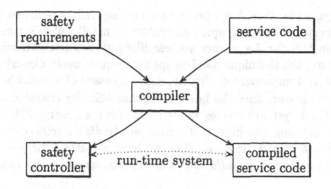

Fig. 2. Overview of the setup.

that we have a very well functioning tool available for doing computations in this logic [4]. Also, since we do not aim for traditional model checking, but rather for synthesizing controllers to be run on fast machines in slow networks, we are in the fortunate position to choose whatever logic provides the most succinct and intuitive syntax. All in all, M2L-Str is very powerful and yet just simple enough to actually allow calculations.

A formula ϕ in M2L-Str over the alphabet Σ will—when interpreted over a finite string w—either evaluate to true or to false and we shall write $w \models \phi$ or $w \not\models \phi$, respectively. The *language* associated with ϕ is

$$L(\phi) = \{\, w \in \Sigma^* \mid w \models \phi \,\}.$$

We shall denote by $pre(\phi)$ the prefix closure of $L(\phi)$.

We will use M2L-Str formulae as safety requirements as follows. Given a safety requirement ϕ we want to restrict the execution of the service S to allow only runs $\sigma = \sigma_0\sigma_1\sigma_2\cdots \in \Sigma^\omega$ for which

$$\{\, \sigma_0\ldots\sigma_{n-1} \in \Sigma^* \mid n \geq 0 \,\} \subseteq pre(\phi).$$

That is, we only allow a run σ if all its finite prefixes, $\epsilon, \sigma_0, \sigma_0\sigma_1, \sigma_0\sigma_1\sigma_2, \ldots$, are in the prefix closure of the language associated with ϕ.

Example 1. A safety requirement formula might look as follows.

$$\forall\textbf{time } t,t'': (t{<}t'' \wedge \text{start-A}(t) \wedge \text{start-A}(t''))$$
$$\implies \exists\textbf{time } t': t{<}t'{<}t'' \wedge \text{end-A}(t').$$

The formula will ensure that at most one session A thread will be allowed to execute at a time.

The above formula will occur automatically once per global variable X with start-A and end-A replaced by take-X and give-X respectively. This will ensure that only one session thread can update a given global variable at a time. One might argue that this could be implemented by simply using a semaphore for each global variable. True, but what we are dealing with here is just one specific safety requirement. Our technique can uniformly handle all safety requirements expressible in M2L-Str, i.e., errors are less likely to occur. Furthermore we will argue later that the technique handles specific requirements like critical regions as efficiently as if implemented directly, e.g., by means of a semaphore.

It has been known since the late sixties that M2L-Str characterizes regularity [8]. The Mona system provides an algorithm for translating M2L-Str formulae into minimal deterministic finite state automata (*mdfa*). Furthermore, regularity is preserved under prefix closure. Thus we have a method for producing from the safety requirements an *mdfa* that will function as our safety controller.

Example 2. The minimal safety controller corresponding to the requirement of Example 1 will thus be

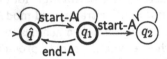

with the convention that non-labeled transitions are implicitly labeled by Σ minus the labels that occur on other outgoing transitions from that state.

As can be seen, it is not possible to start a new session A thread if an A thread is already running.

4 Labeled Services with Safety Requirements

Given a service S with induced automaton A_S and a safety controller A_c we can quite precisely define the restricted behavior that we expect from the composite system. First a definition.

We define the *product automaton* $A_1 \times A_2$ of two automata A_1 and A_2, $A_i = (Q_i, \hat{q}_i, \Sigma, \rightarrow_i, F_i)$ to be

$$A_1 \times A_2 = (Q_1 \times Q_2, (\hat{q}_1, \hat{q}_2), \rightarrow, F_1 \times F_2),$$

where

$$(q_1, q_2) \xrightarrow{\sigma} (q_1', q_2') \text{ iff } q_i \xrightarrow{\sigma}_i q_i' \text{ for } i = 1, 2.$$

Thus the restricted behavior that we want our composite system to have is that of $A_S \times A_c$. For a product $A_1 \times A_2$ of two systems A_1 and A_2 we have $L(A) = L(A_1) \cap L(A_2)$. Thus the product of the service and the controller will allow—among the possible runs of the service—exactly those that also meet the safety requirements.

4.1 Implementing the Naïve Runtime System

The service does not constitute a finite state automaton. Therefore we cannot produce the full runtime system (the combined system consisting of both the service A_S and the controller A_c) by simply computing the product automaton at compile time. What we will do instead is to implement the implicit synchronization of the product automaton directly as part of the runtime system. The runtime system will then consist of three parts:

- a safety controller A_c,
- for each label $\sigma \in \Sigma$ a run-time queue rtq(σ), and
- the current session threads of the service.

All session threads and the controller run in parallel having the queues as shared resources.

- The code for the sessions will then be compiled such that each time a session thread wants to pass a label σ it pushes its session thread *id* onto rtq(σ) and then waits for permission to continue. When permission later is granted by the controller it will pass the label σ and continue its execution.
- The safety controller will be looping while doing the following. Check if any of the queues corresponding to the enabled transitions are non-empty. In case it finds a non-empty queue, say rtq(σ), it
  1. removes a session thread *id* from rtq(σ),
  2. changes its state corresponding to making the enabled σ-transition, and
  3. wakes up the session thread corresponding to the removed *id*.

This way the runtime system will behave as the product of the service and the controller. A diagram of a simple runtime system can be found in Fig. 3.

5 Improvements on the Runtime System

In the following section we will present two major improvements on the runtime system. Since the service part of the runtime system is very hard to reason about at compile time, our improvements will concentrate on the safety controller (which is just a finite automaton) and the shared queues. Both improvements are achieved by using the notion of distributed automata.

- The first improvement concerns the avoidance of the state explosion problem.
- The second improvement increases parallelism of the system by inferring independence information.

First let us define the notion of distributed automata. A *distributed alphabet* $\tilde{\Sigma} = (\Sigma_1, \ldots, \Sigma_K)$ with $K \geq 1$ is a finite collection of finite, non-empty alphabets. We will denote by Loc the set $\{1, \ldots, K\}$ and by Σ the union of the not necessarily disjoint alphabets Σ_i. By loc(σ) we will denote the set of locations where σ occurs, i.e., loc(σ) = $\{ i \in \text{Loc} \mid \sigma \in \Sigma_i \}$.

Safety Controller   Queues   Session Threads

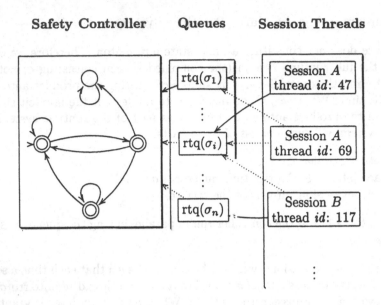

Fig. 3. Sketch of the runtime system.

A *distributed automaton* over $\tilde{\Sigma}$ is a structure $\mathcal{A} = (A_1, \ldots, A_K)$ consisting of finite state automata $A_1, \ldots, A_K$, with $A_i = (Q_i, \hat{q}_i, \Sigma_i, \rightarrow_i, F_i)$. The derived behavior of $\mathcal{A}$ will be as the behavior of the finite state automaton

$$A = (Q_1 \times \cdots \times Q_K, (\hat{q}_1, \ldots, \hat{q}_K), \Sigma, \rightarrow, F_1 \times \cdots \times F_K),$$

where $(q_1, \ldots, q_K) \overset{\sigma}{\rightarrow} (q_1', \ldots, q_K')$ if and only if
- when $i \in \text{loc}(\sigma)$ then $q_i \overset{\sigma}{\rightarrow}_i q_i'$ and
- if $i \notin \text{loc}(\sigma)$ then $q_i = q_i'$.

We will denote by $L(\mathcal{A})$ the language recognized by the distributed automaton $\mathcal{A}$ which is just the language recognized by A, i.e., $L(\mathcal{A}) = L(A)$.

Note that given a distributed automaton $\mathcal{A} = (A_1, \ldots, A_K)$ over $\tilde{\Sigma}$ we also have

$$L(\mathcal{A}) = \{\, w \in \Sigma^* \mid \forall i \in \text{Loc} : (w|\Sigma_i) \in L(A_i) \,\},$$

where $w|\Sigma_i$ denotes the projection of the string w onto the ith alphabet Σ_i.

Note that for $K = 1$ the notion of a distributed automaton coincides with the simple notion of a finite state automaton. The kind of distributed automata that we will be using in this first part to reduce the state space will be automata over distributed alphabets where $\Sigma_1 = \cdots = \Sigma_K$, i.e., the derived behavior of the distributed automaton will simply be as the behavior of the product $A_1 \times \cdots \times A_K$. Later on—when we want to increase parallelism—we will consider general distributed alphabets where the sub-alphabets are not necessarily equal to each other.

5.1 The State Explosion Problem

In model checking, the state explosion problem occurs very often and there have been many attempts to avoid it, e.g., by means of a symbolic representation using BDDs [7, 1]. As a colloquial remark one might mention that we actually already do use BDDs because of the way the Mona system represents its data.

Here we attack the state explosion problem by using distributed automata. The crucial observation that makes it possible to easily use distributed automata in this context is that safety requirements have the form of a big conjunction, i.e., it is a collection of requirements that all have to be satisfied. Also, we can build and use the symbolic representation of the products (the distributed automaton) all the way through when generating controllers. In model checking, though, one needs at some point to actually compute the product.

Let C be a set of safety constraints, i.e., a set of conjuncts. Then, given some partition of C into $C_1, \ldots, C_K$, we can compile each of the smaller conjunctions $C_1, \ldots, C_K$ separately into automata $A_1, \ldots, A_K$. The corresponding distributed automaton $A = (A_1, \ldots, A_K)$ will then behave exactly as the automaton corresponding to the full set C of conjuncts because

$$\begin{aligned}
L(C) &= L(C_1 \wedge \cdots \wedge C_K) \\
&= L(C_1) \cap \cdots \cap L(C_K) \\
&= L(A_1) \cap \cdots \cap L(A_K) \\
&= L(A_1 \times \cdots \times A_K) \\
&= L(A).
\end{aligned}$$

We can thus use A as our safety controller instead. If the partition is chosen appropriately this will lead to a considerable reduction of the state space.

Example 3. Consider the example of having n global variables $X_1, \ldots, X_n$. In order to obey the requirement of mutual exclusion on assignment to globals this will automatically generate the following list of safety constraints.

$$\forall \textbf{time } t,t'': (t<t'' \wedge \text{take-}X_1(t) \wedge \text{take-}X_1(t''))$$
$$\implies \exists \textbf{time } t': t<t'<t'' \wedge \text{give-}X_1(t');$$

$$\vdots$$

$$\forall \textbf{time } t,t'': (t<t'' \wedge \text{take-}X_n(t) \wedge \text{take-}X_n(t''))$$
$$\implies \exists \textbf{time } t': t<t'<t'' \wedge \text{give-}X_n(t');$$

The corresponding safety controller will have $2^n + 1$ states—it will look like the nth dimensional cube plus the "error state". If we use the distributed automaton approach and partition the safety requirements according to the semicolons then the controller will have only a linear ($3n$) number of states. We will have n copies of the following three state automaton.

5.2 Inference of Independence Information

It was shown in the previous section that using distributed automata reduces the state space in frequently occurring cases. In this section we will improve on the fact that we have a central component—the safety controller—which can potentially slow down the performance of the service, e.g., if many session threads are asking for permission to continue at the same time. This can—in many cases—be avoided by exploiting independence in the safety requirements.

We shall call a transition $q \xrightarrow{\sigma} q'$ *state preserving* if $q = q'$. A label σ is said to be *dead* if all σ-transitions are state preserving, i.e., if

$$\to \cap (Q \times \{\sigma\} \times Q) \subseteq \{q \xrightarrow{\sigma} q \mid q \in Q\}.$$

A σ-transition is *dead* if σ is dead.

In a distributed automaton $\mathcal{A} = (A_1, \ldots, A_K)$ a label or transition is said to be *locally dead* in A_i if it is dead in A_i. One can now make the following observation.

Proposition 1. *Given a distributed automaton $\mathcal{A} = (A_1, \ldots, A_K)$. Let $\mathcal{A}'$ be the distributed automaton $\mathcal{A}$ where locally dead labels and transitions have been removed. If $\Sigma' = \Sigma$ then $L(\mathcal{A}') = L(\mathcal{A})$.*

That is, if we do not remove the last occurrence of a label in $\mathcal{A}$ then removing locally dead labels and transitions is a language preserving operation.

The above proposition easily extends to a simple algorithm where we iterate through the automata $A_1, \ldots, A_K$ and for each $i \in \text{Loc}$ remove all locally dead labels and transitions. Running this algorithm on a distributed automaton $\mathcal{A}$ will result in a new distributed automaton $\mathcal{A}'$ with exactly the same overall behavior, but with minimized requirements regarding synchronization between the different components.

Now—to improve performance even further—consider the undirected graph $G = (V, E)$ with nodes $V = \{A_1, \ldots, A_K\}$ and edges $E = \{(A_i, A_j) \mid \Sigma_i \cap \Sigma_j \neq \emptyset\}$. The connected components $C_1, \ldots, C_n$ of G can—since they are collections of finite automata—be considered as distributed automata.

The crucial observation is that—since they have completely disjoint alphabets— these distributed automata $C_1, \ldots, C_n$ can be run completely in parallel while still guaranteeing all safety requirements to be met. Furthermore, inside each of the distributed automata C_i we still have finite state automata that are loosely coupled and thus need very little internal synchronization as well.

A diagram of the runtime system with n global variables, $X_1, \ldots, X_n$, where we have both reduced the state space and exploited independence information can be found in Fig. 4.

As can be seen, we handle the case of critical regions just as efficiently as if we had implemented it using a semaphore, both with respect to space requirements and with respect to the degree of parallelism. Thus we do not lose anything by formulating simple safety requirements in this way. What we gain, however, is a uniform framework in which we can formulate all safety requirements.

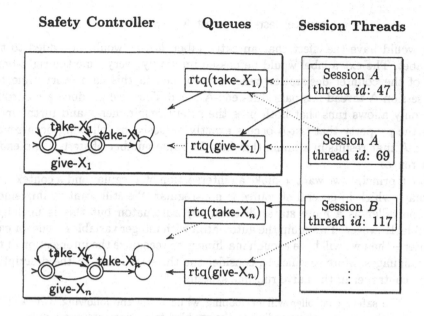

Fig. 4. Runtime system with independent distributed automata.

Inference of independence information via search for locally dead labels and transitions will thus in general lead to a substantial increase of parallelism in the controller. This increase of parallelism will improve on the overall performance of the runtime system, i.e., on the flow capacities of the provided service.

6 Beyond Regularity

In general one can have any number of session A threads. This can of course be constrained to any fixed maximal number by use of safety requirements, e.g., the controller

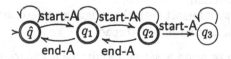

will guarantee that at any time there will be at most two session A threads.

But very often one has requirements like: I only want to enter this part of the code, e.g., pass label foo, if there are no session C threads—without putting a bound on the maximal number of session C threads. This cannot be expressed in M2L-Str. The positions at which there are no session C threads are those where the number of start-C and end-C labels occurring before that position are the same but the standard example of a *non*-regular language is $\{ a^n b^n \mid n \geq 0 \}$ thus the property is not regular and therefore cannot be expressed in M2L-Str.

In order to accommodate the need for these kind of requirements we will introduce the notion of a *counter*. We could declare the counter last-A as follows.

counter last-A : #start-A — #end-A;

This would have the effect that an extra label, last-A, would be added to the alphabet. The extra label would be passed implicitly every time the right-hand side of the counter declaration reaches zero, i.e., in this case every time the last session A thread has passed its end-A label. Thus, we produce a controller that only allows runs that both pass the safety requirements and furthermore have the property that last-A occurs exactly at positions following occurrences of end-A that results in a prefix that has the same number of start-A and end-A occurrences.

So in principle we want to make an intersection of a regular and a context free language which in general of course is non-regular. We still want to implement the controller as a finite state (distributed) automaton but this is no longer possible. However, if we equip the automaton with integer variables—one for each counter—then we will have enough machinery to recognize the intersection of the two languages. More specifically, consider the three step loop in the description of the controller in the naïve runtime system:

> The safety controller will be looping while doing the following. Check if any of the queues corresponding to the enabled transitions are non-empty. In case it finds a non-empty queue, say rtq(σ), it
> 1. removes a session thread id from rtq(σ),
> 2. changes its state corresponding to making the enabled σ-transition, and
> 3. wakes up the session thread corresponding to the removed id.

Apart from the fact that there are now several of these controllers each having a subset of labels to take care of, we must add the following conditional as a fourth step.

> If σ occurs on the right-hand side of a counter declaration, cnt_i, then increment or decrement the variable associated with that counter. If it reaches zero then change the state corresponding to taking the cnt_i-transition.

By using the counter last-A we thus

- add the label last-A and
- in the controller we intersect with the language where last-A occurs after the termination of the last session A thread.

Therefore, one can now write a safety requirement ensuring that there are no active A sessions. E.g., the predicate

$$\text{zero-A}(t'') \equiv \exists \textbf{time } t\!: t \leq t'' \wedge (t=0 \vee \text{last-A}(t)) \wedge$$
$$\forall \textbf{time } t'\!: t \leq t' \leq t'' \implies \neg\text{start-A}(t')$$

will only evaluate to true at positions where there are no active A sessions.

Example 4. We can now formulate the (non-regular) requirement from the beginning of this section, "I only want to pass label foo if there are no active C sessions", as a safety requirement:

$$\forall \textbf{time } t\!: \text{foo}(t) \implies \text{zero-C}(t).$$

7 WSL

The Wig service logic (WSL) is a high-level notation built on top of M2L-Str suitable for writing safety requirements for Wig service code implementing an interactive web service. It inherits from M2L-Str the usual universal and existential quantifications over both first order variables (ranging over instances of discrete time) and monadic second order variables (ranging over sets of instances of time). Also, it has standard boolean connectives like negation, conjunction, disjunction, implication, etc., as well as operations on first order terms, e.g., given an instance of time t one can point out its successor (t+1), operations on second order terms, e.g., taking the union of two sets, plus of course the basic formula that tests membership of a position in a position set. Furthermore WSL provides basic formulae to test whether a label LL is passed at time t: LL(t).

Example 5. Consider some Wig code with a critical region that needs exclusive access to, say, a global resource. The way one makes the region critical is by first adding labels around it.

```
... code ...
label begin-crt-region;
... critical region ...
label end-crt-region;
... more code ...
```

Then, in order to make the code between these labels act as a critical region the following safety constraint is added to the set of requirements.

$$\forall \text{time } beg_1, beg_2:$$
$$((beg_1 < beg_2) \land \text{begin-crt-region}(beg_1) \land \text{begin-crt-region}(beg_2))$$
$$\implies \exists \text{time } end_1: (beg_1 < end_1 < beg_2) \land \text{end-crt-region}(end_1).$$

Example 6. Another thing that WSL is suitable for is formulating requirements regarding priority. We are given some service S with sessions Reading and Writing (See Fig. 5). Reading threads read data from a Database, display the data in a proper way, read some more data, display it, and so forth. Writing threads can only be started by the service administrator. Furthermore, at most one Writing session thread is allowed at a time. This last condition can easily be satisfied, e.g., by the constraint

$$\forall \text{time } t: \text{start-Writing}(t) \implies (t=0 \lor \text{zero-Writing}(t-1)),$$

where zero-Writing and later zero-Reading are defined as the zero-A predicate from the previous section.

Of course Writing must not be started unless there are no active Reading threads and vice versa. This can also be formulated in a straightforward way using, e.g., the constraint

$$\forall \text{time } t: \text{zero-Writing}(t) \lor \text{zero-Reading}(t).$$

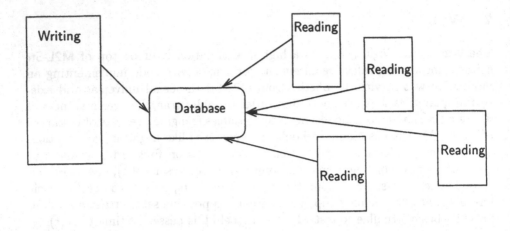

Fig. 5. A Writing thread and several Reading threads accessing a Database.

But what if it is of great importance that the administrator gets access to the database as soon as possible? E.g., if the database contains prices of products that a company sells and corrections have to be made to these prices. Thus, we want to give Writing priority over Reading. This can be managed in the following way (excluding the last WSL-formula above). We assume that the critical regions of Writing, i.e., those that access the database, are surrounded by labels start-Crt and end-Crt.

- Then, in order to make sure that as soon as the Writing thread has started, no more Reading threads will start, we add the constraint

$$\forall \textbf{time } t: \text{start-Reading}(t) \implies \text{zero-Writing}(t).$$

- Of course, we should still make sure that we have mutual exclusion. This is done by adding the constraint

$$\forall \textbf{time } t: \text{start-Crt}(t) \implies \text{zero-Reading}(t).$$

Thus, we make sure that we do not enter any critical region in Writing unless the last Reading thread has ended its execution.

Using the above approach we satisfy the crucial property of mutual exclusion. Furthermore, we impose restrictions that will make sure the administrator gets priority over ordinary users. The corresponding automaton, however, is rather complex, see Fig. 6. Thus, producing it by hand is cumbersome and error prone.

Furthermore, our approach is modular in the sense that requirements can be added and deleted at will without changing the existing requirements. In the automata world small changes can result in extensive changes of the automaton. Solutions using semaphores lack in a similar fashion the property of being modular.

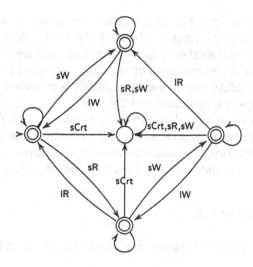

Fig. 6. Automaton corresponding to the Writing/Reading setup.

8 Related Work

Mawl has already been mentioned as an example of a domain-specific language for describing sequential transaction-oriented Web applications. The techniques available for doing synchronization when dealing with concurrency in Mawl is limited to working with critical regions, though. Our work on service logic extends this to working with arbitrary safety constraints.

In general, there are increasingly many systems for doing web-programming, e.g., [6, 5, 3], but so far none of seem of them seem to support proper handling of safety requirements.

The area of control theory is of course huge. We are only dealing with control of discrete systems, though. Ramadge and Wonham give in [9] a good survey on "The Control of Discrete Event Systems". Many of the notions presented here are similar to those of [9].

Distributed automata are simply a special case of the product automata of [10]. They again are a special case of the non-cellular asynchronous automata of [11].

9 Future Work

Writing Wig services results in generation of highly concurrent code which needs lots of synchronization. The implementation of the ideas presented here is in preparation and once we can do experiments writing and using safety constraints, evaluation of the usefulness of our technique can be taken further. The important question is of course: how much do these ideas improve on the quality of the services?

When dealing with inference of independence information, the important part is that of choosing the right partition of the safety requirement. We plan to do static analyses on the safety requirements and combine the achieved information with appropriate heuristics to obtain hopefully good results. Intuitively, the formulae of the safety requirements implicitly say something about which requirements are closely related and which are not.

The idea of having a central controller is proving useful for other aspects of web services. We plan to include support for various kinds of event handling and database locking. Also, the controller may drive an automatically generated service monitor, allow maintenance and performance statistics.

10 Acknowledgments

The authors thank Claus Rasmussen Brabrand and the anonymous referees for useful comments.

References

1. R. E. Bryant. Graph-based algorithms for boolean function manipulation. *IEEE Transactions on Computers*, C-35(8):677–691, August 1986.
2. K. Cox, T. Ball, and J. C. Ramming. Lunchbot: A tale of two ways to program web services. Available from
   http://www.cs.utexas.edu/users/cpg/mawl/doc/lunchbot.ps.gz, April 1996.
3. Brian J. Fox. Meta-html: A dynamic programming language for www applications.
   http://www.metahtml.com/documentation/manifesto.html.
4. J.G. Henriksen, J. Jensen, M. Jørgensen, N. Klarlund, B. Paige, T. Rauhe, and A. Sandholm. Mona: Monadic second-order logic in practice. In *Tools and Algorithms for the Construction and Analysis of Systems, First International Workshop, TACAS '95, LNCS 1019*, 1996.
5. The document *is* the application. Web Site. http://www.htmlscript.com/.
6. D. A. Ladd and J. C. Ramming. Programming the web: An application-oriented language for hypermedia services. In *4th Intl. World Wide Web Conference*, 1995.
7. K. L. McMillan. *Symbolic Model Checking*. Kluver Academic Publishers, 1993.
8. M. O. Rabin. Decidability of second-order theories and automata on infinite trees. *Trans. Amer. Math. Soc.*, 141:1–35, 1969.
9. Peter J. G. Ramadge and W. Murray Wonham. The control of discrete event systems. *Proceedings of the IEEE*, 77(1):81–98, January 1989.
10. P. S. Thiagarajan. PTL over product state spaces. Technical Report TCS-95-4, School of Mathematics, SPIC Science Foundation, 1995.
11. W. Zielonka. *The Book of Traces*, chapter Asynchronous Automata, pages 205–248. World Scientific Publishing, 1995.

A Refinement Calculus for Statecharts *

Peter Scholz

scholzp@forsoft.de

Technische Universität München, Institut für Informatik
D-80290 München, Germany

Abstract. We present a Statecharts dialect with only three syntactic constructs and a semantics that is not restricted to describe reactive systems on an implementation level but allows to model them on an abstract, more specification oriented stage, where design alternatives are still left open. We give a refinement calculus with rules that tell the designer how to come from the abstract specification to the implementation such that the system under development only becomes more concrete but not more abstract; under-specification is eliminated by adding more information. The result of a design process that follows these rules is an implementation that satisfies its specification by construction.

1 Introduction

Statecharts [5] are used in industry to develop reactive systems. A typical application area is rapid prototyping of embedded systems as they occur in avionics and automobile industry. Among other things, their success comes from two facts. First, it is an easy to learn language for design specialists who have more often a degree in electrical or electronic engineering than a solid background in computer science. Those engineers have a considerably better intuition of the meaning of automata than of algebraic specification techniques, for instance. Second, Statecharts are available as description technique in commercial products, like Statemate. Therefore, such specifications are really sturdy for engineers.

In the past years, much scientific work has been invested to improve the Statecharts language. However, up to now most approaches focus more on the implementation aspects of Statecharts than on specification techniques. Several formal semantics for Statecharts and related dialects have been proposed (see [13] for a good but no longer complete overview). Among them some approaches like Argos [7, 8] can be found that are closely related to the reactive programming language Esterel [2, 3].

Our μ-Charts exclude a number of syntactical concepts of Statecharts (as presented in [5]) that lead to semantical problems, such as inter-level transitions,

---

* This work is partially sponsored by the Bavarian Research Foundation (Bayerische Forschungsstifung) as part of the compound project "ForSoft".

priority of transitions w.r.t. state hierarchy, multiple source and target of transitions and so on. When designing our dialect μ-Charts we were inspired by Argos but also tried to modify some basic concepts as discussed in [9]. Our μ-Charts formalism is considered to be a specification mechanism rather than a programming language like Argos, Esterel, Lustre, or Signal. In these synchronous programming languages *unintended* non-determinism that is obtained by composition is avoided by static analysis.

Besides this unintended non-determinism that stems from composition there is also *intended* non-determinism to express underspecification of components. Intended non-determinism is volitional by the user and reflects that design decisions for a component are still left open at the current level of development.

In [9] we have defined the semantics of μ-Charts in terms of sets of I/O-behaviors or, in other words, I/O-histories. The μ-Charts semantics presented here differs in some points with the semantics published in [9]. These modifications have been necessary for a smooth integration of refinement.

In this contribution, we further improve our language concepts. We illustrate that three principal syntactical concepts, sequential automata, hiding, and a composition operator including multicasting, are enough to express more complex Statecharts' constructs; hierarchy and pure parallel composition can be defined as syntactic sugar. This strategy has two main advantages: First, we reduce ourselves to the most essential language concepts and so can motivate that Statecharts are not that complicated as assumed in the hitherto existing literature. Second, we get an easy semantics for the proofs of the refinement rules' soundness.

Moreover, we show how to use this specification formalism in the development process. We demonstrate what it means to incrementally develop a system step by step. We present a refinement calculus with rules that are easy to understand but at the same time describe formal design steps towards the final system. Though this paper is rather theoretically written to motivate that all concepts are sound, also more practical oriented readers should gain from reading this article: For those readers it should be enough to understand which syntactical side conditions have to be fulfilled to make a certain refinement step.

Our goal is to underline that Statecharts are more than a simple twodimensional programming language. What is needed is a design methodology, supported by a set of refinement rules that tell the user how to come from an abstract system description to a more concrete one. In principle, the essential rules we present (for hierarchical decomposition and parallel composition, for instance) are thought to be applicable not only for μ-Charts but also for any other version of Statecharts.

This paper is organized as follows: Section 2 contains the running example, which is used to underline our refinement technique. In Section 3.1 and 3.2 we explain syntax and semantics of the μ-Charts language. The refinement rules are discussed in Section 4. We finally conclude this paper with Section 5.

2 Running Example

As running example we take a simplified specification of a realistic central locking system for two-door cars as already used in [10]. We are aware that this example is much smaller than industrially relevant examples. However, it should be large enough to illustrate all essential points of this contribution. Due to space limitations we are not able to print a larger example.

The system architecture is pictured in Figure 1 and the corresponding μ-Chart in Figure 2. Our graphical syntax for μ-Charts follows the convention that ellipses denote basic states of sequential automata while boxes denote states that are decomposed by other μ-Charts. Later on, we will show that decomposition is in fact only syntactic sugar. Double frames denote default states. Notice that, as we deal with underspecification, more than one default state is possible as demonstrated in the example.

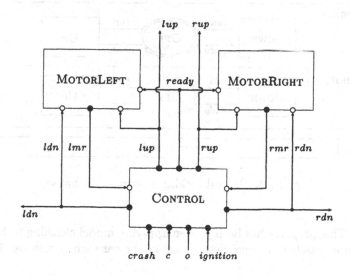

Figure 1. Central locking system — Architecture

Our central locking system consists essentially of three main parts (see Figure 1): the CONTROL and the two door motors. These parts react independently. The default configuration of the system is that all doors are unlocked (UNLD) or locked (LOCKED) and both motors are OFF. Depending on the system's configuration, the driver can (un-)lock the car either from outside by turning the key or from inside by pressing a button. Both actions generate the external signal (*o*) *c*. The CONTROL generates the internal signals *ldn* and *rdn* and enters its locking state LOCKG, which is decomposed by the automaton in Figure 6.

Whenever the crash signal occurs, the CONTROL changes from the NORMAL mode in the CRASH mode and generates the signals *lup* and *rup* and the doors

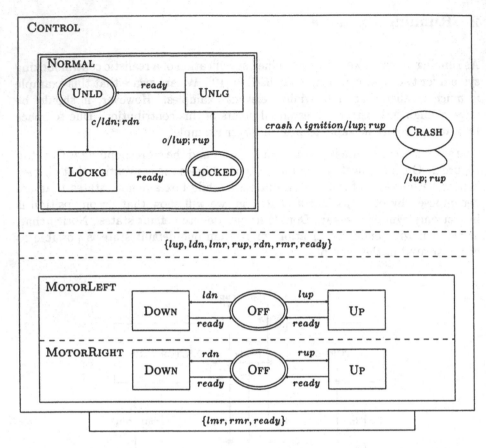

Figure 2. Central locking system — Behavior

will open. This property has been proven applying model checking techniques in [10]. A more detailed informal description of the case study also can be looked up there.

3 The μ-Charts Language

3.1 Syntax

In this section we briefly introduce the essential concepts of our Statecharts dialect. We assume the reader to be familiar with the basic ideas of Statecharts and refer to [5, 6] for a more detailed introduction.

In this paper, all elements in the set $\mathcal{S}$ of μ-Charts can be built from only three syntactical constructs: non-deterministic sequential automata, hiding, and parallel composition including communication between parallel composed charts.

Sequential Automata. In the definition of sequential automata, we use the following syntactical, pairwise disjoint sets: *Ident* is a set of identifiers, *Signals* a set of signal names, *States* a set of state names, and V a set of variable names. The construct $(N, I, O, \Sigma, \Sigma_0, V_l, \varphi_0, \delta)$, in the sequel abbreviated to A, is an element of $\mathcal{S}$ iff the following constraints hold:

1. $N \in Ident$ is the unique identifier of the automaton.
2. $I \subseteq Signals$ is the input interface.
3. $O \subseteq Signals$ is the output interface. We assume I and O to be disjoint.
4. $\Sigma \in \wp(States)$ is a nonempty finite set of all control states of the automaton.
5. $\Sigma_0 \subseteq \Sigma$ represents the set of initial states.
6. V_l is the set of local (integer) variables of the automaton.
7. For each initial state $\sigma_0 \in \Sigma_0$ the function $\varphi_0(\sigma_0) \in V_l \to \mathbb{Z}$ initializes the local variables. We abbreviate $V_l \to \mathbb{Z}$ to $\mathcal{E}(A)$.
8. $\delta : \Sigma \to \wp(Bexp(I + V_l) \times Com \times \Sigma)$ is the finite state transition relation that takes a state and yields a set of triples, where each triple consists of a Boolean expression over I and V_l as transition predicate (guard, precondition, trigger) paired with a command $com \in Com$ and the successor (control-)state.

In this context, arithmetic expressions $a \in Aexp$, Boolean expressions $b \in Bexp$, and commands $c \in Com$ have the form:

$$a ::= n \,|\, Y \,|\, a_1 + a_2 \,|\, a_1 - a_2 \,|\, a_1 * a_2$$
$$b ::= \text{true} \,|\, \text{false} \,|\, a_1 = a_2 \,|\, a_1 \leq a_2 \,|\, s_i \,|\, \neg b \,|\, b_1 \wedge b_2$$
$$c ::= \text{skip} \,|\, Y := a \,|\, s_o \,|\, c_1 ; c_2$$

In the syntax of transitions we have followed the convention that $n \in Int$, $Y \in V_l$, $s_i \in I$, and $s_o \in O$. Note that to permit not only integer variables in Int but arbitrary types is a straightforward extension but is not relevant in the context of this paper and therefore was omitted. The meaning of these expressions and commands is straightforward. In contrast to [6], we use the semi-colon as sequential and not as parallel composition and so avoid racing conditions.

Composition. Suppose that $S_1, S_2 \in \mathcal{S}$ are arbitrary μ-Charts and L is the set of signals that can be possibly transmitted, then the composition $S_1 \lhd L \rhd S_2$ is also in $\mathcal{S}$. Defining the semantics of this operator, we will see that instantaneous communication [2, 3, 7] is achieved by signal feedback (see also Figure 3). Graphically, this construction is denoted as signal set between the dashed lines that separate S_1 and S_2. Though one is totally free in the choice of L, it should be a subset of $(In(S_1) \cap Out(S_2)) \cup (In(S_2) \cap Out(S_1))$ to get meaningful specifications. Here, $In(S_i)$ and $Out(S_i)$ denote the input and output interfaces of S_i, respectively.

Elements in $In(S)$ and $Out(S)$ are called *input* and *output* signals, respectively. If we do not care about the flow direction, we only say *signal*. Each element x

in $\mathcal{I}(S) =_{df} \wp(In(S))$, and $\mathcal{O}(S) =_{df} \wp(Out(S))$ is called an *input* and *output event*, respectively. If we abstract from input or output, we simply speak of *events*. For each signal s an we say s is *present* in event x iff $s \in x$. Otherwise, we say that it is *absent* in x.

Hiding. Output signals that are sent using the ternary operator $. \lhd . \rhd .$ are still visible by the environment of the chart S. If the signal set K shall be hidden for the part of the specification not belonging to S, we use the hiding operator $[S]_K$. The construct $[S_1 \lhd L \rhd S_2]_L$, for instance, hides *all* output signals that are fed back. Likewise for communication, there is also a graphical counterpart for hiding; it is a box, attached to the bottom of S, which contains the signals K that are hidden.

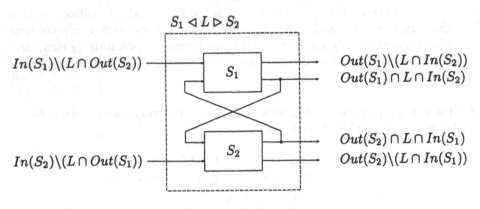

Figure 3. Composition

Hierarchy. To express hierarchical composition, which plays a key role in the concept of Statecharts, we do not need an explicit syntactical construct but derive hierarchy from the above composition operator. This facilitates the definition of both formal semantics and refinement calculus. How this can be achieved will be demonstrated in the sequel.

A hierarchical decomposition A decby (Σ_d, ϱ), where $A = (N, I, O, \Sigma, \Sigma_0, V_l, \varphi_0, \delta)$ can be expressed by composition. Here, the total function $\varrho : \Sigma_d \to S$ defines for each state in $\Sigma_d \subseteq \Sigma$ the sub-chart by which it is decomposed. Thus, hierarchy can be considered as abbreviation mechanism. We can translate hierarchical specifications in flat ones applying the following algorithm (hereby we call A the *master* and $\varrho(\sigma)$ with $\sigma \in \Sigma_d$ the *slave*). The algorithm works differently for weak and strong preemption [1]:

1. Master A and all slaves are composed in parallel.

2. Modification of the master: The fresh signals $go(\sigma)$ for all decomposed states $\sigma \in \Sigma_d$ are added to the output interface of A. In case of weak preemption, for every $\sigma \in \Sigma_d$ the command com of every outgoing edge is replaced by $com; go(\sigma)$. Here, $go(\sigma)$ is a signal which indicates that the slave attached to σ is currently active and is allowed to fire its transitions. This modification is omitted for other edges than self loops when strong preemption is desired. Let t_σ be the disjunction of all trigger conditions on all outgoing edges (inclusive self loops, if they exist) of σ. Then, for every kind of preemption, additionally every state σ is enriched by a self loop with trigger condition $\neg t_\sigma$ and command $go(\sigma)$.

3. Modification of the slave(s): For every $\sigma \in \Sigma_d$ and every sequential automaton in $\varrho(\sigma)$ to every input interface the signal $go(\sigma)$ has to be added. Furthermore, every trigger condition t on every edge has to be substituted by $t \wedge go(\sigma)$ in order to guarantee that the now parallel composed slave only reacts iff it is allowed to. If σ is a non-history [5] decomposed state, additional transitions from every state but the default state of every sequential automaton in $\varrho(\sigma)$ with label $\neg go(\sigma)/\varphi(\sigma)$ have to be introduced. This is necessary to initialize the slave whenever the master is left. Otherwise, all slaves would stay in their current states when the master changes its current step; this, however, is only wanted for history decomposed states [5].

4. In order to enable the communication between master and slave, all above introduced go signals have to be fed back and hidden with respect to the parallel composition of the master and all slaves. Feedback applies to all signals in $In(A) \cap Out(\varrho(\sigma))$, too, to enable communication from slave to master.

Figure 4 shows an example. It is the CONTROL part of the locking system. As once having entered the CRASH mode, the system resides in this state forever. Thus, it makes no difference whether NORMAL is history or non-history decomposed. Figure 4 shows weak preemption; if we omitted the statement $go(\text{NORMAL})$ on the transition between NORMAL and CRASH, we would model strong preemption. In case of nested hierarchy, this algorithm has to be recursively applied.

3.2 Semantics

Steps and System Reactions. Like other Statecharts dialects, μ-Charts are a synchronous language based on a discrete, clock-synchronous time model. It follows the principles of the perfect synchrony hypothesis [3] and uses, similar to [8], instantaneous feedback as semantical model for communication. A *system reaction* of a μ-Charts consists of a sequence of *steps (instants)*. At each step, the system receives a set of signals from the environment. Upon reception of this input set, the system produces a set of output signals, modifies local variables, and changes its control state. The output signals are assumed to be generated in the same instant as the input signals are received. A signal is said to be *present*

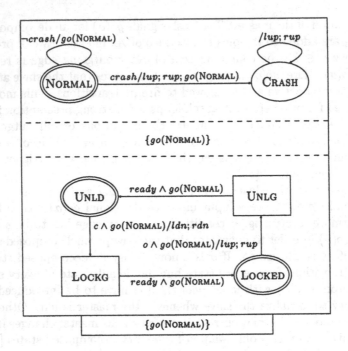

Figure 4. Unpacked hierarchy

in a given instant, if it is either input from the environment or generated by the system. Otherwise, it is said to be *absent*.

Reactive Behavior. Reactive systems have to interact continuously with the environment. Hence, their complete input/output behavior can be described using communication histories. We model the communication history of μ-Charts by streams carrying sets of signals. Mathematically, we describe the behavior of μ-Charts by relations over streams. Thus, we briefly discuss the notion of streams. For a detailed description we refer, for example, to [4].

Given a set X of signals, a stream over X, denoted by X^∞, is an infinite sequence of elements from X. Our notation for the concatenation operator is &. Given an element x of type X and a stream s over X, the term $x\&s$ denotes the stream that starts with the element x followed by the stream s.

For a chart $S \in \mathcal{S}$ we denote the non-deterministic I/O-behavior as relation $[\![S]\!]_{io} \in \wp(\mathcal{I}(S)^\infty \times \mathcal{O}(S)^\infty)$. This pure I/O-semantics is defined by using the auxiliary relation $[\![S]\!] \in \wp(\mathcal{C}(S) \times \mathcal{I}(S)^\infty \times \mathcal{O}(S)^\infty)$:

$$[\![S]\!]_{io} =_{df} \{(i,o) \mid \exists c.c \in Init(S) \wedge (c,i,o) \in [\![S]\!]\}$$

where $Init((N,I,O,\Sigma,\Sigma_0,V_l,\varphi_0,\delta)) =_{df} \{(\sigma_0,\varphi(\sigma_0)) \mid \sigma_0 \in \Sigma_0\}$ and $Init(S_1 \vartriangleleft L \vartriangleright S_2) =_{df} Init(S_1) \times Init(S_2)$ denote the initial configurations. A *configuration* of chart S is an element in $C(S)$, which is inductively defined by:

$$C((N, I, O, \Sigma, \Sigma_0, V_l, \varphi_0, \delta)) =_{df} \Sigma \times (V_l \to \mathbb{Z})$$
$$C(S_1 \lhd L \rhd S_2) =_{df} C(S_1) \times C(S_2)$$

Instead of the explicit tuple we often simply write c to denote an arbitrary configuration. The auxiliary semantics of a sequential automaton A is now defined as the greatest solution of the following recursive equation (∗):

$$[\![A]\!] = \{(c, x\&i, y\&o) \mid \exists c'.((c', y) \in [\![\delta]\!](c, x) \wedge (c', i, o) \in [\![A]\!]) \vee [\![\delta]\!](c, x) = \emptyset\}$$

Informally, $[\![A]\!]$ is the set of all those tuples $(c, x\&i, y\&o)$ such that one of the following two cases is true. Either A generates the output event y and changes its current configuration from c to c' while reacting on input event x and then behaves similarly in the new configuration c' 'eating' the rest of the input event stream or the reaction is (yet) underspecified: In this case, the predicate $[\![\delta]\!](c, x) = \emptyset$ is a characterization for the chaotic behavior of A, as the choice of i, y, and o is not restricted at all. Here, $[\![\delta]\!]$ is defined from the transition relation δ as follows[1]: For all $c = (\sigma, \varepsilon) \in C(A)$ and $x \in \mathcal{I}(A)$:

$$[\![\delta]\!]((\sigma, \varepsilon), x) =_{df} \{((\sigma', \varepsilon'), y) \in \Sigma \times \mathcal{E}(A) \times \mathcal{O}(A) \mid$$
$$\exists t, com.(t, com, \sigma') \in \delta(\sigma) \wedge (\varepsilon, x) \models t \wedge (\varepsilon', y) = \mathcal{R}[\![com]\!]\varepsilon\}$$

$[\![\delta]\!]((\sigma, \varepsilon), x)$ tells us how A reacts upon receiving the input event x in configuration (σ, ε). This reaction yields, due to non-determinism, all possible subsequent configurations (σ', ε') together with the output event y. Here, $(\varepsilon, x) \models t$ is true iff the trigger t can be evaluated to true with respect to the valuation ε and the current event x; $(Y \mapsto 8, \{a, b\}) \models (5 \leq Y) \wedge a$, for example. To join all such pairs in one set, we define:

$$[\![t]\!]_A =_{df} \{(\varepsilon, x) \in \mathcal{E}(A) \times \mathcal{I}(A) \mid (\varepsilon, x) \models t\}$$

The tuple $\mathcal{R}[\![com]\!]\varepsilon$ consists of the next valuation ε' and the output event y that are obtained when the command com is carried out with respect to the current valuation ε. By the predicate $[\![\delta]\!](c, x) = \emptyset$ also chaotic behavior is included in the semantic set $[\![A]\!]$. 'Chaotic' here means that whenever for the automaton A in the current configuration c a transition relation for the current input event x is not defined, it can produce an arbitrary output sequence $y\&o$ and can change to an arbitrary successor configuration c'. Later on, in the design process this underspecification can be reduced; mathematically, this means to transform chaotic behavior in well-defined behavior. To find the greatest solution for the equation (∗) is equivalent to find the greatest solution for $F(X_0) = X_0$, i.e. the greatest fixpoint $\mathrm{gfp}(F)$ of F, where F is defined by the lambda term

$$F =_{df} \lambda X.\{(c, x\&i, y\&o) \mid \exists c'.((c', y) \in [\![\delta]\!](c, x) \wedge (c', i, o) \in X) \vee [\![\delta]\!](c, x) = \emptyset\}$$

---

[1] Note that the brackets $[\![.]\!]$ are overloaded.

Notice that $\emptyset$ is always the least fixpoint, if $[\![\delta]\!](c, x) \neq \emptyset$. Least fixpoints yield finite objects, whereas greatest fixpoints are related to infinite solutions. As we deal with infinite I/O histories, we therefore look for the greatest fixpoint $\mathrm{gfp}(F)$ which is characterized by

$$\bigcup \{X \in \wp(\mathcal{C}(A) \times \mathcal{I}(A)^\infty \times \mathcal{O}(A)^\infty) \mid X \subseteq F(X)\}$$

The monotonicity of F is a sufficient condition for the existence of this fixed point.

Proposition 1 *F is a monotonic function with respect to the subset ordering on power sets.*

As F is a monotonic function on a complete lattice (the power domain), a greatest fixpoint always exists (propositions of Knaster/Tarski and Tarski). The semantics of the composition with instantaneous feedback is defined as follows (see also Figure 3 to get a better intuition):

$$\begin{aligned}
[\![S_1 \lhd L \rhd S_2]\!] =_{df} \{&((c_1, c_2), i, o) \mid \exists o_1, o_2. o_1 \in \mathcal{O}(S_1)^\infty \wedge o_2 \in \mathcal{O}(S_2)^\infty \wedge \\
&o = o_1 \cup o_2 \wedge \\
&(c_1, i|_{In(S_1) \backslash (L \cap Out(S_2))} \cup o_2|_{Out(S_2) \cap L \cap In(S_1)}, o_1) \in [\![S_1]\!] \wedge \\
&(c_2, i|_{In(S_2) \backslash (L \cap Out(S_1))} \cup o_1|_{Out(S_1) \cap L \cap In(S_2)}, o_2) \in [\![S_2]\!]\}
\end{aligned}$$

where $\cup$ here is the pointwise extension of the set-theoretic union on streams of sets and $s|_X$ the pointwise restriction of stream elements (= events) in s to signals in X. Our notion of instantaneous feedback (= feedback in the same instant) was inspired by Argos [8]. It resembles the technique for solving equations in Argos but adds non-determinism and chaotic behavior.

The pure parallel composition $S_1 \| S_2$ of two components S_1 and S_2 is defined as special case: $S_1 \| S_2$ is regarded to be a syntactical abbreviation for $S_1 \lhd \emptyset \rhd S_2$. Just as simple is the definition of signal hiding:

$$[\![[S]_K]\!] =_{df} \{(c, i, o|_{Out(S) \backslash K}) \mid (c, i, o) \in [\![S]\!]\}$$

Having defined the formal semantics for μ-Charts we can discuss some interesting semantical properties of our language:

- Composition is commutative.
- In general, the composition operator does *not* have any associativity-like properties; especially, the following is in general not true:

$$[\![S_1 \lhd L \rhd (S_2 \lhd L \rhd S_3)]\!]_{io} = [\![(S_1 \lhd L \rhd S_2) \lhd L \rhd S_3]\!]_{io}$$

- Other algebraic properties which one would appreciate to be fulfilled but indeed are *false* are, due to non-determinism, redundancy, and distributivity; instead we have:

- $[S\|S]_{io} \neq [S]_{io}$
- $[(S_1\|S_2) \vartriangleleft L \vartriangleright S_3]_{io} \neq [(S_1 \vartriangleleft L \vartriangleright S_3)\|(S_2 \vartriangleleft L \vartriangleright S_3)]_{io}$
- $[(S_1 \vartriangleleft L \vartriangleright S_2)\|S_3]_{io} \neq [(S_1\|S_3) \vartriangleleft L \vartriangleright (S_2\|S_3)]_{io}$

- In contrast, redundant specifications in general increase the non-deterministic behavior of the system: $[S] \subseteq [S\|S]$. The opposite direction $[S\|S] \subseteq [S]$ generally does not hold for non-deterministic specifications; $[S]_{io} = [S\|S]_{io}$ is true only if S is deterministic.
- Furthermore, if the interfaces of two combined specifications do not fit together, they behave as purely parallel composed: For $In(S_1) \cap L \cap Out(S_2) = In(S_2) \cap L \cap Out(S_1) = \emptyset$ the following holds: $[S_1 \vartriangleleft L \vartriangleright S_2] = [S_1\|S_2]$.

4 Specification Refinement

In the previous section we have introduced our automata-oriented specification language. We have defined its semantics, i.e. its input/output-behavior in terms of streams. However, a pure specification formalism is worthless without any system development process. What we need is to know how to develop a concrete implementation or realization from an abstract system specification, that is, how to generate hardware or software from it.

It is usually impossible to carry out this transformation in only one step. In practice, the situation is even worse. For complex systems, even a design specialist may not be capable to write down an abstract specification ad hoc. Rather such a system will be developed by applying subsequent concretization steps, whereby after every single step the overall system behavior is a bit more concrete. Each of these steps is called a *refinement* step. The final implementation then is only the most precise specification that is suitable to run on a certain machine. First ideas on a state-based refinement calculus have been developed in [11, 12].

A specification S_2 is a refinement of another specification S_1 ($S_1 \rightsquigarrow S_2$) iff $In(S_1) \subseteq In(S_2)$, $Out(S_1) \subseteq Out(S_2)$ and the following is true:

$$\{(i|_{In(S_1)}, o|_{Out(S_1)}) \mid (i, o) \in [S_2]_{io}\} \subseteq [S_1]_{io}$$

Notice that there is a good reason to restrict both input and output to $In(S_1)$ and $Out(S_1)$, respectively. Otherwise, one of the most intuitive refinement rules, hierarchical decomposition, would by no means be sound.

We expect our refinement calculus to be stepwise applicable. Therefore, we want to guarantee that also a sequence of refinement steps are a refinement of the original specification again. As $\rightsquigarrow$ is transitive, we can guarantee this in our case.

Besides transitivity, compositionality is a further important property for our semantical framework. It secures that whenever a small part of a large specification is refined, also the entire model is refined:

Proposition 2 *If $S_1 \rightsquigarrow S_2$ then also $S_1 \lhd L \rhd S_3 \rightsquigarrow S_2 \lhd L \rhd S_3$ for arbitrary S_3 and L with $L \subseteq Out(S_1) \cup Out(S_3)$ and $[S_1]_{L'} \rightsquigarrow [S_2]_{L'}$ for arbitrary L'.*

Notice that in the above proposition it is essential that $L \subseteq Out(S_1) \cup Out(S_3)$ and not $L \subseteq Out(S_2) \cup Out(S_3)$. Otherwise, as $Out(S_1) \subseteq Out(S_2)$, S_2 could possibly perform additional behavior due to extra communication that is not possible with S_1.

4.1 The Calculus

In this section, we give a set of purely syntactical rules whose application guarantees the software engineering specialist correct refinement steps. She or he does not need to be aware of the formal semantics but just has to apply the intuitive syntactical rules in a correct way. Hence, the stepwise refinement within a calculus for μ-Charts is not only a mathematically appealing idea but also a realistic procedure to be applied in an industrial environment.

Rules for Sequential Automata. In principle, to show that a sequential automaton A_2 is a refinement of another sequential automaton A_1, where $A_k =_{df} (N_k, I_k, O_k, \Sigma_k, \Sigma_{0k}, V_{lk}, \varphi_{0k}, \delta_k)$ we have to show that $gfp(F_{A_2}) \subseteq gfp(F_{A_1})$. This proof obligation can, whenever both A_1 and A_2 have the same interface and the same configurations, be relaxed to (†):

$$\forall X \subseteq \mathcal{C}(A_1) \times \mathcal{I}(A_1)^\infty \times \mathcal{O}(A_1)^\infty : X \subseteq F_{A_2}(X) \Rightarrow F_{A_2}(X) \subseteq F_{A_1}(X)$$

With this preliminaries we now can present the refinement calculus for automata:

Remove Initial States. The reduction of the initial states Σ_0 to $\Sigma_0' \subseteq \Sigma_0$ is a correct refinement step. In our example, we can reduce the initial states from $\{\text{UNLD}, \text{LOCKED}\}$ to $\{\text{UNLD}\}$.

Add Additional States. The set of states Σ of a sequential automaton can be enlarged by Σ' and the semantics keeps exactly the same as long as the initial states are not modified and the fresh states are not "connected" to the rest of the automaton with already existing transitions. In subsequent refinement steps, however, theses states can be connected with fresh transitions according to the following transition rules. Notice that this rule merely allows to add new states on the same hierarchical level. Whenever new states on an hierarchical different level shall be added, the rule for hierarchy (see below) has to be applied.

In the sequel, let A_i be the automaton $(N, I, O, \Sigma, \Sigma_0, V_l, \varphi, \delta_i)$, for $i = 1, 2$, i.e. A_1 and A_2 only differ in their transition relations.

Delete Transitions. If we obtain A_2 from A_1 by deleting the transition (t, com, σ') from $\delta_1(\sigma)$, i.e. $\delta_1(\sigma) = \delta_2(\sigma) \cup \{(t, com, \sigma')\}$, this is a correct refinement step if $t \Rightarrow \bigvee_{t' \in T_{\delta_2}(\sigma)} t'$ is a tautology, where $T_\delta(\sigma)$ yields the first projection, the trigger condition, of $\delta(\sigma)$. The premise here means that the deleted condition t is already subsumed in the remaining conditions, and therefore, additional non-determinism cannot occur when deleting the corresponding transition[2].

Add Transitions. If we obtain A_2 from A_1 by adding the transition (t, com, σ') to $\delta_1(\sigma)$, i.e. $\delta_2(\sigma) = \delta_1(\sigma) \cup \{(t, com, \sigma')\}$, this is a correct refinement step if $\forall t' \in T_{\delta_1}(\sigma) : t \wedge t'$ is a contradiction. Informally, this premise guarantees that no transitions are introduced, whose triggers are already subsumed in any other existing transition. We want to exemplarily carry out the proof for this rule:

Proof. According to (†), we take an arbitrary $X \subseteq \mathcal{C}(A_1) \times \mathcal{I}(A_1)^\infty \times \mathcal{O}(A_1)^\infty$ with $X \subseteq F_{A_2}(X)$. Now let the following be true: $\exists c'.((c', y) \in [\![\delta_2]\!](c, x) \wedge (c', i, o) \in X) \vee [\![\delta_2]\!](c, x) = \emptyset$. As we must prove $F_{A_2}(X) \subseteq F_{A_1}(X)$ we have to show that $\exists c'.((c', y) \in [\![\delta_1]\!](c, x) \wedge (c', i, o) \in X) \vee [\![\delta_1]\!](c, x) = \emptyset$. This is done by case distinction:

1. First, we assume that $\exists c'.(c', y) \in [\![\delta_2]\!](c, x) \wedge (c', i, o) \in X$. Let $c = (\sigma, \varepsilon)$. We define $\delta_3(\sigma) =_{df} \{(t, com, \sigma')\}$. Since $[\![\delta_2]\!](c, x) = [\![\delta_1]\!](c, x) \cup [\![\delta_3]\!](c, x)$ the tuple (c', y) must either be in $[\![\delta_1]\!](c, x)$ or in $[\![\delta_3]\!](c, x)$. If $(c', y) \in [\![\delta_1]\!](c, x)$ the proof is already completed. Otherwise, $(c', y) \in [\![\delta_3]\!](c, x)$ and so $(\varepsilon, x) \in [\![t]\!]_{A_2}$ must hold. From this we can deduce that $\forall t' \in T_{\delta_1}(\sigma) : (\varepsilon, x) \notin [\![t']\!]_{A_1}$ because $\forall t' \in T_{\delta_1}(\sigma) : t \wedge t' = \text{ff}$ and therefore

$$\forall t' \in T_{\delta_1}(\sigma) : [\![t]\!]_{A_1} \cap [\![t']\!]_{A_1} = [\![t \wedge t']\!]_{A_1} = [\![\text{ff}]\!]_{A_1} = \emptyset$$

   As a consequence, we get $[\![\delta_1]\!](c, x) = \emptyset$ what yields the desired result.
2. Second, we assume that $[\![\delta_2]\!](c, x) = \emptyset$. As $\delta_1(\sigma) \subseteq \delta_2(\sigma)$ implies $[\![\delta_1]\!](c, x) \subseteq [\![\delta_2]\!](c, x)$ also $[\![\delta_1]\!](c, x) = \emptyset$ holds. $\quad\square$

The first case of the proof says that a new transition only can make the specification more precise, but not more chaotic. The second case guarantees that chaotic behavior of A_2 must already have been chaotic in A_1.

Modify Existing Transitions. Let A be as above, σ a state in A, and $e \in \delta(\sigma)$ the transition to be modified; δ and δ' denote the transition relations before and after one transformation, respectively. We then can identify the following rules:

1. The trigger condition t, where $e = (t, com, \sigma')$, σ' not necessarily different from σ, can be refined:

---

[2] Remember that after the application of a refinement rule, the specification only can be more concrete, but not more abstract.

- To $t \vee t'$ if $\forall t''.t'' \in T_\delta(\sigma) \Rightarrow (t' \wedge t'')$ is a contradiction
- To $t \wedge t'$ if $(t \wedge \neg t') \Rightarrow \left(\bigvee_{t'' \in T_{\delta'}(\sigma)} t'' \right)$ is a tautology

for an arbitrary Boolean term t' in $Bexp(I + V_l)$.

2. The trigger condition $a \wedge a'$, where $e = (a \wedge a', com, \sigma)$, can be refined to a for an arbitrary Boolean term a' in $Bexp(I + V_l)$ if $\forall t''.t'' \in T_\delta(\sigma) \Rightarrow (t'' \wedge (a \wedge \neg a'))$ is a contradiction.

3. The trigger condition $b \vee b'$, where $e = (b \vee b', com, \sigma)$, can be refined to b for an arbitrary Boolean term b' over $Bexp(I + V_l)$ if $b' \wedge \neg b \Rightarrow \left(\bigvee_{t'' \in T_{\delta'}(\sigma)} t'' \right)$ is a tautology.

Rule number (1) can be proven from the rules for adding and deleting transitions. Rules (2) and (3) are deduced from (1) when t is substituted by $a \wedge a'$ and $b \vee b'$, respectively and the following equivalences are used:

$$a = a \wedge (\neg a' \vee a') = (a \wedge \neg a') \vee (a \wedge a')$$
$$b = b \vee (b' \wedge \neg b') = (b \vee b') \wedge (b \vee \neg b')$$

In the example we can e.g. modify the transition trigger ldn in MOTORLEFT to $ldn \wedge \neg lup$. As $lup \wedge ldn \Rightarrow ldn \vee (lup \wedge \neg ldn)$ is a tautology, this is a correct refinement step. If we wanted to refine the remaining transition with label ldn to $ldn \wedge \neg lup$, too, we would violate a syntactical refinement condition because $ldn \wedge lup \Rightarrow (ldn \wedge \neg lup) \vee (lup \wedge \neg ldn)$ is no longer a tautology. Finally, we would like to mention that none of the above rules depends on transition commands, but only on trigger conditions.

Rules for Composition. Single components can be composed to more complex specifications using the following rules:

- $S_1 \rightsquigarrow S_1 \triangleleft L \triangleright S_2$ for $Out(S_1) \cap Out(S_2) = \emptyset$ and $In(S_1) \cap L \cap Out(S_2) = \emptyset$
- $S_1 \rightsquigarrow S_1 \| S_2$ and $S_2 \rightsquigarrow S_1 \| S_2$ for $Out(S_1) \cap Out(S_2) = \emptyset$ as direct consequence from the first rule.

Informally, these rules express that S_1 can be composed with any other specifications S_2 whenever S_2 cannot add additional behavior due to message sending to S_1 and the output interfaces are disjoint. If the latter condition would be violated, S_2 could chatter in the output stream of S_1 and one could not distinguish anymore whether events are generated by S_1 or S_2. Again, additional non-determinism possibly would be introduced.

As a consequence, in our running example $S_L \rightsquigarrow S_L \| S_R$, $S_R \rightsquigarrow S_L \| S_R$, and also $S_C \rightsquigarrow S_C \triangleleft L \triangleright (S_L \| S_R)$ and $S_L \| S_R \rightsquigarrow S_C \triangleleft L \triangleright (S_L \| S_R)$, where S_L, S_R, and S_C denote the left and right motor, and the control part of the central locking system, respectively. Due to the transitivity of $\rightsquigarrow$, we also get $S_L \rightsquigarrow S_C \triangleleft L \triangleright (S_L \| S_R)$. Note that, for lack of associativity, we cannot omit brackets as $rdn, rup, ready \in Out(S_C) \cap L \cap In(S_R)$ and $rmr \in In(S_C) \cap L \cap Out(S_R)$.

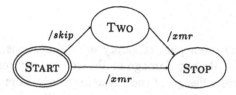

Figure 5. Decomposition of DOWN and UP, $x \in \{l, r\}$

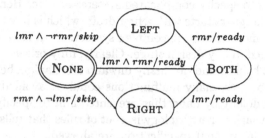

Figure 6. Decomposition of LOCKG and UNLG

Rule for Hierarchy. In the last section we have seen that hierarchical composition can be interpreted as parallel composition plus some extra communication of master and slaves. From the propositions for composition we therefore can deduce the following rule:

Let A decby (Σ_d, ϱ) be defined as in Section 3.1. Then we get

$$A \rightsquigarrow A \text{ decby } (\Sigma_d, \varrho)$$

without any further restrictions in case of strong preemption. For weak preemption this proposition is only true, if

$$\forall k.(1 \leq k \leq |\Sigma_d| \Rightarrow O \cap Out(S_k) = \emptyset = I \cap Out(S_k))$$

where $\{S_1, \ldots, S_{|\Sigma_d|}\} = \bigcup_{\sigma \in \Sigma_d} \varrho(\sigma)$. This rule can be easily derived from the refinement rules for composition, the definition of hierarchy, and the fact that $\{go(\sigma)\} \cap In(A) = \emptyset$ as $go(\sigma)$ is a fresh signal. If we take a look at the central locking system, we ascertain that the automaton in Figure 5 is a correct refinement of DOWN and UP in LEFTMOTOR and RIGHTMOTOR, respectively.

Figure 6 however is no correct refinement of UNLG and LOCKG because $ready \in Out(\text{UNLG}) \cap In(\text{CONTROL})$ and $ready \in Out(\text{LOCKG}) \cap In(\text{CONTROL})$. We see that the restriction $I \cap Out(S_k) = \emptyset$ is really needed as A decby (Σ_d, ϱ) can be embedded in a specification that makes certain signals available for communication which would lead to additional non-determinism. In the example, the signal $ready$ is fed back on the outermost level of hierarchy, which could pander self termination. Therefore, we can conclude that to introduce self termination never is a correct refinement step.

5 Conclusion

Reactive systems are often part of safety critical systems. To obtain correct working systems that do not damage or destroy its environment, it is important to keep the correct design of such systems in eye from the very beginning. One possibility to reduce the number of critical malfunctions is to apply formal verification techniques, such as model checking.

It is hardly possible to specify complicated systems ad hoc. Hence, in a typical design process the designer starts with a first draft, which is later on transformed step by step into a more and more complex system. As a consequence, critical errors can be included in any design stage. Clearly, fully or semi automated verification techniques help to find out many unwanted behaviors before the system is implemented. However, many malfunctions could be avoided if the designer had a design methodology by hand that prevented him to specify unwanted behavior. One part of such a methodology is a set of rules that tells the user which transformations of the original specification are allowed.

In this paper we have proposed a refinement calculus for a synchronous Statecharts dialect that makes a contribution to this task. We have shown that two syntactical constructs are enough to formulate Statecharts specifications. We have described the semantics of μ-Charts mathematically and have described how the notion of refinement can smoothly be integrated in this semantics.

Further work will focus on the question how our refinement calculus can be embedded as part in a more general design methodology for Statecharts.

Acknowledgment

I would like to thank Jan Philipps and Bernhard Rumpe for many fruitful discussions on this and on related topics and for the careful reading of a draft version of this paper. I am also grateful for the inspiring comments of the anonymous referees.

References

1. G. Berry. Preemption in Concurrent Systems. In *Foundations of Software Technology and Theoretical Computer Science : 13th Conference Bombay, India, December 15-17*, volume 761 of *Lecture Notes in Computer Science*, pages 72 – 93. Springer, 1993.
2. G. Berry. *A Quick Guide to Esterel*. Unpublished Esterel Primer, 1996.
3. G. Berry. The Foundations of Esterel. In G. Plotkin, C. Stirling, and M. Tofte, editors, *Proof, Language and Interaction: Essays in Honour of Robin Milner*. MIT Press, 1998.
4. M. Broy. Interaction Refinement - The Easy Way. In *Program Design Calculi*, volume 118 of *NATO ASI Series F: Computer and System Sciences*. Springer, 1993.

5. D. Harel. Statecharts: A Visual Formalism for Complex Systems. *Science of Computer Programming*, 8:231 – 274, 1987.

6. D. Harel and A. Naamad. The Statemate Semantics of Statecharts. *ACM Transactions On Software Engineering and Methodology*, 5(4):293–333, 1996.

7. F. Maraninchi. Operational and Compositional Semantics of Synchronous Automaton Compositions. In W.R. Cleaveland, editor, *Proceedings CONCUR'92*, volume 630 of *Lecture Notes in Computer Science*, pages 550 – 564. Springer-Verlag, 1992.

8. F. Maraninchi and N. Halbwachs. Compositional Semantics of Non-deterministic Synchronous Languages. In Riis Nielson, editor, *Programming languanges and systems - ESOP'96, 6th European Symposium on programming*, volume 1058 of *LNCS*. Springer-Verlag, 1996.

9. J. Philipps and P. Scholz. Compositional Specification of Embedded Systems with Statecharts. In *TAPSOFT'97: Theory and Practice of Software Development*, volume 1214 of *Lecture Notes in Computer Science*. Springer-Verlag, 1997.

10. J. Philipps and P. Scholz. Formal Verification of Statecharts with Instantaneous Chain Reactions. In *TACAS'97: Tools and Algorithms for the Construction and Analysis of Systems*, volume 1217 of *Lecture Notes in Computer Science*. Springer-Verlag, 1997.

11. B. Rumpe. *Formale Methodik des Entwurfs verteilter objektorientierter Systeme (in German)*. Herbert Utz Verlag Wissenschaft, München, Ph.D. Thesis, Technische Universität München, 1996.

12. B. Rumpe and C. Klein. Automata Describing Object Behavior. In H. Kilov and W. Harvey, editors, *Specification of Behavioral Semantics in Object-Oriented Information Modeling*, pages 265–286. Kluwer Academic Publishers, 1996.

13. M. von der Beeck. A Comparison of Statecharts Variants. In H. Langmaack, W.-P. de Roever, and J. Vytopil, editors, *Proc. Formal Techniques in Real-Time and Fault-Tolerant Systems (FTRTFT'94)*, volume 863 of *Lecture Notes in Computer Science*, pages 128 – 148. Springer, 1994.

Refining Formal Specifications of Human Computer Interaction by Graph Rewrite Rules

Bettina Eva Sucrow

Data Management Systems and Knowledge Representation
Dept. of Mathematics and Computer Science
University of Essen, 45 117 Essen, Germany
sucrow@informatik.uni-essen.de

Abstract. Human computer interaction can be specified successfully using the concept of information resources and the formal notation of graph grammars. In order to achieve a precise and continuous specification process between the requirements and design stages, however, a suitable strategy for refining abstract specifications into more concrete ones correctly and consistently is highly necessary.

In this paper it will be proposed to apply graph rewrite rules at a meta level to abstract graph grammar specifications of human computer interaction in order to achieve correct and consistent refinements of the specifications wrt important requirements. A safety-critical system concerning the interaction between the pilot and the flight management system on the flight deck of an aircraft will be used as an example. A graph grammar specification of this interaction at an abstract level will be refined wrt mode visualization by a graph rewrite rule at a meta level.

1 Introduction

A successful design of an interactive system requires a suitable specification of human computer interaction. Specifications using the concept of information resources (cf. [23] and [3]) and the formal notation of graph grammars (cf. [17]) provide a precise understanding of interaction as well as a correct and consistent formal description at least at an abstract level (cf. [21]).

However, in order to achieve a continuous specification process between the requirements and design stages a suitable strategy for refining abstract specifications into more concrete ones in a correct and consistent way is highly desirable.

A variety of techniques for specifying states and behaviour of interactive systems can be found in the literature. As shown in [11] state transition diagrams form the basis of a variety of description techniques for user interfaces. However, as pure sequential techniques they are only suitable for mask and menue dialogs. Describing user interfaces using statecharts permits modelling parallel dialogs but does not show the context between such parallel subdialogs. Dialog nets ([10]), a special form of Petri nets, overcome this problem with the features of modal subdialogs, a clear net structure and hierarchy. However, dialog net specifications of graphical user interfaces result quickly in very complex descriptions of even simple user interfaces. A detailed presentation and comparision of techniques for specifying interaction processes can be found in [18].

Graph grammar descriptions have also been used as specification technique. In [1] a customized user interface design environment is generated. First, a conceptual framework for task-oriented user interface specification is specified as a visual language. The specification is then applied to a visual language generator yielding a visual syntax-directed editor for the specification language. In this approach the visual language is specified with graph transformation systems. Specification and representation of user interfaces based on end user tasks using attributed graphs and related graph rewriting systems can also been seen in [4].

In order to achieve specifications of interaction between human and machine which are expressive enough on the one side and which remain understandable on the other side the formalism of graph grammars is used in [7]. Dialog states describing user interface objects with their current appearance and their respective relationship to the underlying application are formally specified by directed attributed graphs. Transformations of one dialog state into another one by an event are formally specified by graph rewrite rules. Hence, graph grammars provide formal as well as clear interaction specifications allowing correct specification changes and reflecting the intuitive comprehension that designer and customer have about interaction, respectively, in every specification stage. In [15] this approach has been used in order to formalize the control window of a complex real numeric system by graph grammars (see also [19]), and the correct and comprehensive specification led to a far better interaction process. [20] and [22] show an approach for integrating software-ergonomic aspects in formal specifications of graphical user interfaces using graph grammars in order to improve human-machine interaction.

In [21] it has been presented how interaction may be modelled using the concept of information resources and formally specified by the notation of graph grammars. In order to develop a strategy for refining such specifications at an still abstract level the idea of constructing *meta rules* will be introduced in this paper. A graph rewrite rule of this kind specifies a specific task concerning the refinement of the abstract specification wrt a specific requirement. It specifies a refinement resulting from a regular communication between designer and customer during the specification process. A safety-critical system concerning the interaction between the pilot and the flight management system (FMS) on the flight deck of an aircraft will be used as an example for an abstract specification. A meta rule specifying the visualization of modes with the goal of refining the abstract interaction specification correctly and consistently will be constructed.

The formal notation of graph grammars which is based on the algebraic double pushout approach (DPO) will be introduced first. The construction of graph rewriting in this approach will help in understanding the refinement of graph grammar specifications by graph rewrite rules. A short presentation will then be given about how interaction between the pilot and the FMS can be modelled using the concept of information resources and specified formally by a graph grammar at a still abstract level. After the presentation of some proves already at that abstract specification stage wrt some important requirements the specification has to be refined in order to move towards the design stage coming from the requirements stage. For this purpose a graph rewrite rule will be constructed with the goal of refining the abstract specification wrt the visualization of the modes involved. Considering this construction within the DPO will provide a suitable insight into the conditions under which an abstract specification could be refined correctly and consistently by a meta rule.

2 The Graph Grammar Formalism

The graph grammar formalism introduced below is based on the algebraic *double pushout (DPO) approach*. The definitions will sometimes be only semi-formal and incomplete due to lack of space. We therefore refer to [5], [17] and [13] for a detailed and complete description.

Let $Attr_V$ and $Attr_E$ be two type variables denoting types for labelling nodes and edges of graphs respectively. The sets used to actualize $Attr_V$ and $Attr_E$ are not necessarily simple flat alphabets, but could also be sets of functions, relations, etc. as attributes. We define:

Definition 1. An $(Attr_V, Attr_E)$-*graph* M is a system
$M = (V_M, E_M, s_M, t_M, l_M, m_M)$, where
V_M set of nodes,
E_M set of edges,
$s_M : E_M \rightarrow V_M$ source function of edges,
$t_M : E_M \rightarrow V_M$ target function of edges,
$l_M : V_M \rightarrow Attr_V$ node labelling,
$m_M : E_M \rightarrow Attr_E$ edge labelling.
M represents a *directed node and edge labelled* graph.

For describing modifications of graphs by graph rewrite rules we need the definition of a match between two graphs:

Definition 2. A *graph match* g of a $(Attr_V, Attr_E)$-graph M in a $(Attr_V, Attr_E)$-graph N is given by a 4-tupel $g = (g_V, g_E, p_V, p_E)$, where
$g_V : V_M \rightarrow V_N$ and $g_E : E_M \rightarrow E_N$ mappings,
$p_V : (Attr_V \times Attr_V) \rightarrow \{true, false\}$ node attribute match predicate,
$p_E : (Attr_E \times Attr_E) \rightarrow \{true, false\}$ edge attribute match predicate,
such that $\forall e \in E_M, v \in V_M$:
$g_V(s_M(e)) = s_N(g_E(e))$,
$g_V(t_M(e)) = t_N(g_E(e))$,
$p_V(l_M(v), l_N(g_V(v))) \wedge p_E(m_M(e), m_N(g_E(e)))$.

For the induced match $g(M)$ it has to be assured on the one hand that g_V and g_E map consistently the source and target of each edge in graph M onto nodes in the target graph N such that the graph structure of M - i.e. without considering labels - is mapped onto a proper subgraph of N. On the other hand the label of a graph element (node or edge) in M and the label of the corresponding picture of that graph element in graph N (under the mapping g_V or g_E respectively) have to be *compatible* with respect to the predicates p_V or p_E respectively.

Modifications of graphs are described by graph rewrite rules:

A *modification of a graph M* into a new graph N by applying a graph rewrite rule $r = (L, R, K)$ is realized by the following two principal steps:
1) a graph match is chosen between the graph L and the graph M to be modified,
2) the induced match of graph L is removed in graph M and graph R is added. The connection of graph R to the remaining part of graph M is given by the glueing graph K (see below).

As can be seen, a *graph rewrite rule* $r = (L, R, K)$ is a triple of graphs, where graph L is the left hand side of the rule, graph R is the right hand side of the rule and graph K is the so called glueing graph. K takes care that no dangling edges appear in the new graph after applying rule r to the old graph. Hence, K identifies some anchor elements which have to remain unchanged by the modification and is a subgraph of L and R as well.

At this point we have all necessary preliminaries to define:

Definition 3. A *graph grammar* is a system $G = (Attr_V, Attr_E, P, P_r, Z)$, where $Attr_V$, $Attr_E$ are node and edge attributes respectively,
P is a set of graph rewrite rules,
P_r is a set of attribute match predicates required for a graph match,
Z is the start graph (Z is a $(Attr_V, Attr_E)$-graph).

For the sake of simplicity a graph grammar G will be described in the following by $G = (Z, P)$, where Z denotes the start graph and P the set of graph rewrite rules.

In order to prepare the use of the graph grammar formalism for specifications of interaction as well as for refining such specifications a view onto direct derivation diagrams in the DPO helps much in understanding the rewrite mechanism introduced above (see also [2]). Direct derivations, i.e. modifications of graphs by a rewrite rule, are modelled by glueing constructions of graphs, that are formally characterized as pushouts in suitable categories having graphs as objects and graph homomorphisms as arrows. A graph rewrite rule p is given by a pair $L \xleftarrow{l} K \xrightarrow{r} R$ of graph homomorphisms from a common *interface* or *glueing graph K*, and a direct derivation consists of two glueing diagrams as (1) and (2) in the diagram in figure 1. The *context graph C* is obtained from the given graph G by deleting all elements of G which have a pre-image in L, but none in K. This deletion is modelled as an inverse glueing operation by diagram (1), while the actual insertion into H of all elements of R which do not have a pre-image in K is modelled by the glueing diagram (2). The match m must satisfy the so-called *glueing condition* which takes care, that the context graph C will have no dangling edges and that every element of G that should be deleted by the application of p has only one pre-image in L.

Diagrams as the one in figure 1 will help much in investigating the refinement of graph grammars by graph rewrite rules at a meta level as will be seen in

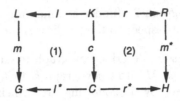

Fig. 1. Direct derivation in the DPO

chapter 4. After this introduction to the graph grammar formalism a specification of the interaction between the pilot and the FMS on the flight deck of an aircraft will be presented using the concept of information resources and the formal notation of graph grammars (for a detailed explanation cf. [21]).

3 Specification of the Interaction between Pilot and FMS

Interaction can be modelled based on the concept of *information resources* (more deeply handled in [23] and [3]). This idea is influenced by the approach of distributed cognition [9] which sees resources as distributed across components of the whole system. The user tries to achieve *goals* by interacting with a system and he has *plans* in his head during certain time periods to achieve these goals. *Action-affordances* refer to the set of possible next actions that can be taken, given the current state of the system. An *action-effect mapping* is a statement of the effect that an action will have if it is carried out. Such information resources are highly suitable criteria for getting an understanding of interaction.

Graph grammars represent a highly suitable formalism for specifying statics and dynamics of interactive systems. Graphs describe states, graph rewrite rules describe changes of states in a powerful but understandable manner (cf. [7]).

Based on these preparations the specification of a safety-critical system, of the interaction between the pilot and the flight management system (FMS) on the flight deck of an aircraft, can be constructed. It comprises the stages beginning with the take-off and ending up with the landing (for a detailed description we refer to [21]). The first state of the interaction may be specified by the start graph G_{Start} in figure 2 where the small pictures denoted by Pilot and FMS are only depicted for orientation purposes.

The root node on the pilot side specifies the top level goal TLG with the meaning of a particular flight. This goal is decomposed into the three subgoals Start, Fly and Land, landing again is decomposed into the subgoals CNM (Changing Navigation Mode), EDI (Entering Descent Input) and TD (Touch Down). All goals not further decomposed are associated to subparts of the system's user interface on the FMS side. Action-effect edges indicate that actions of type <a> can be performed within parts of the system's user interface in order to complete the respective goals. All possible actions constitute the actual action-affordances.

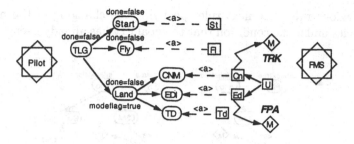

Fig. 2. Start Graph G_{Start}

In the autopilot system the *modes* of the navigation and descent are automatically coupled (cf. [12]). For that reason the corresponding parts of the system's user interface can be grouped together by specifying them, e. g., as subwidgets of a superwidget. Cn and Ed are examples for such subwidgets with a common superwidget U. Moreover, because of the importance of the actual modes of Cn and Ed in every situation during the flight a node M of a new type denoted by a different shape is introduced. It has an attribute indicating the current mode value of its associated system part, e.g. mode value *TRK* (*Track*) for Cn, and a specific edge connects this mode node with its respective user interface part.

Graph rewrite rules specify the interactions. The first rule specifies the start of the flight.

$$P_{Start} : \quad \underset{\text{done=false}}{\text{(Start)}} \leftarrow \overset{\text{<a>}}{-} - \boxed{\text{St}} \quad ::= \quad \underset{\text{done=true}}{\text{(Start)}} \leftarrow \overset{\text{<a>}}{-} - \boxed{\text{St}}$$

This rule matches in a state graph under the condition that the goal Start has not yet been completed as indicated by the value *false* of the attribute done on the left hand side of the rule. In the case of a match the left hand side of the rule will be substituted by its right hand side. This specifies that the action <a> performed within the user interface part St leads to the completion of the goal Start as indicated by the value *true* of the attribute done on the right hand side of the rule. (Glueing graphs necessary due to technical reasons will not be considered further in this context.) The next rule specifies the flying stage.

$$P_{Fly} : \quad \begin{matrix} \underset{\text{done=true}}{\text{(Start)}} \\ \underset{\text{done=false}}{\text{(Fly)}} \leftarrow \overset{\text{<a>}}{-} \boxed{\text{Fl}} \end{matrix} \quad ::= \quad \begin{matrix} \underset{\text{done=true}}{\text{(Start)}} \\ \underset{\text{done=true}}{\text{(Fly)}} \leftarrow \overset{\text{<a>}}{-} \boxed{\text{Fl}} \end{matrix}$$

This rule matches under the condition that the goal Start has already been completed but the goal Fly has not yet been completed, and it works analogously to the previous rule. The next rule specifying the changing of the navigation mode applies under the condition that the goal Fly has already been completed.

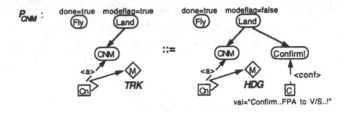

This rule changes the value of the navigation mode from *TRK* to *HDG* (*Track to Heading*) as can be observed by considering the mode node connected to the related subpart Cn of the system's user interface. Such a change is sometimes necessary in order to comply with radar guidance ([12]). But additionally, the rule does something else. A new goal Confirm! appears with related user interface part C within which an action <conf> can be performed to complete this goal. One can imagine C as a modal subdialog or a dialogbox. The goal Confirm! is added here in order to force the pilot to confirm the change of the descent mode from *FPA* to *V/S* (*Flight Path Angle* to *Vertical Speed*) which is automatically coupled with the change of the navigation mode from *TRK* to *HDG*. This is indicated to the pilot by the value of the attribute val attached to the node C. In this specification the pilot ist forced to confirm the automatically coupled change of the descent mode in order to prevent mode errors which in the past have led already to accidents claiming casualties (cf. [12] and [14]).

Now the specification has to assure that the pilot indeed can not do anything else except this confirmation. Therefore, the boolean attribute modeflag is attached to the goal node Land. Its value is always *true* except in the situation that the pilot changes the navigation mode where its value becomes *false*. This can be observed by comparing left and right hand side of the rule P_{CNM}. If the modeflag is *false* in the current state graph then only one specific rule matches, namely $P_{Confirm}$ below specifying the expected confirmation by the pilot as well as the automatically coupled change of the descent mode. The right hand side of the rule shows that after its application the value of the Land.modeflag is *true* again and that the subgraph containing the goal Confirm! has disappeared.

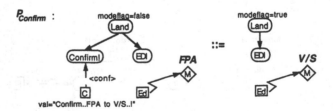

The penultimative rule specifies the entering of the descent input which is a subgoal of the landing stage and is therefore performed under the condition that the goal Fly has already been completed.

Finally, the last subgoal of the landing stage, the touch down goal, is specified by the following rule P_{TD} applicable under the condition that the entering of the descent input has already been completed.

This rule, finally, completes the entire top level goal, the particular flight which is indicated by the value *true* of attribute done attached to node TLG.

Despite existing techniques in the theory of graph grammars for aggregating set of rules differing only in the labels of their graphs (cf. [6]) two further rules $P^\diamond_{CNM}$ and $P^\diamond_{Confirm}$ specifying the change of the navigation and descent modes also in the other direction, from *HDG* to *TRK* (*Heading* to *Track*) and from *V/S* to *FPA* (*Vertical Speed* to *Flight Path Angle*) respectively, are added in this example. Thus, the interaction between the pilot and the FMS can be specified at a still very abstract level by the

Graph Grammar $GraGra = \{G_{Start}, P\}$ with

- G_{Start} Start Graph,
- $P = \{P_{Start}, P_{Fly}, P_{CNM}, P_{Confirm}, P^\diamond_{CNM}, P^\diamond_{Confirm}, P_{EDI}, P_{TD}\}$.

Specifications of this kind are very useful in order to prove already at abstract stages of the development process whether important properties and requirements are fulfilled by the specification or not. In order to give an impression some properties and requirements already considered in [21] will be presented in the following. In the safety-critical system introduced above it is highly important to be able to prove already at early specification stages that certain actions take place before or after other ones. A first claim could therefore concern the required order in which the three goals Start, Fly and Land are intended to be completed.

Claim 4. *The goals Start, Fly and Land will by all means be completed in the required order!*

Proof. The set of nodes and edges of a graph G will be denoted by V_G and E_G.

a) $P_{Start} = (L_{Start}, R_{Start}, K_{Start})$ is the only rule the left hand side L_{Start} of which matches a subgraph of the start graph G_{Start}!

$\forall v \in V_{Start} : v.\text{done} = false \land v.\text{modeflag} = true$
$\forall L_x$ of $P_x \in P \setminus \{P_{Start}\} : (\exists v \in V_{L_x} : v.\text{done} = true \lor v.\text{modeflag} = false)$

b) P_{Fly} is applicable only under the condition that goal Start has been completed!

L_{Fly} only matches graphs of the kind L° where
$\exists v \in V_{L^\circ}$ with $v = \text{Start} \land v.\text{done} = true$

c) All rules contributing to the completion of goal Land are only applicable if goal Fly has been completed!

This has to be shown for all rules in the set $P \setminus \{P_{Start}, P_{Fly}\}$:
The proofs for P_{CNM} (P°_{CNM}) and P_{EDI} work analogously to proof 4b). $P_{Confirm}$ ($P^\circ_{Confirm}$) is only applicable directly after P_{CNM} (P°_{CNM}) (because of the attribute Land.modeflag). P_{TD} is only applicable after P_{EDI} (because of the attribute EDI.done).

One very important requirement is to assure that the pilot is always aware of the actual mode values.

Claim 5. *Any indirect (caused by another action) change of the descent mode will be performed through* **confirmation** *by the pilot!*

Proof. Changing the descent mode is performed by rule $P_{Confirm}$ ($P^\circ_{Confirm}$) forced in turn by rule P_{CNM} (P°_{CNM}). $P_{Confirm}$ ($P^\circ_{Confirm}$) specifies an action $<\text{conf}>$ within a subpart C of the system's user interface to be performed by the pilot.

Finally, it is important to be sure that certain actions are always performable by the pilot at certain stages during the flight. The next claim considers that more concretely.

Claim 6. *The navigation mode can always be changed during the stage* Land.

Proof. A switch between the two navigation modes TRK and HDG is specified by the two rules P_{CNM} and P°_{CNM} respectively. Both work under the condition Fly.done $= true$ according to proof 4b).

A specification describing the interaction between the pilot and the FMS at an abstract level has been constructed so far. Some important requirements could also proved to be true already at this abstract specification stage. In the next chapter it will be investigated how such an abstract specification could be refined continuously by considering a graph rewrite rule at a meta level.

4 Refining the Interaction Specification by a Meta Rule

An important requirement wrt the specification of the interaction between the pilot and the FMS described in chapter 3 is the visualization of the modes involved. The consideration of the start graph G_{Start} in figure 2 shows that modes are specified already but they are not visualized to the pilot who has to be aware of their values in every situation to increase safety for the flight. An idea in order to refine this graph wrt to mode visualization is to apply a graph rewrite rule at a certain meta level. The notion *meta level* indicates that such a rule does not **belong** to the interaction specification, but it has the task to **refine** this specification. A meta rule extending the state graph wrt to mode visualization could look like the graph rewrite rule P_{Meta} in figure 3.

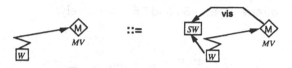

Fig. 3. Graph Rewrite Rule P_{Meta}

The left hand side matches whenever a system's user interface part is connected to a mode node by a respective edge. The free variable W indicates that application of the rule is possible wrt any system part under the conditions specified by the left hand side of the rule. The same holds for the value of the current mode indicated by the free variable MV. Substitution by the right hand side of the rule implies an extension wrt the required mode visualization. An additional system part denoted by the free variable SW will be created by which the current mode value MV becomes visualized. One can think about this new part as a label with a bright background colour or the like. The fact of visualization is explicitly specified by a directed edge labelled by the constant attribute vis and leading from the mode node M to the node SW describing the new system part.

At this point the following should be noted: application of the graph rewrite rule $P_{Meta} = (L_M, R_M, K_M)$ to a graph G leads to a substitution of the induced match $g(L_M)$ (cf. definition 2) in G by R_M for every occurence $g(L_M)$ (the glueing graph K_M is equal to graph L_M in this case). According to a regular communication between designer and customer, however, meta rule P_{Meta} should only be used for refinement in cases in which mode visualization has not yet been integrated into the specification. Thus, to prevent the application of P_{Meta} in cases where modes just have been visualized *negative application conditions* (cf. [8]) can be integrated elegantly into the rule specification. This, however, is omitted here for the sake of simplicity.

Refining the specification of an interaction by a meta rule means applying the meta rule to the respective graph grammar specification, i.e. applying it to

- the *start graph* specifying the first state of the interaction,
- the *set of rewrite rules* specifying the dynamics of the interaction.

Based on these considerations the refinement of graph grammar *GraGra* in chapter 3 by meta rule P_{Meta} in figure 3 will be investigated in the following two sections.

4.1 Refining the Start Graph G_{Start} by the MetaRula P_{Meta}

According to the previous explanations the twofold application of the meta rule P_{Meta} in figure 3 to the state graph G_{Start} in figure 2 would lead to the state graph H_{Start} in figure 4 where the visualization of the navigation as well as of the descent mode is specified now. The visualization of the two modes is realized by the new user interface parts SC and SE respectively.

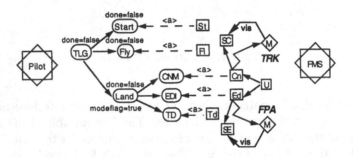

Fig. 4. Start graph H_{Start} (refinement of G_{Start}) with integrated mode visualization

The application of rule P_{Meta} to graph G_{Start} can easily be understood by considering the corresponding derivation diagram in the DPO in figure 5.

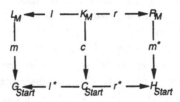

Fig. 5. Application of rule P_{Meta} to graph G_{Start} yielding graph H_{Start} in the DPO

A comparision of the diagrams in figures 1 and 5 provides the proof idea for the fact that applications of graph rewrite rules like P_{Meta} to state graphs like G_{Start} result in correct and consistent refinements of the resulting graphs.

The more complicated question is, how meta rules could refine graph grammar rules specifying interactions. This will be investigated in the next section.

4.2 Refining Set P of Graph Rewrite Rules by Meta Rula P_{Meta}

Application of rule P_{Meta} (cf. figure 3) to the set P of graph rewrite rules (cf. capter 3) at first means application to every graph rewrite rule contained in set P. Obviously, the left hand side L_M of P_{Meta} would only match in graphs involved in the four rules P_{CNM}, $P_{Confirm}$, P_{CNM}° and $P_{Confirm}^\circ$. Additionally, it is intuitively clear that a refinement of either of these rules wrt to mode visualization would make sense: a change of the navigation as well as of the descent mode by the pilot during a flight would have to be reflected in the respective user interface part. Thus, a consistent refinement of a graph rewrite rule $p = (L, R, K) \in \{P_{CNM}, P_{Confirm}, P_{CNM}^\circ, P_{Confirm}^\circ\}$ would require the application of the meta rule P_{Meta} to L as well as to R. Application of rule P_{Meta} to graph rewrite rule $P_{Confirm}$ in chapter 3 would lead to the new rule $P_{Confirm}^\star$ in figure 6.

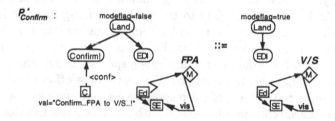

Fig. 6. Graph rewrite rule $P_{Confirm}^\star$ with integrated mode visualization

The DPO diagram in figure 7 describes this idea: the application of the meta rule $P_{Meta} = (L_M, R_M, K_M)$ to a graph rewrite rule $p = (L, R, K)$ yields the refined graph rewrite rule $h = (H_L, H_R, H_K)$ with $H_K = K$.

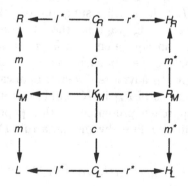

Fig. 7. Refinement of $p = (L, R, K)$ by P_{Meta} to $h = (H_L, H_R, H_K)$ in the DPO

In order to achieve a correct and consistent refinement by the application of the meta rule P_{Meta} to a graph rewrite rule of the kind $p = (L, R, K) \in \{P_{CNM}, P_{Confirm}, P_{CNM}^\diamond, P_{Confirm}^\diamond\}$ the following two requirements have to be ensured for which proof ideas will follow:

- P_{Meta} rewrites L of rule p exactly in the same way as R
  (visualization of a mode has to be updated **together** with the mode value (consistency)).
- $H_K = K$ is a correct glueing graph for the new rule h
  (the new rule is defined correctly).

The first requirement can be ensured by considering the graph homomorphisms m, $m^\star$ and c in figure 7: as in the DPO diagram in figure 1 they take care for constructing a correct graph H_L in case of a match of L_M in L. Thus, because of using exactly the same homomorphisms as well in order to refine the right hand side R of rule p the requirement is ensured.

Generally, also the case in which L_M matches only in one of the graphs L and R has to be considered. Due to the goal of refining interaction specifications according to the result of a regular communication between designer and customer only meta rules within a sensible context are considered. Thus, if L_M matches only in L this would mean that rule p specifies the *deletion* of a specific feature, and this has also to be refined. E.g., switching off a mode by the pilot should also imply the deletion of the respective user interface part for visualizing this mode in the specification **together** with the mode specification part itself. Analogously, if L_M matches only in R this would mean that rule p specifies the *addition* of a specific feature, and this has to be refined as well. E.g., switching on a mode by the pilot should also imply the addition of a respective user interface part for visualizing this mode in the specification **together** with the mode specification part itself.

The second requirement can be ensured by considering the fact that the glueing graph K will not be refined by the meta rule P_{Meta}. The important point here is that P_{Meta} does only add graph elements (nodes/edges), but does not delete such elements. Thus, after application of P_{Meta} to a rule $p = (L, R, K)$ yielding $h = (H_L, H_R, H_K)$, K is still a subgraph of both, H_L and H_R, so that $H_K = K$ is still a correct glueing graph for the new rule h.

The last requirement can not be ensured for meta rules which delete graph elements from graph rewrite rules. In such a case it may happen that K is not a subgraph of H_L and/or H_R anymore. Even, if application of the meta rule to K would be allowed, a match of L_M in K could possibly not exist.

According to the approach presented in this paper[1] the graph grammar *GraGra* in chapter 3 can be refined by the meta rule P_{Meta} in figure 3 yielding the

Graph Grammar $GraGra^\star_{Ref} = \{H_{Start}, P^\star\}$ where

- H_{Start} Start Graph,

---

[1] A similar approach to graph grammar transformation can be seen in [16]

$- P^* = \{P_{Start}, P_{Fly}, P^\star_{CNM}, P^\star_{Confirm}, P^{\diamond\star}_{CNM}, P^{\diamond\star}_{Confirm}, P_{EDI}, P_{TD}\},$

H_{Start} is the refinement of G_{Start}, and $P^\star_{CNM}$, $P^\star_{Confirm}$, $P^{\diamond\star}_{CNM}$ and $P^{\diamond\star}_{Confirm}$ are the respective refinements of P_{CNM}, $P_{Confirm}$, $P^\diamond_{CNM}$ and $P^\diamond_{Confirm}$. In this way the abstract graph grammar specification $GraGra$ of the interaction between the pilot and the FMS on the flight deck of an aircraft could be refined correctly and consistently wrt the so important mode visualization by the meta rule P_{Meta} yielding the more concrete graph grammar specification $GraGra^\star_{Ref}$.

As the main result of this paper refinements using meta rules that do not delete any graph elements can be carried out correctly and consistently. Constructing such meta rules according to the DPO diagrams in figures 5 and 7 and based on the ideas introduced above in order to refine abstract graph grammar specifications of human computer interaction successively into more concrete ones highly encourages the development of a suitable strategy in order to achieve a continuous specification process between the requirements and design stages.

5 Conclusions and Future Work

Specifying human computer interaction in a suitable manner requires a deep understanding of interaction as well as a powerful and understandable formal specification formalism. Interaction can be specified successfully using the concept of information resources and the formal notation of graph grammars.

In order to achieve a continuous specification process between the requirements and design stages a suitable strategy for refining abstract specifications into more concrete ones correctly and consistently is highly desirable. This paper proposes an approach by applying graph rewrite rules at a meta level to abstract graph grammar specifications. A meta rule of this kind refines the start graph as well as relevant graph rewrite rules of an interaction specification by adding new graph elements specifying new requirements resulting from a regular communication between the designer and customer.

As main research goals for future work important issues concerning the correct and complete definition of a strategy or of a calculus in order to achieve a continuous specification process for human computer interaction will be considered. For a requirement arising as a result of discussions between customer and designer it has to be investigated how it could be formulated suitably by a correct meta rule. Beyond the ideas of proofs given in the last chapter the correctness and consistency of this rule has then to be proved. Another important question will concern the problem of how the deletion of certain features of specifications could be specified by suitable meta rules in order to deal with inconsistencies arising during the design process or with contradictory properties possibly being existent from earlier specification stages, becoming evident, however, only later on. Further, the construction of meta rules contributing to collaborative specification processes is one of the most important future goals.

Considering these and future questions highly encourages to develop a suitable specification calculus in order to achieve a continuous specification process of human computer interaction between the requirements and the design stages.

Acknowledgments

I would like to thank Michael Goedicke who always finds the time for discussing ideas, questions and problems, as well as Torsten Meyer for fruitful discussions. Thanks also to Reiko Heckel for valuable conversations and reference hints.

References

1. F. Arefi, M. Milani, and C. Stary. Towards Customized User Interface Design Environments. *Journal of Visual Languages and Computing*, pages 146–151, 1991.
2. A. Corradini, U. Montanari, F. Rossi, H. Ehrig, R. Heckel, and M. Löwe. Algebraic Approaches to Graph Transformation – Part I: Basic Concepts and Double Pushout Approach. In G. Rozenberg, editor, *Handbook of Graph Grammars and Computing by Graph Transformation*, volume 1, pages 163–245. World Scientific, 1997.
3. B. Fields, P. Wright, and M. Harrison. Designing Human-System Interaction Using The Resource Model. In *Proc. APCHI'96: Asia-Pacific Conference on Human Computer Interaction*, Singapore, June 1996.
4. R. Freund, B. Haberstroh, and C. Stary. Applying Graph Grammars for Task-Oriented User Interface Development. In W. Koczkodaj, editor, *Proceedings IEEE Conference on Computing and Information ICCI'92*, pages 389–392, 1992.
5. M. Goedicke. On the Structure of Software Description Languages: A Component Oriented View. Research Report 473/1993, University of Dortmund, Dept. of Computer Science, Dortmund, May 1993. Habilitation.
6. M. Goedicke, T. Meyer, and B. Sucrow. Modularization of Graph Grammars for Describing Grahical User Interfaces. Technical Report 01/96, University of Essen, Essen, 1996. Informatik-Berichte (in German).
7. M. Goedicke and B. Sucrow. Towards a Formal Specification Method for Graphical User Interfaces Using Modularized Graph Grammars. In *Proceedings of the Eighth International Workshop on Software Specification and Design*, pages 56–65, Schloss Velen, Germany, March 22-23, 1996. IEEE Computer Society, IEEE Computer Society Press.
8. A. Habel, R. Heckel, and G. Taentzer. Graph Grammars with Negative Application Conditions. In *Special issue of Fundamenta Informaticae*, volume 26, 1996. no. 3,4.
9. E. Hutchins. *Cognition in the Wild*. MIT Press, 1994.
10. C. Janssen. Dialog Nets for describing Dialog Behaviour of Graphical Interactive Systems. In K.-H. Rödiger, editor, *Software Ergonomics '93*, volume 39 of *German Chapter of the ACM*, pages 67–76, Stuttgart, 1993. Teubner. (in German).
11. C. Janssen, A. Weisbecker, and J. Ziegler. Generation of Graphical User Interfaces using Data Models and Dialog Net Specifications. In H. Züllighoven, W. Altmann, and E.-E. Doberkat, editors, *Requirements Engineering '93: Prototyping*, volume 41 of *German Chapter of the ACM*, pages 335–347, Stuttgart, 1993. Teubner. (in German).
12. V. D. Keyser and D. Javaux. Human Factors in Aeronautics. In F. Bodart and J. Vanderdonckt, editors, *Design, Specification and Verification of Interactive Systems '96*, Editors W. Hansmann and W.T Hewitt and W. Purgathofer, pages 28–45, Wien, 1996. Proceedings of the Eurographics Workshop in Namur, Belgium, June 5-7, 1996, Springer.

13. A. Martini, H. Ehrig, and D. Nunes. Graph Grammars - An Introduction to the Double-Pushout Approach. Technical Report 96-6, Dept. of Computer Science, Technical University of Berlin, Berlin, Germany, 1996.

14. A. Monnier. Rapport préliminaire de la Commission d'enquête administrative sur l'accident du Mont Saint-Odile du 20 janvier 1992. Technical report, Ministère de l'Equipement, du Logement, des Transports et de l'Espace, Paris, France, 1992.

15. U. Nowak, U. Pöhle, R. Roitzsch, and B. Sucrow. Formal Specification of the ZIB-GUI Using Graph Grammars. In W. Mackens and S. Rump, editors, *Software Engineering im Scientific Computing*, pages 290–296. Vieweg, July 1996. (in German).

16. F. Parisi-Presicce. Transformations of Graph Grammars. In J. Cuny, H. Ehrig, G. Engels, and G. Rozenberg, editors, *Graph Grammars and Their Application to Computer Science*, volume 1073 of *Lecture Notes in Computer Science*, pages 428–442. Society for Design and Process Science, Springer, 1996. 5th International Workshop, Williamsburg, VA, USA, November 1994, Selected Papers.

17. G. Rozenberg, editor. *Handbook of Graph Grammars and Computing by Graph Transformation*, volume 1. World Scientific, 1997.

18. C. Stary. *Interactive Systems*. Vieweg, 1994. Software Development and Software Ergonomics (in German).

19. B. Sucrow. Formal Specification of Graphical User Interfaces Using Graph Grammars. In W. Mackens and S. Rump, editors, *Software Engineering im Scientific Computing*, pages 279–289. Vieweg, July 1996. (in German).

20. B. Sucrow. Towards an Integration of Software-Ergonomic Aspects in Formal Specifications of Graphical User Interfaces. In *Proceedings of The Second World Conference on Integrated Design & Process Technology*, volume 1, pages 194–201, Austin, Texas, December 1-4 1996. Society for Design and Process Science, IEEE Computer Society Press.

21. B. Sucrow. Formal Specification of Human-Computer Interaction by Graph Grammars under Consideration of Information Resources. In *Proceedings of the 1997 Automated Software Engineering Conference (ASEC'97)*, pages 28–35, Incline Village at Lake Tahoe, Nevada, November 3-5, 1997. IEEE Computer Society, IEEE Computer Society Press.

22. B. Sucrow. On Integrating Software-Ergonomic Aspects in the Specification Process of Grafical User Interfaces. In *Transactions of the SDPS Journal of Integrated Design and Process Science*. Society for Design and Process Science, IEEE Computer Society Press, 1998. (Accepted).

23. P. Wright, B. Fields, and M. Harrison. Distributed Information Resources: A New Approach to Interaction Modelling. In T. Green, J. Canas, and C. Warren, editors, *Proceedings of ECCE8: European Conference on Cognitive Ergonomics*, pages 5–10. EACE, 1996.

RELVIEW – A System for Calculating With Relations and Relational Programming

Ralf Behnke, Rudolf Berghammer, Erich Meyer, and Peter Schneider

Institut für Informatik und Praktische Mathematik
Christian-Albrechts-Universität Kiel
Preusserstraße 1–9, D–24105 Kiel, Germany

The calculus of relational algebra has its roots in the second half of the last century with the pioneering work on binary relations of G. Boole, A. de Morgan, C.S. Peirce, and E. Schröder. The modern axiomatic development is due to A. Tarski and his co-workers. In the last two decades this formalization has been accepted by many mathematicians and computer scientists as a fruitful base for describing fundamental concepts like graphs, combinatorics, orders and lattices, games in mathematics and like relational data bases and correctness as well as verification of programs in computer science. A lot of examples and references to relevant literature can be found in [6, 2].

Relational algebra has a fixed and surprisingly small set of operations. On finite carrier sets these operations and many others which are based on them can easily be implemented using, for example, two-dimensional Boolean arrays or successor lists. Moreover, concrete relations over finite sets can graphically be represented in a very elegant way as Boolean matrices and directed graphs. Therefore, a computer system for calculating with relations and relational programming can easily be implemented using modern user interface techniques.

In the following, we give an impression of such a computer system, called RELVIEW. Written in the C programming language, it runs under X windows and makes full use of the graphical user interface. The first versions of RELVIEW have been written at the University of the German Forces Munich from 1988 until 1992; see [5]. Based on the experiences with the Munich system, in the last four years RELVIEW was redesigned and extended at Kiel University. It is available free of charge by ftp from host ftp.informatik.uni-kiel.de, where it is located in the directory pub/kiel/relview, and runs on Sun SPARC workstations and INTEL-based Linux systems. Additional information (e.g., a user's and programmer's guide with many examples [4]) and latest news can be found on the World-Wide-Web page http://www.informatik.uni-kiel.de/~progsys/relview.html.

RELVIEW can be used to solve many different tasks while working with relational algebra, concrete relations, relation-based discrete structures, and relational programs. First, it assists the formulation and the proof of relational theorems. In this field, the system can help to construct examples which support the validity of a theorem or to find counter examples to disprove the considered relation-algebraic property. For these activities, "playing" and "experimenting" with relational terms is essential and this is one of the purpose the RELVIEW system has been designed for. In particular, the interactive nature of the system allows to add, change and remove relations and directed graphs, and makes it possible to apply functions and to invoke relational programs at every time within a working session.

Relational program development is a second very important area for the use of RELVIEW. Whereas the relational algebra and especially the relational calculus forms the formal basis for ensuring correctness of the derived programs, the RELVIEW system supports the main validation tasks within nearly all stages of a development of a relational algorithm. In a first step of such a development, a relational specification is constructed, for example, from a logical problem description fixing a desired result of a computation. The resulting specification consists of a relational term which can be prototyped, i.e. evaluated, with RELVIEW. The evaluation not only allows to check the derived specification against the logical description, but also against the requirements of the given problem. Although the relational specification can be considered as an algorithm for solving the problem, it usually has to be improved in efficiency. Therefore, in a second step the specification can be used as a starting point for a formal program development. In spite of the correctness of a derived program established by relational proofs, it normally makes sense to prototype, i.e. execute or test, the resulting program to obtain additional safety.

Altogether, one can say that in the area of relational program development the RELVIEW system is a good means to bridge the gap between classical software engineering tasks like prototyping and testing and objektives of formal methods like assuring correctness.

RELVIEW is a totally interactive and completely graphic-oriented computer system. Although the detailed appeareance of its windows depends on resources defined in a configuration file, typically the four main windows (viz. the menu window, the directory window, the window of the relation editor, and the window of the graph editor) look as in the following screen snapshot:

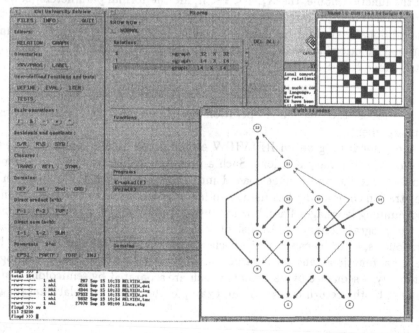

After starting the system, the menu window is presented to the user and the command buttons are available. Conceptually they can be devided into three parts, viz. buttons for system administration (like loading from and saving into files), for function declaration, evaluation and iteration, and for the fundamental operations on relations and relational domain definitions.

The directory window presents the actual state of the system's workspace to the user. It contains four scroll lists showing the names and dimensions of the present relations and possibly existing graphs, globally declared relational functions, loaded relational programs, and, finally, globally declared relational domains. In the above picture, the workspace consists of two relations E and T and two relational programs Prim and Kruskal; there are no globally defined relational functions and no relational domains.

Using the window of the relation editor (resp. the graph editor), the user is able to edit a (homogeneous) relation as a Boolean matrix (resp. a directed graph) using the mouse pointer. In these windows also the results of the computations are shown, where the system provides some additional visualization means like nice drawings of graphs, a labeling mechanism for rows and columns of matrices resp. nodes of graphs, and facilities to emphasize nodes or edges of a graph. As an example, in the above picture the spanning tree with relation T of the depicted undirected graph with relation E is indicated by the boldface edges. The graph itself is drawn with the system's layer graph drawing algorithm.

The main purpose of RELVIEW is the evaluation of relational terms which are constructed from the relations of the workspace using predefined operations (like -, ^, &, |, and * for complement, transposition, intersection, union, and multiplication) and tests (like empty for testing emptiness) on them, user-defined relational functions, and user-defined relational programs.

A declaration of a relational function is of the form $F(X_1, \ldots, X_n) = t$, where F is the function name, the X_i, $1 \leq i \leq n$, are the formal parameters (standing for relations), and t is a relational term over the relations of the workspace that can additionally contain the formal parameters X_i. As an example, an unary relational function Hasse which computes the Hasse diagram $R \cap \overline{RR^+}$ of a partial order R in RELVIEW is

$$\text{Hasse}(R) = R \ \& \ -(R * \text{trans}(R)),$$

where a call of the predefined operation trans computes the transitive closure of its argument.

A relational program in RELVIEW essentially is a while-program based on the datatype of binary relations. Such a program – which is stored in a human-readable text file and can be loaded into the system with the help of an administration command – has many similarities with a function procedure in the programming languages Pascal or Modula-2. It starts with a head line containing the program's name and a list of formal parameters. Then the declaration part follows, which consists of the declarations of local relational domains, local relational functions, and local variables. The third part of a relational program is its body, a sequence of statements which are separated by semicolons and terminated by the return-clause. As an example, the following relational program uses Prim's method to compute the relation of a spanning tree for a nonempty, undirected and connected graph with (symmetric and irreflexive) relation E.

```
Prim(E)
  DECL T, v
  BEG   T = atom(E);
        v = dom(T) | ran(T);
        WHILE -empty(-v) DO
          T = T | atom(v * -v^ & E);
          v = dom(T) | ran(T)
        OD
        RETURN T | T^
  END.
```

In this program, the predefined operations **dom** and **ran** compute the domain resp. range of a relation. Furthermore, the base operation **atom** yields for a nonempty relation a subrelation which contains exactly one ordered pair.

In the last years a lot of case studies have been performed with RELVIEW. These include graph-theoretic questions and algorithms, Petri-net problems, computations on orders and lattices, data flow analysis, computations on finite automata, and relational semantics. See [3, 4, 1]. At Kiel University, RELVIEW was and is also applied in education, i.e., in lectures and seminars. These applications have shown that RELVIEW is a helpful tool for the interactive manipulation of relations and supports many different prototyping tasks within nearly all stages of a development of a relational program. Its main attraction is its flexibility since this property allows to experiment with new relational concepts as well as relational specifications and programs while avoiding unnecessary overhead.

References

1. Behnke R.: Extending relational specifications by sequential algebras – Prototyping with RELVIEW. In: Berghammer R., Simon F. (eds.): Programming languages and fundamentals of programming. Report 9717, Institut für Informatik und Praktische Mathematik, Universität Kiel, 12-22 (1997)
2. Brink C., Kahl W., Schmidt G. (eds.): Relational methods in Computer Science. Advances in Computing Science, Springer (1997)
3. Berghammer R., von Karger B., Ulke C.: Relation-algebraic analysis of Petri nets with RELVIEW. In: Margaria T., Steffen B. (eds.): Proc. TACAS '96, LNCS 1055, Springer, 49-69 (1996)
4. Behnke R., Berghammer R., Schneider P.: Machine support of relational computations. The Kiel RELVIEW system. Report 9711, Institut für Informatik und Praktische Mathematik, Universität Kiel (1997)
5. Berghammer R., Schmidt G.: RELVIEW – A computer system for the manipulation of relations. In: Nivat M., et al. (eds.): Proc. AMAST '93, Workshops in Computing, Springer, 405-406 (1993)
6. Schmidt G., Ströhlein T.: Relations and graphs. Discrete Mathematics for Computer Scientists, EATCS Monographs on Theoret. Comput. Sci., Springer (1993)

ALBERT: A Formal Language and Its Supporting Tools for Requirements Engineering

Eric Dubois

Facultés Universitaires Notre-Dame de la Paix, Institut d' Informatique, Rue Grandgagnage 21, B-5000 Namur, Belgium. Email: edu@info.fundp.ac.be.

1 Introduction

The use of formal specification languages has been proven useful in the development of large and complex software such as safety-critical software. Specification languages like Z, Larch and Statemate propose useful artefacts for modelling and reasoning on the behaviour of the desired *software*. For Requirements Engineering (hereafter RE), similar artefacts are needed but with the objective of capturing customers' descriptions related to a desired *system*.

Albert is (yet another) formal specification language proposed to support RE activities. The design of the language started around 1992 within the framework of the Esprit II project *Icarus*. The validation of the language constructs has been achieved through the handling of non trivial case studies (ranging from CIM to advanced telecommunication systems) performed by the members of the team who developed the language [1]. The language has been the subject of several technology transfer initiatives. In particular, it has been used by two industrial partners in the context of the development and the evolution of two large, distributed, software-intensive, heterogeneous systems (a video-on-demand application and a satellite-based telecommunication system) [2].

Besides the development of the language, we have also started the development of tools in 1995. This development is done within the framework of a 5 years project (25 man/year) where we have adopted an incremental strategy resulting in the delivery of a first version of the tool in December 1997 and and the delivery of second version of the tool in December 1999.

2 The Albert language

Albert organizes an RE specification around the agents identified in the usage environment, where an **agent** is an active entity that can perform or suffer *actions* that change or maintain the *state* of knowledge about the external world and/or the states of other agents. Actions are performed by agents to discharge contractual obligations expressed in terms of *local constraints*, applicable to the agents itself, and *cooperation constraints*, that apply to the interactions between agents. Hereafter, we illustrate the application of the language on the specification of a fragment of a Video on Demand (Vod) system, i.e. a system consisting of a set top box located in the home of a customer, connected to the television set of the customer and which offers roughly the functionality of a video player.

A specification in Albert is made up of (i) a graphical specification component in which the vocabulary of the specification is *declared* and of (ii) a textual specification component in which the admissible behaviors of agents are *constrained* through logical formulas.

Figure 1 contains part of the graphical declaration of the VoD system according to the Albert conventions. Each agent is represented by an oval and multiplicity is indicated by shadowing an oval. Figure 1 also declares the internal structure of the VoD agent. It declares the state structure and the actions that may happen during the lifetime of an agent and which may change the state of the agent. State components are represented by rectangles and actions are represented by ovals. State components are typed and actions can have typed arguments. Types may vary from simple data types to complex data types (recursively built using the usual data type constructors like e.g. set, sequence, table, etc.). From graphical conventions used in fig. 1, we know that *Movies* and *Display* are tables respectively indexed on MOVIE and ENDUSER (the type associated the identity of the End-User agent) while *List-cat* corresponds to a set of CATEGORY and is derived (see below) from the *Movies* component.

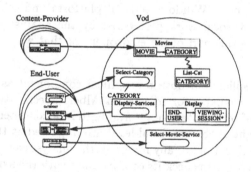

Fig. 1. The graphical declaration of the VoD system.

Besides graphical declarations, textual constraints are used for pruning the (usually) infinite set of possible lives associated with the agents of a system. As explained above, and also because we need this for *naturalness*, Albert supports two styles of specification. Those are reflected in 12 different templates of constraints which are classified into **Local Constraints** describing the internal behavior of an agent and **Cooperation Constraints** (describing the interaction of agents within a society).

State Behaviour templates express restrictions on the possible values that can be taken by the objects and data forming the state of an agent. These restrictions can be static (i.e. invariants which hold at any time) or dynamic (i.e. depending on time). An example is:

> The display of the categories list (lc) to a given End-User (eu) does not last for more than 1'.

$[\neg \text{Lasts}_{1'} \; \text{Display[eu]} = \text{lc}]$

Action composition constraints define how actions may be refined in terms of finely grained actions. Example is the following statement:

> The Select-Movie-service action brought by an End-User has to be
> followed by a Select-Category action made by this End-User or the
> Display-Services-List.

Category-Selection

$\longleftrightarrow$ eu.Select-Movie-Service $<$($>$ eu.Select-Category(c) $\oplus$ Display-Services-List)

The interested reader can find the complete specification of the VoD system in [2]. The semantics of an Albert specification is given by mapping it to a real-time temporal action-based logic called Albert-Kernel.

3   Development of tools for ALBERT

At the moment, we have developed a first set of tools that are available and accompanied by a set of documents including a reference and a user manuals. Basically, the supporting environment has been developed according to an internet-based client/server architecture where The client part is called the "editor". It is running on a Windows 95/NT platform and offers a set of basic facilities which allow local work performed by the analyst. From a practical point of view, this is this part of the environement that we distribute. Facilities include:

- Editing the specification: both a graphical component as well as a textual component are available for editing an Albert specification. In particular, the two kinds of representation are managed in a consistent way (e.g., modifications brought at the graphical level are impacted at the textual level).
- Parsing the specification: at any moment, the analyst can decide to parse the specification in order to check its conformance with the syntax. The scope of the parsing has to be decided by the analyst. It can be concerned with the parsing of one specific Albert statement or with the whole (or a fragment) of the specification.
- Exporting the specification: the specification (both the graphical and the textual parts) can be cut and paste from the editor to any kinds of OLE compliant documents. For example, the graphical part can be put in a Word document. This is also possible to generate the specification in an Ascii format or a LaTeX format.
- Managing traceability links. Facilities are offered by the tools for managing the links existing between fragments of the formal specification and various semi-formal or informal sources of information coming from customers. This is possible, for example, to relate formal Albert statements to informal interviews, fragments of ERA diagrams or even videos capturing real-world scenes.
- Downloading the specification: at any moment, the analyst can decide to download his/her specification on the server through internet. This is when the analyst wants more complex checks (see below) be performed.

At the level of the server, the specification is stored in a deductive object-oriented repository called ConceptBase. On the specification are performed a set of more complex checks including a partial type checking as well as number of heuristics applied for discovering basic incompletenesses and inconsistencies. All results of these checks are presented to the client in a transparent way. The server part is running on top of a Unix platform. From a practical point of view (maintenance and future development), this server is located at the University of Namur.

We plan to achieve a second version of the tool in December 1999. In this version, we hope to integrate more advanced facilities at the validation and verification levels.

At the validation level, we work on:

- a so-called 'paraphrazer' supporting the analyst in a semi-automatic generation process of informal statements from the formal statements written with Albert templates;
- a distributed animation tool allowing the exploration of the different possible lives associated with a specification.

At the verification level, progresses are towards:

- a tool supporting a 'framework' for high-level reasoning. This is to support the analyst in a rigorous (conceptual) reasoning which is at the basis of the skeleton of a proof which can be passed to,
- the PVS theorem prover which will support a complete formal reasoning. To this end, a syntactic embedding of the Albert semantics is done as well a semantic one. The idea is to support both theorem proving and model-checking techniques.

The actual architecture of tools will evolve in order to reach a clean distributed objects architecture. According to the characteristics of the client platform, specific parts of the tool will be downloaded on-demand. With this respect we are investigating Corba, Java and JavaBeans.

Acknowledgements: Thanks are due to all the members of the ALBERT team: P. Du Bois, F. Chabot, L. Claes, P. Heymans, B. Jungen, M. Petit, J.M. Zeippen. This work is supported by the Walloon Region (DGTRE) Project CAT, contract nr. 2791.

References

1. P. du Bois, E. Dubois, and J-M. Zeippen. On the use of a formal requirements engineering language: The generalized railroad crossing problem. In *Third IEEE International Symposium on Requirements Engineering*. IEEE ICS Press, January 1997.
2. R. Wieringa and E. Dubois. Integrating semi-formal and formal software specification techniques. In *Information System Journal*. (to appear), June, 1998.

MOBY/PLC – A Design Tool for Hierarchical Real-Time Automata*

Josef Tapken**

University of Oldenburg, Germany

Abstract. MOBY/PLC is a graphical design tool for PLC-Automata, a special class of hierarchical real-time automata suitable for the description of distributed real-time systems. Besides the modelling language in use and some features of MOBY/PLC, like several validation methods and code generation, the implementational basis which is built up by the C++ class library MCL is sketched. MCL serves for a rapid development of hierarchical editors for different graphical formalisms by providing a modular hierarchical graph editor.

1 Introduction

MOBY/PLC is a graphical design tool for distributed real-time systems which is based upon a formal description technique called PLC-Automata [3]. It is part of the MOBY-workbench which provides several methods to model and analyse distributed systems, e.g. Petri-net based validation methods like simulation and model-checking for SDL-specifications [4].

The kernel of the workbench called MCL (MOBY Class Library) is an application independent C++ class library which comprises, among others, classes for building Motif based hierarchical interactive graph editors [6].

PLC-Automata, a language developed in the UniForM-project [5] and applied to a real-world case study of the industrial partner, are a class of hierarchical real-time automata suitable (but not restricted) to the description of the behaviour of *Programmable Logic Controllers* (PLC) that are often used to solve real-time controlling problems. The automata are tailored to a structural compilation into runnable PLC-code and they are provided with a formal semantics in *Duration Calculus* (DC) [1] to allow formal reasoning about their properties.

This paper gives a survey of MOBY/PLC by introducing its modelling language (PLC-Automata, Sec. 2), by describing its features (Sec. 3) and by making some remarks about its implementational basis (MCL, Sec. 4).

2 PLC-Automata

Programmable Logic Controllers (PLC) are cyclic real-time controllers that frequently poll input values from sensors or other PLCs and compute output values

---

* This research was partially supported by the Leibniz Programme of the Deutsche Forschungsgemeinschaft (DFG) under grant No. Ol 98/1-1.
** e-mail: tapken@informatik.uni-oldenburg.de

for actuators (or other PLCs). To deal with real-time problems, PLCs are enriched by a convenient timer concept.

A PLC-Automaton describes the behaviour of a PLC by an extended finite state machine with three categories of variables, namely input, local, and output variables. A transition is labelled by a condition and by a list of assignments to local and output variables. In every cycle a PLC-Automaton updates its input variables from the environment and performs (exactly) one transition according to the actual state and values of variables. The execution of a transition may be prohibited by a state label which consists of a time value d ($\in \mathbb{R}_{\geq 0}$) and a Boolean expression over the input variables. A state can only be left if it is held for longer than for d time units or the state expression evaluates to **false**.

In order to increase expressiveness as well as for the purpose of structuring PLC-Automata are enhanced by a hierarchy concept which is based on state refinement, i.e. a state can represent a set of substates and its label can also restrict the outgoing transitions of the substates.

The whole system specification consists of a network of PLC-Automata which communicate through channels with each other. Therefore, a channel links an output variable of one automaton to an input variable of another, i.e. communication is performed implicitly by updating every cycle the input variables of a PLC-Automaton with the current values of the corresponding output variables. The system network may also be structured hierarchically.

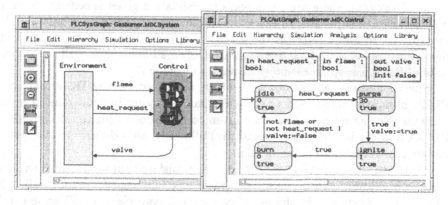

Fig. 1. PLC-automata of the gasburner specification

Fig. 1 shows on the left a system diagram describing a network of two automata (Environment and Control). On the right the Control-automaton is shown in detail. The example is taken from a specification of a control unit for a gasburner, which gets two Boolean inputs from the environment, namely heat_request representing the state of a thermostat changed by the user and flame indicating the status of a sensor monitoring the flame. The control unit delivers one Boolean output valve controlling the gas valve.

3   The MOBY/PLC-Tool

This section gives an overview of the main components which are currently implemented in MOBY/PLC (see Fig. 2).

The central part of the tool is an interactive graphical editor for specifying a real-time system (i). Since the architectural part as well as the behavioural part of a specification may be structured hierarchically the editor comprises several different subeditors, e.g. system editors to describe the network of PLC-Automata or editors to specify automata and subautomata (see Fig. 1).

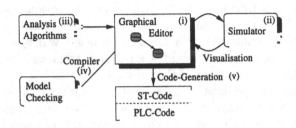

Fig. 2. Components of MOBY/PLC

In MOBY/PLC there are three ways to validate a given specification (ii, iii, iv). A simulator (ii) is able to execute a single or a set of PLC-Automata and to visualize its results directly in the graphical specification. The simulator is designed to support the interactive simulation of small modules as well as extensive tests of the whole specification in background mode [7].

Special analysis algorithms (iii) which are based on the DC-semantics of PLC-Automata can be used to statically calculate certain properties of an automaton, e.g. its reaction time on a given combination of inputs. A compiler of PLC-Automata into timed automata (iv) allows to use existing model checking systems for timed automata, like Kronos [2].

Furthermore, a given specification can be translated automatically by a structural compilation into a special programming language for PLCs called ST (Structured Text)(v). By the use of commercial compilers the ST-code can be transformed into runnable source code for PLCs.

4   The MOBY Class Library

The MOBY Class Library (MCL) is a powerful (Motif based) C++ class library for building graphical applications under the X Window System. MCL adopts several classes and concepts of the SMALLTALK-80 programming environment, e.g. many collection classes and the model view controller concept. Furthermore, it provides runtime class information and dynamic object creation for a given class object or class name.

MCL comprises an editor for hierarchical graphs which is tailored to build a common basis for several implementations of graphical formal description techniques (gFDT), like SDL, statecharts or PLC-Automata. This editor provides a strong modularity by a loose coupling between different hierarchy levels and it serves for a rapid development of editors for gFDTs by a generic description of hierarchy. This description, which is e.g. used for dynamic menu creation, prevents the programmer to reimplement the hierarchy control structure for each gFDT. The programmer only has to define classes of graphs and vertices and to describe what kind of vertices could be inserted into a certain graph and what kind of graphs could serve for a refinement of a certain vertex.

5 Conclusion

In this paper the modelling language, the features and the implementational basis of the design tool MOBY/PLC have been sketched.

Although MOBY/PLC is already usable there are several extensions we are planning to implement. E.g. we want to evaluate and visualize the results of background runs of the simulator. We have to enhance the prototypical implemention of the compiler of PLC-Automata into timed automata. Furthermore, it seems to be promising to expand the static analysis by further algorithms which calculate interesting properties based on the structure of a PLC-automaton.

Currently a graphical editor for Object-Z specifications is developed based on the hierarchical graphs of MCL. This editor should be integrated into MOBY/PLC in order to use Object-Z for the description of data aspects in PLC-Automata.

Acknowledgements. The author thanks H. Fleischhack, H. Dierks, E.-R. Olderog, and the other members of the "semantics group" in Oldenburg for fruitful discussions on the subject of this paper.

References

1. Zhou Chaochen, C.A.R. Hoare, and A.P. Ravn. A Calculus of Durations. *Inform. Proc. Letters*, 40/5:269–276, 1991.
2. C. Daws, A. Olivero, S. Tripakis, and S. Yovine. The tool Kronos. In *Hybrid Systems III*, volume 1066 of *LNCS*, pages 208–219. Springer Verlag, 1996.
3. Henning Dierks. PLC-Automata: A New Class of Implementable Real-Time Automata. In *ARTS'97*, LNCS. Springer Verlag, May 1997.
4. Hans Fleischhack and Josef Tapken. An M-Net Semantics for a Real-Time Extension of μSDL. In *FME'97: Industrial Applications and Strengthened Foundations of Formal Methods*, volume 1313 of *LNCS*, pages 162–181. Springer Verlag, 1997.
5. B. Krieg-Brückner, J. Peleska, E.-R. Olderog, et al. UniForM — Universal Formal Methods Workbench. In *Statusseminar des BMBF Softwaretechnologie*, pages 357–378. BMBF, Berlin, 1996.
6. Josef Tapken. Implementing Hierarchical Graph-Structures. Technical report, University of Oldenburg, 1997.
7. Josef Tapken. Interactive and Compilative Simulation of PLC-Automata. In W. Hahn and A. Lehmann, editors, *Simulation in Industry, ESS'97*, pages 552 – 556. SCS, 1997.

Author Index

Springer
and the
environment

At Springer we firmly believe that an
international science publisher has a
special obligation to the environment,
and our corporate policies consistently
reflect this conviction.
We also expect our business partners –
paper mills, printers, packaging
manufacturers, etc. – to commit
themselves to using materials and
production processes that do not harm
the environment. The paper in this
book is made from low- or no-chlorine
pulp and is acid free, in conformance
with international standards for paper
permanency.

Lecture Notes in Computer Science

For information about Vols. 1–1300

please contact your bookseller or Springer-Verlag

Vol. 1337: C. Freksa, M. Jantzen, R. Valk (Eds.), Foundations of Computer Science. XII, 515 pages. 1997.

Vol. 1338: F. Plášil, K.G. Jeffery (Eds.), SOFSEM'97: Theory and Practice of Informatics. Proceedings, 1997. XIV, 571 pages. 1997.

Vol. 1339: N.A. Murshed, F. Bortolozzi (Eds.), Advances in Document Image Analysis. Proceedings, 1997. IX, 345 pages. 1997.

Vol. 1340: M. van Kreveld, J. Nievergelt, T. Roos, P. Widmayer (Eds.), Algorithmic Foundations of Geographic Information Systems. XIV, 287 pages. 1997.

Vol. 1341: F. Bry, R. Ramakrishnan, K. Ramamohanarao (Eds.), Deductive and Object-Oriented Databases. Proceedings, 1997. XIV, 430 pages. 1997.

Vol. 1342: A. Sattar (Ed.), Advanced Topics in Artificial Intelligence. Proceedings, 1997. XVII, 516 pages. 1997. (Subseries LNAI).

Vol. 1343: Y. Ishikawa, R.R. Oldehoeft, J.V.W. Reynders, M. Tholburn (Eds.), Scientific Computing in Object-Oriented Parallel Environments. Proceedings, 1997. XI, 295 pages. 1997.

Vol. 1344: C. Ausnit-Hood, K.A. Johnson, R.G. Pettit, IV, S.B. Opdahl (Eds.), Ada 95 – Quality and Style. XV, 292 pages. 1997.

Vol. 1345: R.K. Shyamasundar, K. Ueda (Eds.), Advances in Computing Science - ASIAN'97. Proceedings, 1997. XIII, 387 pages. 1997.

Vol. 1346: S. Ramesh, G. Sivakumar (Eds.), Foundations of Software Technology and Theoretical Computer Science. Proceedings, 1997. XI, 343 pages. 1997.

Vol. 1347: E. Ahronovitz, C. Fiorio (Eds.), Discrete Geometry for Computer Imagery. Proceedings, 1997. X, 255 pages. 1997.

Vol. 1348: S. Steel, R. Alami (Eds.), Recent Advances in AI Planning. Proceedings, 1997. IX, 454 pages. 1997. (Subseries LNAI).

Vol. 1349: M. Johnson (Ed.), Algebraic Methodology and Software Technology. Proceedings, 1997. X, 594 pages. 1997.

Vol. 1350: H.W. Leong, H. Imai, S. Jain (Eds.), Algorithms and Computation. Proceedings, 1997. XV, 426 pages. 1997.

Vol. 1351: R. Chin, T.-C. Pong (Eds.), Computer Vision – ACCV'98. Proceedings Vol. I, 1998. XXIV, 761 pages. 1997.

Vol. 1352: R. Chin, T.-C. Pong (Eds.), Computer Vision – ACCV'98. Proceedings Vol. II, 1998. XXIV, 757 pages. 1997.

Vol. 1353: G. BiBattista (Ed.), Graph Drawing. Proceedings, 1997. XII, 448 pages. 1997.

Vol. 1354: O. Burkart, Automatic Verification of Sequential Infinite-State Processes. X, 163 pages. 1997.

Vol. 1355: M. Darnell (Ed.), Cryptography and Coding. Proceedings, 1997. IX, 335 pages. 1997.

Vol. 1356: A. Danthine, Ch. Diot (Eds.), From Multimedia Services to Network Services. Proceedings, 1997. XII, 180 pages. 1997.

Vol. 1357: J. Bosch, S. Mitchell (Eds.), Object-Oriented Technology. Proceedings, 1997. XIV, 555 pages. 1998.

Vol. 1358: B. Thalheim, L. Libkin (Eds.), Semantics in Databases. XI, 265 pages. 1998.

Vol. 1360: D. Wang (Ed.), Automated Deduction in Geometry. Proceedings, 1996. VII, 235 pages. 1998. (Subseries LNAI).

Vol. 1361: B. Christianson, B. Crispo, M. Lomas, M. Roe (Eds.), Security Protocols. Proceedings, 1997. VIII, 217 pages. 1998.

Vol. 1362: D.K. Panda, C.B. Stunkel (Eds.), Network-Based Parallel Computing. Proceedings, 1998. X, 247 pages. 1998.

Vol. 1363: J.-K. Hao, E. Lutton, E. Ronald, M. Schoenauer, D. Snyers (Eds.), Artificial Evolution. XI, 349 pages. 1998.

Vol. 1364: W. Conen, G. Neumann (Eds.), Coordination Technology for Collaborative Applications. VIII, 282 pages. 1998.

Vol. 1365: M.P. Singh, A. Rao, M.J. Wooldridge (Eds.), Intelligent Agents IV. Proceedings, 1997. XII, 351 pages. 1998. (Subseries LNAI).

Vol. 1367: E.W. Mayr, H.J. Prömel, A. Steger (Eds.), Lectures on Proof Verification and Approximation Algorithms. XII, 344 pages. 1998.

Vol. 1368: Y. Masunaga, T. Katayama, M. Tsukamoto (Eds.), Worldwide Computing and Its Applications — WWCA'98. Proceedings, 1998. XIV, 473 pages. 1998.

Vol. 1370: N.A. Streitz, S. Konomi, H.-J. Burkhardt (Eds.), Cooperative Buildings. Proceedings, 1998. XI, 267 pages. 1998.

Vol. 1372: S. Vaudenay (Ed.), Fast Software Encryption. Proceedings, 1998. VIII, 297 pages. 1998.

Vol. 1373: M. Morvan, C. Meinel, D. Krob (Eds.), STACS 98. Proceedings, 1998. XV, 630 pages. 1998.

Vol. 1375: R. D. Hersch, J. André, H. Brown (Eds.), Electronic Publishing, Artistic Imaging, and Digital Typography. Proceedings, 1998. XIII, 575 pages. 1998.

Vol. 1376: F. Parisi Presicce (Ed.), Recent Trends in Algebraic Development Techniques. Proceedings, 1997. VIII, 435 pages. 1998.

Vol. 1377: H.-J. Schek, F. Saltor, I. Ramos, G. Alonso (Eds.), Advances in Database Technology – EDBT'98. Proceedings, 1998. XII, 515 pages. 1998.

Vol. 1378: M. Nivat (Ed.), Foundations of Software Science and Computation Structures. Proceedings, 1998. X, 289 pages. 1998.

Vol. 1379: T. Nipkow (Ed.), Rewriting Techniques and Applications. Proceedings, 1998. X, 343 pages. 1998.

Vol. 1380: C.L. Lucchesi, A.V. Moura (Eds.), LATIN'98: Theoretical Informatics. Proceedings, 1998. XI, 391 pages. 1998.

Vol. 1381: C. Hankin (Ed.), Programming Languages and Systems. Proceedings, 1998. X, 283 pages. 1998.

Vol. 1382: E. Astesiano (Ed.), Fundamental Approaches to Software Engineering. Proceedings, 1998. XII, 331 pages. 1998.

Vol. 1383: K. Koskimies (Ed.), Compiler Construction. Proceedings, 1998. X, 309 pages. 1998.